America Right or Wrong

America Right or Wrong

Second Edition

An Anatomy of American Nationalism

ANATOL LIEVEN

OXFORD
UNIVERSITY PRESS

OXFORD
UNIVERSITY PRESS

Great Clarendon Street, Oxford OX2 6DP,
United Kingdom

Oxford University Press is a department of the University of Oxford.
It furthers the University's objective of excellence in research, scholarship,
and education by publishing worldwide. Oxford is a registered trade mark of
Oxford University press in the UK and in certain other countries

© Anatol Lieven 2012

The moral rights of the author have been asserted

First Edition published in 2012

Impression: 1

British Library Cataloguing in Publication Data

Data available

Library of Congress Cataloging in Publication Data

Data available

ISBN 978–0–19–966025–4

Printed in Great Britain by
Clays Ltd, St Ives plc

For Misha, Beloved Distraction

Contents

Preface

The most important target of this book is Americans themselves. I hope that in a small way it may do something to influence the policy debate in the United States, by revealing some of the underlying myths and historical, cultural, and ideological impulses that drive U.S. thinking and U.S. policy. However, this book is being published not only in the United States, but in Britain. The first edition was also translated into French, Italian, Japanese, and Korean. I have therefore had to explain in some detail a number of things about the United States that will be familiar to educated American audiences, and for this I ask your pardon.

Many people have generously helped with advice during the writing of this book. It would not have been possible without the unstinting help and support of Natasha Fairweather, of A. P. Watt, who worked tremendously hard to find publishers for a highly controversial manuscript, and was a great source of encouragement and strength in moments of discouragement. I am most grateful to David McBride and his colleagues at Oxford University Press for commissioning and editing this new 2012 edition of the book, and to Tim Bartlett, of Oxford University Press, Michael Fishwick, of Harper Collins, and Charlotte Cachin-Liebert, of Lattes for commissioning and editing the original version.

A great debt of gratitude is owed to Michael Lind and Stephen Holmes, who gave me the benefit of their profound insights into the American tradition, and also encouraged me to persevere with this project. Andrew Bacevich, Bill Maynes, Tom Hughes, Walter Russell Mead, William Pfaff, Norman Birnbaum, Stephen Walt, Michael Kraig, Adam Shatz, Justin Vaisse, Tom Geoghehan, Marina Ottaway, Minxin Pei, and my brother, D. C. B. Lieven, all very generously took the time to advise me on one or another part of the manuscript. On Chapter Six, concerning the U.S.–Israeli relationship, David Chambers, of the Middle East Institute in Washington, DC, was of inestimable help, as were Brian Klug, Suzanne Goldenberg, and James Zogby. Responsibility for the statements and arguments made in the book is, of course, entirely my own.

I am grateful to my colleagues in the War Studies Department of King's College London for their help with the production of the second edition of this book, and in particular to Ashley Lait, whose help with the research was indispensable. I thank Jessica Mathews, president of the Carnegie Endowment for International Peace, for allowing me to embark on the original version of the book, and to my colleagues at Carnegie for their help and support. Rashed

Chowdhury and Zhanara Nauruzbayeva worked tremendously hard and diligently on the research. Their intelligence, insights, and perspectives were also a great help to me. Amanda Muller helped gather much information on American domestic politics. Special thanks are due to Kathleen Higgs and the staff of the Carnegie Library. They were not only superbly efficient in procuring books, but extremely patient with a combination of bizarre-sounding requests and extreme lateness in returns.

Finally, my gratitude and love go to my wife Sasha, who bore the twin burdens of a new baby and a book-writing husband with her customary grace, and to my son Misha, to whom this book is dedicated, and who has provided a cheerful background to the writing of this new edition.

America Right or Wrong

Introduction

America will never be destroyed from the outside. If we falter and lose our freedoms, it will be because we destroyed ourselves.

—Abraham Lincoln

This book is an exploration of certain old and deeply rooted features of American political culture that I have grouped together under the term "nationalism." It examines these phenomena against the background of four great and interlinked historical developments of the first decade of the twenty-first century: the reaction of the United States to the terrorist attacks of 9/11; the growing social and economic deterioration of large parts of the white working and middle classes; the radicalization of the Republican Party, which I have argued in this book should really be renamed the American Nationalist Party; and the response of the United States to new challenges, above all the rise of China.

The developments are interconnected. The Bush administration's strategy in response to 9/11 reflected old and deep patterns of American attitudes to the outside world, and right-wing American attitudes to other Americans. The wars launched by Bush were coupled with tax cuts that reflected the swing of the Republican Party away from the New Deal–based policies of the Eisenhower and Nixon administrations and toward radical free-market capitalism—an economic philosophy that progressively undermined the economic and social standing of the Republicans' own white middle class base. These two policies together drove up the U.S. budget deficit under Bush and his successor, Barack Obama, to unprecedented levels, and helped pave the way for the great recession after 2008, which produced a radical downward plunge in white middle class living standards.

The result has been embittered and hysterical politics on the Right in America, which have combined with features of the U.S. Constitution to produce a dangerous stasis in government. Meanwhile, the Bush administration's strategies after 9/11 made it impossible for the United States to mount any serious response to the rise of China.[1] If, as is probable, China overtakes the United States economically

1

and challenges it geopolitically, this may inflame American nationalism still further, in ways that could endanger world peace.

American nationalism has contributed to this crisis in a number of different ways. The chauvinist, religiously, and racially bigoted sides of American nationalism (what I have called in this book the American nationalist antithesis) have stoked aggressive policies abroad and paranoid hatreds at home that are undermining the ability of American democracy to conduct a reasonable discussion of policies and interests.

On the other hand, American civic nationalism (the American nationalist thesis) has also played its part in creating this stasis. The democratic and constitutional values of what has been called the "American Creed" have been of inestimable value to the United States, and through America to the world. In every generation they have inspired Americans to renew their political system and extend its liberties. Throughout history, they have helped produce the traditional American spirit of practical opportunism that has enabled Americans to find answers to new sets of problems. This in turn has established the United States as a model and example that has had a positive influence on people all over the world.

America still does contain immense reserves of imaginative thought and political energy. In our generation, however, the tremendous past success of the American model has combined with the power of American civic nationalism in American society to produce a very different effect as far as a large minority of Americans are concerned. This nationalism has bequeathed to them an essentially mythological version not only of their country's history and role in the world—which is standard for most nationalisms—but of their existing society and economy. This nationalist mythology is not rooted in reality, and is indeed strikingly impervious to it. It prevents many Americans from understanding what is happening to them and their country in rational terms and crafting rational responses. Instead, they are explaining what has happened in irrational terms and crafting irrational responses.

Above all, the quasi-religious veneration for the Constitution and the "founders" that lies at the core of American civic nationalism makes it much harder to think of and discuss limited but essential ways in which it needs to be changed to meet the needs of a society so very different from that of the America for which it was designed more than 200 years ago.[2] In their combination of worship of the Constitution with a new form of old white middle class fears and resentments, the Tea Parties represent a combination or synthesis of the American nationalist thesis and antithesis.

My own work is founded on the work of American scholars of the past and present. In particular, I have looked to that great generation of American thinkers who sought to understand the phenomena of McCarthyism and the Vietnam War in terms of aspects of American history and culture: figures like Richard Hofstadter, Reinhold Niebuhr, C. Vann Woodward, and perhaps most of all Louis Hartz, whose work is of crucial importance for an understanding both of the reaction to

9/11 and the rise of the Tea Parties, but is almost unknown in the United States today outside narrow sections of academia.[3]

"Nationalism" has not been the usual prism through which American political culture has been viewed. Most Americans have spoken of their attachment to their country as "patriotism," in an extreme form as "superpatriotism," or in an ideological form as "Americanism." Critics of the United States, at home and abroad, have tended to focus on what has been called American "imperialism." The United States today does indeed harbor important forces that can be called imperialist in their outlook and aims. However, though large in influence, these people are relatively few in number. They are to be found in overlapping sections of the intelligentsia and the foreign policy and security establishments, with a particular concentration among the so-called neoconservatives.

However, to inspire many Americans to support imperial projects, it is necessary to appeal to them in terms not of imperialism, but of nationalism. Unlike large numbers of Englishmen, Frenchmen, and others at the time of their empires, the vast majority of ordinary Americans do not think of themselves as imperialist, or as possessing an empire. As public disillusionment with the war in Iraq and the growing desire for withdrawal from Afghanistan have demonstrated, they are also simply not prepared to make the massive long-term commitments and sacrifices necessary to maintain a direct American empire. Indeed, Bush's unprecedented combination of war and tax cuts demonstrated very clearly that the Republicans did not in fact expect the American population as a whole to make sacrifices for America's empire.

Apart from the effects of modern culture on attitudes toward military service and sacrifice, American culture historically has embodied a strong strain of isolationism, which is especially strongly marked in the Tea Party movement that developed in 2009, and later in response to the policies of the Obama administration. This isolationism is, however, a complex phenomenon that should not be understood simply as a desire to withdraw from the world—though this sentiment is undoubtedly present. Rather, American isolationism in part forms another face both of American chauvinism and American messianism, in the form of a belief in America as a unique "city on a hill." As a result, it is often closely related to nationalist unilateralism in international affairs. This aspect of isolationism forms part of a view that if the United States really has no choice at all but to involve itself with disgusting and inferior foreigners, it must absolutely control the process, and must under no circumstances subject itself to foreign control, or even advice.

Unlike previous empires, the U.S. national identity and what has been called the "American Creed" are founded on adherence to democracy. However imperfectly democracy may be practiced at home, and hypocritically preached abroad, this democratic faith does set real limits to how far the United States can exert direct rule over other peoples. The United States since 1945 has therefore been an indirect empire, resembling more closely the Dutch in the East Indies in the seventeenth and eighteenth centuries than the British in India.

As far as the mass of the American people is concerned, even an indirect American empire is still "an empire in denial," and in presenting their imperial plans to the American people, the Bush administration was careful to package them as something else: on the one hand, as part of a benevolent strategy of spreading American values of democracy and freedom; on the other, as an essential part of the defense not of an American empire, but of the American nation itself.

A great many Americans are not only intensely nationalistic, but bellicose in their response to any perceived attack or slight against the United States: "Don't Tread on Me!" as the rattlesnake on the American revolutionary flag declared (a slogan taken up by the Tea Parties, though as a statement of antigovernment individualism rather than nationalism). This attitude was summed up by that American nationalist icon, John Wayne, in his last role as a dying gunfighter in *The Shootist*: "I won't be wronged, I won't be insulted, and I won't be laid a hand on. I don't do these things to other people, and I require the same from them."[4]

As an expression of pride, honor, and a capacity for self-defense, these are sympathetic and indeed admirable words. However, it is useful in this context to remember an eighteenth-century expression, "to trail one's coat." This meant deliberately to provoke a quarrel by allowing your coat to trail along the ground so that another man would step on it, thereby allowing you to challenge him to a duel. One might say that American imperialists trail America's coat across the whole world while most ordinary Americans are not looking, and rely on those same Americans to react with "don't tread on me" nationalist fury when the coat is trodden upon. Over the next generation, this combination of U.S. attitudes risks colliding disastrously with a rising Chinese popular nationalism that is also extremely sensitive to real and perceived slights.

This tradition in America also means that it would be highly unwise to assume that the instinctive but unfocused and poorly thought-out isolationism of many in the Tea Parties will lead their representatives to take a more pacific and multilateral approach to international affairs than that of the Republican Party in general.

This is also due to sheer ignorance of the world outside the United States, which—coupled with basic chauvinist prejudices—makes Tea Party representatives in Washington easy subjects of manipulation by Republican foreign policy experts, the great majority of whom—as of 2012—remain essentially neoconservative in their imperialistic and unilateralist approaches to U.S. strategy.

Coupled with particular American prejudices against Islam in the wake of 9/11, public ignorance of the Muslim world allowed the Bush administration to carry out a catastrophic extension of the "war against terrorism" from its original—and legitimate—targets of Al Qaeda and the Taliban to embrace the Iraqi Baathist regime, anti-Israeli groups in Palestine and Lebanon, and quite possibly other countries and forces in future. This reserve of embittered nationalism has also been tapped by the Republicans with regard to a wide range of international proposals that can be portrayed as hurting America or infringing on American national sovereignty, from the International Criminal Court to restrictions on greenhouse gas emissions. The United States under Bush drove toward empire, and the domestic political fuel fed into the engine was that of a wounded and vengeful nationalism.

After the election in 2008 of President Barack Obama, American nationalism was heavily exploited by the Republicans in their battle to undermine him. Particularly striking was the furious Republican attack on the president for his statement in 2009 that "I believe in American exceptionalism, just as I suspect that the Brits believe in British exceptionalism and the Greeks believe in Greek exceptionalism."

In fact, President Obama followed this up with what was in fact a statement of classical American civic nationalism, albeit with a multilateralist tone:

> I'm enormously proud of my country and its role and history in the world. If you think about the site of this summit and what it means, I don't think America should be embarrassed to see evidence of the sacrifices of our troops, the enormous amount of resources that were put into Europe postwar, and our leadership in crafting an alliance that ultimately led to the unification of Europe. We should take great pride in that.
>
> And if you think of our current situation, the United States remains the largest economy in the world. We have unmatched military capability. And I think that we have a core set of values that are enshrined in our Constitution, in our body of law, in our democratic practices, in our belief in free speech and equality, that, though imperfect, are exceptional.

Republicans, however, were able to take the first sentence out of context and use it to argue to great effect that Obama was insufficiently committed to a belief in America's unique greatness. In her book *America By Heart*, Sarah Palin, Republican candidate for vice president in 2008 and a Tea Party activist *avant la lettre*, responded that

> they [i.e., the Democrats] don't believe we have a special message for the world or a special mission to preserve our greatness for the betterment of not just ourselves, but all of humanity. Astonishingly, President Obama even said that he believes in American exceptionalism in the same way "the Brits believe in British exceptionalism and the Greeks believe in Greek exceptionalism." Which is to say, he doesn't believe in American exceptionalism at all. He seems to think it is just a kind of irrational prejudice in favor of our way of life. To me, that is appalling.[5]

This background helps explain tragicomic statistics like the majority of Americans who believe that their country spends more than 20 percent of its budget on foreign aid, and that this figure should be reduced—when the true figure is less than 1 percent and the lowest in the developed world. Combined figures like this allow international critics of American hegemony to portray the United States as a purely selfish imperial power, without generosity and without real vision. This pattern is strange, and very sad, when contrasted with the tremendous generosity of many Americans when it comes to domestic and private charities, and brings out the degree to which chauvinist nationalism can undermine even the noblest of impulses.[6]

The Two Souls of American Nationalism

Like other nationalisms in the world, American nationalism has many different faces, and this book does not pretend to explore all of them. Rather, it concentrates on what I take to be the two most important elements in the historical culture of American nationalism, and the complex relationship between them. Erik Erikson wrote that "every national character is constructed out of polarities," and as I shall show, this is certainly true of the United States, which embodies among other things both the most modern *and* the most traditionalist society in the developed world.[7]

The clash between them is contributing to the growing political polarization of American society. The bitter deadlock in Congress is beginning to have a disastrous effect on the effectiveness of the U.S. government and the health of the U.S. economy. This clash in turn reflects greater differences in social and cultural attitudes than at any time since the Vietnam War. White evangelical Protestants vote Republican rather than Democrat by a factor of almost two to one, with corresponding effects on the parties' stances on abortion and other moral issues. The gap is almost as great when it comes to nationalism, with 71 percent of Republicans in 2003 describing themselves as "very patriotic" compared to 48 percent of Democrats. This reflects in part racial political allegiances, with 65 percent of whites describing themselves as "very patriotic" in that year to only 38 percent of blacks. Gaps concerning attitudes toward crime and faith in American business are even greater.[8]

It is, however, not the opposition, but the combination of these different strands that determines the overall nature of the American national identity and largely shapes American attitudes and policies toward the outside world. This was demonstrated by the Bush administration, which, as chapter 5 will explore, drew its rhetoric from both main strands of American nationalism simultaneously.

The first of these strands in American nationalism is examined in chapter 2. It stems from what has been called the "American Creed," and which I also describe as the "American thesis": the set of great democratic, legal, and individualist beliefs and principles on which the American state and Constitution are founded. These principles form the foundation of American civic nationalism, and also help bind the United States into the wider community of democratic states. They are shared with other democratic societies, but in America they have a special role in holding a disparate nation together, and as the term "creed" implies, are held with an ideological and almost religious fervor.

While Americans' belief in democracy is in itself admirable, the extent of blind faith in the existing form of the Constitution—as reflected in the Tea Parties most especially—blinds many Americans to the extent to which aspects of a constitution drawn up in the late eighteenth century are becoming a crippling problem for the America of the twenty-first century. Even relatively small amendments to the Constitution—such as have been passed several times in American history—now seem ruled out, not only by the deadlock in Washington, but by the fetishism of the Constitution in portions of the public. This problem will be explored in chapter 2.

The second element in American nationalism forms what I have called the American nationalist "antithesis," and stems above all from ethnoreligious roots. Aspects of this tradition have also been called "Jacksonian nationalism," after President Andrew Jackson (1767–1845), and will be explored in chapters 3 and 4.[9] Because the United States is so large and complex compared with other countries, and has changed so much over time, this nationalist tradition is correspondingly complex.

Rather than the simple, monolithic identity of a Polish or Thai ethnoreligious nationalism, this tradition in the United States forms a diffuse mass of identities and impulses, including nativist sentiments on the part of America's original white population, the particular culture of the white South, and the beliefs and agendas of ethnic lobbies. America's highly variegated national and nationalist identity is reflected, among other places, in the diffuse makeup of the Tea Parties.

Nonetheless, these nativist features can often be distinguished from the principles of the American Creed and of American civic nationalism; and although many of their features are specifically American—notably the role of fundamentalist Protestantism and their fanatical faith in the U.S. Constitution—they are also related to wider patterns of ethnoreligious nationalism in the world. The continuing strength of nativist sentiment in the United States was shown in the widespread belief—determinedly cultivated by portions of the Republican Party— that President Obama was not born an American citizen or in the United States. These strands in American nationalism are usually subordinate to American civic nationalism stemming from the creed, which dominates America's official and public political culture. However, they have a natural tendency to rise to the surface in times of crisis and conflict. In the specific case of America's attachment to Israel, ethnoreligious factors have become dominant, with extremely dangerous consequences for the war on terrorism.

The reason why "civic nationalism" rather than "patriotism" is the appropriate name for the dominant strand in American political culture was well summed up in 1983 by one of the fathers of the neoconservative school in the United States, Irving Kristol: "Patriotism springs from love of the nation's past; nationalism arises out of hope for the nation's future, distinctive greatness... The goals of American foreign policy must go well beyond a narrow, too literal definition of 'national security.' It is the national interest of a world power, as this is defined by a sense of national destiny."[10]

In drawing this distinction, Kristol echoed a classic distinction between patriotism and nationalism delineated by Kenneth Minogue, one of the great historians of nationalism. Minogue defined patriotism as essentially conservative, a desire to defend your country as it actually is, whereas nationalism is a devotion to an ideal, abstract, unrealized notion of your country, often coupled with a belief in some wider national mission to humanity. In other words, nationalism has always had a certain revolutionary edge to it. In American political culture at the start of the twenty-first century, there is certainly a very strong element of patriotism, of attachment to American institutions and to America in its present form, but as Kristol's words indicate, there is also a revolutionary element, a commitment to a messianic vision of the nation and its role in the world.[11] This aspect of American civic nationalism will be examined in chapter 2.

As the American historian and social critic Richard Hofstadter (1917–1970) wrote, "the most prominent and pervasive failing [of American political culture] is a certain proneness to fits of moral crusading that would be fatal if they were not sooner or later tempered with a measure of apathy and common sense."[12] This pattern has indeed repeated itself in our time, with the aftermath of the Iraq War leading to a new sobriety in American policies and the American public mood. In the meantime, however, the Bush administration's appeal to this crusading and messianic spirit played a major part in getting the United States into Iraq in the first place.

If Minogue's and Kristol's distinctions between patriotism and nationalism are valid, then it must be acknowledged that nationalism, rather than patriotism, is indeed the correct word with which to describe the characteristic national feeling of Americans. And this feature also links the American nationalism of today to the "unsatisfied," late-coming nationalisms of Germany, Italy, and Russia, rather than the satisfied and status quo patriotism of the British.

But if one strand of American nationalism is radical because it looks forward to "the nation's future, distinctive greatness," another is radical because it continuously looks backwards, to a vanished and idealized national past. A growing tension in American culture is between, on the one hand, a civic nationalism that believes optimistically that America's inevitable greatness is rooted in universal values, and on the other hand, a country that is in many ways in decline compared with other countries in the world and compared to America's status in the past. Indeed, the change in America's fortunes has been astonishingly swift, and deep anxiety and bewilderment at this among Americans have inevitably strengthened the desire to return to the past.

This "American antithesis" is a central feature of American radical conservatism—the world of the Republican Right, and especially the Christian Right and the Tea Parties, with their rhetoric of "taking back" America and restoring an older, purer American society. As explored in chapters 3 and 4, this long-standing tendency in American culture and politics reflects the continuing conservative religiosity of many Americans; it has also, however, always been an expression of social, economic, cultural, religious, ethnic, and racial anxieties. These have assumed a new virulence in the years following 2008, in the context of the economic recession, the rise of Chinese power, and the first black president of the United States.

In part, these anxieties stem from the progressive loss of control over society by the "original" white Anglo-Saxon and Scots-Irish populations, later joined by others. Connected to this are class anxieties—in the past, the hostility of the small towns and countryside toward the new immigrant-populated cities; today, the economic decline of the traditional white middle and working classes, which dates back to the 1970s but accelerated greatly after 2008.

As a result of economic, cultural, and demographic change in America, the supremely victorious nation of the modern age, large numbers of Americans feel defeated. The domestic anxieties this generates spill over into attitudes toward the outside world, with 64 percent of Americans in 2002 agreeing that "our way of life needs to be protected against foreign influence," compared to 51 percent of British and 53 percent of French. These figures lie between those for Western Europe and those for developing world countries like India (76 percent)—which is piquant, because the "foreign influence" that Indian and other cultural nationalists in the developing world most fear is, of course, that of the United States.[13]

These fears help give many American nationalists their curiously embittered and defensive edge, so curiously at odds with America's image and self-image as a land of success, openness, wealth, and generosity. Over the years, the hatred generated by this sense of defeat and alienation has been extended to both domestic and foreign enemies.

This too is a very old pattern in different nationalisms worldwide. Historically speaking, in Europe at least, radical conservatism and nationalism have tended to stem from classes and groups in actual or perceived decline as a result of socioeconomic change. One way of looking at American nationalism, and America's troubled relationship with the contemporary world America dominates, is indeed to understand that many Americans are in revolt against the world that America itself has made, because—for reasons that they cannot understand and that in many ways the American Creed prevents them from understanding—they feel that this American-made world has now turned against them, their families, and America as a whole.

However, it should be noted that with the exception of the extreme fringe among the various "militia" groups, the neo-Nazis, and so on, these forces of the American antithesis are not in public revolt against the American Creed and American civic nationalism as such.[14] Most radical nationalist and radical conservative movements elsewhere in the world have in the past opposed democracy and demanded authoritarian rule. In contrast, Americans from this tradition generally believe strongly in the American democratic and liberal creed. Indeed, among the Tea Parties it has become a reigning obsession. However, they also believe—consciously or unconsciously, openly or in private—that it is the product of a specific white American civilization, which is threatened by immigration, racial minorities, and foreign influence. And I am not saying that they are necessarily wrong; a discussion of this point lies outside the scope of the present book. I am only pointing out that people with this belief naturally feel embattled, embittered, and defensive as a result of many contemporary trends.[15]

American Protestant fundamentalist groups also do not reject the creed as such. In terms of their attitude toward culture and the intellect, however, their rejection of contemporary America is even deeper, for they reject key aspects of modernity itself. For them, modern American mass culture is a form of daily assault on their passionately held values, and their reactionary religious ideology in turn reflects the sense of social, cultural, and racial embattlement among their white middle class constituency. Even as America is marketing the "American dream" to the world, numerous Americans at home feel that they are living in an American nightmare.[16]

America is the home of by far the most deep, widespread, and conservative religious beliefs in the Western world, including a section possessed by wild millenarian hopes, fears, and hatreds—and these two phenomena are indeed intimately related. As a Pew Research Center Survey of 2002 demonstrated, at the start of the twenty-first century the United States as a whole in terms of religious belief is much closer to the developing world than to the industrialized countries (though, of course, a majority of these believers are not fundamentalist Protestants, but Catholics and "mainline," more liberal Protestants). This continues a pattern evident since the early nineteenth century and remarked on by Tocqueville, when religious belief among the European populations had been shaken by several decades of the Enlightenment and the French Revolution, but American religious belief was fervent and nearly universal.[17]

As of 2002, with 59 percent of respondents declaring that "religion plays a very important role in their lives," the United States lay between Mexico (57 percent) and Turkey (65 percent), but was very far from Canada (30 percent), Italy (27 percent), or Japan (12 percent). In terms of sheer percentage points, it was indeed closer on this scale to Pakistan (91 percent) than to France (12 percent).[18] When a U.S. senator exclaimed (apocryphally) of the Europeans, "What common values? They don't even go to church!," he was expressing a truth, and this is as true of the U.S. political elites (though not of the cultural or economic ones) as of the population in general. Among the fundamentalist Protestant portions of the United States, there has been a strong historical connection to American nationalism, and within this is an inclination to a "paranoid style," originally directed against Catholics, Freemasons, and others, and perpetuated by the cold war and the Communist threat.[19]

In our own time, "the recent Evangelical engagement with public life reflects religious and cultural habits that Anglo-American Protestants, both liberal and Evangelical, learned when threatened by Americans of different religious and ethnic backgrounds."[20] While it is not true that most American populist movements in modern times have been dominated by evangelical elements, they have all drawn on them for much of their support, and that remains true of the Tea Parties in 2011. Some leaders of the Tea Parties, like Michelle Bachmann, are shaped above all by their religious faith. The great majority of Tea Party leaders have been influenced by this tradition to some extent, or feel obliged to pay public respect to it because of its presence among their followers.

The extreme tension between these fundamentalist religious values and the modern American mass culture that now surrounds them is an important cause of the mood of beleaguered hysteria on the American Right that so bewilders outside observers. Across large areas of America, these religious beliefs in turn form a central part of the identity of the original white American colonist population, above all in the Greater South, or what Lady Bird Johnson described simply as "*us*—the simple American stock."[21]

The religious beliefs of large sections of this core population are under constant, daily threat from modern secular culture, above all via the mass media. And of equal importance is the decline in recent decades in the real incomes of large parts of the white American middle and working classes—a decline that has accelerated sharply with the great recession that began in 2008. This decline, and the wider economic changes that began with the oil shock of 1973, have had the side effect of helping force more and more women to go to work, thereby undermining traditional family structures even among those groups that are most devoted to them.

The relationship between this traditional white Protestant world and the forces of American economic, demographic, social, and cultural change may therefore be compared to the genesis of a hurricane. A mass of warm, humid air rises from the constantly churning sea of American capitalism to meet a mass of cooler layers of air, and as it rises it sucks in yet more air from the sides, in the form of immigration. The cooler layers are made up of the white middle class and their small-town and suburban worlds in much of the United States, the old white populations of the Greater South, and the especially frigid strata of old Anglo-Saxon and Scots-Irish fundamentalist Protestantism.

The result of this collision is the release of great bolts and explosions of political and cultural electricity. Like a hurricane, the resulting storm system is essentially circular, continually chasing its own tail, and essentially self-supporting, generating its own energy until, at some unforeseeable point in future, either the boiling seas of economic change cool down or the strata of religious belief and traditional culture dissolve, or the American system itself disintegrates. Among these bolts is hatred, including nationalist hatred.[22]

Externally directed chauvinist hatred must therefore be seen as a by-product of the same hatred displayed by the American Right at home, notably in their pathological loathing of Presidents Bill Clinton and Barack Obama. In Europe, Clinton was generally seen as a version of Tony Blair, a centrist who "modernized" his formerly center-Left party by stealing most of the clothes of the center-Right and adopting a largely right-wing economic agenda. Similarly, Obama was seen as a moderate conservative, engaged in highly limited reforms to preserve the existing system. And indeed this was not simply a perception. The program of Obama *has* in fact been a moderate conservative one, which would have been wholly acceptable to President Dwight Eisenhower, and in many respects to President Richard Nixon—both, of course, Republicans. Indeed, many more radical Democrats have accused their own president of "governing like a Republican."

To radical conservatives in America, this has been irrelevant. They have hated both Clinton and Obama principally not for what they *did*, but for what they *are*: the representatives of a multiracial, pluralist, and modernist culture and cultural elite that they both despise and fear, just as they hate the atheist, decadent, unmanly Western European nations not only for what they do, but for what they are.

In the U.S. context it is also crucial to remember that, as in a hurricane or thunderstorm, rather than simply being opposing forces, the two elements that combine to produce this system work together. The unrestrained free-market capitalism that is threatening the old conservative religious and cultural communities of Protestant America with dissolution is being urged on by the political representatives of those same communities. This is especially true of the Tea Parties, with their cult of low taxes (including for the rich), deregulation, and small government.[23]

This was not always so. In the 1890s and 1900s, this sector of America formed the backbone of the Populist protest against the excesses of American capitalism, and in the 1930s it voted solidly for Roosevelt's New Deal. Today, however, the religious Right has allied itself solidly with extreme "free-market" forces in the Republican Party—though it is precisely the workings of unrestrained American capitalism that are eroding the world the religious conservatives wish to defend.

In the economic sphere, the populist tradition has abandoned its former critique of free-market capitalism (except in the form of an empty rhetoric directed against banks) in favor of an exclusive concentration on debt as the source of the nation's economic woes. This focus on debt owes much to old cultural traditions, but it has also been deliberately and systematically fostered by right-wing portions of the U.S. media and the corporations and elites they represent—to the extent where the Tea Party obsession with the issue is beginning to threaten the U.S. economy and the long-term interests of those same elites.[24]

The clash between cultural and social loyalties and the imperatives of capitalist change is an old dilemma for social and cultural conservatives who at the same time are dedicated to the preservation of free-market economics. As Garry Wills has noted, "there is nothing less conservative than capitalism, so itchy for the new."[25] Karl Marx wrote of the inexorably shattering effects of capitalism on traditional societies in words that remind us that "globalization" and consequent unending and disruptive change are as old as capitalism itself:

> The bourgeoisie cannot exist without constantly revolutionizing the instruments of production, and thereby the relations of production, and with them the whole relations of society . . . All fixed, fast, frozen relations with their train of ancient and venerable prejudices and opinions, are swept away; all new-formed ones become antiquated before they can ossify. All that is solid melts into air, all that is holy is profaned, and man is at last compelled to face with his sober senses his real conditions of life and his relations with his kind . . . the bourgeoisie has through its exploitation of the world market given a cosmopolitan character to production and consumption in every country. To the great chagrin of Reactionists, it has drawn from under the feet of industry the national ground on which it stood. All old established national industries have been destroyed or are daily being destroyed.[26]

A vital function of myth in political culture is to reconcile such conflicting pressures, or rather to create an appearance of doing so that is sufficiently convincing to the society concerned.[27] Chapter 2 will examine how American national and nationalist myths do so in the case of the contemporary United States.

The Threat of Nationalism

The historical evidence of the dangers of unreflecting nationalist sentiments should be all too obvious, and are all too relevant to U.S. policy today. Nationalism thrives upon irrational hatreds, and upon the portrayal of other nations or ethnoreligious groups as congenitally, irredeemably wicked and hostile. Yesterday, this was true of the attitudes of many American nationalists toward Russia. Today, it risks becoming the case with regard to the Arab and Muslim worlds, and most dangerously of all, to China. Chauvinism in the Republican Party was at its height in the years immediately following 9/11, but as of 2012 there was very little sign that Republican leaders and their advisors had seriously rethought the attitudes of the Bush administration.[28]

In a striking essay, Fouad Ajami in 2003 unwittingly summed up the central danger of chauvinist American nationalism in imperial guise for the United States and the world, and also placed this nationalism squarely in the context of nationalist and imperialist history. The only specifically American aspect of this is his own non-American origins—and even this would have been entirely normal for great civilizational empires of the past. As chapter 1 will show, like America today, these empires did not distinguish between the racial origins of their subjects as long as they served the imperial state and accepted unreservedly the imperial ideology. To take a historical example from the Middle East, Ajami could be seen as a contemporary Arab Josephus working as an imperial propagandist for America's Rome.[29]

Ajami's essay ostensibly concerned anti-Americanism. He dismissed out of hand the evidence of Pew, Gallup, and other respected survey organizations demonstrating that hostility to America had increased greatly as a result of the policies of the Bush administration. Instead, Ajami argued, across the world—not just the Arab and Muslim worlds, but in Europe, Asia, and Latin America too—anti-Americanism is congenital, ingrained, and a response to America's wealth, success, and modernity, which is forcing other countries to change their systems. The essay suggests that U.S. policies are completely irrelevant to international attitudes toward the United States, and the sympathy displayed by France and other countries after 9/11 was completely hypocritical: "To maintain France's sympathy, and that of Le Monde, the United States would have had to turn the other cheek to the murderers of Al Qaeda, spare the Taliban, and engage the Muslim World in some high civilisational dialogue. But who needs high approval ratings in Marseille?"[30]

Ajami's argument was taken up in an even cruder form in an article for *Time* magazine by the leading right-wing commentator Charles Krauthammer, entitled simply "To Hell With Sympathy." In this he both attacked "the world" and sought to tar his domestic political opponents with the same anti-American brush:

> The world apparently likes the US when it is on its knees. From that the Democrats deduce a foreign policy—remain on our knees, humble and supplicant, and enjoy the applause and "support" of the world...The search for logic in anti-Americanism is fruitless. It is in the air the world breathes. Its roots are envy and self-loathing—by peoples who, yearning for modernity but having failed at it, find their one satisfaction in despising modernity's great exemplar. On September 11th, they gave it a rest for one day. Big deal.[31]

Or as Fox News star Bill O'Reilly put it, explaining the great difference between coverage of the push for war with Iraq in the U.S. media and internationally, "Well, everywhere else in the world lies."[32]

The whole point of such arguments is that—like all such nationalist discourses—they are intended to free America from moral responsibility for the consequences of its actions, and therefore to leave America free to do anything. To this end, facts are falsified or ignored (e.g., that France strongly supported the United States in Afghanistan) and usual standards of evidence suspended. Thus reputable opinion polls, used as basic sources of reliable information in every other context, are suddenly declared to be irrelevant—leaving national prejudice and an assumption of national superiority as the only standards of judgment.

Other nations are declared to be irrationally, incorrigibly, and unchangingly hostile. This being so, it is obviously pointless to seek compromises with them or to try to accommodate their interests and views. And because they are irrational and barbarous, America is free to dictate to them or even conquer them for their own good. This is precisely the discourse of nationalists in the leading European states toward each other and lesser breeds before 1914, which helped drag Europe into the great catastrophes of the twentieth century. It was also a central part of the old hideous discourse of anti-Semitism.

Thus it is especially depressing that arguments of this kind in the United States are often linked to very similar ones on behalf of Israel, and intended to absolve Israel of any responsibility for the consequences of its actions—a theme that will be explored in chapter 6. In the words of Brian Klug:

> If Israel is basically the victim of persecution in an anti-Semitic world, then it bears no responsibility for the situation in which it finds itself: the object of widespread condemnation...Nothing that the Jewish state does or refrains from doing could produce it or prevent it. All Israel can do, if it really is "the collective Jew among the nations," reprising the role of pariah, is fight for its survival, defying the world and keeping it at bay.[33]

What also links this kind of radical nationalist discourse in both America and Israel is that the enemy is seen by its proponents as almost universal. Nationalists in other countries restrict their hostility to a limited number of other nations—and indeed, over the years I have seen this accusation of incorrigible and wicked anti-Americanism applied to Russians, Arabs, and Chinese as an excuse for America adopting whatever policies it likes toward them. But only in America, and Israel perhaps, could an influential political writer like Charles Krauthammer declare the world itself to be the mad enemy. And this language did not appear on some backwoods talk show, but in America's leading news magazine and one of its foremost foreign policy journals.

If such visions come to dominate the politics of the United States, they will be disastrous not only for American interests and American security, but for America's soul. Pathological hatred and fear of the outside world will feed the same emotions in American domestic politics, until America's moral and cultural greatness lies in ruins and America's legacy to the future is also ruined beyond repair.

The dangers of a chauvinist version of American nationalism may be greatest of all when it comes to relations with China. Here, the United States is experiencing a situation that it has never faced before in its history, that of a declining power confronted with a rapidly rising one. The historical precedents for such a situation are not at all good. Managing it will take immense restraint and moderation in both China and the United States. If, on the other hand, an embittered, resentful, and chauvinist American nationalism runs into an edgy and aggressive Chinese nationalism still obsessed with past Chinese defeats and humiliations, the results could be catastrophic for modern civilization.

One

An Exceptional Nationalism?

Nations, as individuals, who are completely innocent in their own esteem, are insufferable in their human contacts.

—Reinhold Niebuhr[1]

The terrorist attacks of September 11, 2001, struck a country in which the strength of its nationalism already made it very much the "outlier" in the developed world.[2] Under the Bush administration, this feature of American political culture was one of the most important factors in alienating the United States from some of its closest allies in Europe and elsewhere. This nationalism separates the United States from what Europeans have come to think of (in their own Eurocentric way) as central patterns of post-1945 modernity, namely the overcoming of a culture of bellicose nationalism by "modern" civilization, and the replacement of nationalist unilateralism with international cooperation. To disagreements over policy, it adds the perception of profound cultural differences.

This general, deeply felt, and rather unreflective American nationalism was inflamed by the attacks of 9/11, and then exploited by dominant sections of the Bush administration for their own purposes: abroad, the expansion of American imperial power; at home, the further consolidation of the power and wealth of what Michael Lind has called the American "overclass."[3] According to the Pew Research Center in 2011, "the proportion [of Americans polled] saying they are very patriotic has varied by just four percentage points (between 87 percent to 91 percent) across 13 surveys conducted over 22 years."[4]

Closely related is the very widespread presence in U.S. popular culture of national symbolism and national language. This extends from the most obvious symbol—the flag—through the patriotic celebrations and primers to be found at supermarket checkout counters. All of this is far more reminiscent of Europe in 1904 than Europe in 2004. The endless references to the nation also extends in small and unrecognized ways throughout American life, just as they did in Europe before 1914.

16

Visitors to the US are frequently impressed by the outward show and symbols of conscious nationalism. Children are taught to salute the flag, and it is flown by private individuals to demonstrate their patriotism. The word "American" is used with a wealth of overtones, so that to describe oneself or a custom or an institution as "American" is to claim a whole set of positive values. The all American boy has become something of a joke, but it is a character which most American parents covet for their sons. Conversely, to be "un-American" is not to be merely foreign or unfamiliar, but dangerous, immoral, subversive and deluded. Fourth of July orations are the classic expressions of American patriotism, but hyperbole is not confined to these rhetorical exercises; and to foreign ears, the discourse of public men seems to be marked to an extraordinary degree by appeals to the special character and destiny of the American people.[5]

William R. Brock wrote this in 1974, but it is no less true a generation later. As of 2012, there is no sign that the economic recession (including most notably the collapse of the housing market, of which Freddie Mac was a leading booster) has had any effect on these attitudes.

In my local supermarket I bought "A Celebration of America: Your Helpful Guide to America's Greatness," part of the "Better Your Home" series.[6] The children's section of Dalton's Booksellers at Union Station in Washington, DC, in the fall of 2003 also contained a "Celebrate America" stand, with books with titles like *American Patriots*, *God Bless America*, and *America's Promise*, a small hagiography of Laura Bush, *America's First Lady*, and a *Patriotic Primer* "for reading levels 4–8" by Lynne Cheney, wife of Vice President Dick Cheney. The last stretches from "A is for America, the land that we love" to "Z is the end of the alphabet, but not of America's story. Strong and free, we will continue to be an inspiration to the world."[7]

Just as in Europe in the past, emotional support for the American armed forces (though, of course, not necessarily for their specific missions) is virtually omnipresent in the mainstream media. *Time* magazine made its "Man of the Year" for 2003 "The American Soldier." The *Washington Post* Sunday *Parade* section regularly carries cover articles on military and patriotic themes. In an absolutely classic image of this kind, its last issue of 2003 carried a cover picture of an avuncular American military medic holding a wounded Iraqi child.

Another issue of *Parade* featured the former prisoner of war (POW) Jessica Lynch on the cover, declaring "The Pledge [of Allegiance] Will Never Be Just Words For Me" (months by the way after most of the details of her capture and recapture as reported by the *Post* had been admitted to be wild patriotic exaggerations).[8] Advice columnists like "Dear Abby" often feature pieces about how readers can support the troops abroad. Very little of this kind of thing now remains even in Britain and France, the most military-minded of the European states, though once such images were omnipresent.[9]

Also entirely characteristic of old Europe are traditional ritual affirmations of American nationhood, like the daily recital of the Pledge of Allegiance in schools and the celebration of Memorial Day in smaller towns. "The sentiment that is continually reaffirmed by these sacred ceremonies is the conviction that America is a nation called to a special destiny by God."[10] Of course, all European nations have their own national rituals and ceremonies. Only rarely, however, are these celebrated as widely or with so much emotional force as in the United States.

In the words of the great Russian-born student of America and editor of *The Nation* Max Lerner, "the cult of the nation as social myth has run as a thread through the whole of American history."[11] Alexis de Tocqueville noticed its strong presence in the 1830s, and traced it to the fact that "democratic institutions generally give men a lofty notion of their country, and of themselves." (In an irritated moment, he also remarked that "it is impossible to conceive of a more troublesome and garrulous patriotism."[12]) At that time, even in France, ordinary country people often still had no real conception of France or French identity, and were attached instead to purely local loyalties.[13]

The greater age of American mass nationalism is closely related to other key features of American "exceptionalism." The North American colonies inherited from Britain strong elements of a relatively clear-cut national cultural identity centered on a mixture of the Protestant religion and belief in the institutions of law, liberty, and representative government.[14] This was incarnated both in their own institutions and later in the American Constitution.

The fact that as colonists in a new land Americans were in some sense truly "born equal" has been advanced by many scholars from Tocqueville on as the fundamental difference between the political traditions and cultures of the United States and Europe; the United States, lacking a feudal tradition and an aristocracy, also escaped violent social revolution, socialism, and most of the political forms and traditions that stemmed from these movements and collisions.

The result was that under the froth and spume of political clashes lay a remarkably homogeneous, continuous, basically unchanging, universally held civic nationalist ideology—"an absolute Americanism as old as the country itself."[15] By the early twentieth century, as Herbert Croly wrote in 1909,

> the faith of Americans in their country is religious, if not in its intensity, at any rate in its almost absolute and universal authority. It pervades the air we breathe. As children, we hear it asserted or implied in the conversation of our elders. Every new stage of our educational training provides some additional testimony on its behalf. Newspapers and novelists, orators and playwrights, even if they are little else, are at least loyal preachers of the Truth. The skeptic is not controverted; he is overlooked. It constitutes the kind of faith which is the implication, rather than the object, of thought, and consciously or unconsciously, it enters largely into our personal lives as a formative influence.[16]

This tendency has been strongly marked in the response of conservative Americans to the combination in recent years of economic recession, long-term decline of the middle class, and the relative decline of the United States on the international stage. It has encouraged a desire for a return to the past, based on a deep but unthinking attachment to a supposedly perfect and therefore unchangeable U.S. Constitution. This, in turn, has discouraged deeper thinking about America's problems and how address them, and has tremendously served the short-term interests of economic elites concerned with preventing any reform of the existing U.S. system. This need on the part of the elites has grown still further as a result of the economic recession starting in 2011, which might have been expected to lead to a fundamental rethinking of aspects of the American capitalist system, comparable to the changes introduced by Roosevelt's New Deal.

The nationalist cult of American "exceptionalism"—which in populist and Republican discourse is a barely veiled euphemism for American superiority to all other nations—also legitimizes ferocious criticism of anyone who suggests that America in some respects has fallen behind other countries, and can learn from them. Thus the public debate on health care reform was greatly hampered by the difficulty supporters of reform have found in publicly comparing the U.S. health care system to those of other Western countries, and thereby bringing out how much more the United States pays for worse results. Such a comparison would be instinctively felt to be unpatriotic by many Americans.

Imperialism and Nationalism

As stated in the introduction, the Bush administration and its intellectual backers—who as of 2012 continue to dominate thinking on foreign and security policy in the Republican Party—also exploited American nationalism to tremendous effect in the service of what was in fact an imperialist agenda. This does not, however, necessarily reflect conscious hypocrisy or cynical and cold-blooded manipulation of the public, though these elements have certainly been present.

The point is rather that, as with their equivalents in the Europe of the past, the nationalist Right in the United States absolutely and sincerely identify themselves with their nation, to the point where the presence of any other group in government is seen not as a defeat, but as a usurpation, as something profoundly and inherently illegitimate and "un-American." They feel themselves to be as much "America" as the Kaiser and the Junkers felt themselves to be "Germany" and the Tsar and the Russian noble elites to be "Russia."

In European history, closely linked to this identification of elites with their countries has been the exploitation of nationalism for the purposes of imperialism—also seen by elites as a higher national good that the ignorant masses cannot understand and into which they have to be led, if necessary by deceit. Rudyard Kipling and other imperialists notoriously despised the ordinary people of their countries, with their pathetic ordinary lives and dreams, their banal indifference to imperial visions, and their unwillingness to die for such visions.

This is how the Bush administration seemed at heart to view the American people too. As a range of observers from historian Andrew Bacevich to humorist Bill Maher pointed out, from the first days after 9/11 the Bush administration carefully omitted calls for sacrifice from its rhetoric to the American people, and indeed urged them to resume normal spending patterns to help the economy: "The primary responsibility of the average citizen for the duration of the emergency remained what it had been in more peaceful times: to be an engine of consumption." Sacrifice was to be restricted to the armed forces.[17]

Public disillusionment with the wars in both Iraq and Afghanistan has revealed yet again the lack of appetite of ordinary Americans for direct empire, with all its costs in blood and treasure.[18] This was despite the fact that—without any evidence, but with the encouragement of leading Bush administration officials and the pro-war media like Fox News—a great many Americans believed that Saddam Hussein was directly involved in the 9/11 attacks, and therefore—by extension—that the war with Iraq was a legitimate act of traditional self-defense. In a Harris poll in February 2004, 74 percent of respondents still believed that a link between Iraq and Al Qaeda before the war was either certain or likely. An NBC poll in March 2004 showed 57 percent still believing that Iraq had possessed weapons of mass destruction.[19]

In the 2000 American election campaign, foreign and security policy was overwhelmingly absent both from the debates and from the concerns of U.S. voters as expressed in opinion polls. Even declared Bush voters polled in September 2000 put seventh on their list of priorities, with only 6 percent saying the candidate's stand on this issue mattered most to them. Top concerns were taxes and abortion, at 22 percent each. Al Gore voters polled did not mention defense as a priority at all. Neither set of voters mentioned foreign policy as such.[20]

As the *New York Times* commented on Bush's neglect of these issues, "but then, Bush may have decided that too much talk about foreign policy is bad business. He has talked often to friends and acquaintances about his father's loss to Bill Clinton eight years ago, when the elder Bush focused on foreign affairs and the Arkansas neophyte emphasized the economy."[21]

An unwillingness on the part of the masses to make serious sacrifices for empire is not new. Until the World War I, the British empire was conquered and run very much on the cheap (largely by local native auxiliaries—not unlike the United States in Afghanistan after 2001), and this was true of the other colonial empires as well. The Royal Navy was, of course, expensive, but it doubled as the absolutely necessary defense of the British Isles themselves against invasion or blockade.

Then as now, given the overwhelming superiority of Western firepower and military organization, enormous territories could be conquered at very low cost and risk. When European empires ran into areas that would be truly costly to conquer and hold—the British in Afghanistan, the Italians in Ethiopia—they tended to back off. In the view of the British imperial historian Niall Ferguson, the unprecedentedly heavy British casualties in the Boer War can be seen as beginning the process of British disillusionment with empire.[22]

This absence of a willingness to make sacrifices for empire among the European masses was something of which the general staffs and the conservative establishments of Europe were well aware. Students of both Clausewitz and of the reports of their police on the mood of the proletariats, they knew the importance of mass support for any serious war, and the limits on how far empire could be used for purposes of mass mobilization. So sensible governments with the ability to do so always used volunteer troops and foreign mercenaries, not conscripts, for colonial wars.

The French Foreign Legion was created for this explicit purpose. The British Army was a small volunteer force, but also used Indian troops as much as possible for the task of colonial war and policing. When countries did use conscripts in colonial wars, the results were often disastrous both to the campaign itself and to domestic political stability—witness Italy after the defeat at Adowa in Ethiopia, Russia after the Russo-Japanese war, and Spain after the catastrophe of Anual in Morocco in 1921, which in some ways began the historical process leading to the Spanish Civil War.[23]

The U.S. adoption of the "Revolution in Military Affairs" from the 1990s on, coupled with the use of local auxiliaries in Afghanistan and elsewhere, has been seen as a new imperialist version of the British use of "gunboats and Gurkhas" intended to spare the use of the imperial power's troops.[24] But as the debacle in Iraq after the initial conquest demonstrated, high technology and local auxiliaries only go so far. In a truly imperial strategy, the use of large numbers of U.S. troops will also be necessary—and this will not be popular at home, unless they can be shown to be fighting not for an empire, but for the nation itself.

In Douglas Porch's work on the French conquest of Morocco, the author presents a fascinating description of the various stratagems Marshal Hubert Lyautey and the other French imperialists used to convince a thoroughly skeptical French public to support this adventure, which many regarded as economically pointless and a costly distraction from the need to strengthen France's defenses against the real national threat, Germany. French conscripts did serve to a limited extent in Algeria (legally not a colony, but part of France), and this was extremely unpopular with French youth. Fear of colonial military service fed in turn on much older hatreds of military service, especially among peasants, which extended across Europe.[25]

The French ultranationalist Paul Deroulede declared that in Alsace and Lorraine he had lost two sisters, and all the French colonialists were offering him in return were "twenty black servants."[26] Hence the prominence of the propaganda concerning France's *mission civilisatrice* and the need to create a modern Moroccan state and abolish "barbarism" there, but also suggestions that because Germany too had designs on Morocco, the wider struggle with Germany required French control of that country.[27]

The central domestic political strategy of capitalist elites in Europe before 1914 was to rely much less on imperialism than on nationalism to rally democratic support as a defense against socialism. And in 1914, the impulse that drove the European masses to support the war and to immolate themselves in it was nationalism, universally expressed in the genuine belief that the homeland itself was in imminent danger of attack.

As Jean-Jacques Becker stresses in the case of France, despite the intense nationalism of much of French culture in 1914, the initial popular response to the crisis of July 1914 was worried and very desirous of peace. Only when the German ultimatum appeared as a clear case of aggression against the *patrie* herself did mass enthusiasm for war develop.[28] Despite all the periodic flare-ups of tension over colonial rivalries, the great European powers in the decades before 1914 never did in fact go to war over a colonial issue (with the exception of Russia and Japan in 1904). One key reason for this was a well-based doubt in the minds of European governments and militaries about the response of the masses to a bloody war that had obviously begun as a squabble between two greedy predators in an unpronounceable African swamp.

The terrorist attacks of September 11, 2001, were a real and atrocious attack on the American homeland. Any U.S. administration—indeed, any self-respecting country in the world—would have had to respond to this attack by seeking to destroy the perpetrators. The war to destroy the Al Qaeda forces in Afghanistan and their Taliban backers was therefore a completely legitimate response to the 9/11 attacks, as are U.S. actions against Al Qaeda and its allies elsewhere in the world. What the Bush administration did, however, was to instill in the U.S. public a fear of much wider threats to the U.S. homeland from states like Iraq, Iran, and North Korea that had no connection to Al Qaeda. By doing so, they created a belief that anything America does is essentially defensive and a response to "terrorism." By foisting this belief on the American people, the latter could therefore to some extent be mobilized for imperial war.[29]

But even the Bush administration had to remain within certain limits. The common paradigm of hostility toward Muslims and the inability to distinguish between Muslims made it possible to mix up Iraq and Al Qaeda in the minds of a majority of Americans, but not even Bush would have gotten away with declaring that the terrorists on 9/11 were really Russians, or Chinese, or North Koreans. For that matter, Bush's first election campaign deliberately concealed his followers' imperial ambitions—as in his remark that the United States should adopt a more "humble" approach to international affairs, and that "I am worried about overcommitting our military around the world. I would be judicious in its use."[30]

The distinction between imperialism and nationalism is therefore an important one to keep in mind; and one key way of understanding the political strategy of the Bush administration after 9/11 is that—like some of their European predecessors before them—they essentially tried to drive a program of imperial hegemony with the fuel of a wounded but also bewildered and befuddled nationalism.

Spared by History

Like European imperialists of the past, many Americans genuinely see their country's national interests and ambitions as coterminous with goodness, civilization, progress, and the interests of all humanity.[31] Communal self-deception among members of a shared political culture, driven by a mixture of ideology and self-interest, is the issue here. Or, in the wonderful phrase of Max Weber: "Man is an animal suspended in webs of significance he himself has spun."[32]

To put it another way: the heightened culture of nationalism in the European countries was in part the product of deliberate strategies of the then European elites to combat the socialist movements and preserve their dominant positions by mobilizing mass support in the name of nationalism. But the resulting nationalism was a cause for which the sons of these elites, the officer corps of old Europe, sacrificed themselves in uncounted numbers and with sincere faith.[33]

Self-sacrifice is admittedly not a thing for which America's right-wing nationalist elites have shown much appetite, but their discourse at least has some sinister echoes of that of their European predecessors. This is especially true of two linked obsessions: cultural and moral decline, and domestic treachery—which together are used to explain national decline. Both have very old cultural, racial, and religious roots; were reshaped, strengthened, and perpetuated by the cold war; and have attained new force as a result of 9/11. Thus Sean Hannity links gay marriage somehow with Adolph Hitler as evil threats to the United States and declares "we have a battle within our country with those that want to tear down the foundation, the Judeo-Christian values that made this country strong."[34]

The Catholic right-winger William Bennett exemplifies this concern with "decadence" as a source of national weakness, with particular focus on the liberal intelligentsia and the universities.[35] Now it must be said that some of the criticism leveled by these forces at American left-wing academia is justified. The next chapter will touch upon some of the lunatic excesses of academic "political correctness," and even the veteran radical Richard Rorty has denounced the fact that "we now have, among many American students and teachers, a spectatorial, disgusted, mocking Left rather than a Left which dreams of achieving our country."[36]

Rather than aiming at stimulating an engaged debate on improving the United States and U.S. policy, however, the approach of Bennett and his allies, like Lynne Cheney, was clearly intended to shut down debate. It also had some extremely troubling antecedents. Its language about the healthy, patriotic American people as opposed to the deracinated, morally contemptible intellectuals could be taken almost directly from European documents of the past, such as a German nationalist statement of 1881, with its talk of "sinister powers" sapping the religion, morality, and patriotism that formed the "ancient, sound foundation of our national character."[37] This kind of thinking in the United States was also enormously strengthened by the cold war, which saw repeated waves of anxiety that the United States was becoming too morally and physically soft to compete with the supposedly "purposeful, serious and disciplined" Soviet society.[38]

Former Republican Congressman and House Speaker Newt Gingrich used to teach a course on "Renewing American Civilization" at conservative colleges in Georgia, the tapes of which were distributed to Republican activists. They suggested the following words to describe political opponents: "decay, failure, shallow, traitors, pathetic, corrupt, incompetent, sick."[39] And this is indeed the standard language of right-wing media stars to their immense audiences concerning Democrats, liberal intellectuals, and Europeans.

The language is strongly reminiscent of what George Mosse has called the "rhetoric of anxiety" among nationalists before 1914, focused both on external threats to the nation and on moral, sexual, and political subversion from within. This is also true of its markedly hysterical tone.[40] And this is not just a matter of a few media squibs. In its anti-intellectualism, antielitism, antisecularism, and antimodernism, this rhetoric strikes very deep chords among that large minority of Americans who feel deeply alienated from the world in its present shape.

As Mosse's work recalls, closely linked to this traditional nationalist "rhetoric of anxiety" is one virtually universal aspect of right-wing nationalist language throughout history, namely its obsession with threats to national virility and with the supposed effeminate weakness of critics at home and abroad: "Americans are from Mars; Europeans are from Venus" in Robert Kagan's phrase. More crudely, Europeans are "Euroweenies." Lee Harris sees "Spartan ruthlessness" as the "origin of civilization." Robert Kaplan calls for Americans to recover the "pagan virtues" in war fighting.[41]

In British historian and journalist Timothy Garton Ash's summary of this kind of language about Europe in the United States, "if anti-American Europeans see 'the Americans' as bullying cowboys, anti-European Americans see 'the Europeans' as limp-wristed pansies. The American is a virile, heterosexual male; the European is female, impotent or castrated ... The word 'eunuchs' is, I discovered, used in the form 'Eunuchs.'"[42]

Much of this could be seen as merely silly, though as Donald Rumsfeld's attitudes and language concerning Europe as secretary of defense demonstrated, it does have serious consequences in the real world. Of much greater, and grimmer, significance is right-wing nationalist language about domestic treachery. In America and so many other countries in the past, such language has fuelled and justified domestic repression, and as some of the behavior of the Bush administration indicated, 9/11 and a war against terrorism with no foreseeable end have once again made this a matter of real concern.[43]

Not surprisingly, 9/11 led to a great increase in anti-Muslim feeling in the United States. Despite the wars in Iraq and Afghanistan, this might have been expected to diminish with time, given the lack of further Islamist terrorist attacks on the U.S. homeland (the only serious exception being the shootings by Major Nidal Hasan at Fort Hood, Texas, in November 2009). However, in the years following 9/11 there grew a network of right-wing nationalist groups, linked to the Israel lobby and fundamentalist Christian groups, that dedicated themselves to keeping fear and hatred of Muslims at the boiling point.

These campaigns included not only warnings about the threat of terrorism, but also a systematic attempt to block the building of new mosques in the United States and agitation over the alleged spread of Sharia law among U.S. Muslims. This latter agitation drew strength from growing anti-Muslim political movements in Europe, but against a quite different background. In Europe, both the much higher level of Muslim immigration and the concentration of working-class, poorly integrated Muslims from particular countries in particular European regions has made the issue of separate Muslim identities a real one.

In contrast, the Muslim population of the United States is smaller, far more fragmented, and on the whole much better educated and better integrated. The threat of the introduction of Sharia law in America is in fact a nonissue, approximately as realistic as past McCarthyite fears of Communist revolution. Yet the agitation against it has attracted not only leading representatives of the Israel lobby, like Daniel Pipes, but also former Central Intelligence Agency (CIA) Director James Woolsey and leading Republicans including Newt Gingrich. In 2010 this campaign was responsible for a 70 percent majority of voters in the state of Oklahoma passing a resolution to ban the use of Sharia law in the state. The campaign against Sharia law was in origin quite separate from the Tea Parties, but many leading Tea Party figures added their voices to it, including Sarah Palin and Michelle Bachman. As with the Tea Parties, tremendous—indeed indispensable—help was given by Rupert Murdoch's Fox News network and its associated media outlets, which relentlessly propagandized this issue.

This was also true of the protest campaign against plans to build a Muslim prayer center in lower Manhattan, not far from the site of the former World Trade Center. The most striking thing about this furor was that the leader of the Sufi body that planned to build the center, Feisal Abdul Rauf, had been sponsored by the State Department under the Bush administration to conduct speaking tours of the Middle East dedicated to condemning terrorism and advocating reconciliation between Muslims and Christians.

This formed part of a wider U.S. strategy of trying to back Sufism and other "moderate" forms of Islam against Islamist radicalism. None of this prevented leaders of the agitation—including many who certainly knew the facts very well—from branding him and his organization as extremists and terrorist sympathizers, undermining U.S. strategy in the "war on terror" and increasing hostility toward the United States in the Muslim world. Moreover, the New York agitation was only one of a number of movements in different cities against the construction of new mosques and Muslim community centers, including ones intended to serve America's sizable population of Muslim African Americans. As with these agitations in general, the storm in Boston over plans to build a mosque in Roxbury, an African American neighborhood of the city, was to a great extent driven by the Murdoch-owned *Boston Herald* newspaper in alliance with Fox News.

This anti-Muslim tendency in the United States was in one sense quintessentially American, in that what is at the bottom of a movement of nationalist chauvinism has been largely couched in the language of the defense of law and liberty, and in particular the freedom of women. In parts of Europe like Holland, anti-Muslim feeling has also been bound up with homosexual fears of Muslim repression, but for obvious reasons this has emphatically not been the case on the American Right. The greatest danger of this movement is that in the event (God forbid) of another major terrorist attack on the United States, the fear and hatred it has inspired would burst the bounds of law altogether, and in certain parts of the country would lead to pogroms against local Muslim institutions and against Muslims themselves.

Even the hostility directed at Muslims in the United States by the Right is dwarfed by the campaign to denounce American liberals as traitors. Ann Coulter's amazing book *Treason* is a sustained attempt to portray liberals and Democrats, categories which she treats as identical, as traitors to America both in the cold war and the "war against terrorism." As noted, this accusation is the common stuff of right-wing media stars like Sean Hannity, Bill O'Reilly, Rush Limbaugh, and Michael Savage, figures who have huge and appreciative audiences and, at their back, the tremendous power and reach of networks like Fox News.[44]

In the wake of 9/11, a body headed by Lynne Cheney produced a list of 117 statements by American academics and students that they deemed "morally equivocal" or anti-American, or both: for "college and university faculty have been the weak link in America's response to the attack." The statements cited for denunciation ranged from the genuinely wicked and unacceptable, like "Anyone who can blow up the Pentagon gets my vote" (no. 14) to "We should build bridges and relationships, not simply bombs and walls" (no. 19), and "Ignorance breeds hate" (no. 49).[45]

Influential former officials and respected commentators like Richard Perle, David Frum, and Irving Kristol also made it a central part of their rhetoric, with Frum denouncing not only liberals, but "unpatriotic" conservatives who opposed the Iraq War for carrying out "a war against America."[46] Sean Hannity's book of 2005 was entitled *Deliver Us From Evil: Defeating Terrorism, Despotism and Liberalism*.[47] The spirit behind the old, ugly German nationalist insult *nestbeschmutzer* (someone who "dirties his own nest") is much in evidence in America today.

The willingness of large numbers of American politicians and intellectuals to use such language, and America's difference in this regard from Europe and other parts of the developing world—though this difference is diminishing with the rise of extreme rightist thought and language in Europe—has been closely linked to what is also the most important root of American "exceptionalism" in its positive sense, namely that the United States has been spared the greatest European disasters of the past two centuries, "kindly separated by nature and a wide ocean from the exterminating havoc of one quarter of the globe," in Jefferson's phrase.[48]

The first, and critical, salvation, as Tocqueville noted, was from the French and other European revolutions after 1789, and the extreme reactions to which they gave rise. Thereafter, of immense importance in distinguishing the United States from the rest of the developed world is that the United States avoided the truly searing effects of war and revolution in the twentieth century. Of course, the United States participated in both world wars—the U.S. armed forces fought with magnificent courage and dedication in both, and individual units suffered terrible losses—but overall American casualties in proportion to the U.S. population were very small compared to those of the leading European states, and above all America itself was spared invasion or bombardment.

As memories of the first half of the century fade and economic discontent and fears of immigration grow, extremist politics are increasing in Western Europe. As of 2012, differences between the United States and Western Europe in this regard remain noticeable. Too many Europeans and Japanese were tortured, imprisoned, or executed for some form of "treason"—or did the torturing and shooting—for this word to be one that people from these countries use lightly. Too many people were killed, maimed, raped, or starved to death in wars for the language of militant, outwardly directed nationalism to be acceptable, not merely in political or intellectual circles, but in the vast majority of the population. Even the least-educated European can preserve a family memory of a grandfather killed at Ypres or an uncle maimed at Stalingrad, a home destroyed in Cologne or Warsaw, and rapes and forced prostitution from Naples to Berlin and Krasnodar.

Precisely because such language as that of Bennett was used incessantly by intellectuals and politicians in all the major European states in 1914–1915, and again by Germany and Italy in 1939–1941, it is very difficult indeed for any European today to write or speak in the terms used by William Bennett and quoted above. This is not just a question of thoughts that may be strongly held in private, but which can no longer be publicly expressed, like racism in the United States. It is *psychologically* extremely difficult for educated Europeans even to think in these terms.[49] And this is as true of the European elites as the population at large. The European nationalist death ride unleashed in 1914 began by destroying the sons of those elites, and by 1945 had destroyed their dominance, and in many cases their countries as well.

American capitalists, however, like America as a whole, escaped the European catastrophes of the first half of the twentieth century. This was, of course, very fortunate for America, but it also means that the United States and its rulers escaped perhaps the most searing lessons the world has ever known in the need to keep social, class, economic, and national ambitions and passions within certain bounds. The greater radicalism of American capitalism therefore also stems in part from America having been spared the horrible consequences to which such capitalist excesses can contribute; and this form of American capitalism feeds in turn the greater radicalism of the American Right and the culture of American nationalism. This complex of radical attitudes can be seen in the editorial pages of the premier newspaper of American business, the *Wall Street Journal*. For a taste of the difference between the culture and politics of American capitalists, taken as a whole, and those of their European equivalents, one could not do better than to compare those pages with those of the *Journal's* European equivalents—the *Financial Times, Frankfuerter Allgemeine, Corriere della Sera,* and so on. This difference was displayed, for example, in the horrified reaction of leading articles in the *Financial Times* to the Bush tax cuts.

Above all, what is striking in the *Journal*—a paper representing a presumably satisfied and dominant capitalist class—is its writers' capacity for both radicalism and sheer hatred. *Wall Street Journal* editorials treated both President Bill Clinton and President Barack Obama as cultural aliens, dangerous radicals, and national traitors. This resembled the treatment meted out in the 1930s by the *Journal* and much of the capitalist classes in general to the "Communist" Franklin Delano Roosevelt—a man who probably did more than any other to preserve and extend American capitalism in the world. The explanation for this feral behavior is to be sought partly in the conservative cultural and racial anxieties that will be examined in the next chapter, but equally importantly in the pre-1914-style assumption of American capitalists of an unqualified right to dominate the state and to retain profits.

Since this is the behavior of a large section of the economic elites and the media that they control, it is not surprising that in the minds of the Tea Parties and the people they represent, the idea has taken hold that the moderate conservative Barack Obama is a Socialist or even a Communist.

The particular nature of American capitalism is reflected in the contemporary character of the Republican Party. Like so many party labels around the world, the historic names of the main U.S. political parties have long since lost whatever descriptive value they once possessed. As of 2012, it would not be easy to find a truly descriptive name for the Democrats, given the enormous and curious mixture of class, ethnic, cultural, and ideological viewpoints they represent. "Progressive Liberals" would perhaps be closest, and not very close at that, given the conservatism of many of their members. If, however, one were to seek a name for the Republicans that would situate them accurately in a wider historical and international context, there would be no doubt at all as to what that name should be: the Republicans would be renamed the American Nationalist Party.

This is not just because of the Republicans' external policies and the political culture that underpins them, but rather, the entire contemporary Republican mixture is reminiscent of the classic positions of past conservative nationalist movements in Europe and elsewhere. Abroad, these stood for "assertive nationalism" and often supported imperialist policies. At home, they were devoted to defending private property in general and the interests of the upper classes in particular, with a special stress on hereditary wealth.

Of course, they also portray themselves as the defenders of traditional national, religious, and family values against the rising tide of cosmopolitan, liberal, socialist, and foreign decadence. Especially in times of heightened national emotion, public adherence to these values was used to present themselves as "apolitical," transcending political and class differences and appealing to the nation as a whole. Thus in the wake of 9/11, William J. Bennett wrote of

> the spontaneous upwelling of national feeling that followed upon September 11th, the day of trauma. Quite suddenly, as if in the twinkling of an eye, everything petty, self-absorbed, rancorous, decadent, and hostile in our national life seemed to have been wiped away. Suddenly, our country's flag was everywhere, and stayed everywhere. Suddenly, we had heroes again—and what heroes: policemen and firemen, rescue workers, soldiers and civilian passengers who leapt from their seats to do battle with evil personified.
>
> It was true; for weeks and even months after September 11, partisan political issues seemed to fade in urgency, racial divisions to be set at naught. Cynicism and irony were declared out, simple love of country in... Something in those events, wrote an uplifted Peggy Noonan, "something in the fact that all the different colors and faiths and races were helping each other, were in it together, were mutually dependent and mutually supportive, made you realize: we sealed it that day. We sealed the pact, sealed the promise we made long ago... We are Americans."[50]

In the same spirit, Kaiser Wilhelm II declared in August 1914 that "I know no parties, I know only Germans." In the same spirit, in 2009, the radical conservative media star Glenn Beck founded the 9/12 Project, appealing to the common spirit that supposedly existed in the United States on the day after 9/11. The project's mission statement reads:

> The 9/12 Project is a volunteer based, non-partisan movement focusing on building and uniting our communities back to the place we were on 9/12/2001. The day after America was attacked we were not obsessed with political parties, the color of your skin, or what religion you practiced. We were united as Americans, standing together to protect the greatest nation ever created. Our goal is to bring us back to that same feeling of togetherness again.

Among the principles to which the 9/12 Project wishes to recall Americans are

1. America is good.
2. I believe in God and He is the center of my life.
   "The propitious smiles of Heaven can never be expected on a nation that disregards the eternal rules of order and right which Heaven itself has ordained."—George Washington's first Inaugural address....
6. I have a right to life, liberty and pursuit of happiness, but there is no guarantee of equal results.
   "Everyone has a natural right to choose that vocation in life which he thinks most likely to give him comfortable subsistence."—Thomas Jefferson
7. I work hard for what I have and I will share it with who I want to. Government cannot force me to be charitable.[51]

It hardly needs pointing out that these supposedly "apolitical," "nonpartisan" appeals to "all Americans" are intended, among other things, both to encourage hostility to Americans who do not share these particular beliefs and to encourage people to vote for the Republican Party.

Chosen Peoples

Underlying the nationalism not only of the American Right, but of American culture in general, is a belief that America has been specially "chosen" and is therefore, in Madeleine Albright's words, the "indispensable nation"—whether chosen by God, by "destiny," by "history," or simply marked out for greatness and leadership by the supposed possession of the greatest, most successful, oldest and most developed form of democracy. In Woodrow Wilson's words, in World War I "America had the infinite privilege of fulfilling her destiny and saving the world." This messianism will be explored in the next chapter.[52]

One reason for the persistence of this belief in America is that in the mid-twentieth century it was actually true. When the popular evangelist Billy Sunday declared at the outbreak of war with Germany in 1917 that "America is placed in a position where the fate of the world depends largely on our conduct. If we lose our heads, down goes civilization," he was engaging in nationalist hyperbole. In the 1940s and early 1950s, this was no exaggeration.[53]

This sense of America not just as an unfulfilled dream or vision, but also as a country with a national mission, is absolutely central to the American national identity, and also forms the core of America's faith in its own "exceptionalism."[54] It was inscribed on the Republic's Great Seal at America's birth as a united nation: *Novus Ordo Seclorum* (A New Order for the Ages).

Today this belief does indeed make Americans exceptional in the developed world. In the past, however, this was emphatically not the case: "From time immemorial, nations have conceived of themselves as superior and as endowed with a mission to dominate other peoples or to lead the rest of the world into paths of light." A great many nations throughout history—perhaps even the great majority—have had a sense of themselves as especially "chosen" by God, or destiny, for great and special "tasks," and have often used remarkably similar language to describe this sense of mission.[55] Indeed, some of the most articulate proponents of America's universal mission are British subjects, repeating very much the same lines that their fathers and grandfathers used to employ about the British empire.[56] In the words of Hermann Melville (1819–1891):

> We Americans are the peculiar chosen people—the Israel of our time; we bear the ark of the liberties of the world. God has predestined, mankind expects, great things from our race; and great things we feel in our souls. The rest of the

nations must soon be in our rear. We are pioneers of the world; the advance guard, sent on through the wilderness of untried things, to break a path into the New World that is ours.[57]

As the leading religious historian Conrad Cherry writes, "the development of the theme of chosen people in both Germany and the United States between 1880 and 1920 illustrates the protean character of the myth of religious nationalism. It has proven itself able to assume the identity of multiple biblical and non-biblical images without loss of its mythic power." The difference today is of course that in Germany this myth was killed off completely (at least in its nationalist form) by the horrors of 1933–1945, and to a very considerable degree this was true in the rest of Western Europe as well. In the United States this myth is still very much alive.[58]

The Protestant form of this myth was to be found in sixteenth- and seventeenth-century Holland, Sweden, and Britain before it migrated to the United States. In Milton's words of the mid-seventeenth century, "let England not forget her precedence of teaching nations how to live." As in America, this usually involved the explicit identification of the country concerned with biblical Israel. Such Protestant and biblical imagery pervaded British imperial rhetoric, including on the part of the not very religious (indeed, Masonic) Rudyard Kipling. It always strangely blended themes of Christianization, liberation, and development with racial superiority and celebration of victorious force.

Present in all the great powers in modern history has also been an American-style sense of themselves as "universal nations," summing up the best in mankind, and also embracing the whole of mankind with their universally applicable values. This allowed them in turn to claim that theirs was a positive nationalism or patriotism, while those of other nations were negative, because they were morally stunted and concerned only with the interests of their own nation.

Germans before 1914 believed that "Germany may heal the world" with its own particular mixture of legal order, technological progress, and spirit of organic, rooted "culture" and "community" (*gemeinschaft*). These values were opposed by German thinkers to the allegedly decadent, shallow "civilization" and atomized, rootless "society" (*gesellschaft*) of England, France, or the United States, and to the "barbarism" of Russia. In the words of Johann Gottlieb Fichte a century earlier: "The German alone therefore can be a patriot; he alone can for the sake of his nation encompass the whole of mankind; contrasted with him from now on, the patriotism of every other nation must be egoistic, narrow, and hostile to the rest of mankind."[59]

Russia too had its own sense of universal mission and nationhood under the tsars, closely linked as in some other cases to religion; the belief in Russia as the heir to the Christian Empire of Rome and Constantinople. Konstantin Aksakov wrote that "the Russian people is not a nation, it is a humanity; it only appears to be a people only because it is surrounded by peoples with exclusively national essences, and its humanity is therefore represented as nationality."[60] Dostoyevsky wrote that Russians were "the only God-bearing people on earth, destined to regenerate and save the world." This spirit was later to flow into Soviet Communism, which envisaged the Russian language and selected aspects of Russian culture as forming essential building blocks of a new socialist nation that would in turn set a pattern for all mankind.

The most interesting parallel to the American sense of universal national mission is to be found in the history of France. Indeed, to a pragmatic and empirical latter day British subject, the long-running alienation between the United States and France often resembles two brothers quarrelling over a shared inheritance.[61] For the French state too, like the American, has claimed for most of the past 200 years to represent the heritage of the Enlightenment with regard to liberty, democracy, and progress, and to have the right to spread these ideals to other nations. This belief dates from the French Revolution, but is built on the older conviction of Royal France in the 17th and 18th centuries that it was *La Grande Nation*, with a cultural mission to lead Europe. Indeed, the ultimate roots can be traced still further back, to medieval Catholic and protonational images of France as "the eldest daughter of the Church."

For many years after the revolution, France was seen as a "glorious mother who is not ours alone and must deliver every nation to liberty."[62] As Thomas Jefferson put it: "Every man has two countries—his own and France"; words that could well be applied, culturally speaking, to much of the world today with reference to the United States.[63] Or in the very American words of General de Gaulle, inscribed on the base of his statue on the Champs Elysees: "There exists an immemorial covenant between the grandeur of France and the freedom of the world."[64] As in the United States, this particular belief can also be made into a domestic political weapon. Thus in January 2004, the former Socialist minister Jack Lang, attacking the conservative government for excessive friendliness to China, declared that "the [French] National Assembly has embodied for two centuries the fight for the rights of man"—a sentiment entirely characteristic of the U.S. Congress, and in both cases, equally surprising to the Vietnamese, among many others.[65]

General de Gaulle shared a long-standing French belief that France was intended by Providence to enjoy "an eminent and exceptional destiny." This belief still exists, albeit to a considerably reduced extent, in the French elites, though as the poll cited at the beginning of this chapter suggests, at the start of the twenty-first century mass nationalism is very much less in France than in the United States. According to Edgar Quinet, only France had "the instinct of civilization, the need to take the initiative in a general way to bring about progress in modern society...It is this disinterested though imperious need...which makes French unity, which gives sense to its history and a soul to the country."[66]

Such feelings still exist to a degree not only in France, but in Western Europe more widely, but with a crucial difference from their nature in the contemporary United States. This lies in the fact that since World War II they have, on the whole, separated themselves from the self-images of particular nations and attached themselves to the "European Project" as a whole, as expressed through the European Union (EU) and its predecessor bodies.

In its overt commitment to spread democracy, human rights, and development, the EU resembles to some extent the United States, and has taken on some of the former *mission civilisatrice* of its former imperial member states—though this may now be collapsing as a result of the economic recession that began in 2008 and a basic lack of commitment to this project among ordinary Europeans. For the elites who still believe in this project, unlike in the United States, an absolutely central part of this mission is precisely to overcome and transcend nationalism and individual nationalist missions. This was, after all, the most important reason why the "European Project" was started in the first place, to ensure that there would be no repetition of the catastrophic national conflicts that had wrecked Europe in the past: "Europeans have done something that no one has ever done before: create a zone of peace where war is ruled out, absolutely out. Europeans are convinced that this model is valid for other parts of the world."[67]

France too has sunk in the EU and the "European Project" the greater part of its old sentiments of *mission civilisatrice*, and of its great power ambitions. This has been both because of sheer weakness and because, as far as large-scale unilateral intervention in the non-European world is concerned, these sentiments had in any case been largely bled out by the wars of 1946–1954 in Indochina and 1954–1963 in Algeria. As the French and British intervention in the Libyan civil war of 2011 demonstrated, these countries still possess the will to use independent military force in support of their national interests and ideas of civilization, but only if the costs in human life are small or nonexistent.

Thesis and Antithesis

There is, however, another way in which France provides some very interesting parallels with a feature of American nationalism that is a core subject of this book: namely its historical separation into very different and frequently opposed ideological and cultural streams. Because of the political and ideological convulsions that repeatedly gripped France between 1789 and 1958, these have been more clearly defined and radical than in the United States, but in some ways they are rather similar.

Since 1789 France, like the United States, has possessed what could be called a national ideology or creed, a civic nationalist thesis about itself that France has presented to its own citizens and to the world—albeit one that, unlike in the United States, was for a long time not shared by all Frenchmen. This is the tradition of the core values of the French Revolution, later incorporated to greater or lesser extents in Bonapartism and the French republics: popular sovereignty (even when expressed through a form of plebiscitary monarchy or other leadership), the "Rights of Man," equality before the law, secularism, and "career open to the talents."[68]

These principles thus became central to the dominant strand of French nationalism, to France's official sense of universal mission, and to a concept of French identity and citizenship at home that was rooted in loyalty to the French state, and not in ethnicity or religion. As a result, France was for a long time the most open society in Europe (except for Russia) when it came to the assimilation of foreigners.[69] This, however, was intended to be *assimilation*, not mere tolerance: because aliens could become French, they were expected to become French.

France was the first country in Europe by many years to emancipate its Jewish minority, but with the explicit intention, voiced by Napoleon, that they would thereby merge into the mass of the French people—a very different approach from that of Britain, for example. In recent decades this tension has reappeared with regard to France's Muslim minority, as symbolized by the highly controversial decision of 2003 to ban Muslim girls from wearing headscarves in schools, on the principle of the role of the state education system in preserving the secular and assimilatory values of the Republic.[70] French civic nationalism therefore is assimilationist, but not pluralist. As we shall see, this is also true of some strains in American civic nationalism.

Like the United States, France has also harbored political tendencies, cultures, and ideologies that run counter to this French "thesis." These were most obviously represented in the long refusal of conservative and Catholic forces in the nineteenth century to accept the French Republic and the values on which it was based. However, as in the United States, continuities of political allegiance are not the central feature of this "antithesis." The last watered-down remnants of French monarchism flowed gently enough into loyalty to de Gaulle's Fifth Republic, and the Catholic Church too has long since made its peace with the Republic and democracy. Moreover, for long historical periods, even the French extreme Right has largely merged with the center-rightist mainstream.

It would therefore be wrong to draw any kind of straight political line between the antirevolutionary royalist Chouans of the Vendee in the 1790s and the National Front of Jean-Marie Le Pen in the early twenty-first century. Indeed, as Hans Rogger has emphasized, because historically and internationally the Right has tended to be composed of communities or movements of sentiment rather than of formal ideology, "differences on the Right are even more pronounced than those on the Left, and it is this which makes it so difficult to generalize about the Right, to arrive at universally valid definitions."[71]

Rather, one can trace certain continuities of sentiment that have taken different political forms in different generations. These tendencies have stressed a French national identity based not on secular ideology, but on a more-or-less closed ethnic cultural identity. For a long time this meant adherence to Catholicism: for several decades beginning in the later nineteenth century and culminating in Vichy, it was anti-Semitic; today it means being white, speaking good French, and not being a Muslim. It has generally been extremely hostile to the administrative, business, and cultural elites of Paris, and indeed to Paris itself, with its multiethnic population and modern culture (even when the leaders and ideologists of this tendency have been Parisian intellectuals).

In America, as Walter Russell Mead of the Council on Foreign Relations has written: "The belief that the essence of American nationality lies in dedication to universal principles is constantly at war with the idea that Americanism belongs exclusively to the American people and must be defended against alien influences rather than shared with mankind."[72]

This belief has also been quintessentially true of France.[73] Like every other tendency of its kind, these traditions in both the United States and France have seen themselves as representing the *pays reel*, the true, authentic, immemorial nation, against the *pays legale* of the administrative and cultural elites—a prejudice endlessly appealed to by right-wing American politicians in their diatribes against Washington.[74] Like its conservative nationalist analogues elsewhere in Europe, this French tendency is strongly hostile in spirit towards the EU, and toward globalization—both seen as projects of the cosmopolitan elites and hostile to the interests of ordinary, "true" Frenchmen. The natural home of this tendency in the past was the traditional aristocracy and sections of the petty bourgeoisie and peasantry. Today, it embraces many workers, often ex-Communists.

And just as the roots of France's sense of transnational mission can be seen to originate long before the Revolution, so the roots of this tendency can also be traced back to provincial resistance not only against the Revolution, but against previous attempts at royal centralization, standardization, conscription, and taxation. Here too is a parallel with the world of the "antithesis" in the United States.

The strong distrust of government characteristic of so many Americans—and so powerfully manifested in the Tea Parties—has been generally attributed, following Frederick Jackson Turner, to the individualist tradition of the American frontier. and this is of course correct. However, this distrust also embodies elements of the old European peasant distrust for state authority, which had generally appeared to peasants in old Europe—as in much of the "developing world" to this day—in the form of corrupt tax collectors, savage policemen, brutal conscripting sergeants, and looting, raping armies (even those of one's own state), all of them speaking in alien languages or dialects. One way of looking at the violently individualistic and antistatist inhabitants of parts of America is to see them as traditional European peasants who ran away into the forests and mountains to escape the demands of the state. They just ran a bit further.

These "antithetical" tendencies in France have had a natural tendency to rise to the surface in times of economic depression, and when France is defeated, humiliated, or is felt to be in decline. This occurred after France's defeat by Prussia in 1870–1871, and culminated in the Dreyfus case.[75] In 1872 Sully Prudhomme repudiated his former internationalism in verse: "I wrote with Schiller:/'I am a citizen of the world'.../But I have repented at last/Of my perverted love./From now on my love will be/For my country alone./For those men whom I betrayed/Through love of the human race."[76]

This swing to the antithesis happened again in a much more disastrous way with the mass rally to Marshal Petain and his Vichy regime after France's defeat in 1940. The last time it has threatened or transformed the state came in the 1950s, with defeat in Indochina and quagmire in Algeria. But as the popularity of Le Pen's movement indicates, it is by no means certain that some combination of economic depression, immigration, and terrorism could not raise it to truly dangerous heights once again in the future.

Today, like other such movements elsewhere in Western Europe, this nationalist tendency in France is profoundly defensive, even to a degree isolationist. It is focused on defending the "traditional" national culture and ethnicity (that is to say, as in the United States, the established ethnic mixture bequeathed in part by previous generations of immigration) against new immigration, new forms of culture, and new economic patterns. This form of nationalism shades easily into various forms of "skinhead" violence.

But this violence too is both portrayed and felt by its exponents as a matter not of aggression or expansion, but of the defense of vital collective interests: using ferocious measures to defend the national core community, jobs, law and order, and so on, against aliens. They are not really dreaming of marching off to recover Breslau for Germany, or Lvov for Poland. And this reflects not only ideology, international reality, and contemporary culture, but also prudence, and strong and bitter historical memories that permeate European society. Kicking immigrants on street corners is a rather less formidable proposition than marching off to fight a war.

At present, it seems unlikely that this French antithesis could come to power, at least for a good many years to come. For an intriguing example of a nationalist antithesis that has succeeded, India is a good place to look. There too, as in France and the United States, the Indian state and elites after 1947 put forward a civic nationalist thesis about India to the Indian public and the world. Unlike in France and the United States, this thesis was fostered under foreign imperial rule, but much of its content was the same: India as a secular democracy—indeed, "the world's largest democracy"—dedicated to progress and human rights, and with equal rights and opportunities for all its citizens. For some three decades after independence, closely associated with this Indian civic "creed" was also a moderate, nontotalitarian form of socialist economics. Internationally, this was associated with a desire to provide enlightened leadership for the former colonial world in its struggle against Western hegemony and neo-colonialism.

This democratic civic nationalism has been associated above all with the name of Jawaharlal Nehru and the Congress Party, which he led (and which at the time of this writing was led by the widow of his grandson, who, in a testimony to the openness of this tradition, is Italian by birth). However, from the start, even the Congress Party harbored elements of a nationalist "antithesis," based on an idea of India not as a civic, but as a religious, cultural, and to some extent ethnic community. Outside the Congress Party, much more extreme variants were represented by a variety of Hindu political groups, often tinged with fascistic beliefs and modes of organization, which eventually came together to form the Bharatiya Janata Party (BJP), which from 1998 to 2004 led India's federal government.

As in the French and American nationalist antitheses, this nationalist tradition rejects the openness and universalism of the Nehruite civic nationalist creed in favor of a vision of India as a closed cultural community; in this case, of Hindus. It therefore explicitly or implicitly excludes Muslims, Christians, and others from the "true" Indian political nation. Unlike other such movements, it has become dedicated to modern economic growth and openness (largely because of its desire to challenge China for the role of the Asian great power), and enjoys great support among the Indian diaspora in the United States, but it greatly dislikes the more ostentatiously Westernized and secular elites in India itself. Like the "antithetical" tendencies in France and the United States in the past, it can have a very violent edge in dealing with minorities that are seen as threatening the interests and control of the "core" community—as demonstrated in a long tradition of bloody communal riots and pogroms.[77]

As with their analogues in the United States, Hindu nationalists have, over the years, come to accept considerable elements of Indian civic nationalism. These include what seems to have become a genuine attachment to basic democratic practice—albeit a specifically Indian kind of "*herrenvolk* (master race) democracy," in the form of rule by a dominant religious group rather than a race or ethnicity. This partial merger of civic and religious nationalism was certainly not true at the time of independence. In the decades since, leaders of the BJP have seemingly come to recognize that democracy, or at least constitutionalism, is the only system that can hold a country like India together. They also see India's status as a democracy as an integral part of the Indian national greatness of which they are so proud—and not least Indian superiority to the hated Pakistan and the feared China.

The second resemblance to the United States is the complex relationship between this tradition and ethnicity. The roots of the BJP remain chiefly among the Hindi-speaking Hindus of North India, usually of the upper and middling castes. But after some weak attempts to make Hindi the Indian national language—abandoned in the face of stiff resistance from South India—the BJP now seems to have settled for a vision of India based on Hindu nationalism, democracy, economic success and military pride. Neither of the Indian nationalisms therefore is an ethnic one—which just shows the limited relevance of models of nationalism drawn from the "classic" ethnic nationalisms of central Europe for the study of much of the rest of the world.

From *Herrenvolk* Democracy to Civilizational Empire

This attachment to democracy and the universalist principles of the "American Creed" has in turn played a central role in America's ability to transcend its racist past and transform itself from a *herrenvolk* (master race) democracy, based on rigid and savagely oppressive rules of racial exclusion and superiority, into a great "civilizational empire." A highly symbolic—but also highly conflicted—moment in this transformation was Barack Obama's election as the first black president of the United States in 2008.

The former European national visions of great missions and callings all had a certain guiding image before their inner eyes: that of the Roman Empire. This is a parallel that also has a long history in American thought, and which has spread enormously in the U.S. public debate as a result of America's emergence as the world's only superpower.[78] Like China and the early Islamic caliphates, Rome not only united many different ethnicities under one language and culture, its legacy continued to shape the history and character of Europe long after the Roman empire itself passed away. These empires were not just states, but whole civilizations, transcending racial and ethnic divisions within their borders and projecting their cultural influence far beyond their frontiers in space and time.

As civilizational empires, they are to be distinguished both from purely military empires like the Mongols, and also from European seaborne *herrenvolk* empires, which while undoubtedly transformative of many cultures and societies, also drew a sharp and ruthless dividing line between the master European races and their dark-skinned subject peoples. The Soviet ambition was also that of a civilizational empire: to create a new kind of civilized man, multiethnic in origin but speaking one language and bound by one culture, which in turn would spread beyond the borders of the Soviet Union to influence all mankind.

The sheer size of the United States, its economic dynamism, and its ability to assimilate huge numbers of alien (white) immigrants to its creed and culture have always given America certain features of such an empire. As Justice Oliver Wendell Holmes declared early in the twentieth century: "We are the Romans of the modern world—the great assimilating people."[79]

Beyond its borders, the tremendous economic success of the United States and the vitality of its culture also created an informal version of such a civilizational empire. This was shown in the way in which admiration for the United States helped to undermine the belief in Communism and the Soviet Union in Russia's younger elites in the late 1980s and early 1990s. In terms of the global reach of its "hard" and "soft" power—of American fleets, American language, American food, American popular culture, and American versions of economics—the United States today does indeed match the civilizational empires of the past.

In the past, however, U.S. aspirations to play the role of a civilizational empire were long crippled by racism, and this was recognized by many Americans, even if they did not speak in imperial terms. The intense, specifically Southern racism of Woodrow Wilson, for example, deeply compromised his liberal internationalism in the eyes of the Japanese and many other nonwhite peoples of the world in his own time and since.[80] As Reinhold Niebuhr wrote in 1943, "our racial pride is incompatible with our responsibilities in the world community. If we do not succeed in chastening it, we shall fail in our task." Gunnar Myrdal's great work of 1944,

An American Dilemma, was also motivated in part by anxiety at the way in which racism at home was weakening the American struggle against totalitarianism.[81]

During the early years of the cold war, a realization of the way in which domestic treatment of blacks undermined U.S. power and influence in the struggle with Communism was a very major factor in the decision of the American national elites to eliminate the public face of this racism in the 1950s and 1960s.[82] Much earlier, Abraham Lincoln had warned that slavery weakened America's world democratic mission by exposing her to the charge of hypocrisy.[83]

When comparing the contemporary United States to other great civilizations of the past, it is vitally important to make a distinction between racism and cultural prejudice. The Han Chinese harbored strong prejudices against "barbarians," both beyond and within their frontiers, but these prejudices ceased when these "barbarians" successfully learned the Chinese language and culture, adopted the official Confucian ideology (if they aspired to join the elites), and thus became Chinese. A central requirement of civilizational empire is a willingness to replace qualifications for membership based on race and ethnic origin with ones based on language, creed, and culture: something that was formally achieved by the Roman Empire with the grant of citizenship to all its free subjects in 212 AD.

Unlike blacks, Native Americans, or Chinese in the America of the past (and of course in the other West European seaborne empires), barbarians could always be assimilated by the elites of the great empires of Asia. Hence the fact that so many of the great Russian aristocratic names are of Tartar or Circassian origin: Yussupov, Nabokov, Kochubey, Turgenev. Lenin, of course, was a complete ethnic hodge-podge, but also culturally speaking entirely Russian. The Chinese chief minister who led the revolt of 755 AD that wrecked the early T'ang dynasty, An Lu-Shan, was a sinified Turk from Central Asia; the greatest T'ang poet, Li Po, was also most probably of Turkic origin.[84]

The principle that "one drop of blood" made you black, and therefore excluded you—whatever your education, property, military valor, or even beauty—from joining or intermarrying with the dominant people and its ruling class would have been simply impossible for these states. So too would the elaborate racial codings of Dutch colonial Java, New Orleans, Brazil, or the West Indies (quadroon, octaroon, mulatto, and so forth). Such rules would have made the expansion of these empires impossible (to be fair, of course, the cultural differences between Han Chinese and Miao, or Russians and Bashkirs, were also vastly less than those between white Americans and red Indians, or newly enslaved blacks).[85]

These civilizational empires accepted into their elites anyone who accepted their culture, but they retained intense hostility to internal groups—like the Jews in Russia—who were seen either as rejecting that culture or as infiltrating and subverting it for their own national ends. Like the United States today, they were also strongly hostile to those external "barbarian" peoples who rejected their culture. Indeed, the entire official identity and ideology of these empires was largely built around the distinctions between themselves and the barbarian "other."

The public elites of America today conform rather closely to this historical pattern of real racial diversity coupled with intense cultural conformity in certain key areas: worship of the creed and the official imperial gods. Thus the presenters on CNN, picked for their racial diversity, are in fact diverse only in the color of their skin. They represent a real breakthrough of equality in terms of outward race, but certainly not of culture or even in any real sense of ethnicity. Their presence is a real celebration of America's civilizational achievement—and is, consciously or unconsciously, intended to be seen as such.

Tremendously positive changes in this regard have occurred in the United States over the past two generations. A striking example of this is public attitudes toward marriage between whites and blacks—like the one that produced Barack Obama. In 1963, 64 percent of Americans believed in the maintenance of laws against such marriages, which did indeed still exist in many states. In 1998 only 13 percent believed that there should be such laws—even though a rather higher proportion expressed private unease about interracial "dating."[86] Moreover Republicans and Democrats were both equally committed to the legality of interracial marriage.

Racist attitudes still remain deeply embedded in the white South and in the Republican Party. However, they have also had to become modified and coded, usually expressed through policies that are not ostensibly racist (especially regarding welfare, immigration, crime, and the "war on drugs") rather than directly. If they had retained their old crude frankness, then it seems likely that, far from helping to make the Republicans the normal "party of government" in the United States from 1968 to their defeat in 2008 (holding the presidency for 24 years to the Democrats' 12), it would in fact have turned them into pariahs and doomed them to minority status. This is demonstrated by the speed with which the Republican Party forced Trent Lott to resign as Senate majority leader in December 2002 after he publicly praised the segregationist campaign for president of Strom Thurmond in 1948.[87]

Nor has this transformation been simply the work of liberals. On the contrary, a key role has been played by institutions with great right-wing and nationalist prestige: the military, certain Hollywood directors and actors, and some of the evangelical churches. Even in the white South there has been a development from prejudice based on the color of one's skin to one based on culture (though these two prejudices are deeply entwined).[88] Starting in the 1990s, some of the leading figures and journals of the Christian Right made what seems to be a sincere effort in this regard, with Ralph Reed apologizing for the past racism of the evangelical churches, and *Charisma* and *New Man* magazines both publishing articles on successful interracial marriages.[89] The prominent black appointments to George W. Bush's administration therefore were by no means just tokenism. They did mark a real and very positive change of heart.

In the evangelical religious field, a pioneering role was played by the so-called televangelists, who have used mass media to appeal to a wider audience than ever before. Starting with Billy Graham, several of these figures have made a point not only of reaching out to different races, but of including blacks and others in their church choirs, where the cameras would be sure to pick them up. Graham in particular has been very supportive of a number of black causes.[90]

One reason for this has been their own version of America's move from *herrenvolk* democracy to civilizational empire—for although from a deeply Southern conservative background in North Carolina, Graham was both passionately devoted to the cause of anti-Communism, and well aware of the ammunition that American racism gave to Communist appeals in the "Third World." His move to a form of bland multiracialism also formed part of a shift on his part away from overt and hardline fundamentalism and towards a form of bland ecumenism that made him acceptable to Eisenhower and later presidents and turned him into "a sort of informal national chaplain."[91]

Moreover, Graham and many of the other televangelists have deliberately aimed at audiences in the developing world; and in the age of globalization, it is no longer possible to keep a missionary appeal abroad completely separate from behavior at home, especially since within the United States some have also set out to woo Latino immigrants away from Catholicism. Some of the Pentecostalists had already begun to reach out to blacks in the 1950s and 1960s.[92]

In other words, blacks and others who conform to certain forms of respectable behavior—including patriotism and religious practice—are now regarded even by most conservative nationalist white Americans as part of the American "folk," in Walter Russell Mead's phrase.[93] General Colin Powell and Condoleezza Rice are genuinely accepted as good Americans, though of course only by what black radicals would call "acting white"—in other words, accepting the culture, creed, and gods of the civilizational empire.

Of great importance in this shift have been three other institutions with great prestige in the South, and to a lesser extent the "heartland" more generally: the military, the sports industry, and the patriotic and macho strain in Hollywood. Thus in stages beginning in the 1940s, the U.S. military has deliberately turned itself into the most genuinely multiracial of all U.S. institutions, and one where blacks and others can advance to the highest ranks without having accusations of unfair preference thrown at them.[94] Starting with Truman's decision to desegregate the military in 1948, this development has been encouraged by all U.S. presidents, with the conscious intention of strengthening America's civilizational appeal to "colored" peoples tempted by Communism.[95]

For the military, this has increasingly become a matter of necessity as well as ideology. After the military abandoned conscription in the wake of Vietnam, it became highly dependent on low-income groups for its recruits—among whom the racial minorities are overrepresented. More recently, military service has even become a way for American immigrants (including illegal immigrants) to gain early citizenship—a practice that recalls late imperial Rome.

The military also remains deeply mindful of the bitter racial tensions that split the troops in Vietnam, when (thanks to class bias in the conscription system) an army containing a very high proportion of blacks was commanded by an officer corps that was overwhelmingly white. During the attempt in 2003 to get the Supreme Court to rule against racial preference in higher education, a key part in this played by "friend of the court" briefs filed by senior retired military officers, who argued that the well-being of the armed forces requires a large pool of black university graduates to provide officer material.

Apart from the actual record of courage, success, and self-sacrifice on the part of blacks and other racial groups in the military, of great importance has always been Hollywood's presentation of this, which in turn forms part of a wider pattern by which Hollywood films with a populist nationalist cultural tinge (Westerns, police films, sports) have deliberately sought to include a wider and wider range of Americans and present them as valuable citizens.

A recurrent theme of John Ford's work is the integration of old and new Americans (and of former Confederates and Unionists) through military service, settlement, and defense of the white frontier. Particular attention was paid to the Irish—not surprisingly, since his original name was Sean Feeny. By 1956 and *The Searchers*, the slow acceptance by the protagonist (played by that arch Jacksonian film icon, John Wayne) of a part Cherokee relative as a comrade has become a central theme, though only because this character is both culturally completely white and his ally against the savage Comanche, who were to be fought without mercy. One of Ford's last films, *Sergeant Rutledge*, has as its subject a brave and dedicated black soldier on the frontier, wrongly accused of the murder of a white girl; it is essentially a nationalist treatment of the theme of Harper Lee's *To Kill a Mockingbird*, with its backdrop being the U.S. Army rather than the U.S. legal system.[96]

During and after World War II, Hollywood made a point of stressing the courageous war service of American Jews (e.g., William Wellman's *The Story of GI Joe*, 1945, with Robert Mitchum). More generally, American war films—like their Soviet equivalents—turned the multiethnic American unit into a formula, with stock white Anglo-Saxon Protestant (WASP), Southern, Irish, Italian, Jewish, and other elements.[97]

Over the past decade American television soap operas have begun to play a not wholly dissimilar role in promoting racial mixing, though here the field is that of love—or sex—rather than battle. After some four decades of television in which it was wholly absent, interracial "dating" on television has become, if not common—it is hardly common in society—then at least present (though more between whites, Latinos, and Asians than whites and blacks).[98]

Another great patriotic film hero, Clint Eastwood, has made a point in some of his films of making a black (or, in his great *The Outlaw Josie Wales*, an Indian) into his character's closest friend and helper, and not as a "Tonto" caricature, but as a dignified, honorable, and intelligent character who provides ironic comments on white society and hypocrisy.[99] Eastwood's *Heartbreak Ridge* is a very Soviet-style example of the mixed-race platoon genre. His late masterpiece *Gran Torino* is almost a locus classicus of belief in new, multiracial integration through adherence to middle-class values, telling the story of how an affectionately caricatured deeply conservative elderly veteran combines with decent, hardworking Hmong immigrants against a Hmong youth gang. Coming from directors and actors whom the South and the Heartland have revered, this approach probably had a greater effect than the more overt antiracism of directors like Norman Jewison and Denzel Washington.[100] For if Billy Graham and Clint Eastwood both suggest a change in racial attitudes, even the most benighted conservative white American must feel somewhere in his heart that his God too is speaking.

However, two critically important sets of qualifications need to be added to this picture of benign change, and both had a great impact on Obama as first black president. The first set is the well-researched difference between conscious and unconscious prejudices, and between the explicit expression of such prejudices and their rendering in a coded and indirect form. The second, which brings us back to the comparison with the Russians and Chinese, is the complex relationship between racial prejudice and cultural prejudice, linked in turn with questions of state loyalty.

In the case of white conservative hostility toward Obama, this can be summed up by saying that while there have been very few public racist attacks on him (since American public culture now strongly discourages this), there has been an enormous amount of indirect racism rendered through doubts expressed as to whether he truly shares American culture (especially the persistent propaganda that he is Muslim, encouraged by his father's identity and his Muslim middle name), and whether he was actually born in the United States.[101] Moreover, in a strikingly brilliant—and deeply evil—maneuver, some right-wing commentators like Glenn Beck have managed to play the racist card—while shielding themselves from accusations of racism—by accusing Obama himself of being the antiwhite racist. In Beck's words, President Obama "has exposed himself as a guy...who has a deep-seated hatred for white people."[102] In the words of Nicholas Kristof:

> Religious prejudice is becoming a proxy for racial prejudice. In public at least, it's not acceptable to express reservations about a candidate's skin color, so discomfort about race is sublimated into concerns about whether Mr. Obama is sufficiently Christian. The result is this campaign to "otherize" Mr. Obama. Nobody needs to point out that he is black, but there's a persistent effort to exaggerate other differences, to de-Americanize him.[103]

These campaigns had an effect. In a poll from October 2010, 58 percent of white respondents expressed some doubt about Obama's place of birth.[104] Even more worrisome, by August 2010 almost 20 percent of Americans—and a majority of registered Republicans—believed that Obama is Muslim; and for such Americans, "Muslim" equates instinctively and almost automatically with "potential traitor." In a tribute to the power of Fox News and other conservative outlets, 60 percent of those who believed this said that they had learned it from the media. This is a continuation of the McCarthyite tradition of branding liberals as traitors to America, but—thanks to 9/11—with an even uglier edge. This prejudice has been diminished by President Obama's role in authorizing the successful operation to kill Osama bin Laden in May 2011, but assiduous attempts are being made to keep it going.[105]

However, the surprising thing about the election of a black president of the United States in 2008 was not that it happened, or that it happened when it did. As already mentioned, General Colin Powell could have had the Democratic or Republican nomination virtually for the asking, and would most probably have won. The surprising thing is that the first black president was not a retired general or admiral—both because military service has been the passport into establishment careers for so many blacks, and because, for reasons set out above, patriotic service partially defuses remaining racial hostility in the white middle classes.

And indeed, while Powell would probably have won a majority of white as well as black votes, in the 2008 election Obama lost among whites (though he won among younger white voters) but was carried to victory by the support of an overwhelming majority of blacks and (to a lesser extent) Latinos. By October 2010, the difference between support for Obama among whites and blacks had widened enormously, with only 34 percent of whites giving Obama a positive rating compared to 84 percent of blacks.[106]

More widely, successful service in the military is implicitly seen as acceptance of that complex of cultural attitudes that self-define the U.S. "middle classes," and of which patriotism is the single most important factor. By curious paradox, however, Obama has not suffered from the middle-class prejudice normally associated with his skin color—that directed against the supposedly lazy, shiftless, criminal, drug-taking black underclass—but from a quite different but equally old one that will be discussed in following chapters: that is, white "middle class" (in U.S. terms, embracing what in Europe would be called working class) resentment directed not downwards but upwards, against the supposedly arrogant, domineering, atheist, liberal, "bleeding-heart," multicultural and culturally alien "East Coast elite."

And indeed, through his mother this is in fact to a great extent the class to which Obama belongs—while his Kenyan father, who separated from his mother not long after he was born, bequeathed him very little except the color of his skin. Barack Obama's mother did not come from the hereditary East Coast moneyed classes, but with her two interracial marriages, long residence abroad, and love of Indonesian culture, in other ways she conformed all too closely to certain hate images among white middle-class conservatives. In present day America, the focus of Republican slurs has been on the fact that Obama's father was a Muslim. A generation or two earlier, it would have been that his parents met at a Russian language class.

The perception of Obama as elitist also comes from choices that he himself made—and probably had no choice but to make if, as a black who was not a member of the armed forces, he wished to join the U.S. establishment. His career path included Columbia University and Harvard Law School (perhaps the single greatest source of members of the Democrat establishment), where he was president of the *Harvard Law Review*, as well as a period as a community organizer in Chicago.

In his personal style, Obama is entirely a member of America's liberal establishment—not just in his policies, which by historical standards are in fact those of a moderate conservative with a love of compromise and consensus, but even in his dress. Trying to explain the hatred that this arouses among the lower-middle-class white constituency of the Tea Party, an old-style Republican friend of mine said the following: "You know, leaving aside the color of his skin, Obama would have been a natural invitee to Hyde Park (the aristocratic country residence of President Franklin Delano Roosevelt). And so would Sarah Palin. The difference is that Obama would have been invited to the front door, and Palin to the servants' entrance."

Here then lies the tragic paradox of Obama's presidency: To dispel prejudices against him as a black outsider, he had to conform to the white establishment, abandoning in the process any real economic radicalism, and thereby any real ability to appeal to the class resentment of lower-class white Americans against the capitalist elites. But by conforming to the white establishment, Obama has associated himself with a class that many lower-class white Americans have always hated. If, on the other hand, Obama were to run on a platform of economic radicalism, capitalist interests would use coded language to brand him in the eyes of the white middle class as the representative of a radical, shiftless, and un-American black underclass.

It is impossible to say at the time of this writing whether this hatred will lose Obama the November 2012 presidential election, but since 2008 it has been proved again and again how these white resentments, assiduously fomented, shaped, and directed by right-wing capitalist interests and their media, have largely crippled his ability to implement what has in fact been a program of moderate conservative reform. The fact that the Republican Party of the early twenty-first century has so savagely and comprehensively rejected reforms that would have been promoted by Republican presidents Eisenhower and Nixon is also a stark sign of the radicalization of that party since the 1970s. The roots of this radicalization will be the subject of subsequent chapters.

Just as at home, an absence of overt racism based purely on skin color has not diminished cultural prejudice, so attitudes toward the outside world among conservative white Americans in some respects conform to the old Roman or Chinese pattern of attitudes to barbarians. That is to say, foreigners are accepted only if they themselves accept the primacy of the United States and U.S. civilization, and are indeed willing to become Americans, if only culturally. Clyde Prestowitz has written of contemporary Americans' "implicit belief that every human being is a potential American and that his or her present national or cultural affiliations are an unfortunate but reversible accident"—a very imperial Chinese or Roman attitude.[107] Consequently, if other people refuse to behave like Americans, then it means that there must be something seriously wicked and malignant about them. In other words, this new order in the United States is a recipe for tolerance within the United States, not outside it. One good definition of solipsism, after all, is "someone [who] believes that he is the world."[108]

Max Lerner's words of the 1950s remain true today:

> One of the American traits is the recoil from the unfamiliar … This seems the more curious when one remembers that America is itself a "nation of nations" and contains a multitude of diverse cultural traditions. Yet this fact only serves to increase the bafflement of the Americans abroad: since he has seen people of foreign extraction in his own country abandoning their customs and becoming "Americanized," he cannot understand why people of foreign countries should not do the same.[109]

Lerner adds that "there is little real hatred of outsiders in this attitude," but that is only as long as outsiders appear completely nonthreatening, which is certainly not the case after 9/11 as far as many Americans are concerned.

The most important qualification of all for becoming an American is to accept the U.S. Constitution and the democratic and legal values associated with it, which have been summed up in the quasi-religious phrase "the American Creed." A naive belief has also existed that all over the world, people who become Democrats would also naturally associate themselves with the United States, not only culturally, but in terms of support for U.S. geopolitical goals. This belief in the universal power of American values provided the cultural and moral underpinnings for America's global role in the twentieth century. It has also helped lead the United States into some notable disasters, including the war in Iraq. The American Creed and its political implications are the subject of the next chapter.

Two

Thesis: Splendor and Tragedy of the American Creed

Even a good idea can be a little frightening when it is the only idea a man has ever had.

—Louis Hartz[1]

The American thesis has also been called the American Creed and the American ideology. It is the set of propositions about America that America presents to itself and to the outside world: "Americans of all national origins, classes, religions, creeds, and colors have something in common: a social ethos, a political creed."[2]

For most Americans, a central part of the creed, if only implicitly, has been the belief that the United States is the supreme example of democratic values and institutions in the world, and as such has the right and duty to show the way to other nations when it comes to achievement of these goals: "Americans see history as a straight line and themselves standing at the cutting edge of it as representatives for all mankind."[3]

This belief has been nurtured over two centuries of American growth and expansion. A vital question for the American psyche and for American domestic and foreign policies will be the effects of this faith in an era of relative decline for America as a whole, and for the American white middle class in particular. Closely linked to this is the question of whether the creed remains, as it was in the past, a continual inspiration to Americans to renew and reform their institutions and their social and economic system, or whether for too many white Americans it is ossifying into a blind fetishism of their Constitution, economic system, and way of life as they presently exist—something that is strongly marked in the Tea Party movement. It would indeed be a tragic irony if a constitutional system that was the greatest expression of Enlightenment rationalism in politics should become an obstacle to rational thought; but alas, such ironies are not uncommon in history.

The danger of such a development is rooted in the very depth of Americans' faith in their system. Ralph Waldo Emerson wrote of adherence to American governing principles as a form of religious conversion. This thesis or creed, with its attendant national myths, forms the foundation for American civic nationalism, and indeed makes the public face of the United States an example of civil nationalism par excellence.[4] In theory, anyone who assents to the American thesis can become an American, irrespective of language, culture, or national origin, just as anyone could become a Soviet citizen by assenting to Communism.[5]

The principles of the American thesis are also rationalist and universalist principles, held by Americans to be applicable to peoples and societies everywhere, and indeed throughout time. In Tocqueville's words, the Americans "are unanimous upon the general principles that ought to rule human society," and this is no less true at the start of the twenty-first century than it was when Tocqueville made his observation in the 1830s.

Partly in consequence, this set of assumptions is also basically optimistic. It suggests both that the United States has achieved the highest possible form of political system, and that this great system can be extended to the rest of mankind. Centuries before Francis Fukuyama recoined the phrase, a certain belief that America represented the "end of history" was already common in American thought, and still more in the American subconscious. "I alone inaugurating largeness, culminating time," as Walt Whitman put it, speaking for his country.[6]

In Richard Hofstadter's words, "it has been our fate as a nation not to have ideologies but to be one."[7] This American thesis is also, both in American belief and in reality, the core foundation of America's "soft power" in the world, and of America's role as a civilizational empire; the American version of *Romanita*. Both in the past and at present, the American Creed has deeply shaped the conduct of American foreign policy.[8]

The essential elements of the American Creed and American civic nationalism are faith in liberty, constitutionalism, the law, democracy, individualism, and cultural and political egalitarianism. They have remained in essence the same through most of American history.[9] They are chiefly rooted in the Enlightenment, and are derived in turn from English roots; the liberal philosophy of John Locke and much older beliefs in the law and in the rights of free-born Englishmen.

Economic egalitarianism is definitely not a part of the creed. On the contrary, it has also been closely associated with belief in the absolute superiority of free-market capitalism, unlimited economic opportunity, and consumerism.[10] However, these facets of the creed are contested by larger numbers of Americans than are its political elements, which are believed in by overwhelming majorities. In recent decades, racial tolerance and equality have also come to be seen as essential components of the creed, and the rights of women are also mentioned—though these too are contested, in private at least, by considerable numbers of Americans. Informally, an important part of the creed is also the belief that America embodies and exemplifies the only model of successful modernity in general.

At the start of the twenty-first century, the contents of the American thesis are, of course, not exceptional to America; most are also held by the other developed democracies, and indeed in public at least, by most of the world. In its ultimate origins the creed is overwhelmingly indebted to a mixture of the British legal and religious tradition, and the British and French enlightenments. American democracy forms part of a subworld of Western democratic states, just as American capitalism, though it has highly specific features, is inextricably entwined with the world capitalist system as a whole.

However, two features of the creed are exceptional: the absolutist passion with which these beliefs are held, and the degree to which they are integral to American nationalism. Louis Hartz wrote of the creed's "compulsive nationalism" and the "fixed, dogmatic liberalism of a liberal way of life."[11] The myths attendant on the creed include a very widespread belief that America is exceptional in its allegiance to democracy and freedom, and that America is therefore exceptionally good. And because America is exceptionally good, it both deserves to be exceptionally powerful and by nature cannot use its power for evil ends. The American Creed or thesis is therefore a key foundation of belief in America's innate innocence, which is due in turn to the innate qualities of ordinary Americans. This faith underpins the belief of ordinary Tea Party members that "if only government would get off our backs" these qualities would allow American society and the American economy to flourish.[12]

According to Samuel Huntington, "it is possible to speak of a body of political ideas that constitutes 'Americanism' in a sense in which one can never speak of 'Britishism,' 'Frenchism,' 'Germanism,' or 'Japaneseism.'" Americanism in this sense is comparable to other ideologies and religions...To reject the central ideas of that doctrine is to be un-American...This identification of nationality with political creed or values makes the United States virtually unique."[13]

In fact, as noted in chapter 1, other states have also embodied their own versions of such a thesis in their own versions of civic nationalism. However, in most of these cases the thesis has either been publicly contested by many people, as in the case of France, or, as in the case of imperial China, has been, historically speaking, mainly the faith of national or imperial elites. What is unusual about America is the sheer unanimity of belief in these guiding national principles.

The Canadian sociologist Sacvan Bercovitch has described discovering in America "a hundred sects and factions, each apparently different from the others, yet all celebrating the same mission." This ideological consensus, he said, is invested with "all the moral and emotional appeal of a religious symbol." Discovering it gave him "some of the anthropologist's sense of wonder at the symbol of a tribe."[14] At the start of the twenty-first century, the United States may indeed be the most truly ideological society on the face of the earth.

America is not, of course, the most ideological state on earth. A number of other states still claim an infinitely more rigorous, ruthless, and extensive right of control over the thoughts of their subjects than the American state ever has, or ever could. So did the Communist states in their prime. But even in their prime, these ideologies were resisted by large parts of the populations concerned, and after a few decades not only most of the intelligentsia, but most ordinary people as well lost all genuine belief in them, while continuing to go through the required motions in public. The same became true of theocratic Iran in the course of the 1990s.

Russian and Chinese intellectuals of my acquaintance who came to America in the 1990s after living in this atmosphere of private cynicism toward public ideology often reacted with utter astonishment, and some fear, to the way in which ordinary Americans glorify their country's beliefs, institutions, laws, and economic practices in private conversations, not just as a matter of defensive patriotism, but with a sincere belief in their validity for all mankind: "They actually believe all this! No one is forcing them to say it!"[15] Closely related to this is the sense of national mission: "All nations... have long agreed that they are chosen peoples; the idea of special destiny is as old as nationalism itself. However, no nation in modern history has been quite so consistently dominated as the United States by the belief that it has a particular mission in the world."[16]

Even most American dissidents throughout history have sincerely phrased their protests not as a rejection of the American Creed as such, but, on the contrary, as a demand that Americans, or American governments, return to a purer form of the creed or a more faithful adherence to it. Groups that really step outside the creed soon find themselves marginalized or even suppressed. The mass of the white population at least simply takes the creed for granted.

Given the general stereotype of the United States as a new, young, and everchanging country, it is important to note that one of the sources of the immense strength of American loyalty to American institutions is their antiquity. They have an older and less changed existence than in almost any other state in the world. For since the American Constitution was adopted in 1787, the great majority of states have undergone revolutionary institutional change. Even the British political system has changed far more fundamentally than the American system over these two centuries.

The principles underlying these institutions, and the American thesis that these institutions embody, are much older still. According to Huntington, "the principal elements of the English constitution were exported to the new world, took root there, and were given new life precisely at the time that they were being abandoned in the home country. They were essentially Tudor and hence significantly medieval in character... The institutional framework established in 1787 has, in turn, changed remarkably little in 175 years."[17]

Far from being a "new" or "young" state, America therefore has some claim to be almost the oldest state in the world. It is "the oldest republic, the oldest democracy, the oldest federal system; it has the oldest written constitution and boasts the oldest of genuine political parties."[18]

The origins of these American institutions go back to medieval and, more importantly, Tudor England, before the rise of centralizing monarchies on the continent of Europe and of centralizing parliamentary government in Britain.

Huntington links the continuing belief of Americans in a fundamental, essentially unchanging law to the English medieval tradition: "*nolumus mutare leges Angliae*," that is, "we do not wish to change the laws of England," as the barons declared at Runnymede; thus "this old idea of a fundamental law beyond human control was given new authority by identifying it with a written constitution."[19] These then are the ancient beliefs and sentiments that filled the dry, rationalist carapace of the American Constitution.[20]

American civic nationalism has been central both to the assimilation over the centuries of huge numbers of immigrants and to America's eventual transition from *herrenvolk* democracy to civilizational empire. As Dr. Martin Luther King, Jr., declared at the Lincoln Memorial on August 28, 1963, "I still have a dream. It is a dream deeply rooted in the American dream that one day this nation will rise up and live out the true meaning of its creed."[21]

Thus the contents of the American Creed are of tremendous importance to America and to humanity. On many occasions throughout American history, the creed has led Americans not just to make sacrifices for their own countrymen and for humanity, but to question their national motives and improve their institutions and behavior. It also helps stand between the United States and certain imperial crimes, and indeed makes the exercise of direct empire by the United States less likely, for it enforces at least a surface respect for democracy and self-determination.

It could be said that the American thesis, like democracy in India, is also a matter of necessity for America. It is essential to preventing America's immensely disparate and sometimes morally absolutist social, cultural, religious, and ethnic groups from flying apart. Creedal civic nationalism and belief in the value of the American thesis for America and mankind are perhaps the only things on which Pentecostalists in Texas and gays in San Francisco can agree.[22]

The American Creed, and the institutions it underpins, are indeed America's greatest glory, and will be America's greatest legacy to mankind after the United States itself has disappeared. The fruits of American economics may prove ambiguous or even disastrous in the long run, but the principles that have allowed masses of diverse people in an enormous land to live together and prosper without coercion will always have positive lessons to teach.

Restoring Innocence

Despite its great virtues, however, this civic nationalism, and the ideological consensus that underpins it, carry with them certain grave interlinked dangers. As Reinhold Niebuhr wrote:

> Irony consists of apparently fortuitous incongruities in life which are discovered, upon closer examination, to be not merely fortuitous...Our moral

perils are not those of conscious malice or the explicit lust for power. They are the perils which can be understood only if we realize the ironic tendency of virtues to turn into vices when too complacently relied on; and of power to become vexatious if the wisdom which directs it is trusted too confidently.[23]

Of these perils, two in particular have been remarked on by American historians and commentators: conformism and messianism. To these can now be added the growing danger of ossification. Historically these dangers have usually been somewhat latent and held in check by American traditions of empiricism, pragmatism, and open debate.[24] In moments of national shock and trauma, like 9/11, however, they tend to become active, and do much to shape America's response. This may also be the case with the less sharp, but perhaps even deeper long-term trauma of America's relative decline in the world, and the decline of the white middle class in America.

These tendencies inherent in U.S. civic nationalism draw on a set of common myths so deeply embedded as to operate beneath the level of most Americans' consciousness. These myths are not strictly speaking part of the formal thesis or creed, but help give them much of their emotional force. These myths affirm, among other things, the idea of America's innocence;[25] or as President George W. Bush put it, "I'm amazed that there's such misunderstanding of what our country is about that people would hate us. I'm—like most Americans, I just can't believe it because I know how good we are."[26]

As the Bush administration's National Security Strategy of 2002 stated: "Today, the United States enjoys a position of unparalleled military strength and great economic advantage. In keeping with our heritage and principles, we do not use our strength to press for unilateral advantage. We seek instead to create a balance of power that favors human freedom: conditions in which all nations and societies can choose for themselves the rewards and challenges of political and economic liberty."[27]

This belief in American innocence, of "original sinlessness," is both very old and very powerful.[28] It plays a tremendously important role in strengthening American nationalism and in diminishing America's willingness to listen to other countries, viewed in turn as originally sinful.

This is in origin a New England puritan or "Yankee" myth stemming from the idea of the settlers as God's elect, born again in the New World and purged of the sins of England and Europe. It was later enthusiastically adopted by grateful refugees from Europe and elsewhere fleeing persecution or war in their homelands.[29] It received an early European endorsement in 1782 from Hector St. Jean de Crevecoeur, who celebrated the American as a "new man," reborn in a kind of Rousseauian natural state in the wilderness and purged of the European past.[30]

The white South was historically suspicious of this myth, because they saw it as responsible for the (in their view) high-minded, high-handed, hypocritical Yankee moralizing that led the North to condemn the South first over slavery, then over civil rights. A strong, though unacknowledged echo of this historical position is to be found in the deep skepticism of the Southern patrician Senator William Fulbright of Arkansas concerning the messianic follies that in his view helped embroil the United States in Vietnam and other unnecessary disputes.[31] This attitude is also reflected in the continuing skepticism of many Southern conservative Republicans concerning "nation building." At the same time, however, the passionate American nationalism of this Southern tradition has also led them to strongly identify with the "city on a hill" image of America as part of their belief in America's unique greatness and moral supremacy in the world.

As Richard Cohen wrote in 2003, asking how America could have gone to war with Iraq in the face of all evidence and warnings, "this [the Iraq War] was no mere failure of intelligence. This was a failure of character. Why?... Finally, there was our smugness—the sort of American exceptionalism that so rankles non-Americans. No one better exemplified that than Bush himself."[32]

In 1980 Conor Cruise O'Brien quoted *New York* magazine as lamenting that "we lost our innocence in the seventies, and, for the first time, a war," and commented,

> the lost war is not hard to identify, but the lost innocence is worthy of respectful and inquisitive wonder. The French lost a war (admittedly not for the first time) in the Sixties, in Algeria, in much the same way and for much the same reasons as those for which the United States, ten years later, lost a war in Indochina. Negative generalizations are usually hazardous, but I offer confidently the proposition that no Frenchman wrote, and no French periodical published, at the end of the Sixties, any claim that France had lost its innocence as well as a war during that period... Yet the theme of American innocence—whether lost, preserved, or to be recaptured—is not a mere mawkish conceit, but represents a powerful and active ferment of meaning that has worked throughout American history.[33]

An unwillingness or inability among Americans to question American sinlessness feeds in turn a culture of public conformism in the United States, commented on across the centuries. "In the abstract we celebrate freedom of opinion as part of our patriotic legacy; it is only when some Americans exercise it that other Americans are shocked...Intolerance of dissent is a well-noted feature of the American national character."[34] Or to quote Louis Hartz: "Here is a doctrine which everywhere in the West has been a glorious symbol of individual liberty, yet in America its compulsive power has been so great that it has posed a threat to liberty itself. Actually Locke has a hidden conformitarian germ to begin with, since natural law tells equal people equal things, but when this germ is fed by the explosive power of modern nationalism, it mushrooms into something pretty remarkable."[35]

This conformism is certainly true in my experience for large sections of the political, intellectual, and media worlds of Washington, DC, and the American ruling elites. Tocqueville (the most famous European *admirer* of America, it should be noted) declared that "I know of no country where there is so little true independence of mind and freedom of discussion as in America... The majority raises very formidable barriers to the liberty of opinion: within these barriers an author may write whatever he pleases, but he will repent it if he ever step beyond them."[36]

Like the description of Nicolas I's Russia by Tocqueville's compatriot and contemporary the Marquis de Custine, this could be described as an exaggeration of the truth. After all, America has throughout its history produced famous dissidents. However, their spheres have tended to be rather more limited than in many other developed countries, and restricted mainly, though not entirely, to the worlds of the intellect and the arts. The great dissident wave of the 1960s and early 1970s was to a considerable extent an epiphenomenon that was rejected by the mass of the American people. Moreover, dissent can be identified in part with certain regional and ethnic traditions in the United States that do not extend to the mass of the American people as a whole: "For all the lip service given to respect for cultural differences, Americans seem to lack the resources to think about the relationship between groups that are culturally, socially or economically quite different."[37]

One source of the immense power of the American Creed and civic nationalism in American society is that they combined both the Enlightenment and the "protestantoid" religious strands of the old American tradition in a way summed up in Julia Ward Howe's "Battle Hymn of the Republic," with its melding of biblical and liberal imagery. The kingdom of God became identified with the American Republic.[38] As "mainline" Protestantism in most of the United States (but not, as we shall see, in the greater South) became more liberal and latitudinarian in the course of the twentieth century, so a diffuse form of vaguely protestantoid "civil religion" also came to form a central part of this national consensus. This in turn owed something to the deism of the Republic's founders, who had also emphasized the central importance of religion for the survival of the Republic, without stipulating what it should be (though they certainly meant some variety of Protestant).

In President Eisenhower's much-quoted words, "our government makes no sense unless it is founded on a deeply felt religious faith—and I don't care what it is."[39] This identification of the positive civic virtue of religion with nationalism was strengthened still further by the struggle against "atheist Communism."[40] This diffuse, nondenominational Judeo-Christian religious culture in turn became part of what Will Herberg, Robert Bellah, and others have called America's "civil religion," composed of a mixture of the principles of the American Creed with a set of historical and cultural myths about America.[41] This became the essential cultural underpinning of America's present version of civic nationalism.

One social studies textbook for fourth graders (10 year olds), entitled *Our People*, sums up aspects of this civil religion, including deliberately targeted national integration: "It opens with a discussion of a major national ceremony, the inauguration of a president, and a visit to the Lincoln Memorial and other

Washington sites. This presentation is clearly intended to elicit feelings of membership in a national community. The chapter concludes with a comment by a fictitious character: 'Yes,' said Maria to Pedro, 'This is a great country. We are all Americans.'"[42]

The conformism of ideological attitudes reflects in part the self-definition of the great majority of Americans as "middle class." This definition by now has little to do with class in the economic sense, but everything to do with being "respectable," which means, above all, sharing a certain set of common values, including the American Creed and American nationalism.

The legacy of the 1960s and of older radical traditions lives on today in American universities—though these often suffer from their own form of liberal conformism. Moreover, it must be noted that these myths are both in their origin and in their location today principally *white* myths. Like President Barack Obama and General Colin Powell, blacks and others who wish to join the establishment must worship the gods of the American civilizational empire, at least in public; but as Richard Hughes has noted, although blacks believe in and have appealed to the American Creed, every one of its attendant myths takes on a highly ironic aspect when viewed from the perspective of black or Native American history.[43]

As far as the official and semiofficial world of Washington, DC, is concerned, I can testify from my own experience to the continuing truth of the following passage from Louis Hartz, written in the 1950s:

> When one's ultimate values are accepted wherever one turns, the absolute language of self-evidence comes easily enough. This then is the mood of America's absolutism: the sober faith that its norms are self-evident. It is one of the most powerful absolutisms in the world...It was so sure of itself that it hardly needed to become articulate, so secure that it could actually support a pragmatism which seemed on the surface to belie it. American pragmatism has always been deceptive because, glacierlike, it has rested on miles of submerged conviction, and the conformitarian ethos which that conviction generates has always been infuriating because it refuses to pay its critics the compliment of an argument.[44]

There is a strong tendency in consequence to treat even licensed dissidents essentially as jesters. They ring their bells, and even dare on occasions to hit the democratic sovereign over the head with a bladder and tell him that he is a fool. The king laughs loudly and tosses them a chicken bone, but does he listen to them? Often, like King Lear, he listens only when evident facts have given him no choice, and the jester's advice is too late to be of much use to him. And perhaps one should not complain. America is not at present *physically* repressive of dissent, and it is, after all, better to wear a jester's cap than a prisoner's chains, let alone a hangman's noose.

This conformism is nonetheless dangerous both to liberty and to the frank and honest discussion of public issues, especially in time of war, when it is exacerbated by a heightened nationalism.[45] It is particularly alarming when combined with the loyalty and trust that many Americans in time of war instinctively feel toward their president and administration, and which was reflected for many months in the deference paid to the Bush administration by the mainstream American media after 9/11.[46]

One consequence of a national language based on a rigid ideological consensus is that it gives to certain words the power of what W. H. Auden called in 1967, "black magic"—the power to suspend a capacity for independent thought in audiences: "More deadly than the Idle Word is the use of words as Black Magic...For millions of people today, Communism, Capitalism, Imperialism, Peace, Freedom and Democracy have ceased to be words the meaning of which can be inquired into and discussed, and have become right or wrong noises to which the response is as involuntary as a knee reflex."[47]

When President Eisenhower, in his Inaugural Address of 1952, declared that "freedom is pitted against slavery; lightness against the dark," he was of course expressing a truth about Stalinist Communism, but he was also summoning up a spirit of absolutism in America that he himself seemed later to regret.[48] Indeed, this later repentance from messianism has been true of some of the most famous praise-singers of that messianism, including Herman Melville (in his poem *Clarel*), Walt Whitman, and indeed Reinhold Niebuhr, who coined the phrase "the children of light and the children of darkness" for the battle against totalitarianism during World War II, but later became one of the most incisive critics of American arrogance, mythopoeia and self-deception.[49]

It has been widely remarked how the Bush administration's use of the words "terrorism" and "evil" after 9/11 partially shut down the possibility for intelligent discussion of American strategy. But this is no less true of their use of the word "freedom" and identification of this word both with America and with American policies in the Middle East. Under Barack Obama, "the Constitution," "individualism," and "the American way of life" were used by the Right in a largely successful attempt to stifle serious debate on economic reform and the terms of state revenue collection. The Bush administration composed rhetorical spells drawn from the basic elements of the American ideological consensus, and until the situation in postwar Iraq spoiled the magic, this allowed them for a while to play the Pied Piper to much of America.

Lines written by the historian of the South and political thinker C. Vann Woodward on this subject during the Vietnam War are no less valid today: "The characteristic American adjustment to the current foreign and domestic enigmas that confound our national myths has not been to abandon the myths but to reaffirm them. Solutions are sought along traditional lines...Whatever the differences and enmities that divide advocates and opponents (and they are admittedly formidable), both sides seem predominantly unshaken in their adherence to one or another or all of the common national myths."[50]

It may seem surprising that passages like these should still ring so true decades later, given both the horrible lessons that the experience of Vietnam supposedly taught, and the great example of Franklin Roosevelt in successfully reforming the American system in response to economic crisis. Like so many of the better literary and cinematic works on Vietnam, Francis Ford Coppola's *Apocalypse Now* (1979) is, among other things, a profound questioning of civic nationalist myths about America, including inevitable American success, American innocence, American benevolence, and America's national mission. And as its protagonist, Captain Willard (Martin Sheen), says of his task, "I wanted a mission, and for my sins they gave me one...It was a real choice mission. And when it was over, I'd never want another."[51]

At the time, this conclusion would have been agreed to by the vast majority of Americans. A quarter of a century later, in the wake of 9/11, it sometimes seemed as if this entire historical episode had been erased from American public memory. In Loren Baritz's bitter words of 1985, in a chapter entitled "The American Lullaby":

> Our power, complacency, rigidity and ignorance have kept us from incorporating our Vietnam experience into the way we think about ourselves and the world...For one brief moment, later in the 1970s, it looked as if we had developed some doubts about our international and cultural moorings. It looked as if we might have the nerve and wisdom to be concerned not only about Vietnam, but about ourselves. But there is no need to think unless there is doubt. "The era of self-doubt is over," President Reagan assured the West Point cadets. Freed of doubt, we are freed of thought. Many Americans now seem to feel better about themselves.[52]

This initial impression is, in part, a false one. Some of the bitter lessons of Vietnam have in fact sunk deeply into the American consciousness. In the years after 2003, the bloody and chaotic aftermath of victory in Iraq and Afghanistan recalled them to life. In the two years after 9/11, however, they were largely swept away by a tide of myth-based nationalism against which it was very difficult to argue. The period when the memories of Vietnam were suspended was not very long—but it was long enough to get America into Iraq.[53]

The figure of Ronald Reagan is critical to an understanding of how America dealt with the legacy of Vietnam, and the consequences for America today and in the future.[54] On the one hand, Reagan's external policy demonstrated that he and most of his administration were determined not to get involved in any major conflict, and realized full well how bitterly unpopular this would be with a majority of Americans. The common left-wing image of Reagan as a warmonger is therefore quite wrong.[55]

The Reagan administration conforms to a key feature of the American security elites and military–industrial complex that will be examined in chapter 5: namely, that they tend to be "militarist, but not bellicose." In Reagan's rhetoric, however, the "Great Communicator" was a superb restorer of the founding myths of American nationalism, so badly tarnished by Vietnam, and this was without question because he believed them to the full himself. Above all, this was true of his beliefs in American innocence, American beneficence, and America as the heartland of human freedom and progress. He held "an innocent and unshakeable belief in the myth of American exceptionalism."[56] In Garry Wills' superb phrase, Reagan was "the demagogue as rabble-soother."[57]

Reagan's mixture proved the perfect one to reassure Americans after the combined traumas of defeat in Vietnam, bitter political divisions at home, Watergate, and the Iranian hostage crisis. But by far the most important ingredient in the mixture was that, in Woodward's words, Reagan "reaffirmed" America's national myths. He also did so in a style that not only calmed, but united most Americans. In this, Reagan's geniality, his acting skill, and his genuine identification with his country and countrymen made him a far more uniting figure than George W. Bush, who represents the same nationalist mixture, but in a considerably harsher form.

In his brilliant essay of 1982, "The Care and Repair of Public Myth," William H. McNeill examined classic American myths of superiority and benevolence, and remarked that "no one is likely to reaffirm these discredited notions today, even though public rhetoric often assumes the reality of such myths without expressly saying so. Politicians and journalists really have little choice, since suitably revised national and international myths are conspicuous by their absence."[58]

This passage depicts the character of Reagan and indeed those who voted for him. After all, they elected him in part precisely because he was so good at restoring their myths about their country, including the belief that Vietnam had been a noble crusade.[59] As a result, while Americans remember in their guts that Vietnam was an unpleasant experience that should be avoided, its deeper lessons have remained largely unlearned, and in our own time it has proved entirely possible to "reaffirm these discredited notions."

One reason for this was that while the Vietnam War was a dreadful experience for those Americans who fought in it, their numbers were small, and—quite unlike, once again, European and Asian wars, or for that matter the experience of the Vietnamese—Americans at home were physically unaffected: "for most Americans the tangible consequences of the debacle in Southeast Asia seem inordinately slight."[60] This lack of personal knowledge of war was of course true of Reagan himself, and was true of George W. Bush and all the other men in his administration of 2000–2004 who were of military age during the Vietnam War, but for some reason failed to serve.

In another way, however, the trauma of Vietnam is, if anything, too deep to be addressed: nothing less than "the death of the national god" and the national religion of American innocence, goodness, and God-given success. Without this, it was feared at some deep, semiconscious level that American civic nationalism itself would also wither and die. This fallen national god therefore had to be laboriously pieced back together and returned to its pedestal.[61]

It is interesting from this point of view that both McNeill in his essay and John Hellmann in his fascinating study of American literary and cinematic approaches to Vietnam call for American myths to be reformulated on a new basis—more progressive, honest, and morally courageous. Neither, however, suggest trying to do without national myths altogether.[62] Clint Eastwood's distinctly post-Vietnam western *The Outlaw Josie Wales* (1976) can also be seen as an attempt to heal the wounds of Vietnam by merging Hollywood western traditions with new cultural and social attitudes to create a more humane, open, and multicultural American mythology.[63]

Conformism and Political Correctness: Ignorance Is Myth

Perhaps a society as diverse and as bitterly culturally divided as America, with its diversity continually increased both by immigration and by the creative and destructive surges of capitalist change, cannot in fact live without strong common myths and a strong civic nationalism that depends on them. Thus, even as memories of Vietnam were being suppressed, other developments within U.S. society and culture were also encouraging a tendency to propagate soft, conflict-free, lowest-common-denominator versions of American nationalist myths and of American history. These have been based on a projection of the contemporary form of the American Creed back into the past.[64]

Curiously enough, Reagan's own style can thus be seen as related in some ways to a phenomenon that at first sight appears absolutely alien to it: "political correctness" on the part of the academic Left and representatives of racial and ethnic minorities, especially when applied to American schools. In its original form, this was supposed to correct the prejudices, reflected in demeaning and contemptuous language, that for so long humiliated and oppressed a range of minorities in the United States. In this the political correctness movement has largely succeeded, though only in the context of much wider changes in society and culture. And this is an unequivocal good, if one remembers the revolting racist language of the past and the revolting treatment it encouraged.

The problem is, however, that the picture presented to schoolchildren as a result tends to conform to nationalist myths about America as an innocent, happy, conflict-free society, and propagates the American thesis in its purest and most basic form. Thus Frances FitzGerald paints a quite Soviet picture of the photography selection in school textbooks about the United States:

> The treatment of European minorities is far more realistic than that of non-European minorities, whose sensibilities the publishers are anxious not to offend. The photographs in the mass-market texts rarely show a non-White person who is brutalized, dirty or even poor—unless the photograph specifically illustrates "pockets of poverty in America"...Most of them are smiling. You can find pictures of Chicano farmworkers, but the workers are always clean and look as if they're enjoying their work. They're always smiling at Cesar

Chavez. The Puerto Ricans are smiling and healthy. The Chinese are smiling at healthy-looking vegetable stands. Indeed, everyone is smiling so hard you would think that all non-White people in the United States took happy pills. (The Russians, by contrast, appear to be a somber lot. Their grimness dates from a time in the fifties when a group of right-wing organizations made an enormous fuss about a photograph of smiling Russian children.) ... Not only fundamentalists but progressives as well have a strong tendency to think that the schools should present the world, or the country, as an ideal construct. The censorship of schoolbooks is simply the negative face of the demand that the books portray the world as a utopia of the eternal present.[65]

Diane Ravitch describes how an American history textbook by Gary B. Nash, an historian of impeccable progressive credentials, was attacked by left-wing and minority representatives in the late 1980s, accused of being "anti-black, anti-Semitic, anti-Muslim, anti-American Indian, anti-gay and anti-Christian."[66]

A few years later, in the mid-1990s, Professor Nash and his colleagues came under savage attack from the nationalist Right—with Lynne Cheney yet again playing a leading role—for their work in drawing up proposals for a new set of National History Standards for teaching in classrooms that allegedly ignored America's heroes, cast doubts on American myths, and undermined American patriotism. The groups responsible were largely the same as those that in 1994–1995 had forced the Smithsonian in Washington, DC, to abandon an exhibition showing the effects of the atomic bombing of Hiroshima, and compelled the director of the Air and Space Museum to resign.[67]

This tendency toward a bland patriotic picture of America—of "authorless crimes and sideless conflicts," in FitzGerald's words—is of long standing.[68] Her portrait of smiling America was first published in 1979, but a British journalist, Andrew Gumbel, recorded similar feelings in 2003 when his son first went to school in California. His article is worth quoting at some length, as the appalled reaction of a politically centrist citizen of a vital English-speaking ally of the United States to behavior that most Americans take for granted:

> Even after five years in the United States, I continue to be surprised by the omnipresence of patriotic conformism ... With my son's education at stake, I can't help pondering the link between what is fed to children as young as six and what American adults end up knowing or understanding about the wider world. There is much that is admirable in the unique brand of idealism that drives American society, with its unshakeable belief in the constitutional principles of freedom and limitless opportunity. Too often, though, the idealism becomes a smokescreen concealing the uglier realities of the United States and the way in which it throws its economic, political and military weight around the globe. Children are recruited from the very start of their school careers to believe in a project one might call Team America, whose oft-repeated mantra is: we're the good guys, we always strive to do the right thing, we live in the greatest country in the world. No other point of view, no other cultural mindset, is ever seriously contemplated ...

The manipulation of education is more subtle and, arguably, more insidious than it was 50 years ago at the height of the Cold War and the great Red Scare. Then, the battle for hearts and minds was about the straightforward exclusion of certain books and topics in pursuit of a political agenda...These days, the issue is no longer banning books, even if that still goes on in parts of the heartland dominated by the Christian right, but rather systemic conformism. It used to be that an inspiring teacher could overcome the shortcomings of bland textbooks and blinkered administrative madness. But with the curriculum now much more closely defined and homogenized...[teachers] are effectively forced into complicity with the textbook pretense that every historical struggle has now been settled and can be summarized in a few soothing lines of near-meaningless analytical blancmange.[69]

Gumbel quotes a song from his son's elementary school class:

America, I love you!
From all sorts of places,
They welcomed all the races
To settle on their shore ...
To give them protection
By popular election,
A set of laws they chose.
They're your laws and my laws,
For your cause and my cause
That's why this country rose.[70]

These words would cause any historically aware black or American Indian to grind his or her teeth—but, as Gumbel points out, are taken by most American children as simply natural. This nationalist tendency is greatly encouraged by a wider decline in historical studies and, indeed, in general culture (a decline of course not confined to the United States). As a result, Americans' knowledge of the world, and their own history, has not declined over the past 60 years—but it has also not improved from the miserable level of that time. In 2001, 57 percent of American high school students were graded "below basic" in history, with only 11 percent rated proficient or advanced.[71] In many individual cases, the result of this is pure ignorance; but this cannot be true of a society as a whole, which needs some kind of basic cultural operating principles in order to function. For America as a whole, the absence of historical knowledge does not mean ignorance, but the presence of myth.

Michael Lind has also argued cogently that a combination of political correctness with a system of (very limited and selective) positive discrimination for minorities actually serves the interests of what he calls the "overclass." This overclass is still overwhelmingly white, and even white Anglo-Saxon Protestant (WASP), but creams off and co-opts small numbers of black and other elites while diverting the energies of radicals into essentially pointless struggles over symbols—and away from concrete transracial issues like immigration control and raising the minimum wage, which would genuinely help ordinary members of the racial minorities, who on average remain markedly poorer than the white population.[72] In a way, the supreme example of a content-free multiracial symbol has proved to be the election of Barack Obama. Endlessly celebrated as demonstrating American progress and achievement, apart from a very limited health care reform he has proved unable to do anything much at all for most black Americans.

Political correctness of this type is not simply the result of a swing to the left in academia, on the one hand, meeting a newly radicalized Right on the other. It also reflects profound changes in U.S. society from the 1960s on: the freeing of the blacks as a serious political force, and the resumption of mass immigration without racial restrictions. The resulting new society is one to which Americans of many different political allegiances have had to respond.

Thus not just official U.S. patriotic propaganda, but the visual propaganda of the nationalist and religious Right is also now in general deliberately multiracial (Lynne Cheney's patriotic primer is full of drawings of black and Asian American toddlers waving flags and playing at being U.S. soldiers).[73] Indeed, to be fair, one could almost say that America over the past generation or so has become so complicated that its education system is more or less *forced* back upon simplistic myths, for trying to teach or discuss the full reality would simply be physically impossible.

This connection between diversity and conformism is not only involuntary, but also quite deliberate. American public culture is so conformist *because* America is so diverse, and also because, concerning other races, its history is so foul. In this sense, political correctness can be seen as an aspect of what Ernest Renan said about the creation of modern nations: "Forgetting, I would almost say historical error, is a crucial factor in the creation of a nation, which is why progress in historical studies often constitutes a danger for [the principle of] nationality...The essence of a nation is that all individuals have many things in common, and also that they have forgotten many things."[74]

Precisely because a good many of the people and groups making up contemporary America actually have very little in common, in order for them to become a nation it may be necessary for Americans to be even more forgetful than other peoples. The example Renan used was that of the French religious wars of the past. Had he still been around in France after World War II, he could have used the treatment of the memory of the German occupation and Vichy; and this is true with even greater force of past racial oppression in the United States. In this sense, Americans can be said to be "held together only by ideas" in the same way that Soviet citizens were. The ideas of American civic nationalism are, happily, much more positive and valuable ones than those of Soviet Communism—but that does not change the fact that they cannot be seriously questioned without endangering the stability of the entire structure.[75] Their absolutist character influences, in turn, the underlying ideology of American foreign policy, making it even more difficult for even highly educated and informed Americans to form a detached and objective view of that policy; for to do so would also risk undermining the bonds uniting diverse Americans at home.[76]

America's Mission: Exemplary and Interventionist

So pervasive is the American Creed or ideology in American culture that even Henry Kissinger, no great idealist, has been moved to write that

> the rejection of history extols the image of a universal man living by universal maxims, regardless of the past, of geography, or of other immutable circumstance...The American refusal to be bound by history and the insistence on the perpetual possibility of renewal confer a great dignity, even beauty, on the American way of life. The national fear that those who are obsessed with history produce self-fulfilling prophecies does embody a great folk wisdom.[77]

At least since President Woodrow Wilson took America into World War I in 1917, belief in American values and institutions has intermittently taken the form of a desire to spread them to the rest of the world as a matter of government policy, and even through by military means. This has usually occurred as a result of America going to war, or—in the case of the cold war—becoming engaged in intense rivalry with an antidemocratic state. According to Seymour Martin Lipset (in his great study of American exceptionalism), Bush and his leading officials possessed, and expressed, a boiled down, simplified and extreme version of a vision of America that is in fact held very widely in American society, and has deep historical roots: "The US primarily goes to war against evil, not, in its self-perception, to defend material interests."[78]

The apogee of this tendency in recent times came in the wake of 9/11, when the Bush administration—rhetorically at least—made the "Freedom Agenda" a central part of U.S. strategy in the "Global War on Terror." The locus classicus of American civic nationalism in messianic mode is to be found in Bush's address to the U.S. Congress on September 20, 2001, when he identified America with freedom, and said that this was why America had been attacked:

> Americans are asking, why do they hate us? They hate what they see in this chamber—a democratically elected government...Great harm has been done to us. We have suffered great loss. And in our grief and anger we have found our mission and our moment. Freedom and fear are at war. The advance of human freedom—the great achievement of our time, and the great hope of every time—now depends on us.[79]

This idea was then set out formally in the Bush administration's National Security Strategy of 2002, the prologue to which read:

> The great struggles of the twentieth century between liberty and totalitarianism ended with a decisive victory for the forces of freedom—and a single sustainable model for national success: freedom, democracy and free enterprise. In the twenty-first century, only nations that share a commitment to protecting basic human rights and economic freedom will be able to unleash the potential of their people and assure their future prosperity. People everywhere

want to be able to speak freely; choose who will govern them; worship as they please; educate their children—male and female; own property; and enjoy the benefits of their labor. These values of freedom are right and true for every person, in every society—and the duty of protecting these values against their enemies is the common calling of freedom-loving people across the globe and across the ages.[80]

This belief found an even more strident and messianic expression in Bush's speech at West Point on June 1, 2002, which also ushered in the "doctrine" of preventive war and helped lay the propaganda groundwork for the attack on Iraq:

> Wherever we carry it, the American flag will stand not only for our power, but for freedom (applause). Our nation's cause has always been larger than our nation's defense. We fight, as we always fight, for a just peace—a peace that favors human liberty...The twentieth century ended with a single surviving model of human progress, based on non-negotiable demands of human dignity, the rule of law, limits on the power of the state, respect for women and private property and free speech and equal justice and religious tolerance.[81]

Like the Soviets, and like so many Americans—liberal as well as conservative— over the years, Bush cast America as the agent of a historical teleology.[82] Statements that "our nation is on the right side of history" echo the Soviet Communist cliché, "the winds of history are in our sails."[83] Much of this language on the part of Bush and other administration officials might have come—word for word— from the Clinton administration, as expressed by Madeleine Albright and others, and indeed from President Woodrow Wilson, who declared in January 1917 that "these are American principles, American policies. We could stand for no others. And they are also the principles and policies of forward-looking men and women everywhere, of every modern nation, of every enlightened community. They are the principles of mankind and must prevail."

The argument that America needed to invade Iraq in order to liberate its people was used by the Bush administration and its supporters as a subsidiary justification for going to war. After the war, and the failure to find Iraq's alleged weapons of mass destruction, it became the principal justification.[84] Nor was support for the liberation argument confined to Republicans. On the contrary, it proved extremely useful in winning support for the war from many intellectuals from the Democratic Party. In this there was nothing new. Woodrow Wilson was of course a Democrat. Until the Vietnam War split the Democrats and recast the American party system, the chief home of a more active and interventionist version of America's mission was the Democratic Party. The Republicans, in contrast, generally tended more toward the realist thinking of Eisenhower, Nixon, and Kissinger.

The neoconservative movement originated among Democratic intellectuals (often former Marxists) who supported the bitterly anti-Communist, pro-Vietnam War, and pro-Israel Democratic Senator Henry "Scoop" Jackson.[85] Although the neoconservatives soon gravitated to the Republican Party, this tradition remained strong among some Democrats. Many of the policies of the Clinton administration were based on a belief in America's right and duty to lead other countries toward democracy, although Clinton in general attempted to do this with the help of multilateral alliances, and the Clinton administration's rhetoric lacked the harsh nationalism of Bush's followers. In the years immediately after 9/11, however, the language of more hawkish Democratic intellectuals about America's role in the world was often barely distinguishable from that of the neoconservatives. This was especially true of members of the Progressive Policy Institute (PPI), an institution close to Hillary Clinton.

In the years afterward, the experience of Iraq and Afghanistan, and anger at the way in which the Bush administration exploited the language of America's mission for its own advantage, led to a revulsion of feeling among many Democratic intellectuals who had supported the Iraq War, and stronger opposition toward military intervention in the name of democratization. This was also because of the way in which the revolutions of the "Arab Spring" succeeded (with the exception of Libya) without U.S. support and encouragement, and even in the face of U.S. opposition. By the later years of the Bush administration, the contrast between the administration's rhetoric of democratization and its actual Middle East strategy—that of supporting Sunni Arab autocrats hostile to Iran—had become glaring.

The shift of many Democratic intellectuals to an anti-interventionist position, however, implied not an abandonment of belief in America's mission, but rather a reversion to an older version of it, that of America as example. For if belief in America's uniquely valuable role in the world pervades American political culture (and has indeed often been justified by reality), this by no means necessarily implies a desire to carry out this role by active means, let alone military ones. Equally strong, and indeed historically more common, has been the belief that America's mission to humanity consists above all of the force of her example.[86] In the debates between Al Gore and George Bush in the presidential election campaign of 2000, both candidates stressed America's mission to the world, but both also stressed that it should be exercised by example, with Bush famously declaring:

> I think they [the people of the world] ought to look at us as a country that understands freedom, where it doesn't matter who you are or how you're raised or where you're from, that you can succeed...So I don't think they ought to look at us in any other way than what we are. We're a freedom-loving nation. And if we're an arrogant nation, they'll view us that way. But if we're a humble nation they'll respect us as an honorable nation.[87]

One of the earliest and most famous expositions of this view was by President John Quincy Adams in 1821:

> America does not go abroad in search of monsters to destroy. She is the well-wisher to the freedom and independence of all. She is the champion only of her own. She will recommend the general cause by the countenance of her

voice, and the benignant sympathy of her example. She well knows that by once enlisting under other banners than her own, were they even the banners of foreign independence, she would involve herself beyond the powers of extrication, in all the wars of interest and intrigue, of individual avarice, envy, and ambition, which assumed the colors and usurped the standards of freedom...She might become the dictatress of the world. She would be no longer the ruler of her own spirit.[88]

As these words imply, one underlying concern of many Americans who have opposed overseas interventions—including ones in the name of the American Creed—has been that they would tarnish the force of America's example, and thereby in the long run make it more difficult to spread the lessons of the creed around the world.[89] This is an argument that I would endorse from my own observation of how the prestige of American democracy and American material culture destroyed the faith of the younger Soviet elites in the Soviet system, and thereby helped destroy that system. This bore out the prediction of George Kennan: "The most important influence the United States can bring to bear upon internal developments in Russia will continue to be the influence of example: the influence of what it is, and not only what it is to others, but what it is to itself."[90]

The alternation of activist and exemplary versions of America's mission as the dominant intellectual force in the United States is heavily influenced by the course of America's international experience. After World War I, the Wilsonian period was followed by almost two decades in which most Americans held to an isolationist view of American policy. In our time, the bitter experiences of the wars in Iraq and Afghanistan, while they have not led to isolationism (at least in the policy elites), have certainly led to an immense reduction in the belief that America can successfully promote democracy through war, and can itself create new democracies from the ground up.

The Afghan experience in particular also damaged belief in a much wider intellectual trend that helped underpin Bush's democratizing rhetoric, that of rational choice theory. This ostensibly scientific and objective approach to social and economic analysis is in fact both heavily ideological and rooted in American culture. Rational choice theory is really founded on an almost theological faith in the universal validity of a dogmatic (and in part imaginary) American-style economic individualism. In the traditional Christian faith, all human beings if taught properly and protected from the lures of the devil will become Christians. That is their default mode. In rational choice theory—and in the instinctive belief of many ordinary Americans—the default mode of humanity is to become Americans. This quasi-religious, utopian belief was strengthened still further by the fall of Communism.[91]

The extremely abstruse, "scientistic" style of this and other related approaches, however, makes it very easy to hide such basic assumptions within the model.[92] As Edward Shils commented two generations ago, "it is not difficult to understand how the adoption of the scientist tradition can prepare the way to the acceptance of a secularized millenarianism and thus lead on to ideological politics." He was speaking of the link between scientism and Communism, but it is no less true with regard to the American ideology.[93] Thus the great majority of official and semiofficial discussions on the subject of democratization that I attended in Washington, DC, between 2000 and 2005 were conducted as if no serious work of history, sociology, or political anthropology had ever been written.

President Obama, however, though he repeatedly stressed his belief in America's unique democratic mission, also greatly toned down the Bush administration's rhetoric of democratization as a central aspect of foreign policy, emphasizing that America needs to work closely with allies and, whenever possible, give regional states the lead—as in the Libya War, where America took a back seat to Britain and France. Obama's inaugural address of January 2009 provided a good summary of contemporary American civic nationalism, expanded to take in multiracialism and softened so as to add a greater element of multilateralism:

> As for our common defense, we reject as false the choice between our safety and our ideals. Our founding fathers, faced with perils that we can scarcely imagine, drafted a charter to assure the rule of law and the rights of man, a charter expanded by the blood of generations. Those ideals still light the world, and we will not give them up for expedience's sake. And so, to all other peoples and governments who are watching today, from the grandest capitals to the small village where my father was born: know that America is a friend of each nation and every man, woman and child who seeks a future of peace and dignity, and we are ready to lead once more.
>
> Recall that earlier generations faced down fascism and communism not just with missiles and tanks, but with sturdy alliances and enduring convictions. They understood that our power alone cannot protect us, nor does it entitle us to do as we please. Instead, they knew that our power grows through its prudent use. Our security emanates from the justness of our cause, the force of our example, the tempering qualities of humility and restraint.
>
> We are the keepers of this legacy. Guided by these principles once more, we can meet those new threats that demand even greater effort, even greater cooperation and understanding between nations ...
>
> What is required of us now is a new era of responsibility—a recognition, on the part of every American, that we have duties to ourselves, our nation, and the world, duties that we do not grudgingly accept, but rather seize gladly, firm in the knowledge that there is nothing so satisfying to the spirit, so defining of our character, than giving our all to a difficult task.
>
> This is the price and the promise of citizenship.
>
> This is the source of our confidence—the knowledge that God calls on us to shape an uncertain destiny.
>
> This is the meaning of our liberty and our creed—why men and women and children of every race and every faith can join in celebration across this magnificent mall, and why a man whose father less than sixty years ago might not have been served at a local restaurant can now stand before you to take a most sacred oath.[94]

These are noble and inspiring words, which certainly do not contain any chauvinist spirit. Their emphasis on humility and restraint contrasts sharply with the approach of the Bush administration. Nonetheless, they embody a continued claim to American global leadership, even if it is a leadership that must be earned and not asserted as a right.

Wolfish Wilsonians: The Bush Administration and America's Mission

While American civic nationalism has indeed been part of the foundation of America's prestige in the world and of its consensual leadership, it has also been used on occasions to underpin American chauvinism and aggression—as by the Bush administration in its push to launch the Iraq War. As noted, this strategy helped Bush and his supporters to undermine opposition to the war among the Democrats and among the U.S. intelligentsia. For the future, two important questions for the United States and the world are whether belief in America's role as leader of the world toward freedom can be mobilized as part of anti-Chinese propaganda, and as an argument—within the United States at least—for the creation of a NATO-style "democratic alliance" against China, and for a strategy of encouraging revolt against the Chinese Communist state.

Connected to this is the question of the attitude of Republicans toward America's mission in the world. As of 2012, two quite distinct tendencies can be seen—even if, bewilderingly, within the Tea Parties especially, they often seem to coexist within the same head. The first reflects the growing disenchantment of a majority of Americans with overseas wars and interventions, focused above all on hostility to a continuation of the U.S. military campaign in Afghanistan. This was shown, for example, by the vote in the House of Representatives on Afghanistan in May 2011, when 26 Republican congressmen joined 178 Democrats to urge accelerated U.S. withdrawal.

On the other hand, the Republican intellectual establishment shows almost no signs of rethinking the ideological approach of the Bush administration. As of 2012, it is very difficult to find old-style realists among the Republican staffers in Congress, and impossible to find them at the Heritage Foundation and the American Enterprise Institute. The rhetoric remains entirely that of America's right and duty to lead the world toward democracy. As with Bush, absence of democracy is used as a matter of course to deny the legitimacy of rival states. In the words of Newt Gingrich, attacking Colin Powell and realists within the State Department and the Republican Party:

> The United States should actively stand for and promote its values around the globe. Every person deserves safety, health, prosperity, and freedom. The United States supports the core values of constitutional liberty, the right to

> free speech (including a free press), independent judiciaries, free markets, free elections, transparency in government, the equality of women, racial equality, and the free exercise of religious beliefs. Without these values, it is very hard to imagine a world in which U.S. safety can be secured. We should not confuse respect for others with acceptance of their values if they violate these principles.

This passage formed part of a determined attempt by the Republican Right to reduce still further respect in the U.S. government for the opinions even of democratic Western allies, to undermine the chief government department entrusted with international relations, to open the door wider to unilateral American military actions, and to reduce genuine support in the administration for President Bush's "Road Map" for peace between Israel and Palestine.[95]

This was part of what might be called a "Jacobin" tendency in the neoconservative movement and the Bush administration: a refusal to grant any legitimacy to regimes that did not share America's political system, unless they displayed complete subservience to American foreign and security policy. The dangers of this for international peace and order were described by the great historian of nationalism Elie Kedourie, writing of the effects of the French Revolution:

> The [traditional] society of European states admitted all varieties of republics, of hereditary and elective monarchies, of constitutional and despotic regimes. But on the principle advocated by the [French] revolutionaries, the title of all governments then existing was put into question; since they did not derive their sovereignty from the nation, they were usurpers with whom no agreement need be binding, and to whom subjects owed no allegiance. It is clear that such a doctrine would envenom international quarrels, and render them quite recalcitrant to the methods of traditional statecraft; it would indeed subvert all international relations as hitherto known.[96]

C. Vann Woodward echoed this warning in writing about U.S. attitudes during the Vietnam War:

> The true American mission, according to those who support this view, is a moral crusade on a worldwide scale. Such people are likely to concede no validity whatever and grant no hearing to the opposing point of view, and to appeal to a higher law to justify bloody and revolting means in the name of a noble end. For what end could be nobler, they ask, than the liberation of man ... The irony of the moralistic approach, when exploited by nationalism, is that the high motive to end justice and immorality actually results in making war more amoral and horrible than ever and in shattering the foundations of the political and moral order upon which peace has to be built.[97]

This tendency among powerful sections of the modern American Right does not date from 2002. The most important historical moment in this regard was

Ronald Reagan's adoption of the language of democratic revolution and human rights as a key part of his struggle against the "evil empire" of the Soviet Union, involving a deliberate and open repudiation of the "realist" considerations that had supposedly governed the policies of the previous Republican administrations of Ford, Nixon, and Eisenhower.

Above all, a strong movement is afoot among the Republicans to concentrate on China the same degree of hostile rhetoric—in the name of support for "democracy" and hatred of "dictatorship" that was previously directed against the Soviet Union, Russia and parts of the Muslim world. This is not, of course, to say that a future Republican administration will necessarily adopt a much more anti-Chinese policy, or seek to subvert the Chinese state from within. The general pattern from the 1980s on has been for the U.S. party in opposition (whether Republican or Democrat) to attack China and to damn the government in power for being too pro-Chinese, and for not defending human rights and promoting democracy in China—only to pursue the same "pro-Chinese" policies themselves when next in power. However, this pattern was formed in a period when China, though growing greatly, was still very much inferior to the United States in wealth and power. Whether it can survive a period in which China overtakes the United States is another matter.

Hawkish Republican views are distributed to the general public through Fox News and a huge array of conservative radio stations, but also through the media alleged by conservatives and the Tea Parties to be part of the "liberal establishment." Thus, even in the comment pages of newspapers such as the *New York Times* and the *Washington Post*, hard-line right-wing nationalists like George Will, William Kristol, Robert Novak, William Safire, and Charles Krauthammer are to be found day after day.[98]

In a softer and more diffuse way, the ideology of American democratic supremacy and America's mission in the world is also enshrined in institutions created during the cold war as part of the ideological campaign against Communism. These include a range of private organizations, but also two congressionally funded institutions, the National Endowment for Democracy and Freedom House. Their origins meant that they were built around the idea of America's struggle with the Soviet Union, and their propaganda tends to have a harshly nationalist tone toward any country seen as a rival of the United States, while being notoriously soft on U.S. allies. Despite extensive and detailed critiques of their work, their publications tend to be seen in the United States as possessing a mixture of intellectual objectivity, guaranteed quality of research, and semiofficial gravitas.

Thus Freedom House's annual survey of freedom and democracy in the world is treated as a kind of biblical authority by many American journalists and commentators. Yet this is an institution that from the 1970s to the 2000s advanced China precisely one grade in its freedom rating, from seven to six. That is to say, according to Freedom House, Chinese in 2004, after a generation of economic liberalization and the transition from fanatical totalitarianism to authoritarianism, were only very slightly more free than they were in the depths of the Cultural Revolution in 1972. India in 2002 rated a two, despite severe repression in Kashmir, and the massacre in Gujarat of more than 2000 members of the Muslim minority, with the active complicity of the local government and police. And so on.[99] In this, Freedom House was simply following the pattern of many U.S. institutions during the cold war, when a range of dictatorships in Africa, Latin America, and elsewhere were classified as part of the "Free World" because their allies were geopolitical allies of the United States.[100]

And, of course, at the level of policy discussions, human rights abuses, whether real or exaggerated, can be cited in almost any circumstances as a reason to display hostility against a given country. Thus, in a small but typical example, a writer in the *New York Times*, arguing for a hostile American attitude to the Chinese space program, declared "amid calls for joint scientific or commercial ventures in space to improve Chinese–American relations, officials in Washington should consider what kind of cooperation is appropriate with a regime that does not share the United States' tradition of freedom and respect for human rights."[101]

This kind of thing filters down through U.S. society. Thus in February 2004, the *Washington Post*'s "Parade" section asked its readers, "Who Would *You* Say is the World's Worst Dictator?"—lumping together indiscriminately—just like Freedom House—Hu Jintao of China with Kim Jong Il of North Korea, Robert Mugabe of Zimbabwe, Than Shwe of Burma, Teodoro Obiang Nguema of Equatorial Guinea, and Crown Prince Abdullah of Saudi Arabia. In other words, this was a selection made with no reference whatsoever to the nature of the given regime, the role of the leader within that regime, or, most of all, the success of the regime in advancing the material well-being and economic freedom of its subjects—which when applied to themselves, Americans have defined as part of the essence of liberty.[102] Hu Jintao came in third, counted as worse than the leaders of the catastrophic regimes in Zimbabwe and Guinea and the Wahabi Islamist totalitarianism of Saudi Arabia. Coupled with the incessant rhetoric of politicians, the media, and human rights groups concerning freedom in other countries, the effect is both to feed American chauvinist hostility toward other countries and to pour a continual nourishing rain of self-praise on Americans' belief in their own country's superiority.

Many people from the former colonial world in particular are bound to see this mixture as simply a repeat of former European *missions civilisatrices*, as a hypocritical cover for imperial aggrandizement, and they are often right to do so. Moreover, as the next chapter will explore, America's universal mission contains within itself certain elements of "universal values" that are in fact not universal at all, but very visibly part of a purely American culture and "way of life."[103] This too is clearly perceived by many people in the countries that Americans propose to liberate in the name of these supposedly universal values.

The merger of the selective use of "democratization" with strategies based on ruthless "realism" has been central to the approach of the "neoconservatives" since the inception of this political tendency during the first decades of the cold war. In their program, the Soviet Union was to be driven to destruction by a mixture of military and economic pressure, the ruthless repression of Communist-backed rebellions against U.S. client regimes—including, where necessary, U.S. military intervention—and the rigorous preaching of democracy and liberty to Soviet subjects.

The selective or instrumental use of moral outrage and calls for liberation— what Jeane Kirkpatrick, candidly enough, called "the utilitarian value of democracy" to U.S. foreign policy—is a very old pattern in human affairs, and especially perhaps in the Protestant and Anglo-Saxon worlds.[104] Rarely, however, has it been used so systematically, or with such contempt for even the appearance of consistency or intellectual honor, as by American nationalists, especially from the neoconservative camp. Thus, in 1980, when attacking President Jimmy Carter's attempts at consistency in the treatment of U.S. allies and rivals concerning their human rights abuses and lack of democracy, Irving Kristol sounded like George Kennan, Samuel Huntington, and other realist conservative critics of American messianism:

> It is the fundamental fallacy of American foreign policy to believe, in the face of all the evidence, that all peoples, everywhere, are immediately "entitled" to a liberal constitutional government—and a thoroughly democratic one at that...As a matter of fact, it is only since World War I—a war fought under the slogans of "self-determination for all nations" and "make the world safe for democracy"—that American foreign policy began to disregard the obvious for the sake of the quixotic pursuit of impossible ideals. Before World War I, intelligent men took it for granted that not all peoples, everywhere, at all times, could be expected to replicate a Western constitutional democracy.[105]

Two years earlier, as part of the same hard-line campaign against Carter, Kristol had expressed himself categorically in favor of America's mission as example, not intervention:

> The proper extent of political rights in any nation is not something that our State Department can have any meaningful opinion about. It can only be determined by the people of that nation, who will draw on their own political and cultural backgrounds in arriving at a suitable disposition of this matter. We can try to set them a good example by making our democratic republic as admirable as possible—as our Founding Fathers urged. But that is about all we can do—as our Founding Fathers recognized.[106]

But, of course, Kristol and his school have reserved such moderation for U.S. allies, however savage. Precisely such realist statements as Kristol's have been attacked by neoconservatives when these have been applied to countries that they wish to weaken or undermine, and these attacks have been not only ferocious, but also phrased in terms of the most strident version of America's messianic mission as intervention, and not merely example.[107]

The most shameless example of this is the way in which the neoconservatives and other former anti-Communists in the United States have played around with the distinction between "totalitarian" and "authoritarian" regimes. During the 1980s, this was advanced by a number of anti-Communist intellectuals as a key difference between the dictatorial, but still culturally, intellectually, and economically open pro-American regimes of Latin America and the Communist states. And this is indeed a valid distinction.[108]

The amusing thing is that when Russia and China both in their different ways abandoned Communism, it turned out that the Americans who had most fiercely argued for this distinction did not really take it seriously themselves. Instead, in these and other cases (like Iran) they did their utmost to blur the line between totalitarianism and authoritarianism. For them, this had been nothing more than a cheap debating trick, intended to demonstrate that Washington's Latin American dependents were better than Moscow's in Eastern Europe.

Ossification, Race, and the Tea Parties

In the future, as U.S. power declines and domestic problems grow, the dangers of ideologically driven U.S. aggression seem likely to decrease—though it is easy to imagine how the language of an American-led crusade for democracy could be mobilized in the context of increasing hostility between the United States and China.

As of 2012, however, a greater danger fuelled by American civic nationalism is a domestic one: that the creedal foundations of that nationalism are ceasing to be, on balance, a force for renewal of the United States, and instead are becoming a force for ossification, and from a force for expansion of the American identity to take in broader and broader groups of Americans, as absolutist attachment to the American Constitution is once again becoming a weapon to exclude much of the American population from real power. There is a real risk that aspects of American civic nationalism will both speed up America's decline and embitter relations between Americans. This could in turn lead future American governments to seek to unite the nation again through foreign conflict.

These dangers are very evident in the Tea Parties and the sections of the white "middle class" that they represent. This part of American society has suffered very badly in recent decades. Absolutist faith in both the formal and informal elements of the American Creed, however, help make it impossible for many of these people to explain what is happening to them and to America in rational terms.

A perfect constitution can by definition not have become an obstacle to effective government and a contribution to political paralysis. The free-market, individualistic capitalism, which has supposedly been responsible for America's economic greatness, cannot need qualification in order to meet new challenges. People who are suffering and cannot explain their suffering in rational terms and seek rational solutions will adopt irrational answers and solutions: on the one hand, demon-ologies and conspiracy theories, and on the other, theologies and nostalgia for a return to supposedly perfect pasts.

Such nostalgia is characteristic of right-wing populism all over the world, and in some ways has fed into left-wing populism as well. What makes America special is that the nostalgia has before its eyes not just a vague vision of a better past, but for-mal, written political texts that were supposedly bound up with and even respon-sible for that better past: the Constitution and the Declaration of Independence. The Constitution, on the one hand, has mythic, quasi-religious force, but on the other hand, contains the detailed, specific rules that regulate U.S. democracy and government.

It is important to note that while the Tea Parties are not supported by a majority of Americans and have taken worship of the Constitution to extreme lengths, they have only been able to do so because of a quasi-religious language in this regard that already permeated American civic nationalism and political culture. Thus the signatories of the Declaration of Independence and framers of the Constitution are generally known as the "founders" or the "founding fathers," and these documents as "founding texts." Declarations of allegiance to these universally worshipped texts allow the Tea Parties to seize for themselves the banner of Americanism, and to portray themselves as representing everything that is truly American.

This kind of language in itself tends to discourage analysis of the founders as members of the elite in the British colonies, products of a particular society and economy at a particular time. Instead, the Constitution becomes "a lesson in time-less wisdom," in the words of a Tea Party supporter.[109] When the Republicans took up the majority position in the House of Representatives after the 2010 midterm elections, they began by reading the Constitution, and passed a rule requiring that every new proposed bill contain a statement by the lawmaker who drafted it cit-ing the constitutional authority to enact the new law—something that under the Constitution is actually a matter for the Supreme Court to decide.[110]

The attachment of the Tea Parties and their allies in the Republican Party to these texts is indeed religious rather than political in tone, and gives strong endorsement to Louis Hartz's argument about the danger that the creedal elements in American nationalism, while devoted in principle to liberty, will lead to a crush-ingly illiberal conformism. The sight of people at Tea Party rallies waving copies of the Constitution and Declaration of Independence brings irresistibly to my mind pictures of Mao's followers waving his Little Red Book. Tea Party supporters meet to read these documents aloud together—once again, traditionally a religious rather than a political pattern of behavior. In the words of Michele Bachmann:

> To those who would spread lies, and to those who would spread falsehoods
> and rumors about the Tea Party movement, let me be very clear to them. If you

are scared of the Tea Party movement, you are afraid of Thomas Jefferson who penned our mission statement, and, by the way, you may have heard of it, it's called the Declaration of Independence. [Cheers, applause.] So what are these revolutionary ideas that make up and undergird the Tea Party movement? Well, it's this: All men and all women are created equal. We are endowed by our creator—that's God, not government [applause]—with certain inalienable rights.[111]

Bachmann's statement reflects a widespread sentiment in the Tea Party movement that attributes the founding texts to divine inspiration, and perhaps the tendency in the Tea Parties to quote the Declaration of Independence over the Constitution is because, unlike the Constitution, the second phrase of the Declaration speaks of the Creator. The influential book *The Five Thousand Year Leap*, by the late Cleon Skousen, argues that the Founding Fathers based the Constitution on divinely ordained Natural Law, and that this was responsible for

> the 28 fundamental beliefs of the Founding Fathers which they said must be understood and perpetuated by every people who desired peace, prosperity, and freedom. These beliefs have made possible more progress in 200 years than was made previously in over 5,000 years. Thus the title *"The 5,000 Year Leap"* ...
>
> **Principle 1**—*The only reliable basis for sound government and just human relations is Natural Law.* Natural law is God's law. There are certain laws which govern the entire universe, and just as Thomas Jefferson said in the Declaration of Independence, there are laws which govern in the affairs of men which are "the laws of nature and of nature's God."[112]

This book is relentlessly plugged by right-wing media star Glenn Beck, whose views have great influence among the Tea Parties. The same argument is made in *Christianity and the Constitution: The Faith of Our Founding Fathers*, by John Eidsmoe, a book that had a great influence on Michele Bachmann.[113]

An especially potent melding of religious and constitutional faith into a hysterical American chauvinist nationalism is to be found in the speeches and writings of Phyllis Schlafly, one of the leaders of the Christian Right. She linked hostility to foreigners to a quasi-religious faith in the U.S. Constitution in an attack on Clinton's desire to sign a range of international treaties:

> Global treaties and conferences are a direct threat to every American citizen... The Senate should reject all UN treaties out of hand. Every single one would reduce our rights, freedom and sovereignty. That goes for treaties on the child, women, an international court, the sea, trade, biodiversity, global warming, and heritage sites ...
>
> Our Declaration of Independence and Constitution are the fountainhead of the freedom and prosperity Americans enjoy. We Americans have a constitutional republic so unique, so precious, so successful that it would be total folly to put our necks in a yoke with any other nation. St. Paul warns us (II Corinthians 6.14): "Be ye not unequally yoked together with unbelievers, for

what fellowship hath righteousness with unrighteousness? And what communion hath light with darkness?" The principles of life, liberty, and property must not be joined with the principles of genocide, totalitarianism, socialism, and religious persecution. We cannot trust agreements or treaties with infidels.[114]

This passage beautifully illustrates both the intertwining of democratic and religious exceptionalism in parts of American society and the deep nationalist isolationism that helps feed nationalist unilateralism.

For the bulk of the Tea Parties, however, it would be truer to say that the founding texts *are* the religion; and indeed the reverence for these texts does have echoes of the fundamentalist Christians' reverence for the literal word of the Bible. A fundamentalist faith in the original Constitution, and a belief that this mandates small government and low taxes, are the ideas that tie together what in other ways is a very disparate movement—indeed, hardly a movement at all, but rather a loose alliance of local groups.

Thus, while according to CNN, 57 percent of Tea Party supporters polled agreed with the statement that "America is and always has been a Christian nation," according to the Pew Research Center, 46 percent of Tea Party supporters polled in August 2010 did not have an opinion about the "religious Right." However, on issues like gay marriage and abortion, majorities of between 59 and 64 percent of Tea Party supporters agreed with conservative religious positions, while 44 percent of self-declared conservative Christians polled agreed with the Tea Parties, against only 4 percent who disagreed. However, there is also a libertarian streak in a fair number of Tea Party supporters, which opposes government regulation of morality. This tendency is represented by Ron Paul, who is also at odds with most of the Tea Parties on military spending and America's superpower role.[115]

A quasi-religious faith in the Constitution is not only present in the less-educated ranks of the Tea Parties, but it also permeates the language of many American conservative intellectuals. Thus the Mount Vernon Statement ("Constitutional Conservatism: A Statement for the Twenty-First Century") of February 2010, drawn up by a long list of such intellectuals, and backed by, among other institutions, the Heritage Foundation, begins as follows:

> We recommit ourselves to the ideas of the American Founding. Through the Constitution, the Founders created an enduring framework of limited government based on the rule of law. They sought to secure national independence, provide for economic opportunity, establish true religious liberty and maintain a flourishing society of republican self-government.
>
> These principles define us as a country and inspire us as a people. They are responsible for a prosperous, just nation unlike any other in the world. They are our highest achievements, serving not only as powerful beacons to all who strive for freedom and seek self-government, but as warnings to tyrants and despots everywhere.[116]

It should hardly need pointing out that while the spirit of the Constitution does indeed provide a great inspiration for future generations, the text and its detailed provisions were drawn up by late eighteenth-century aristocrats and haut bourgeois for a small, overwhelmingly rural, preindustrial and in part slave-owning society with 13 federal units, a total population of around three million people, and almost no regular armed forces. It hardly seems controversial to suggest that to govern a society with a population of more than 300 million, a vastly expanded territory, a completely different economy, vast military forces, and a far more culturally and ethnically diverse population will probably require significant changes to that constitution. When it comes to voting rights, to return to the original Constitution would disenfranchise not just most blacks, but Michele Bachmann and Sarah Palin.

As Michael Lind has cogently argued, "freedom rests on a culture of constitutionalism, not on a particular document." He points out that not only has the U.S. Constitution been amended 27 times, these amendments include some beloved by the Tea Parties, like the Second, establishing the right to bear arms, and the Tenth, reserving to the states and the people all powers not explicitly vested in the United States. Moreover, the constitutions of individual states have been repeatedly and radically changed—seven times, in the case of Texas.[117]

These criticisms of the Tea Parties' understanding of the Constitution and of American history are accurate, but also to a great extent irrelevant, for the Tea Parties are neither a political party nor an organized movement. Rather, they are an incoherent shout of protest and anger that appeals to certain deep and ancient strains of American political culture.

These features of the Tea Parties have led them to be dismissed with contempt by many liberal observers. In addition, there is a widespread—and well-based— liberal view that this movement is in many ways a tool of sections of the capitalist elites, who are far more concerned with deregulation of the economy and low taxes for the rich than with love of the Constitution. Special attention has been drawn in this regard to the role of the Koch industrial group in funding the Tea Parties and institutes associated with them.[118]

This analysis would see the Tea Parties as essentially ignorant tools of big capitalism, promoting a vision of small government that in fact works against their own middle class economic interests. Thus the origins of the Tea Parties owed much to public anger at the governments' bail out of crippled banks in 2008–2009, an anger with deep roots in traditional left-wing populism; but by 2011, criticism of the banks had been completely swamped in the Tea Parties by hysterical attacks on Obama's health care reform—but without focusing on its most negative aspect, namely the failure to rein in the profits of the big pharmaceutical companies.

On the other hand, while the ideological backers of the Tea Parties in the right-wing intelligentsia are strongly hostile to *all* aspects of big government except the military, the Tea Parties and their representatives generally steer clear of attacks on the key programs that support the middle classes, especially Social Security and

Medicare. Bizarrely, but understandably, the elderly, white, middle class beneficiaries of these government programs do not see them as part of the big government that they want to reduce.[119]

The Right's fetishism for the Constitution is especially dangerous since aspects
of the Constitution (at least, as interpreted by the conservative-dominated
Supreme Court over the past 25 years) and rules associated with it are contributing strongly to the inability of *any* government of the United States—Republican
or Democrat—to govern effectively. The constitutional guarantee of free speech,
interpreted to mean that there can be no effective limit on election contributions
or spending, condemns politicians to an endless search for money that inevitably
puts them in the pockets of special interests. Midterm Congressional elections
and short presidential terms turn the entire political system into one continuous
election campaign, boosting still further the role of money, lobbyists, and focus
groups, and reducing the chances of crafting long-term policies with long-term
results.

Above all, both the power of the U.S. Senate and its internal rules (especially
the filibuster) give immense power to a minority in that body to block legislation
by the majority. This not only frustrates the entire democratic process, it boosts
the wasteful government spending the Tea Parties and the Right say they desire
to reduce—because it helps give senators the ability to extract massive subsidies
and benefits for their states in return for their votes. The increasing radicalization
of the Republican Party, and the retaliation it has provoked by the Democrats, has
led to an immense expansion of the use of the filibuster. The only precedent for
this was the battle of Southern senators to block civil rights for blacks in the 1950s
and 1960s, and that was essentially a one-issue campaign. Current Republican use
of the filibuster extends across much of the field of legislation and federal appointments—and Democrats are likely to follow suit when they are in the minority. In
the 1960s, around 8 percent of bills were faced with a filibuster; in the 2000s, it has
been around 70 percent. This is not a recipe for the decline of progressive government, it is a recipe for the decline of government in general.[120]

Fetishism of the Constitution makes it even less likely that Tea Party–influenced
Republicans will contemplate even small changes to the Senate's rules, let alone the
Constitution in general. Their refusal to do so is not, however, irrational—at least
if one assumes that, as the next chapter will argue, considerations of race and ethnicity have been a central thread of U.S. politics for much of the past 200 years. For
any serious consideration of a change to the U.S. Senate is bound, sooner or later,
to come to the conclusion that bad as they are, it is not the *rules* of the Senate that
are the greatest barrier to the will of democratic majorities in America, it is the
composition of the U.S. Senate.

The existing distribution of U.S. Senate seats is colossally weighted in favor of
white conservatives. The rule that every state in the United States has two senate seats irrespective of population was framed at a time when the largest state
(Virginia) had 12 times the population of the smallest (Delaware). Moreover,

the distribution of states and populations meant that there was a rough balance between the Senate representation of the different regions of the original United States. As of 2012, the largest U.S. state, California, has more than 70 times the population of the smallest, Wyoming—but they both have two senators. The smallest 21 states of the United States *put together* have a smaller population than California, which makes 42 senators to California's 2. Above all, this means that six western states with only 3 percent of the U.S. population have 12 senators between them and are thus in a position to block any legislation that displeases their mainly white conservative populations.

This has already contributed enormously to blocking legislation on a range of issues that affect the populations of those states either emotionally or materially, from gun control to carbon taxing. As long however as the United States as a whole has an overwhelmingly white majority, the issue of disproportionate representation will not become couched in racial terms.

This is very unlikely to remain the case, however, as whites decline steadily from a majority to a plurality of the U.S. population—unless, that is, they also lose their majorities in the upper belt of western states, which does not seem likely. The white proportion of the U.S. population has declined from 75 percent in 2000 to 72 percent in 2010. According to projections of the U.S. Census Bureau, whites will cease to be a majority (while remaining a plurality) sometime between 2040 and 2050. Meanwhile, the proportion of Latinos will have grown to almost a quarter of the U.S. population.[121] Even in times of growing economic prosperity, a shift on this scale would have been bound to cause tensions (especially when a sizable proportion of the change is due to illegal immigration)—and the next three decades do not seem likely to be ones of growing prosperity for many less-educated whites. Moreover, this shift in the United States coincides with a shift in global power toward the non-white states of China and India. This shift reverses the pattern of the past 500 years and overthrows deeply rooted assumptions that exist at a subconscious level in the minds of even liberal white Americans and Europeans.

Already, while explicit racism is relatively rare in the Tea Parties (though clear enough in the mouths of right-wing media figures like Glenn Beck and Rush Limbaugh, with their talk of the Obama administration supporting a new Black Panther party), white anxieties about the United States having a black president are very clear indeed, even if they take the form of coded fears that he is "not Christian" or "not born in the United States." It hardly needs stressing how infuriating these attacks are to both blacks and Muslims.[122]

The constitutional principle of states' rights has been used as a racial tool before, in one way or another, for most of U.S. history. From the 1840s to the 1960s, this was the white South's principal tool and argument in trying to block freedom and then civil rights for blacks. Indeed, the current Republican and Tea Party obsession with states' rights is one aspect of the much-remarked "southernisation" of the Republican Party since the 1960s.

In both the 1860s and the 1960s, however, white majorities in the United States as a whole eventually overcame Southern white resistance. In the future, there is a real risk that as a result of white middle class anxieties about economic, demographic, and national decline, a majority of whites will come together in defense of an increasingly dysfunctional and unrepresentative constitution that is more and more obviously being used to defend white dominance at the expense of non-whites. Such a development would mark the end of America's greatness and her democratic example to the world. In such circumstances, the wild rhetoric of the Right about resorting to arms in defense of the Constitution might also turn into something more than rhetoric.

Thankfully there is nothing certain about this. As this chapter has noted, a central theme in America's history has been the overcoming of ethnic and racial divisions and the gradual expansion of the categories of people considered to be true U.S. citizens. On the other hand, as the next chapter will explore, an equally central theme has been the bitter tensions and anxieties that have accompanied this process.

Three

Antithesis Part I: The Embittered Heartland

Defeat of the aspen groves of Colorado valleys,

The blue bells of the Rockies,

And blue bonnets of old Texas,

By the Pittsburg alleys.

Defeat of the alfalfa and the Mariposa lily.

Defeat of the Pacific and the long Mississippi.

Defeat of the young by the old and silly.

Defeat of tornadoes by the poison vats supreme.

Defeat of my boyhood, defeat of my dream.

—Vachel Lindsay, "Bryan, Bryan, Bryan, Bryan" (on the defeat of William Jennings Bryan's Populist campaign for president, 1896)[1]

Radical nationalism has many fathers, but its mother is defeat, and her milk is called humiliation. From this poisoned nourishment comes in part the tendency to chauvinist hatred that has streamed through so many of the world's nationalisms. This is self-evidently true of the nationalisms of the former colonies, which grew out of their conquest and occupation by the European and other empires, and the destruction or forced transformation of their previous economic structures and traditions of moral and political authority.

It is no less true, however, of those countries that avoided direct conquest, but in order to defend themselves were forced, as best they could, to imitate Western forms and reshape themselves radically in the process. Religiously ordered social and state traditions were particularly threatened. Where these survived, it was often by associating themselves with modern nationalism, sometimes—as in Japan—of a quasi-totalitarian kind.

Russia, Japan, and Turkey are the best-known examples in this category. In the case of Russia, despite great military victories, the repeated failure of the country as a whole to "catch up" with its Western European and North American rivals produced an inferiority complex that has haunted Russian society and culture for almost three centuries.

In a wider sense, this pattern has been true not only of most of the globe, but even of most European countries: in recent centuries all have been forced to adapt themselves as best they could to a model of modernity and progress that they did not create and over the shape of which they have had little say—whether that model was set by Holland, France, Britain, or most recently the United States.

The tensions, insecurities, and hatreds produced by this pattern sometimes endure long after the country concerned has in fact liberated itself from its oppressors, and even in those rare cases where it has caught up with its Western rivals. Thus German nationalism was born in the later eighteenth and early nineteenth centuries in large part out of a profound sense of inferiority and vulnerability to France. Culturally speaking, this was produced by the overwhelming dominance of French language and culture in eighteenth century Europe, leading in Germany to that humiliating aping of French words and forms that was so bitterly denounced by Herder, Fichte, and the rest.

For ordinary Germans, there was the repeated and unpleasant experience of invasion by French armies, culminating in those of Revolutionary and Napoleonic France. And for the German elites, there was the ruthless reshaping of Germany's political and social structures by French diktat—all of which was made possible by Germany's radically disunited condition, compared to the "*grande nation*." The resulting resentments were watered by a steady drizzle of French contempt for German boorishness, drunkenness, and general absurdity, well publicized by German nationalists.[2]

As a consequence, Germans developed a national inferiority complex that persisted even after Germany's unification in 1871 and emergence as Europe's most militarily powerful and economically successful nation: the psychological pattern by which, as Bismarck put it sardonically, "a German generally needs to drink two glasses of champagne before he feels himself to be his full height." This legacy was not least among the causes of the edgy arrogance, restlessness, and paranoia of Wilhelmine German foreign policy, which, when combined with overwhelming German power, did so much to alarm other European powers and unite them against Germany. There is reason to fear today that this may be true of China, as it rises to become the world's greatest economic power even while many of its peoples are still obsessed with their country's past humiliations at the hands of Europe, the United States, and Japan.

In the case of the United States, such tendencies are extraordinary not in the context of the history of nationalisms in the world, which has obviously thrown up infinitely much worse examples. What makes it remarkable is once again the fact that the U.S. population seems at first sight to have had so little underlying reason—when compared to the historical sufferings and humiliations of other peoples—for a spirit of embittered, mean-spirited resentment at the outside world, and in particular at foreign countries that have in any way crossed their national will.

Regarding particular animosities, one needs to examine the role of specific U.S. ethnic lobbies, and that of the American military–industrial–academic complex (Eisenhower's original phrase). These two factors combined to prolong a widespread spirit of inveterate malignity against Russia for a decade after the Soviet Union collapsed and Moscow ceased to present any real threat to the United States. Clearly the Israeli lobby has also played its part over the decades in generating hostility toward Arabs and Muslims.

However, it would be a mistake to accord either of these factors a central place in the overall pattern, which was shaped long before World War II and the cold war transformed the American state, and before the ethnic lobbies attained their full power. These groups would not have achieved their objectives had they not been able to tap the support of much larger bodies of Americans who have a natural tendency in the face of any disagreement to adopt harshly adversarial stances and who, when confronted with opposition from any other country, feel impelled automatically to take up positions of fear, hostility, militancy, intransigence, and self-righteousness: in other words, classically nationalist positions.

This nationalist culture, and not only public ignorance, helps to explain how the Bush administration could transfer the anger Americans felt after 9/11 to targets that had nothing to do with that attack, and why the opposition by much of the world to the Iraq War caused such an outburst of chauvinist fury in portions of the American media and public opinion.

This capacity for chauvinist nationalism in the United States is largely to be explained by the fact that the role of defeat in the genesis of nationalism resides not only in the defeat of nations as a whole, but of classes, groups, and indeed individuals within them; the hatred and fear directed abroad by nationalism often emanates in large part from hatreds and tensions at home, and this is strikingly true in the case of the United States.

The appearance of nationalism in many countries has been correctly attributed in large part to the ascendancy and needs of new bourgeois classes, but it is equally true that many of nationalism's darker features have been produced by classes in relative or absolute decline, or with good reason to fear such decline, and who have seen not only their status and security, but their cultural worlds undermined by economic and social change.[3] This feeling is liable to become radicalized if a period of economic growth ends and is replaced by depression or stagnation; thus many of Europe's modern radical conservative and radical nationalist movements had their origins in the first "Great Depression," which lasted from the mid-1870s to the 1890s.[4]

If one defining feature of many nationalisms has been a belief in a glorious future for the nation, another that is equally common has been the desire for a return to an idealized past of a culturally and ethnically purer nation, a stable, traditional society, and a "moral economy" in which decent, hardworking people are guaranteed a decent job: a shimmering, golden, ungraspable mirage, ever present, ever receding. In Germany, for example, this was the old world of the independent small towns, with their homogeneous religious cultures and their guilds guaranteeing employment to respectable insiders and the exclusion of outsiders. This sentiment lies at the heart of the Tea Parties' desire to return America to an imagined previous age of small government and middle class responsibility, effort, and prosperity.

In the United States, this sense of defeat and embattlement resides in four distinct but overlapping elements of the American national tradition. These are the original "core" white Anglo-Saxon and Scots-Irish populations of the British colonies in North America; the specific historical culture and experience of the white South; the cultural world of fundamentalist Protestantism; and the particular memories, fears, and hatreds of some American ethnic groups and lobbies.

Daniel Bell's words of 1963 remain true today: "What the right wing is fighting, in the shadow of Communism, is essentially 'modernity'—that complex of beliefs that might be defined most simply as the belief in rational assessment, rather than established custom, for the evaluation of social change—and what it seeks to defend is its fading dominance, exercised once through the institutions of small-town America, over the control of social change. But it is precisely those established ways that a modernist America has been forced to call into question."[5]

Nativism and White Middle Class Anxieties

In America, the vision of an ideal past has developed and changed with almost every generation, as formerly "outsider" groups join the white middle classes and form a new synthesis with the older Protestant culture. Like the Hindu nationalist tradition in India, this tendency today is no longer narrowly ethnic. The stream of feelings of dispossession, however, has flowed continually from one cup to another, from the old "Protestant nativism" through McCarthyism to the Christian and nationalist Right of our own day.

In each generation, a new fear of being "swamped" or invaded arises. Nor is this by any means restricted to poorer or more ignorant whites. In March 2004, Samuel Huntington issued a stern warning that the United States is in danger of losing its political culture and even its language as a result of Mexican immigration, and declared roundly that both the American Creed and the American dream are purely products of "a distinct Anglo-Protestant culture." He warned of the risk of a fierce white "Anglo" backlash if this trend continues. The same theme was indeed present less explicitly in Huntington's *Clash of Civilizations*, in which he effectively classified not only American Latinos and Asians, but even blacks as members of non-American civilizations.[6]

The radical edge that this lends to American conservatism also allows us to speak of the associated American right-wing nationalism as a "nationalism" and not merely a "patriotism."[7] Hence the phenomenon—so strange at first sight, but perfectly sincere, and entirely characteristic of the history of radical nationalism worldwide—of deeply conservative defenders of the American capitalist system like Newt Gingrich describing themselves as "revolutionary republicans," and adopting a style and rhetoric of radical alienation from the supposed ruling elites and dominant culture. Hence the popularity on the American Right of speeches, books, and manifestos on the theme "taking America back"—a most revealing formulation. The demand to "take back our country" is at the heart of Tea Party rhetoric and sentiment.[8]

As the right-wing conservative politician Patrick Buchanan put it at the 1992 Republican Convention: "We must take back our cities and take back our culture and take back our country," the way (he said) that the U.S. military had recently "taken back" Los Angeles from the black and Latino mobs during the Rodney King riots.[9] Ralph Reed has spoken of the need for Christians to "take back this country, one precinct at a time." Laments about "the loss of the America we grew up in" are a staple of Rush Limbaugh's broadcasts. This kind of radical Rightist sentiment was perfectly expressed by Charles Maurras, who declared in the 1930s that "in order to love France today, it is necessary to hate what she has become."

As such words reflect, this attitude stems from a feeling of dispossession and even alien occupation. It is common in this segment of American politics to hear talk of America being ruled by a "liberal (or gay, or feminist) dictatorship." Such sentiments in turn feed dark fantasies about America being secretly ruled by the United Nations or other international conspiracies, and contribute to the general apocalyptic tendency of parts of American culture and the intense hatreds that suffuse the American radical Right. Barry Goldwater, who exploited this tendency in America, was once called "the favorite son of a state of mind."[10]

The Tea Parties too can be best described as the reflection of an anguished white middle class state of mind, rather than a political movement in any traditional sense, let alone one with a program for government. Sarah Palin's highly emotional books, for example, are astonishingly free of specific policy prescriptions of any kind, beyond a vague and general demand for tax cuts and smaller government.[11]

This tendency in U.S. political culture can be summed up by the wonderful name of a Texas-based right-wing organization of the 1960s: the "National Indignation Committee." It is a tendency with numerous and extremely dangerous parallels in the history of radical conservatism and nationalism in Europe. Like such movements in the late nineteenth and early twentieth centuries, it also stems from the moral and cultural confusion of deeply traditional people (largely, but by no means exclusively, petty bourgeois and peasants) desperately trying to make sense of a world that has become alien, and doing so with the help of the only culture and ideas available to them.

One could say therefore that the ethnic anxieties of sections of the original American stock created an enduring cultural mood in American society, a kind of rich layer of sediment that was later added to by other assimilated ethnic groups, and in which, over the generations, many different kinds of paranoia, fanaticism, and national ambition have been planted and have flourished.[12]

In the mid-nineteenth century, the nativist "Know-Nothings" dreamed of a return to an earlier Protestant America without Irish Catholics and without the growth of the new capitalism.[13] In the early twentieth century, a complex of Protestant nativist tendencies dreamed of an America without a whole set of new immigrant groups, and also without the automobile (or at least its back seat) and its corrosive effects on sexual morality. Today, much of the white middle class in general (including, of course, Irish and many other ethnicities and mixtures) dream of an idealized version of the Eisenhower years of the 1950s, before the sexual revolution and the rise of African Americans, gays, feminists, and other hated groups. This particular nostalgia suffused the language of the "Republican Revolution" of the mid-1990s, and the memoirs by Pat Buchanan and other Rightists.[14]

The real or perceived defeats that fuel such nostalgia have affected and harmed important groups within America just as badly as they have similar groups elsewhere. The American middle class may not have suffered so badly economically—though that may be changing as the economy ceases to generate adequate numbers of "middle class" jobs—but America's openness to immigration means that they have suffered even more from demographic pressure and the cultural tension and change that this has encouraged.

This clash has generated much of the electricity that drives the turbines of nationalism and other radical political tendencies across the world. A classic example of this is the role of the endangered and declining nobility, peasantry, and traditional middle class (*mittelstand*) of Germany in generating German "radical conservatism," and the new nationalism that was its intimate partner, in the later nineteenth century.[15] These social strata generated movements that often combined radical economic protest against the new capitalism with intense nationalism and cultural conservatism.[16] And as the example of the Prussian nobility shows, absolute decline does not necessarily have to occur to drive an old elite in a radical direction—the threat can be enough.

Anti-Semitism has been described as the "socialism of the petty bourgeois," but in fact it formed part of a much wider complex of radical attitudes and resentments. Ultranationalism, and reproaches to "cosmopolitan elites" for not being nationalist enough, have long formed one path for the expression of socioeconomic grievances on the part of groups that for whatever reason could not turn to Socialism: "Having gained a foothold in the world of bourgeois respectability, they stood in danger of being plunged back into what they viewed as an abyss of powerlessness and dependence. It was that fear that made the middle class, even more than those who were truly rootless and indigent, a politically volatile group."[17]

The United States is not only the home of rapid, unceasing capitalist modernization and unceasing change, it also contains large middle class groups who at certain times in history—including today—have suffered badly as a result of the workings of this same capitalism; especially when compared to other developed societies, this capitalism is also less restrained and softened by state controls and state-funded social support mechanisms.

Over the centuries, the socioeconomic anxieties of the white middle class and rural populations have often been suffused with ethnic and racial fears. These fears stemmed originally from what used to be called the "native" Americans—not the American Indians, but the white Anglo-Saxon and Scots-Irish populations of the eighteenth-century British colonies.[18]

At the time of independence from Britain, the 13 colonies, far from representing great diversity of ethnicity and culture, were, if anything, rather less diverse than the kingdoms of Britain and France. This statement is not true if one includes the blacks and the Indians—but then, nonwhites were *not* included in the American states as they then understood and defined themselves, nor would they be for almost another 200 years.

Leaving aside the blacks and Indians, white America at independence was over-whelmingly made up of two ethnicities, Anglo-Saxon and Scots-Irish (Protestant Scots who had settled in Ireland as part of the wars against the native Gaelic Catholic Irish), with significant numbers of Dutch in New York and Germans in Pennsylvania and a few other places. And although overwhelmingly Protestant at this stage, even these Germans attracted considerable hostility and fear from the English colonists, including the supposedly pragmatic and tolerant Benjamin Franklin, who was not even sure that the Germans and other Europeans were really white: "The number of purely White people in the world is proportionally very small...In Europe, the Spaniards, Italians, French, Russians and Swedes are gen-erally of what we call a swarthy complexion, as are the Germans also, the Saxons only excepted, who with the English make the principal body of White people on the face of the earth. I could wish their numbers were increased."[19]

However, the vast majority of the white American population spoke English, and equally important, were Protestant. These were divided into different churches and sects, and displayed very considerable cultural differences (especially between the English of New England and the Scots-Irish of the frontier and the South). They also shared a great many attitudes, not least their deep distrust of Catholicism. Especially in the South and on the frontier, Americans perpetuated not just the Protestant religious culture of sixteenth- and seventeenth-century England and Scotland, but also aspects of their language and folk culture. And the English had already developed strong elements of a common national identity even before the first settler set foot in North America.[20]

Compared to Britain and France, America lacked the huge Gaelic-speaking Catholic population of most of Ireland, the still Welsh-speaking population of Wales, the numerous mutually incomprehensible languages and dialects spoken by ordinary Frenchmen, and even the suppressed but still considerable and deeply disaffected Protestant minority of central and southern France.

By historical standards then, the population of the new United States was rel-atively homogeneous ethnically and culturally. By European standards it was also relatively homogeneous socially. Except for the great plantation owners of the Southern states, there was no aristocracy—and even the Southern planters were vastly closer to the mass of the white population than the Duke of Norfolk and the Prince de Rohan were to their tenants.

In reality, if not legally, this was a Protestant nation in which Catholics and others were protected and tolerated, and for many years even toleration "was regarded more as an arrangement among the Protestant sects than a universal principle" (for that matter, it may be remembered that John Locke, philosophical father of the American political Enlightenment and national creed, had explicitly denied toleration to Catholics).[21] "Most of the proponents of the various religious positions did not really believe in either freedom or toleration. Freedom came to the Western world by the providence of God and the inadvertence of history."[22] To this extent it must be said that Glenn Beck, Michele Bachmann, and others on the extreme right are correct about the America of the "founders"—though how they think that this can be re-created in the United States of 2012 is another matter.

This belief in America as a Protestant country was, if anything, only encouraged as more and more German Protestants immigrated and later joined the elites. The view of the United States as "an essentially Protestant nation with free exercise rights constitutionally guaranteed to minorities" remained widespread well into the twentieth century, and in many ways up to the election of the nation's first (and to date, only) Catholic president, John F. Kennedy, in 1960.[23]

Of course, this nativist stream has changed greatly over time. Most notably, it has continually attracted to itself sections of those immigrant populations that formerly were precisely those that stoked the fears of the "true stock." In the process, it has infected these groups with some of its own "paranoid style."[24]

Although sections of the old core groups felt embattled and even defeated, such was the strength and conviction of their culture that over two centuries they were able to turn even a largely immigrant America into a "protestantoid" nation, in which the white middle class (including the upper proletariat) across large parts of the country in fact now share a culture that is rather homogeneous and above all, as already noted, very conformist.

As Walter Russell Mead has written, the American sense of "folk community" (in the German sense of *volk*), from having been originally not merely white but Protestant and Anglo-Saxon or Scots-Irish, has gradually become synonymous in the minds of its proponents with "the American middle class." However, it has still retained the meaning of a community of shared and narrowly defined cultural values, closed to many categories of outsider.[25] This conformism gives tremendous opportunities to any political force that can seize upon key symbols of public consensus for its own ends. The whole ideology and self-perception of the Tea Parties stems from their belief that the white middle class from whom they stem represents the true American people.

Furthermore, from the first, both the size of America and the nature of the American system made compromises between these groups a necessity. Thus, despite pathological fears of Catholicism among nineteenth-century American evangelical Protestants, a political alliance has existed on and off between the "Jacksonian" tradition in the South and West and sections of the Catholic Irish in the Northeast ever since the 1820s. The ethnic and regional background of right-wing Fox News talk show hosts is a good representation of the traditional Jacksonian alliance: Rush Limbaugh, with his family's Confederate ancestry, from the South; Sean Hannity and Bill O'Reilly for the Irish; and Glenn Beck (until he was removed from Fox for being too inflammatory even for them) for the West. One essential ingredient in the glue holding this alliance together has always been common hatred of the "East Coast elites."[26]

In our own time, too, a determined and partially successful attempt has been made to create an alliance between this tradition and American Jewish groups on the basis of support for Israel and a strong U.S. military policy in the Middle East, and of hostility to Muslims and Arabs, and to Americans and Europeans who criticize Israel.

One aspect of this history has indeed been the attempt of older immigrant groups to ingratiate themselves and deflect hostility by attacking either more recent immigrants, racial minorities, or both. The Jacksonian alliance of Southern whites with the Irish and other Northern "ethnics" has always owed much to shared fear of and hostility toward blacks. After World War I, "even liberals such as Fiorello LaGuardia and Representative Samuel Dickstein began to bait Asians and Mexicans in order to protect Jews and Italians."[27]

In the mid-nineteenth century, the most important targets of nativist Protestant movements like the Know-Nothings were Irish Catholics. A century later, the descendants of this tradition had taken up a German–Irish Catholic as one of their great heroes. Progress? Not entirely. His name was Senator Joseph R. McCarthy. Similarly, it is at first sight wonderful that the Christian Right tradition has shed much of its ancestral anti-Semitism and come to identify closely with Israel. The problem is that the Israel in question is that of Ariel Sharon, the Likud, and even more extreme forces in Israeli society and among the settlers in the Occupied Territories.

The "Jacksonian" and Frontier Traditions

As chapter 5 explores, sympathy for Israel on the part of the American nationalist Right also owes a great deal to the ferocious history of racial conflict on the North American continent. This history also created the figure who more than any other has been seen to symbolize the populist nationalist tradition in the United States, and who has indeed given his name to one of its dominant elements: President Andrew Jackson (1767–1845).

The Jacksonian tradition continues to have an impact on conservative populist politics in the United States. During the campaign for the Republican primary in

South Carolina in January 2012, a supporter of the victorious candidate, Newt Gingrich, wrote as follows on FoxNews.com:

> It is no accident that Gingrich made frequent mention of one of South Carolina's favorite sons, Andrew Jackson. Jackson, born in the Appalachian foothills in South Carolina's upstate, was the father of the Democratic Party as it existed from the 1820s until the turn of the 21st Century: a party for poor folks with blue-collar white voters at its core.
>
> Jackson, bearing a saber-scar on his face delivered by a redcoat when he was a lad, was the angry attack muffin of his day. He stole his wife from another man and horsewhipped and shot some of those who called her an adulteress for it.
>
> He brawled and battered his way through his life as a lawyer and a military officer. His presidential candidacies were fueled by rage at the vested powers in Washington, which were either mercantile elites from Boston, New York, and Philadelphia, or planter aristocrats from Virginia.
>
> But a wave of immigration from Jackson's fellow Scotch-Irish Presbyterians, fueled by the availability of land to the West, had changed the composition of the electorate dramatically. He promised these poor voters, mostly subsistence farmers and "mechanics" (the blue collar voters of the day) that he would go to Washington and smash the establishment that was leaving them out.[28]

The Jacksonian tradition stems above all from the experience of the American frontier, an experience that at one time or another affected all the states of the nation, and which remains strong to this day in the South and West.[29] But as recorded by David Hackett Fischer and others, it also has older roots in the traditions and experience of the "Scots-Irish" Protestants, who after settling Ulster and largely exterminating its Gaelic Irish Catholic population, later brought both their fundamentalist Protestantism and their ruthless attitude to warfare with them to the Americas. In the words of one of Jackson's early biographers, which would be endorsed by any student of recent Northern Irish history, "it appears to be more difficult for a North-of-Irelander than for other men to allow an honest difference of opinion in an opponent, so that he is apt to regard the terms opponent and enemy as synonymous."[30]

Born in North Carolina into a prominent Scots-Irish lineage, and later settled in Tennessee, Jackson's entire career was shaped by conflict with the American Indians of the South and their British, French, and Spanish backers. Although General Jackson's greatest victory was against the British at New Orleans in 1815, most of his campaigns were against the Cherokees, Creeks, and other Native Americans. It was as an Indian fighter and leader of local militias that Jackson emerged to prominence in Tennessee. And although Jacksonian nationalism contains other important elements, including nativism, anti-elitism, anti-intellectualism, and dislike of the Northeast, a strong sense of white identity and violent hostility to other races has also been at its core.[31]

A classic collision between this strand of "Jacksonian" nationalism and the core principles of the American Creed as publicly formulated occurred in 1831, during Jackson's own presidency. The Cherokee Nation, resident in what had become northern Georgia and parts of Tennessee and Alabama since long before whites landed in the Americas, appealed to the Supreme Court of the United States against new laws passed by the state of Georgia making them subject to its law and laying the basis for the Indians' expulsion beyond the Mississippi to make way for white settlers. The Cherokees' lawyers argued—quite correctly—that this was in violation of several treaties with governments of the United States. In accordance with the unarguable legal facts, a majority of the Court, led by Chief Justice John Marshall, ruled in favor of the Cherokees.

To this Jackson reportedly replied, "John Marshall has made his decision; now let him enforce it." And although Jackson may not have actually said this, these words certainly reflected the spirit in which he acted. The U.S. government refused to defend the Cherokees against Georgia, and Jackson warned them that they had no choice but to leave, and within a few years (though after Jackson himself had left office) they were driven out of their ancestral homeland on the "Trail of Tears" to Oklahoma, on which a large number died of disease and malnutrition.[32]

Jackson's reported words, however, not only reflected his own implacable hostility toward the Indians, more importantly, his statement was descriptive of the actual situation in the South and West, and the attitudes of the vast majority of Jackson's constituency, the white inhabitants of these sections. They were determined to drive out the Indians irrespective of what the U.S. government or U.S. law said. Folk law called for the expansion of white land and civilization at the expense of the "savages," and protection of the white community from any possibility of a revival of the Indian raids of the past, or Indian alliances with foreign enemies of the United States.

This folk law took precedence over the written code of the United States (even when the Indians concerned had been allies of the United States in war, and had in fact made great strides toward the adoption of "civilization," including the creation of a written language). Together with this came a deep hostility toward humanitarian East Coast, or "Yankee," lawyers and intellectuals, who, having gotten rid of their own Indians more than half a century before, now felt free to criticize and restrict the behavior of the West and South in this regard—a regional hostility that has replicated itself over numerous different issues up to the present.

The other elements that over time have shaped the populist nationalist tradition in America include the Southern experience of slavery, the specific cultural and historical traditions of the Protestant Scots-Irish, who dominated on the Southern frontier, and a communal culture heavily influenced by evangelical Protestantism.[33] This tradition has reflected the culture, interests, and anxieties of the original Anglo-Saxon and Scots-Irish settler stock, though it has also been willing to forge political alliances with specific immigrant groups and, over time, accept as full members of the community aliens who are held to conform to communal and "civilized" values. In the past, this always meant white aliens, but in the last three decades it has expanded to include some nonwhites as well.

Another element is a "producerist" ethos with very strong resemblances to the ideologies thrown up by lower middle class and agrarian-based radical conservative and nationalist movements in Europe of the past. As with the Tea Parties' combination of hatred of government programs and adherence to the white middle class welfare programs of Social Security and Medicare, so the Jacksonian tradition's public celebration of rugged frontier individualism masked the ways in which it was the state that in fact subsidized and largely enabled the expansion of white settlement on the frontier.[34] In Orange County, the main base of right-wing conservatism in California, the great postwar boom was very largely fueled by state military spending.[35]

This producerist ethos involved bitter hostility to "parasitic" elements of society—concentrated in the Northeast—that supposedly drained away the wealth from those who actually produced it: "finance capitalists," snobbish "silk stockings," hereditary *rentier* elites, overpaid intellectuals, "experts," bureaucrats, and lawyers—all of them with suspect foreign contacts, influences, or antecedents (in the past, this tradition often involved anti-Semitism)—and also the equally "parasitic," shiftless, lazy, drunken (or addicted) urban lower proletariat, above all when of alien or immigrant origin. Hostility toward the elites stemmed from the society of the frontier and the newly settled areas, but it also had roots in seventeenth-century English and Scottish Puritan hostility to the Anglican (and sometimes crypto-Catholic) English elites of that time, not only in the nobility and the clergy, but also in the universities and the legal profession.[36]

In America, these attitudes are also closely related to regional interests and prejudices; the hostility of the "honester South and West," as Thomas Jefferson phrased it, toward the decadent, exploitative, and above all commercial East.[37] In our own time, some of these sentiments have found expression through the term "the heartland." Geographically this means the states of the Midwest and the high plains, from Ohio to the Rockies. However, as its name indeed suggests, in political rhetoric it often carries with it the suggestion that this territory is also the home of true, core American people and values, of which nationalism is one of the most important.[38]

Jacksonian language pitting these regions against the East Coast elites continued in the Democratic Party for more than a century: in the 1948 elections (drawing also on bitter Confederate memories), Harry Truman declared in North Carolina that the Republican Party and business elites "treat the South and West as colonies to be exploited commercially and held down politically."[39] Over the past 40 years this attitude has been taken over by the Republican Party. For obvious reasons to do with the economic interests of their own leadership, the Republicans have taken a somewhat different group of Jacksonian hate objects—Washington bureaucrats and liberal intellectuals rather than bankers—but the appeal to regionalist hatred of metropolitan elites remains the same. These hate objects were indeed always somewhat flexible and protean. Thus Thomas Jefferson has been seen as in many ways a precursor of Jacksonianism, in his thoroughly racist version of an egalitarian white society and *herrenvolk* democracy based on the "healthy" producerist farmers and artisans. However, Jefferson—Virginia aristocrat, former ambassador to France, and admirer of the French Revolution—was also himself attacked by his enemies both as a frenchified Jacobin revolutionary atheist and as a frenchified, decadent, parasitic intellectual aristocrat.[40] During the campaign for the Republican nomination in 2012, a TV advertisement by supporters of Newt Gingrich, entitled "The French Connection," attacked his wealthy, "moderate" opponent Mitt Romney as an East Coast elitist who would say anything to win, "and just like John Kerry [Democratic presidential candidate in 2004] he speaks French too."[41]

Indeed, the association of France not only with atheism and decadence, but also with East Coast elitism dates back to American reactions against the French Revolution. Notable among these was the first "Great Fear" of independent America, the hysteria surrounding the passage of the Alien and Sedition Act of 1798, directed against supposed French revolutionary plotters in the United States.[42] Hostility toward European decadence, when contrasted with American purity and honesty, found its way into the American education system at an early date through one of its fathers, Noah Webster.[43] The attacks on France in the context of the war with Iraq therefore had a long pedigree, and even some of the language about French decadence, atheism, and elitism has remained much the same (in the words of one right-wing nationalist attack on France after 9/11, "most Americans find it difficult to take the French critique seriously, coming as it does from men who carry handbags.")[44]

In his classic work on the populist tradition in America, Michael Kazin characterized Jacksonian ideology as one of American populism's most important and enduring elements. Jacksonian beliefs and rhetoric were rooted in a particular moral frame, the elements of which were drawn from a mixture of Scots-Irish Calvinism and the frontier experience. This morality championed the honest producers against "the consumers, the rich, the proud, the privileged" and American "aristocrats" corrupted by European atheism and decadence. It advocated equal *access* to wealth—above all, Indian lands—for all white Americans, but certainly not economic egalitarianism, and it celebrated "toughness, maleness, and whiteness" in defense of family, race, and nation.[45] In the later 1960s and 1970s, the Republican Party revived the Jacksonian alliance of Southern whites and Northern "ethnics" (in Jackson's own time and after, Irish Catholics) in hostility toward blacks.[46]

It was on the strength of this appeal that Jackson won election to the presidency in 1828. His election has been taken as symbolizing, in myth and to some extent in reality, America's transition from the oligarchical rule of the founding elites to mass democracy; a transition closely related to the emergence of new forms of evangelical Protestant popular religion, which radically downgraded the position of the old elite-dominated churches and which had strong anti-intellectual and antimodern biases. This democracy categorically excluded Indians, blacks, and women.[47]

As Jackson's own mixture of Southern and frontier origins indicates, the American frontier and the American South might be treated almost as one cultural complex in terms of their cultural impact on American nationalism. Gunnar Myrdal, in 1944, described the South as a "stubbornly lagging American frontier society."[48] Jackson himself was a product both of the Indian frontier and the upper South, as these existed from his birth in 1767 to the deportation of the southern Indians in the 1820s to 1830s. What we have been taught by Hollywood to think of as the classic frontier, in the West, was largely settled by Southerners with Southern Cultural traits.

The mingling of the Southern and western traditions is at its most obvious in Texas, the home state of George W. Bush, and the source of much of his political culture and attitudes. Texas has been described as "a southern state masquerading as a western state."[49] It was one of the Confederate states, and its eastern section, close to the border with Louisiana, has a strongly Southern flavor, with a large black population and a plantation tradition of agriculture. Central and western Texas, however, was still Indian territory at the time of the Civil War.

Western frontier culture was molded by the previous experience of the Southern frontier in the Appalachians and the Southern forests. On the other hand, the frontier tradition as a whole also had aspects that had nothing to do with the South. The northeastern states also had an Indian frontier from their foundation in the early seventeenth century to the expulsion of the French and then the British 150 years later. The frontier also generally lacked the other defining factor in the South, namely a black population and (before 1865) an institution of black slavery to be defended. The need to defend slavery and black subordination produced a Southern tradition of conformism—enforced democratically and spontaneously, but with ruthless determination—which has not been as characteristic of the West.[50] Closely connected with this is the fact that the West is also far more religiously diverse than the South.

One of the most important legacies of the frontier for American nationalism was a history of exceptionally ferocious warfare, often amounting to genocide, in which both sides committed appalling atrocities. This has bred in sections of the American tradition both a capacity for ruthlessness and a taste for absolute and unqualified victory of the kind that was, in the end, won over all the indigenous adversaries of white America. A second feature was constant expansionism, often pushed for by the frontier white populations against the wishes of administrations in Washington. As Newt Gingrich said of Andrew Jackson during the South Carolina primary campaign: "Andrew Jackson had a pretty clear-cut idea about America's enemies: kill them."[51] This might seem an empty piece of rhetoric, except for the fact that he was speaking of his desire to launch a raid into Pakistan to kill the Afghan Taliban leader Mullah Omar, even at the price of a complete end to Pakistani cooperation against terrorism.

In the South especially, this expansionist spirit was directed not just toward the Indian and Mexican lands, but also toward European colonial possessions in the

Caribbean. In the twentieth century, as T. R. Fehrenbach has written, it carried over into support for far wider agendas:

> Since 1900, Texas had increasingly fused back with the nation in foreign policy, especially when foreign policy was basically imperial—whatever name was put upon it. Texans instinctively supported anything that seemed to support American power and prestige. Both the domination of the banana republics and the destruction of Imperial Germany were parts of the same policy, blended of self-interest, self-defense, and an arrogant form of goodwill... Those who had in some sense carried the American flag West did not metamorphose overnight when they had no more worlds to conquer on their shores.[52]

Moreover, as far as the American mainland itself was concerned, this expansion was completely successful—in part because it very cannily stopped short of annexing regions with large, Catholic, Spanish-speaking populations that could be neither exterminated, swamped, nor assimilated.

In contrast, the record of successful settlement on the part of other white nations has been a mixed one. In parts of the world where the indigenous peoples were similar to those of the Americas (and had been decimated by Eurasian diseases before the settlers even arrived), white settlement was successful and seems quite likely to prove long-lasting. Everywhere else, in the long run the white settlers have been either kicked out again, as in Algeria, Zimbabwe, and Soviet Central Asia, or subordinated to the indigenous population, as in South Africa and Kazakhstan. In America, the record of settlement has been one of unqualified victory through ruthless violence—with all the effects that this is bound to have on a nation's psyche.

The bestial atrocities to which Indian tribes like the Comanche and Kiowa subjected their prisoners also did much to shape long-term attitudes toward aliens in Texas and elsewhere:

> Survivors of Indian raids were unable to rationalize a brotherhood of man that included American Indians... The dominant view of the Amerindians among the English became one of inhuman savages who were unpredictable and dangerous predators. Since the whole frontier population—not a protecting line of soldiers—became involved in endemic Indian wars, the entire population was predictably brutalized. Suffering terrible wrongs themselves, the frontier people inflicted terrible wrongs on the Amerindians.[53]

The Scots-Irish in particular had already experienced one savage frontier war with genocidal overtones. Their ancestors (together with some English Puritans and French Huguenots) had initially settled in Ireland as part of the Elizabethan and Jacobean clearances of the native Irish population of Ulster, and the Cromwellian and Williamite settlements of the rest of the island, and had mixed with protestantized elements of the Irish population.[54]

From their original settlements in central Pennsylvania, the Scots-Irish eventually settled much of the old frontier of Virginia and the Carolinas (where Jackson was born), before moving on to Tennessee, the lower South, Texas, and the Southwest. Indeed, the Southern historian Grady McWhiney has gone so far as to attribute most of the cultural difference between the South and the rest of the United States to their Gaelic cultural heritage.[55] Discriminated against by the Anglo-Irish Episcopalian elites on the grounds both of class and religion, they brought with them to America a legacy of dislike of educated elites, whether English or Yankee (Northeasterners of overwhelmingly English origin).[56]

This tradition in America remains closely akin to the Ulster Protestant community, from which it stemmed, in its conflation of religion and nationalism, and (until recently) its bitter hatred of Catholicism. Now that the Boer tradition of South Africa has surrendered to the black majority, the Ulster Protestant Loyalists are today the only people anywhere else in the developed world whose culture and ideology resembles that of American evangelical Christianity.[57]

The Old Testament gave these settlers in Ireland, America, and South Africa both a language and a theological framework to describe and justify their dispossession of the native inhabitants of the land. The biblical tones of Jackson's addresses to the Cherokees and Creeks demanding their removal across the Mississippi were prefigured 150 years earlier in Cromwell's addresses to Irish Catholics demanding their removal "to Hell or Connaught."[58] As chapter 6 explores, this tradition creates a natural affinity with the harsher aspects of Israeli attitudes toward the Palestinians.

The frontier also helped perpetuate a belief in private weaponry, which—as orchestrated by the National Rifle Association (NRA)—has become an article of faith for the Republican Party. This belief has always been closely associated with a certain kind of egalitarianism and belief in every man's right and duty to defend his personal and familial honor—a classic theme of Hollywood versions of the West, but one with a real existence and with real roots in the Southern and frontier traditions.

These traditions in turn derive ultimately from the world of late medieval and early modern England and Scotland, which was extremely violent by contemporary standards. Especially in northern England and Scotland, crimes were very often crimes of "honor," or forms of the *lex talionis* (law of retaliation): collective family revenge or self-defense, often on the part of respectable gentry families. "Stuart England was a country in which violence was endemic even when it was not being torn apart by Civil War."[59] Gentry and poor alike displayed the "ferocity, childishness and lack of self-control of the Homeric age."[60] Stuart Scotland and Ireland were a great deal worse. As in the South and West of the United States and in many tribal societies across the world, this concern with honor was often indistinguishable from intense quarrelsomeness. The duel proper lasted in the South for several generations after it had died out in most of the Western world.[61]

Writing in the 1960s, Warren Leslie described the traditional Texan character as follows:

> Frontier days in Texas are not so far in the past...Challenged, [the Texan] fought with his gun or his fists, and he fought the land, too, as he would an enemy. He was a man of action rather than contemplation; he was an individualist, and he took great pride in victory—over the land and over other men. His life was made up of elemental facts, and fundamentalist preaching confirmed his conviction that things were either Black or White...The man who acts, who fights, who resists trespass, who takes no orders from groups or from other men and who will not compromise—he is the frontier man, and he is still around in Dallas, and in Texas.[62]

This is a tremendously important part of the self-image of George Bush, of Dick Cheney (from Wyoming, another tough frontier state), and indeed of their administration as a whole, and it shaped that administration's aggressive stance in international affairs—though, of course, unlike their ancestors, its leading members showed no desire to fight themselves. A former senior official of the Bush administration from a state of the upper South once declared in my presence that even if it had been possible after 9/11 to use police and intelligence methods to hunt down and kill or capture Osama bin Laden and his chief lieutenants, wars would still have been necessary, because "a handful of deaths would not have been sufficient compensation for our culture for the losses we suffered on 9/11."

As John Shelton Reed remarked of Appalachian society in the mid-twentieth century: "It has been found impossible to convict men of murder...provided the jury is convinced that the assailant's honor was aggrieved and that he gave his adversary notice of his intention to assail him." In other words, the code of the duel: once again, an essentially premodern cultural tradition continues to exist in the standard-bearer nation of world modernity.

Reed has described this as "lawful violence," in the sense of violence that is socially sanctioned, is a predictable response to certain actions, and observes codes and limits. It is, in other words, another aspect of community or "folk" law, as opposed to that of the state, and closely related to the right of the community as a whole to administer its communal version of "justice" where the state, for whatever reason, is unwilling or unable to follow the popular will. The resulting tradition of lynching has been associated above all with the bestial terrorization of blacks in the South in the century after the Civil War, but the tradition on the frontier was much older, and had usually been deployed against deviant whites (and Indians, of course).[63]

This culture of violence has declined greatly in the South and West over the past century, but it remains very high compared to the rest of the United States (except for the inner cities, which were largely peopled from the South), let alone the rest of the developed world, and this has carried over to the outside world.

As W. J. Cash wrote in his great study of 1941, *The Mind of the South*, Southern violence was not only personal:

> The Southerner's fundamental approach carried over into the realm of public offences as well. What the direct willfulness of his individualism demanded, when confronted by a crime that roused his anger, was immediate satisfaction for itself—catharsis for personal passion in the spectacle of a body dancing on the end of a rope or writhing in the fire—now, within the hour—and not some ponderous abstract justice in an abstract tomorrow. And so, in this world of ineffective social control, the tradition of vigilante action, which normally lives and dies with the frontier, not only survived but grew.[64]

In one respect, the frontier, like the South, embodies a tradition that is quite at variance with the popular image of a triumphant march westward, and which links the roots of American populist nationalism to radical nationalisms elsewhere in the world. This is a tradition of repeated and sometimes shattering defeats, though on the frontier these were at the hands of nature, provoked by human mismanagement and greed: the defeat of whole populations on the agricultural frontier by soil exhaustion, erosion, and drought.

The most internationally famous episode of this was the "dust bowl" on the lower plains in the 1930s, which led to the westward migration of "Okies" and others described by John Steinbeck in *The Grapes of Wrath*; but this was only part of a much wider and longer pattern. Indeed, many of the Okies moved to the plains from the lower South in the first place, not only because they were drawn by the lure of land taken from the Indians, but also because they were *driven*: driven first from the fertile lands of the South to the thin soils of the hills by the spread of slave-worked commercial plantations, then driven from the hills by the erosion of that soil due to deforestation and overfarming. When they arrived on the plains, the same pattern would repeat itself.

When the Okies arrived in California, they found themselves treated by the existing white Californian population (itself originally very largely from the Midwest) as an inferior and despised underclass, almost like the Mexicans, and this treatment lasted into the 1960s—with inevitable results for Okie alienation, antielitism, and of course racial hatred of the Mexicans. This Southern and Midwestern background of "Anglo" Southern California explains in part the flavor of religious and political conservatism in that region, and its differences from Northern California, with its far more mixed white population.[65]

A brilliantly evocative picture of this process of defeat in one section of the agricultural frontier, the Texas Hill Country (Edwards Plateau), is to be found in Robert Caro's monumental biography of Lyndon B. Johnson, who came from that country. Caro describes the deceptively fertile soil of the Hill Country as "a trap baited with grass and water," which, having attracted the settlers, doomed their descendants to generations of poverty and a continual, grinding struggle against drought and erosion.[66]

In the late 1880s, a decade or so after the trap began to close on the inhabitants of the Hill Country, a defeat by drought more sudden and on a much larger scale struck the new settlers of the high plains of the Dakotas, Nebraska, Colorado, and western Kansas. Hundreds of thousands of people had to abandon their dream of an honorable life of farming for wage slavery in the factories of the cities. Those who remained fell deeper and deeper into debt to the hated banks.[67] This pattern was repeated in a less dramatic way across large parts of the rural Midwest in the last decades of the twentieth century.[68]

This defeat (repeated in a fresh drought after 1910) produced one of the great heartland revolts against the East Coast elites in American history, the Populist movement led by William Jennings Bryan. His defeat as the Democratic candidate by the Republicans (backed by a combination of East Coast financial–industrial interests and the big city populations) in the presidential elections of 1896 was mourned by Vachel Lindsay in the poem quoted at the head of this chapter.[69] Just as the Democrat Al Smith was defeated in 1828 in large part because of his Catholicism, which led to the defection of many Protestant heartland and southern supporters, so Bryan lost in part because his intense evangelical Protestant culture, and barely veiled dislike of the cities and the Catholic immigrants, alienated the Democrats' big city voters, especially the Irish.

In fact, Bryan picked up and reunited a good deal of the Protestant nativist tradition of the "American Party" or Know-Nothings, which had collapsed when their northern and southern wings split in the run-up to the Civil War. In the interval, however, the number of immigrants—and especially Catholic immigrants—in America had increased greatly, increasing the difficulties of this approach.

The 1880s and 1890s were years in which while farmers in the Midwest suffered badly, overall, not just the American economy, but American agricultural production grew enormously. In the same way, the incomes of many ordinary Americans from the 1970s to 2008 stagnated and fell, even while the overall American economy grew greatly. My point is therefore not to suggest that the American tradition of national and individual success is somehow imaginary. It is only to point out that this tradition also contains within it innumerable personal and collective defeats, and that these too have had their place in shaping the American national psyche.

For every family that moved West and made good, there was another "decent, feckless family that had left a century of failed farms, male suicides, and infant graves across the land from Ohio to the Coast, pushing always unprofitably westward."[70] Furthermore—though this is something that cannot be established statistically—the sting of defeat has probably been more bitter in a country where success really did depend to a much greater extent than elsewhere on character and determination, not just on the frontier, but in the cities as well. Failure in America has thus been attended by both shame and Protestant-flavored guilt, for "to fail is to acknowledge some deep flaw in the self, for responsibility cannot lie with a society whose promise of happiness and possibility is its reason for being."[71]

In the still hierarchically influenced societies of Europe, no small German farmer needed to feel bad about not being a Prince von Hohenlohe or a Count Preysing. A new Texan settler who remained a small farmer—or was forced off the land altogether to become an urban proletarian—while Charlie Goodnight created in less than a generation a ranch larger than some European countries would naturally have a different feeling about himself, and seek all the harder, perhaps, to soothe this feeling by a conviction that, all the same, he was part of God's chosen elite—culturally, religiously, and nationally.

The White South

The South has often been treated both by foreign analysts and by Americans themselves as if it were a culturally quite separate part of the United States, without influence on that country's wider national identity. And the South does indeed have a very special historical and cultural character—but one that cannot be somehow cut out from America's wider political culture and American nationalism: "No small part of the reactionary nationalism of the twentieth century United States can be directly attributed to the South's pronounced conservatism and its comparative isolation from contact with foreigners and foreign ideas."[72]

The white South occupies a very considerable portion of the United States, and a very much bigger portion of what I have called the "American Nationalist Party," or Republicans.[73] According to the 2010 census, the 11 former Confederate states made up 31.53 percent of the U.S. population, with the Greater South (including Oklahoma, Missouri, Kentucky, and West Virginia) making up 36.69 percent. Only 19.79 percent of the Old South and 18.13 percent of the Greater South was black, and 17.6 percent and 15.75 percent, respectively, was Latino.

This means that white Southerners make up more than one-fifth of the total U.S. population; not a dominant portion, but certainly a potentially very powerful one. In terms of political power, the position of the South (and the often allied West) is strengthened by the American federal system, which gives disproportionate weight to states with small, mainly traditional white populations.[74] Since the 1970s, only a handful of Southern states have ever voted Democrat in presidential elections.

As Michael Lind, Kevin Phillips, Peter Applebome, and others have pointed out, over the past two decades the "southernization" of the Republican Party has given these traditions a very considerable new importance in the politics of America as a whole, and consequently in U.S. international behavior.[75] The Tea Parties draw support from all over the United States, but their attitudes display strongly marked Southern trends—in particular, their belief in the power of the states over that of the federal government. And, of course, Barack Obama's identity—a black Yankee intellectual from Abraham Lincoln's state of Illinois—makes him almost a composite hate figure for many white Southerners.

Among the effects of this "southernization" has been a harsher form of nationalism. The growing Southern-style religiosity of the Republicans has also had its effect, both in alienating the United States from "atheist" Europe and in increasing commitment to Israel. This transformation of the Republicans has contributed greatly to the increasing polarization of Americans along party lines. As indicated in the Introduction, it also reflects strongly contrasting attitudes to religion, morality, culture, economics, and nationalism.

This division was symbolized in 2003 by the public condemnation of the Democrats for moral decadence and lack of patriotism by their last senior conservative Southern representative, Senator Zell Miller of Georgia. Or as Thomas Schaller put it in 2003, "trying to recapture the South is a futile, counterproductive exercise because the South is no longer the swing region. It has swung: Richard Nixon's "Southern strategy" of 1968 has reached full fruition."[76] This picture may change, however, as an influx not only of Latinos, but of blacks from northern cities reduces white dominance. Thus in 2008 Obama carried North Carolina thanks in part to a much higher than usual black turnout.

The white South has not, of course, regained the political dominance enjoyed by Virginia's aristocracy from the 1780s to the 1820s, but it has recovered and indeed exceeded the power exercised by the white South's representatives from the end of post–Civil War Reconstruction in the late 1870s to civil rights and the collapse of the South's allegiance to the Democratic Party in the mid-1960s.

A key reason for Southern power is the way in which the South has been able to exercise disproportionate political influence through its grip on one of the two major parties. From 1877 to the 1960s (albeit with diminishing strength from the 1940s), the white South was solidly Democratic, thanks to bitter hostility toward the Republican Party of Abraham Lincoln. However, during all that period, lingering prejudices related to the Civil War, and unease about the South's racial record, meant that no Southerner from the 11 Confederate states could aspire to the presidency (unless, like Woodrow Wilson, he had moved north in his youth).[77]

Because a majority of the white South switched its allegiance to the Republicans in the 1960s and 1970s in reaction against Democratic advancement of civil rights and multiculturalism, its role has become a good deal more activist. The critical importance of this section to Republican hopes has been demonstrated in a series of presidential elections—most notably in 2000, when Al Gore's failure to win a single southern state (despite coming from Tennessee himself) helped doom his presidential hopes.[78]

The region's importance to hard-line conservative influence in the Republican Party is indicated by the fact that in a survey of senators and congressmen compiled by the *National Journal* in 2004, of the 16 senators dubbed "most conservative" by that journal (one-third of the Republican total), 10 came from the Greater South; of 21 senators dubbed "centrist," only 5 were from the South.[79]

If only because southern blacks now have the vote and use it to vote solidly Democrat, the South today is not as overwhelmingly Republican as it was once

Democrat. In recent years, the end of discrimination and the economic rise of the South (compared to the "Rust Belt" cities of the Midwest and Northeast) has led to blacks returning to the South. If this process continues, then it will seriously undermine the white conservative political grip on the South.

As of 2012, however, Southern whites form the most solidly and reliably major Republican voting bloc in the country, which naturally gives them immense influence over that party. The political power and longevity of the Southern conservatives in Congress has been unintentionally increased by the redrawing of congressional districts intended to create solidly black areas and therefore strengthen black representation, the result of which has also created more solidly white districts. From the late 1970s, and more importantly since the "Republican Revolution" led by the Georgian Newt Gingrich in 1994, and the formation of the Texan-led Bush administration in 2001, this influence has been used to advance programs with their roots in white southern culture.

As noted by Applebome, Mead, and others, this process has been greatly facilitated by the fact that important parts of that culture have, in recent decades, spread far beyond their original homelands: this is true, for example, of southern evangelical Protestant religion, the cult of personal weaponry, country and western music, and stock car racing (which apparently originated among Appalachian mountain bootleggers of moonshine whisky). The South has also long been the home of a particularly intense form of American nationalism, strongly flavored by respect for the military and military values, and part of a wider culture that believes in traditional values of religion, family, manhood, and honor.[80]

The South in this sense was never coterminous with the 11 states that in 1861 seceded from the Union and for four years formed the Confederate States of America. The Greater South extends beyond the borders of the former Confederacy and even the Mason-Dixon Line (dividing slave from free states before 1861) to cover large parts of the Midwest and the West. According to some cultural geographers, the northern cultural border of the Greater South lies roughly along Route 40, which runs from east to west across the middle of Ohio, Indiana, and Illinois. In the West, the Greater South includes Oklahoma and other states largely settled from the Old South.[81] George C. Wallace appealed to Southerners "from Baltimore to Oklahoma City to St. Louis."

This region forms the heartland of evangelical Protestant religious belief, or the so-called Bible Belt, and the picture of America as a deeply religious country is to a considerable extent derived from the Greater South.[82] This was a region that until fairly recently lacked many large cities, and in consequence did not undergo the massive immigration that poured into the cities of the North and East from the mid-nineteenth century on. In many areas, and especially of course in the countryside and small towns, its white population therefore remained homogeneous.

W. J. Cash declared that the white South "is not quite a nation within a nation, but it is the next thing to it."[83] That was in 1941, but decades later John Shelton Reed could still speak of Southern whites constituting a form of ethnicity and possessing a form of ethnic consciousness.[84] And it is worth remembering in this context that if a couple of battles in the Civil War had gone the other way—by no means a historical impossibility—the South would in fact have become an independent nation, with its own (white) national consciousness.

Because the white South's bid for nationhood was crushed in war, and the region's particular nationalism was later reincorporated into that of the United States as a whole, the development of Southern identity before 1865 has never been properly addressed by students of nationalism. This is a pity, for in many ways it provides a fascinating case study and adds interesting nuances to the debate between the "primordial" and "constructivist" approaches to the explanation of nationalism's origins.

On the one hand, the Southern "national identity" was clearly a "constructed" one. It was constructed moreover in response to a particular threat, that to the South's "peculiar institution," slavery. Moreover, though Southern whites genuinely hated and feared the blacks, slavery was an issue that affected above all the Southern slave-owning elites. The Antebellum South can well be seen therefore as a good example of the model of elitist construction of modern nationalism argued for by Eric Hobsbawm and other left-wing scholars of the "constructivist" tradition in nationalism.

Of course, issues other than slavery were also involved in the North–South split before 1861. Nonetheless, take slavery, and Northern antislavery, out of the equation, and there is no real reason to think that the Southern elites would have devoted such intense effort to the construction of a separate identity, nor that the Southern states would have gone so far as to fight for independence through four years of catastrophic warfare.

But the South is also an example of the fact that while national identities can be "constructed," they cannot—*pace* Hobsbawm—be "invented." They have to be put together, or "imagined" out certain previously existing elements, and if these elements are not old and strong, then the resulting nationalism will be a weak one for which few are willing to sacrifice and die. This is one key reason why the invented nationalisms of postcolonial Africa, based on completely artificial colonial territories, have usually proved so weak, while many old tribal and religious loyalties have proved so strong.[85]

The antebellum white Southern "protonational" identity was based on three main foundations. The first, obviously, was a *herrenvolk* determination to keep the blacks in a subordinate and helpless position—what Cash called the "Doric" tradition of the South, after ancient Sparta and its ferocious suppression of the Helot population. The second, closely linked to the first, was a desire to preserve the South's agrarian economy, and with it the domination of the plantation-owning class. This in turn generated intellectual and cultural defenders who self-consciously looked to European traditions of aristocratic conservatism, very different indeed from the kind of liberal pseudoconservatism prevalent elsewhere in the United States.

As in Europe, rather than explicitly defending aristocratic rule, this tradition instead attacked the soullessness, atomization, and exploitation of Northern capitalism, and contrasted this with real or invented Southern values of continuity of tradition and rootedness in the soil.[86] (Or in the words of T. R. Fehrenbach about twentieth-century Texans, "the great majority knew where their grandparents lay buried."[87]) This kind of critique of Western capitalism has of course been very characteristic not only of declining agrarian and aristocratic social orders, but of nationalist movements from wholly or partially "defeated" societies throughout modern history, from German ideas of Teutonic community (*gemeinschaft*) against the soulless, exploitative French and British "society" (*gesellschaft*) to the nineteenth-century Slavophils in Russia and a host of "third world" writers in our own time.[88] Thus, already by 1825 there had been created among the South Carolinian gentry "just that atmosphere of pride, poverty and resentment which in the 20th century has favored the growth of Arab and African nationalism."[89]

This tendency in the Southern identity overlapped with one that has been obscured both by defeat in 1865 and by the fact that in the Civil War Americans of Anglo-Saxon and Scots-Irish descent fought on both sides, as did evangelical Protestants. This is the specifically ethnic element in the white Southern tradition. In my view, if the white South had prevailed in the Civil War and established itself as an independent nation, the assertion of an ethnic identity based on a composite of the Anglo-Saxon and Scots-Irish strains and fundamentalist Protestantism would have emerged as *the* central public face of white Southern nationalism.

As the North, or the remaining United States, became more and more ethnically mixed due to immigration, so the "purity" of the Southern ethnic tradition would have been asserted against Northern "mongrelization." Indeed, this purity–mongrelization opposition was already widely used in Southern rhetoric during the Civil War. It was shared by the Southerner Woodrow Wilson, and was continued in rabid form by Southern anti-Semitic nativists like Governor Tom Watson of Georgia.[90] In these circumstances, the South would have lost its remaining liberals to the North, but would have attracted in turn conservative Northern whites appalled by the transformation of America by immigration, like the novelist Owen Wister or the painter Frederic Remington, with his ferocious talk of "Jews, Injuns, Chinamen, Italians, Huns—the rubbish of the Earth I hate."[91]

But as recent scholars of American historical demography have stressed, the Scots-Irish ethnic tradition was neither constructed nor invented, but very ancient, perpetuating until well into the twentieth century "folkways" that long predated the modern age, and in some cases even Christianity. Moreover, the violent circumstances in which the Scots-Irish found themselves on the American frontier in the eighteenth and nineteenth centuries replicated in many regards those they had left behind, both in the savage wars against the Gaelic Irish and in the much older tradition of feuding along the English–Scottish border, and among Scottish and northern English clans.[92] This was a tradition of which the Scots-Irish themselves in the nineteenth century were well aware. Andrew Jackson reportedly "required his wards to read the history of the Scottish chieftains whom he deeply admired and made the models for his own acts."[93]

The figure of Sir Walter Scott is a fascinating one in this regard. The craze for his historical novels and poems in the Antebellum South has been generally seen—and mocked—as part of the attempt of the Southern plantation-owning class to invent a British aristocratic and "Cavalier" tradition for themselves. For the Scots-Irish frontiersmen, however, his role was rather different: to "reimagine" in suitably sanitized form their own historical tradition, and thereby also to romanticize their actual lives on the southern frontier, which, as noted, reproduced in many ways those of their wild ancestors.

If the white South had gained its independence, Scott might be studied today from some of the same angles as those nineteenth-century nationalist poets and novelists who helped "imagine their nations" by weaving genuine but fragmented stories and legends into nationalist myths—like Elias Lonnnrot in Finland, or Andrejs Pumpurs in Latvia. Or as a nineteenth-century Estonian nationalist declared, "let us give the people the epic and the history, and everything is done!" That Sir Walter himself, of course, had no idea that he was performing this role in the American South only indicates the extremely tortuous cultural paths by which nations come into being.[94]

A Vignette of the Deep South

In 1979 I spent several months at a college in the small town of Troy in southern Alabama (on an English Speaking Union scholarship named for soon-to-retire Governor George C. Wallace). Not only was society rigidly divided between blacks and whites, but the absolutely overwhelming majority of locally born whites I met were of mixed Anglo-Saxon and Scots-Irish descent, and Southern Baptist by religion. A survey of 1982 shows religious adherents in Pike County, where Troy is located, as 67.5 percent Southern Baptist and 15.7 percent United Methodist. No other church reached 5 percent of the total. Eighteen years later, the figures for the Southern Baptists and Methodists were almost identical, with fundamentalist believers in the Assembly of God and Church of Christ growing to 3.8 percent and 4.9 percent, respectively.[95]

The public spirit of the place was strongly marked by this religion. Thus the county was "dry" (not completely, but to the extent that alcohol could not be advertised or drunk in public, and bars were highly restricted). Neither this, nor the fact that we were mostly under 21 years of age seemed to have the slightest effect on the drinking habits of my peers. The great majority of white students were self-described "rednecks," and proud of it. They were very far indeed from the centers of American wealth, power, culture, and influence. They knew this, and their response differed from prickly pride to bitter resentment.

They possessed a very strong sense of ethnoreligious community and local tradition. Although very few were of wealthy or aristocratic descent, very many were able to trace their ancestry back beyond the creation of Alabama, to settlers who had originally moved from Tennessee, Georgia, or the Carolinas. Surprisingly, some were even proud of the possession of Cherokee or Creek ancestry, since this constituted proof of ancient establishment—whereas black ancestry, though perhaps sometimes present, was emphatically not talked about. Despite state relief programs, a large part of the rural population, white as well as black, was also still appallingly poor by the standards of the "developed" world, with extremely high levels of illiteracy.

Except for time spent in military service, a quite astonishing number had never been outside Alabama, except for visits to Pensacola and the beaches of the Florida panhandle, and still more had never traveled outside the South. Given the greater distances in the United States, Troy's isolation was in some ways comparable to that of small European towns before the coming of the railroads.

People were extremely kind and hospitable to the individual visitor (at least from Britain, a land that seemed to enjoy an almost mystical prestige both as an ally in war and as their own ancestral land of origin), but many were deeply suspicious of outsiders in general, and deeply ignorant of America beyond the Lower South. The world beyond America's shores was a kind of magic shadow play, full of heroes and demons, but without real substance. "Demons" in some cases is a literal rendering of how they saw America's enemies, for millenarian views of history were also present, though less at the college than among the surrounding population.

This was therefore a society as different from the common image both of American prosperity and the American "melting pot" as could be imagined. This picture was, and to a considerable extent still is, mirrored in small towns across the Deep South, and certain parts of Texas and the West, reflecting what Oran Smith has called the continuing "incredible homogeneity among White Southerners."[96] Blacks had been accepted into the university, and were not subject to overt discrimination, but were still in a thoroughly subordinate position, with little local influence.[97]

Over the past 60 years, the tremendous economic changes initiated by World War II have changed the South greatly. The shift of industries from the Rust Belt of the Northeast and Midwest have transformed parts of the South into some of the most industrialized areas in America, and this transformation has been widely publicized by boosters from the region and beyond.[98] Economic development has sucked in new immigrants, including not only Latinos, but also South Asians, so that for the first time since the expulsion of the Indians, Southern society is not simply split along black–white lines.

However, a glance at the political, religious, and ideological map of the white South reveals a society that has not changed nearly as much as figures for economic change would suggest. Although both the Latino and South Asian minorities have grown enormously, in 2000 the Southern Focus Poll still found that 65 percent of Southerners declared themselves Protestant, and more than half the population of Mississippi, Alabama, and Georgia belonged to one denomination, Southern Baptist. Six of 10 southerners still say that they prefer the biblical account of creation to evolutionary theory (a figure, of course, including Southern blacks).[99]

The region has continued to elect a range of politicians of strikingly conservative, religious, and nationalist caste. Older representatives of this culture, like Strom Thurmond and Jesse Helms, have retired, but only to be followed by figures like James Inhofe, Jim DeMint, and Roy Blunt, who perpetuate their tradition. These are indeed "lively dinosaurs," as one observer put it. They are not fading remnants of a dead tradition and a lost cause.

One reason for this continuity may be that in one respect the South has become, if anything, more homogeneous over the past century. Before the Civil War, blacks were a majority in two Southern states (South Carolina and Louisiana) and very close to a majority in two more (Alabama and Mississippi). By the 1960s, black emigration to the North, pulled by Northern jobs and pushed by Southern white oppression and harassment, had radically reduced these figures—a change that helps explain why the achievement of civil rights for blacks under federal pressure, savagely resisted though it was by many whites, did not lead to the Balkan-style eruption of white mass violence of which Southern racists and conservatives had so often warned. According to the census of 1880, blacks made up 41 percent of the population of the Old South. By the 1960s, this had fallen by more than half.[100]

For a century and a half, however, the desire to preserve first slavery and then absolute black separation and subordination had contributed enormously to the closing of the Southern mind, with consequences for America as a whole that have lasted to the present. They led to a situation both before the Civil War and in the mid-twentieth century in which the social system of the South was "on the defensive against most of the Western world" and white Southerners saw "outside aggression" against the South everywhere.[101] The effects of this long experience of embittered defensiveness continue to this day.

Racial solidarity gave poor whites pride in belonging to the superior, ruling race, and helped deflect resentment against the wealthy plantation owners. Cultural, racial, political, and economic defensiveness reached the point where the South became the pioneer in the modern world of the mass public burning of "dangerous books" from the abolitionist North. "In place of its old eagerness for new ideas and its outgoing communicativeness the South developed a suspicious inhospitality toward the new and the foreign, a tendency to withdraw from what it felt to be a critical world."[102]

Southern Defeat and Reconciliation

The defense of slavery and its effects on culture, in combination with the other specific features of Southern culture noted above, led the South into its attempt at independent nationhood in 1861, and to crushing defeat. The losses suffered by the South during the Civil War were fully comparable with those of European nations during the great wars of the twentieth century. Some 260,000 Confederate soldiers—more than one-fifth of the entire white adult male population—were killed in action or died of disease (some 350,000 Union soldiers died, but from a much larger population).

Hundreds of thousands of civilians, white and black, also died of disease brought on by malnutrition. Several of the South's largest cities were destroyed, along with numerous smaller towns, and extensive tracts of the countryside were deliberately stripped bare by the strategies of Sherman, Sheridan, and other Northern generals. The real value of all property dropped by one-third, the number of horses by 29 percent, and pigs by 35 percent. The South's cotton production did not recover its prewar levels until 1879, 14 years after the war ended.[103] Moreover—as in so many neocolonial monoculture economies around the world—the Southern economy as a whole was depressed by a drop in the price of cotton that lasted for several decades, just as the same thing was happening to wheat farmers of the Great Plains.

It was more than a century before even parts of the Confederate South "caught up" with the rest of America, both in terms of income and development, and in access to political power. Indeed, extensive areas have still not done so. For a century the South was reduced, in reality and still more in the perception of Southerners, to a position of almost colonial dependence on the North and the East Coast, symbolized above all by railway freight rates that discriminated against the South and in favor of the Northeast—a gross injustice that was not rectified until World War II.[104]

Moreover, the period of radical reconstruction under military rule in the South, with its establishment of black voting rights and advancement of blacks to political office, was a terrible shock to the white South. The "tragic legend of Reconstruction" was immensely exaggerated and embroidered in subsequent Southern propaganda (most famously in Thomas Dixon's novel *The Clansman* and the film *Birth of a Nation*, which was based on it). Nonetheless, it had a solid basis if not in real black behavior, then certainly in real Southern white fears.[105]

Absolute white dominance was reestablished in the 1870s with the help of a campaign of terrorism by the Ku Klux Klan, directed against supporters of the Republican administrations in the South, both black and white. Thereafter, a determination to eliminate any possibility of even limited black political power led to the establishment at a formal level of the "Jim Crow" apartheid laws, which were to rule in the region until the 1960s. Informally these laws were reinforced by the tradition of public lynching, which in the Antebellum South had been used more often to control white criminals (slaves being valuable private property and punishable by their owners).[106]

Typically of colonized territories, with a feeling of economic exploitation came bitter resentment of cultural patronization and insults, focused chiefly but not exclusively on criticism of the South's racial record and habits. This resentment lingers on, though now rather than race, the feeling is of a general sneering at the

South by East Coast and California liberals, intellectuals, and not least, film makers. And such sneering has indeed occurred continuously—albeit at varying levels of intensity—since the 1830s, with a new crescendo being reached in the 1960s.

Specifically, Southern resentments of Northern elites have fed into the wider social and cultural resentments of the "heartland" to create a mixture that is very prominently on display in the Tea Parties. And these resentments are not without cause. East Coast liberal contempt for the heartland and the religious middle class is often crude and ostentatious. The Midwest in general is widely known among the East Coast elites as "the Great Flyover," something you cross at 30,000 feet as you fly between Boston, New York, or Washington and California. The daughter of a rare surviving elected Democratic official from Idaho once described to me her fury on arriving at an Ivy League university to be asked by fellow students, "Idaho—that's next to Iowa, right?" sometimes as a put-down, but more often out of genuine ignorance.

A century and a half earlier, in the run-up to the Civil War, a Northern supporter of Abraham Lincoln had called the South "the poorest, meanest, least productive, and most miserable part of creation, and therefore ought to be continually teased and taunted and reproached and reviled." The great satirist H. L. Mencken derived much pleasure from slashing at Southern barbarity, ignorance, and fatuity, with fundamentalist religion receiving the sharpest strokes. Even when justified, such approaches are unlikely to create good feelings.[107]

During his campaign for the presidency in 1968, George C. Wallace declared in Georgia that "both national parties have been calling us peckerwoods and rednecks for a long time now…and we gonna show them we resent being used as a doormat." He said that these parties represented "the Eastern moneyed interests that have done everything they could to keep the people of our region of the country ground into the dirt for the past hundred years."[108] Senator Zell Miller's public attack on the Democrats was motivated in part by what he saw as their elitist Yankee sneering at Southern culture:

> Democrat leaders are as nervous as a long-tailed cat around a rocking chair when they travel south or get out in rural America. They have no idea what to say or how to act. I once saw one try to eat a boiled shrimp without peeling it. Another one gagged loudly on the salty taste of country ham…We're like the alcoholic uncle that families try to hide in a room up in the attic: after the primaries are over and the general election nears, national Democrats trot out the South and show us off—at arm's length—as if to say, "Look how tolerant we are; see how caring? Why, we even allow people like this in our party of the big tent. We still love that strange old reprobate uncle." As soon as the election is over, the old boy is banished to the attic and ignored for another two years.[109]

In Troy, acquaintances would complain bitterly that every Southern character in a Hollywood movie was likely to be a variant on half a dozen stock and hostile types: the sadistic police chief, the bestial swamp-dwelling "cracker," the fanatical and/or hypocritical preacher, the corrupt political boss, or—at best—the corny, simple-minded hillbilly and the eccentric aristocratic lady on her decaying Gothic plantation (of course, certain Southern actors have themselves made careers by playing "white trash" parts, and often celebrating their culture and attitudes— notably Robert Mitchum and Burt Reynolds).[110]

More recently, the Coen Brothers' film *O Brother Where Art Thou?*, though praised for its love of Southern music, was also criticized by Southerners for portraying some of the same old shallow stereotypes. The unforgiving reader is admittedly at liberty to find a certain poetic justice in white Southerners sharing some of the cultural experience of American blacks and Indians at the hands of Hollywood.[111]

As has often been pointed out, this collective regional experience of comprehensive defeat and humiliation is unusual in a white American history characterized by continuous national success. In Richard Weaver's phrase, "the South is the [American] region which history has happened to." Equally unique is the sense of guilt for past collective crimes of slavery and racism felt by more liberal Southerners, including those like William Faulkner, whose pride in their regional tradition was fundamental to their identity and culture. The psychological and cultural anxiety that this produced is comparable to the position of a Westernized, humane, and patriotic Russian serf-owning noblemen in the nineteenth century.[112] As in that case, these profound contradictions and ironies contributed enormously to the richness of the Southern literary tradition after the Civil War.[113]

Once the Southern threat to the United States had been eliminated, and for that majority of Americans who were prepared to overlook the white South's record on race, the attitudes of the rest of America toward the Old South were by no means as hostile as Southern defensiveness would suggest—the enormous popularity of the prettied-up plantation romanticism of the *Gone with the Wind* tradition being one example. As part of the reconsolidation of America as a white *herrenvolk* democracy, Northerners joined with Southerners in denouncing the period of Radical Reconstruction as a disastrous mistake and the blacks as unfit for government.[114]

The Confederacy's glorious military struggle against overwhelming odds was quite soon reincorporated into the military legend of the United States as a whole: a process symbolized by joint meetings of Union and Confederate veterans, by mass Southern enlistment to fight in the War of 1898, and, somewhat later, in a tradition of literary, Hollywood, and television portrayals of the Civil War that continues to the present.[115]

This was something in which the white South was glad to join. Having itself abandoned the dream of independence, the South responded to Yankee patronization by seeking to outdo the Yankees in American nationalism, and especially to outdo the effete and gutless Yankee in a willingness to fight for America. Linked to this was a return to pre–Civil War patterns in which Southerners were the most ardent proponents of American imperial expansion.

At the same time, however, other schools of Americans were beginning to celebrate the South almost precisely for the fact that it had been defeated: as a kind of badge of honor and tradition for those who in a range of different ways felt alienated from or defeated by the dominant values of bourgeois America. This tendency might be dubbed Henry Adams on a Harley-Davidson, and has been heavily colored by the romance of the "Lost Cause."

At one end of the spectrum, it has included Yankees and others who reacted against the greed, corruption, vulgarity, materialism, and self-satisfaction of the post–Civil War "Gilded Age" and have continued to react against these features of American life until the present day. In the process, some of them rediscovered the conservative and aristocratic critique of capitalism developed as part of the South's intellectual and cultural defenses by writers like George Fitzhugh before the Civil War, and perpetuated by Southern intellectuals like Allen Tate in the mid-twentieth century, and to some extent by Eugene Genovese and others in our own day.[116]

At the other end of the social and intellectual spectrum, as John Sheldon Reed has noted, for many southerners and others, Confederate symbols came to represent a version of the "Don't Tread On Me" slogan:

> Sometime around the middle of the last century [i.e., the twentieth century], the Confederate battle flag took on yet another meaning: Especially in the South, but not only there, it began to send a message of generalized defiance directed at authority, and to some extent at respectability. People who use it in this way may not care for Black folks or Yankees, but those groups are somewhere behind high-school principals on their list of targets...As one girl said, "When I see the Confederate flag I think of a pickup truck with a gun rack and a bumper sticker that says "I Don't Brake For Small Animals."[117]

The adoption of Confederate symbolism by alienated members of the Northern white working class (including many Irish, Poles, and others from outside the old white core ethnicities) reflects three elements in the Confederate tradition. The first is, of course, white racial supremacy. The others, however, are more attractive. One is the "good ole boy" or redneck Southern tradition described above and celebrated, for example, by the popular TV series *The Dukes of Hazzard* (1979–1985). This is a tradition of great innate attraction to hell-raisers everywhere, and dignified by the Confederate "Rebel" label—as in the choice of name for "Rebel Yell" Bourbon whisky.

"Redneck" culture, often originally rooted in that of the less respectable Scots-Irish, is much more attached to country music, fishing, and beer than to evangelical religion, or at least church attendance—which is, of course, not necessarily the same thing, as the record of many country singers who have mixed deeply religious sensibility with utter wildness tends to demonstrate.[118]

Another aspect of Southern culture that has spread to sections of the wider American working classes, and fed strongly into American nationalism, is the picture of stoicism, tenacity, and gallantry against overwhelming odds presented by the Confederate soldiers of the Civil War.[119] This is an image of great emotional force for many white Americans who feel defeated by economic and other circumstances beyond their control and excluded from wealth, power, influence, and fashion. And, of course, those who feel this are also, by instinct, culture, and tradition, American nationalists. When they felt let down by their rulers and generals during and after Vietnam, they listened to ballads of betrayed working class patriotism by Bruce Springsteen or Johnny Cash, not to the protest anthems of Don McLean or Bob Dylan. Such people therefore require a symbol that is rebellious and yet part of the American national, and especially the military, tradition.

My own acquaintances in Troy, though overwhelmingly of Confederate descent and very proud of it, had also by the 1970s moved a long way toward this wider identity and sentiment. Though they still harbored certain old Southern prejudices against "Yankees" in general, these had become something of a self-confessed joke, although one that retained a bitter flavor.[120] Their most intense and vivid loathings had become of a more generic "heartland" kind: of the "East Coast elites" and unpatriotic liberal intellectuals in general; of the "fruit and nut states" of California and (southern) Florida, and the homosexual and hippy lifestyles they were held to represent; and of New York City, for which the hope was frequently expressed that it would be towed out to sea and sunk. Cultural, religious, ethnic, economic, historical, and geographical distance meant that they only to a very limited extent regarded the people of New York as fellow countrymen.

Because of the Iranian hostage crisis, the people of Troy were in a more than usually nationalist mood, and "Iranians" had joined the existing gallery of international hate figures. However, in a sign of what were to prove extremely dangerous confusions after 9/11, a commonly used word for "Iranian" was "Arab."

The General Will

The United States therefore possesses strong elements of an antithesis to its publicly accepted national "creed." Indeed, this antithesis appears to fit all three of what Eugen Weber called the "three Rs" of extreme nationalism: "Reaction against the tendencies of the present; Resistance to Change; and Radicalism, which has radical change in mind." As of 2012, these are very strongly marked features of the Tea Party movement.[121]

Compared to conservative and nationalist radicalism in the history of most of the rest of the world, however, one very important and widespread element has been absent in the United States: namely, the impulse to authoritarian dictatorship characteristic of the vast majority of radical nationalist and radical conservative movements in the world. The autocracies that have been pursued by different movements at different times have differed greatly, taking the form of traditional royal autocracies, military *caudillismo*, the Fascist Duce principle, or the charismatic leadership of groups of young nationalist radicals, à la Garibaldi (which later in turn fed into Italian Fascism). In most countries, however, the impulse to authoritarianism and the leadership principle has seemed inherent to this kind of nationalist tendency. Nor has this been wholly lacking in America, if one remembers the number of successful (and unsuccessful) American generals elected to high office, or encouraged to aspire to it.[122]

But in the United States, such threats have in the end always been contained by the institutions of American democratic constitutionalism, and this has been thanks not only to the institutions themselves, but to the strength and uniformity of the democratic national political culture and ideology sustaining them. Although at their further fringes the forces of the American antithesis shade over into fascistic manias like that of the terrorist Timothy McVeigh and the various militia movements, the great majority are not opposed to the formal democratic aspects of the American Creed; on the contrary, they take enormous pride in them, and regard them as the core of American grandeur. As the last chapter explored, the Tea Parties worship the Constitution, or rather what they take it to be.

For most of American history, American tendencies to authoritarianism have taken what might be called a communal form, and have been phrased and even thought of in terms of a defense of the American liberal democratic system—what Seymour Martin Lipset has called episodes of "Creedal passion"—not a revolt against it. In Louis Hartz's words, America's commitment to an absolute form of liberal nationalism "does not mean that America's General Will always lives an easy life. It has its own violent moments—rare, to be sure, but violent enough. These are the familiar American moments of national fright and national hysteria when it suddenly rises to the surface with a vengeance, when civil liberties begin to collapse, and when Fenimore Cooper is actually in danger of going to jail as a result of the Rousseauan tide."[123]

As this passage suggests, certain collective aspects of democratic America have a close affinity with Jean-Jacques Rousseau's prescription for the ideal state, and with the role of the general will in the life of that state: that each individual citizen should, when making up his or her mind on a public issue, ask him- or herself what decision would be in accordance with the general will. In Rousseau's conception, this is a mechanism based on the shared moral and ideological consensus of society—which in turn is shaped by a universally held civic religion. This "saves the ideal of liberty, while preserving discipline" and also preserves a national capacity to make decisions.[124] As noted by J. L. Talmon, Rousseau's vision possesses implications that point to a form of collective authoritarianism, or even totalitarianism, though this suggestion has been widely viewed as overdrawn.[125]

Rousseau's portrait of the general will is not only prescriptive, but also to a degree descriptive—of the ethnically, culturally, and religiously homogeneous world of his native Swiss city-state of Geneva (an insight that would not have pleased Rousseau himself, at least after Geneva burned his books for immorality). The idea of the general will as formulated by Rousseau can therefore be seen as an attempt to extend the powerful and admirable, but also stifling and repressive atmosphere of a culturally homogeneous small town to the life of an entire nation. But as it actually existed in Geneva—and in other closed, homogeneous communities where homogeneity is maintained not by repression from above, but by the community itself—a form of general will has emerged naturally from the community's history.

For many populist nationalist Americans, the general will, and "liberal nationalism," have never been just about an absolutist adherence to liberal democratic institutions. They have also involved a conviction that being American means adherence to a national cultural community, one defined by its values, and in the past at least, also by race, ethnicity, and religion. And this has been true from the start. Whatever one thinks of his present agendas, when Christian Coalition leader Ralph Reed writes that "the centrality of faith to the maintenance of democratic institutions was once considered axiomatic," he is being completely accurate historically.[126]

This combination explains how many Americans can combine in themselves elements of both the American thesis and its antithesis; Americans can, as Louis Hartz has argued, be genuinely devoted followers of the American Creed, on a basis laid down by John Locke and developed by the Enlightenment, and yet can combine this with a sense of cultural, religious, and national community that is decidedly pre-Enlightenment. After all, if the Enlightenment contributed critically to the American Revolution and the national institutions it generated, it is equally true that many Americans felt—as their Parliamentarian ancestors in England had done during the Civil War 130 years previously—that they were fighting for ancient English liberties against the innovations of an autocratic monarch. At least some aspects of the American Revolution itself were founded in a "dread of modernity."[127]

And the numerous descendants of this tradition have had a strong sense, fostered originally by many years of racial warfare in North America, that this community is threatened by alien and savage "others." They also have a sense that they constitute in some way the genuine American people, or folk—the backbone of the American nation, possessing a form of what German nationalists called the *gesundes volkssinn* ("healthy consciousness of the people"), embracing correct national forms of religion, social behavior, and patriotism. With time they have come to accept people first of different ethnicities, then even of different races as members of the American community—but only if they conform to American norms and become "part of the team."[128] Hence the attempt by the Right and the Tea Parties not to attack Barack Obama's race and color as such, but rather to brand him as a Muslim and non-American.

Although this culture is devoted to freedom, it is not devoted to "negative freedom," as Isaiah Berlin defined it, but to a kind of "positive freedom." First, freedom is restricted to members of the moral, cultural, and (formerly) racial and ethnic communities: "Free, *White*, and Twenty-one" was the old saying. The racial qualification has disappeared, but a sense that freedom can only be exercised in certain ways and by certain kinds of people is still very much alive.[129] In the words of Merle Haggard's song Okie from Muskogee, they believe not only in "bein' free" but also in "livin' right." One might almost say that they believe in being free *in order* to live right.[130]

Second, and as a consequence, freedom is tightly circumscribed by communal culture. It is a form of "positive freedom," a freedom to—in Immanuel Kant's phrase—"obey the laws you yourself have made." The freedom of aliens, who do not share this culture, or deviants, can therefore legitimately be circumscribed by authoritarian and even savage means, as long as this is to defend the community and reflects the will of the sound members of the community.[131] A survey of Southern Baptist ministers with premillenarian beliefs in 1987 revealed rather low levels of willingness to allow Socialists, civil liberties activists, and "secular humanists" even to speak in public, run for public office, or teach in schools.[132]

The following description by Walter Russell Mead has deep implications for the Tea Party movement and for American nationalism abroad as well as at home:

> Death to the enemies of the community! It is a legacy from colonial times, confirmed by the experience of two centuries of American life, and one of the most deeply ingrained instincts in the Jacksonian world...Jacksonian realism is based on the very sharp distinction in popular feeling between the inside of the folk community and the dark world without. Jacksonian patriotism is an emotion, like love of one's family, not a doctrine. The nation is an extension of the family. Members of the American folk are bound together by history, culture and a common morality. At a very basic level a feeling of kinship exists among Americans. We have one set of rules for dealing with one another; very different rules apply in the outside world.[133]

This is the tradition that produced figures such as John Ashcroft, former governor of Missouri and attorney general in the Bush administration. Ashcroft was responsible for formulating laws and measures that greatly increased federal powers of surveillance, interrogation, and detention without trial, which would seem hostile to the legalism that is a core element of the American Creed and self-image, in which Ashcroft himself professes to believe passionately.

Nor is this belief in the rule of law on the part of figures like Ashcroft hypocritical. It is merely qualified by two very large conditions: that in a crisis, written laws can be suspended for the sake of the defense of the community; and that the law in any case only applies to a limited extent to aliens, above all those who are suspected of being enemies and of having behaved in a "barbaric" manner.

The most dramatic and chilling result of this historically derived attitude has been seen since 9/11 in the approach of the Bush administration to the torture of prisoners captured in the course of the war on terrorism and the response of a section of the American public to what happened. In the spring of 2004, hard on the heels of the evidence of gross maltreatment of Iraqi detainees by U.S. interrogators and guards at the prison of Abu Ghraib, came the exposure of secret memos by administration lawyers advocating the torture of prisoners. This episode also encapsulated some of the contrast between the forces of the American Thesis and those of the American Antithesis.[134]

On one hand, probably a majority of Americans, and certainly a majority of the media, seemed not only outraged by what had happened but also genuinely and deeply surprised that U.S. troops could do such things. Mainstream papers and television channels gave extensive coverage to agonized discussions of the brutalizing effects of war on ordinary, decent people. The outrage was of course both understandable and correct. The surprise, however, was somewhat surprising, given the record of the U.S. military in Vietnam. Certainly Abu Ghraib would not have come as a surprise to the Vietnam veterans with whom I spoke in Alabama.[135]

But another very considerable section of Americans were not surprised at all by what had happened and indeed approved it. In an opinion poll commissioned in May 2004 by the *Washington Post* and ABC News, 34 percent of respondents said that torture is acceptable in the case of "people suspected of involvement in recent attacks on U.S. forces in Iraq or Afghanistan," with 64 percent rejecting this. When asked if physical abuse short of torture is acceptable, 45 percent said yes and 53 percent no.[136]

What happened can also clearly have come as no surprise to White House Counsel Alberto Gonzales, who in a memo to the president of January 25, 2002, described articles of the Geneva Convention regarding the treatment of prisoners as "quaint" and advised that they be abandoned (Colin Powell strongly dissented). Later, lawyers in the Justice Department (August 2002) and in the Pentagon (March 2003) advised the administration that a U.S. President in his capacity as commander in chief has the right to override both U.S. and international law and sanction physical abuse of prisoners as part of the war on terrorism.[137]

These memos were intended to be kept secret. There was nothing secret, however, about the reaction of numerous right-wing politicians and media commentators to the Abu Ghraib revelations. Senator James Inhofe (Republican, Oklahoma) declared to his colleagues on the Senate Armed Services Committee: "I'm probably not the only one at this table that is more outraged by the outrage than we are by the treatment....You know, they [the prisoners at Abu Ghraib] are not there for traffic violations...they're murderers, they're terrorists, they're insurgents."[138]

Senator Inhofe attacked the International Committee of the Red Cross (ICRC) as "humanitarian do-gooders right now crawling all over these prisons looking for human rights violations while our troops, our heroes, are fighting and dying."

His fellow Republican senator, Trent Lott (Mississippi), declared: "Frankly, to save some Americans' troops lives or a unit that could be in danger, I think that you should get really rough with them." Reminded that at least one prisoner had been beaten to death by U.S. troops at Abu Ghraib, Lott replied: "This is not Sunday school. This is interrogation. This is rough stuff."[139] Similar statements came from right-wing media figures such as Rush Limbaugh, Bill O'Reilly and Michael Savage. Limbaugh declared:"Maybe the people who ordered this [the abuses at Abu Ghraib] are pretty smart. Maybe the people who executed this pulled off a brilliant maneuver... boy, there was a lot of humiliation of people who are trying to kill us—in ways they hold dear. Sounds pretty effective to me if you look at us in the right context."[140]

Right-wing radio star Michael Savage described Arabs as "non-humans" and declared that "conversion to Christianity is the only thing that can probably turn them [Arabs] into human beings." He said: "Smallpox in a blanket, which the U.S. Army gave to the Cherokee Indians on their long march to the West, was nothing to what I'd like to see done to these people."[141] Savage's talk show is broadcast on 350 radio stations and has an audience of some 7.5 million people. Limbaugh's goes out on 680 stations and has an audience of around 20 million.[142]

Senator Inhofe's attack on the ICRC was echoed two days later by the *Wall Street Journal* in an editorial entitled "Red Double Cross," which decried the organization's "increasing politicization" and warned that it was at risk of becoming "just another left-wing advocacy group along the lines of Human Rights Watch or Amnesty International" (the *Journal* has always been glad to cite these bodies as respectable authorities when it comes to attacking countries which its editors hate and wish to target).[143] Of course, these statements did not represent the views of all Republicans. They drew a sharp rebuke from former prisoner of war Senator John McCain, who praised the ICRC's record and stressed America's duty to abjure torture and respect international conventions.[144]

This tradition is clearly antithetical to the formal aspects of the American Creed when it comes to both the administration of justice and the equality of rights—it certainly does not believe either that fundamental rules of justice are to be found in law books or that "all men are created equal." However, in the past it has usually coexisted comfortably enough with the creed at home, because the eruptions of popular fury and folk justice have been short-lived responses to particular real or perceived threats.

The exceptions were the Frontier, where the threat from the Indians and the tradition of vigilanteeism and collective punishment which it produced, lasted as long as the Frontier itself, and the South, where the constructed threat from the Blacks required collective repression that lasted from the origins of these colonies to the 1960s. The implication of these traditions for the "war on terrorism" will be among the subjects explored in the following chapters.

The Tea Parties

The Tea Parties that developed in the United States in 2009 embrace much of the old Jacksonian tradition, but also extend well beyond it.[145] They represent the latest stage in the shift of American populism to the Right, visible since the 1960s and analyzed by Michael Kazin, Kevin Phillips, and others. Kazin's work on the history of populism in the United States links the American nationalist thesis and antithesis in a way that applies perfectly to the Tea Parties (which emerged 14 years after his book was published):

> The first element in the shared language of politics was *Americanism* itself. This was the creed for which independence had been won and that all genuine patriots would fight to preserve. It was breathtakingly idealistic: in this unique nation, all men were created equal, deserved the same chance to improve their lot, and were citizens of a self-governing republic that enshrined the liberty of the individual. It was also proudly defensive: America was an isolated land of virtue whose people were on constant guard against the depredations of aristocrats, empire-builders, and self-aggrandizing office-holders both within and outside its borders.[146]

The Tea Parties are indeed an especially powerful synthesis of the American nationalist thesis and antithesis of the American Creed described in the last chapter and the racial, regional, and class anxieties described in this one. At the same time, however, the Tea Parties as such—like previous populist movements—seem highly dependent on the specific circumstances that gave them birth, and unlikely to last for very long. Apart from tax cuts and a passionate but extremely vague commitment to the Constitution, they wholly lack a program for government, and they almost pride themselves on their lack of a national organization. Moreover, polls seem to suggest that while they are supported by a very large minority of Americans, the more a majority get to know about them, the more a majority has swung against them—as their lack of a program and the extremism and sheer ignorance of some of their leaders have come under increased media scrutiny.

The experience of recent decades, however, suggests that while radical conservative movements within the Republican Party may not succeed in seizing control of that party, let alone winning the presidency, each populist wave has pulled the party another step toward the Right—to the point where many aspects of the party today would not be recognizable to Presidents Eisenhower or Nixon. This has certainly been true of the Tea Parties, whose role in encouraging the Republicans to reject compromise with the Obama administration in the debate over raising the U.S. debt ceiling in July 2011 almost led to a national default. The conservative commentator David Brooks wrote:

> If the Republican Party were a normal party, it would take advantage of this amazing moment. It is being offered the deal of the century: trillions of dollars

in spending cuts in exchange for a few hundred billion dollars of revenue increases…But we can have no confidence that the Republicans will seize this opportunity. That's because the Republican Party may no longer be a normal party. Over the past few years, it has been infected by a faction that is more of a psychological protest than a practical, governing alternative. The members of this movement do not accept the logic of compromise, no matter how sweet the terms. The members of this movement do not accept the legitimacy of scholars and intellectual authorities. A thousand impartial experts may tell them that a default on the debt would have calamitous effects, far worse than raising tax revenues a bit. But the members of this movement refuse to believe it. If responsible Republicans don't take control, independents will conclude that Republican fanaticism caused this default. They will conclude that Republicans are not fit to govern. And they will be right.[147]

At the same time, if the Tea Parties themselves do not triumph or survive, the underlying trends that gave them birth will remain and even intensify. For while the immediate impulse for their creation was the economic recession after 2008, the election of a black president, and the Obama administration's health care reform, all three of these developments were reflections of deeper patterns that will continue and may even intensify in the decades to come: the long-term economic decline of large sections of the white middle and working classes, dating back to the 1970s, and the growing inequality of U.S. society; the demographic decline of the white population; and the increasingly unsustainable nature of government programs that favor the middle classes. So far, despite widespread fears, the government has not in fact begun to reform Medicare and Social Security. Sooner or later it will have to do so or face fiscal collapse.

The radicalization of the Republican Party visible since the 1970s is linked to this slow economic decline of its white middle class base, as well as to the cultural and religious factors that I will describe and analyze in the next chapter. Compared to the decades before the Great Depression and from the 1940s to the 1970s, most individual middle class and working class incomes from the 1970s to 2008 stagnated or declined. Overall real median household income peaked in 1999 at $53,252. By 2009 the U.S. male median wage had dropped 28 percent in real terms since 1970.[148] This has been a truly shattering decline, which was only made bearable for a while by the entry of married women into the workforce, which supported overall family income, while at the same time increasing childcare costs and strains on family life. Adding enormously to the strain has been the increase in job insecurity even for those in good work, with unionized labor being replaced by short-term contracts.

Associated with these trends has been a steep rise in social inequality, which had decreased in every year but two between 1947 and 1968, then stabilized, before rising steeply after 1981. This trend was principally due to the decline of manufacturing jobs in the face of Asian competition and the growing importance of "knowledge-based" businesses closed to those without higher education.

The especially steep increases in inequality after 1981 and 2001 also reflected the beginnings of the Reagan and Bush administrations, with their programs of tax cuts for the wealthy.[149]

Closely associated with this trend has been a decline in social mobility and the opportunities for children of the working and middle classes to better their social and economic status compared to their parents. As of 2012, the United States is now almost at the bottom among the developed economies. As has often been pointed out, the belief in America as a model of universal economic opportunity compared with other countries, so beloved of the Tea Parties, no longer has any basis in fact. Once again, this is essentially a mythological understanding of the United States, handed down from a vanished golden age of the past.[150]

These trends sharpened after 2000. Despite overall U.S. economic growth and an improvement in productivity, between 2000 and 2008, real median income decreased by 1.6 percent, while the percentage of gross domestic product (GDP) going to wages declined to its lowest levels since records began. By 2003–2004, median incomes no longer increased even when the economy was growing well—while incomes for the already wealthy top 5 percent of Americans soared.[151] This was partly because of a decrease in manufacturing jobs of 22 percent between 1998 and 2008—in other words, before the beginning of the recession. To put it simply, even when the U.S. economy is growing, far fewer of the benefits are now going to most Americans than at any time in America's history. This in turn led to a pessimism about personal and familial prospects with no precedents in times of overall growth.[152]

The resulting conservative populism, however, itself seems likely to drive both the economy and white middle class prospects down further—as already seems clear from what has happened in California since the rise of the antitax movement in the 1980s. Unable either to raise additional revenue or to make deep cuts in middle class entitlements, governments will be forced to cut even more deeply in the only areas where they can cut (other than the military, which is still not threatened by truly deep cuts): infrastructure, research and development, education, and strategic investment. This is likely to drive the United States still deeper into relative and even absolute decline.

If the response of large parts of the white middle class is yet more right-wing populism, and if the U.S. Constitution continues to allow them a blocking vote in Congress, then a vicious circle may be created in which decline leads to populism and more populism leads to more decline. Closely linked is the way in which growing economic inequality embitters the white middle and working classes, who react by insisting on tax cuts for the rich and cuts to government programs, thereby producing yet more inequality, yet more bitterness, and yet more populism. This is a process analogous to the crew of a listing ship shifting the cargo in the direction of the list and not against it, until eventually the ship capsizes.

A more complex question is the impact of continued conservative populism on U.S. foreign policy. As already mentioned, the white population of the U.S. heartland has very strong traditional impulses toward isolationism. The wars in

Iraq and Afghanistan have had a strong effect in turning people away from more invasions and occupations. A representative figure in this regard is the country singer Merle Haggard, who reacted with belligerent fury to the 9/11 attacks, but by 2005 was already singing "America First," in which he pays tribute to U.S. troops, but also laments America's crumbling infrastructure and economy, and calls for America to "get out of Iraq, and get back on track."[153]

C. Vann Woodward, writing in the 1960s, described most white Americans as having traditionally been "bellicose but not militaristic." They are willing—even overwilling—to fight if America is attacked or even insulted, but are not committed to the permanent celebration and projection of military power and values.[154] Even after the militarizing effects of the cold war, this remains true to a considerable extent today. It is closely linked to the fact that many Americans can also be said to be "bellicose but not imperialistic," and are indeed very unwilling to recognize that they possess even an indirect empire.[155] Open exaltation in empire, and celebrations of parallels with the British and other empires, remained restricted to a few neoconservatives and others.[156]

Bellicose nationalism, however, is a different matter, and certainly is very widely present in the white population and in the populist tradition. Michael Kazin makes the point that even some left-wing populists like "Mother Jones," who were strongly opposed in principle to militarism and standing armies, could respond with strong and even ferocious support for particular wars (in her case, American involvement in World War I) after they had actually started.[157]

This gut bellicosity, the "Don't Tread on Me" or "Spread Eagle" position, and the opportunities this gives for political manipulation and exploitation, were summed up with amazing frankness by Irving Kristol, writing in 1989:

> If the president goes to the American people and wraps himself in the American flag and lets Congress wrap itself in the white flag of surrender, the president will win... The American people had never heard of Grenada. There was no reason they should have. The reason we gave for the intervention—the risk to American medical students there—was phony but the reaction of the American people was absolutely and overwhelmingly favorable. They had no idea what was going on but they backed the president. They always will.[158]

While often an embarrassment to U.S. foreign policy, the "Don't Tread on Me" tendency is also extremely useful to any U.S. leader planning a war. Many of these figures can be counted on to support almost any war, as long as they can somehow be convinced that the United States has been attacked or insulted. The stance of some conservative Republicans over the Kosovo War is a revealing example. This attitude is also reflected in the demand of Republicans that Obama should either have avoided involvement in the Libyan conflict of 2011 altogether or engaged with much greater force.

Most Republicans opposed the Kosovo War, out of hostility to the Clinton administration and out of opposition to "humanitarian" wars in which U.S. national interests did not seem to be at stake (the importance of preserving NATO as a vehicle for U.S. influence in Europe, and therefore for giving it something to do, was missed). It might have been expected therefore that when the Chinese embassy in Belgrade was bombed, and the Chinese reacted with bitter criticism of the United States, these men would have explained this as a lesson of the dangerous wider "unintended consequences" of supposedly minor, limited military operations. Not at all. The reaction was one of furious belligerence, strongly flavored with traditional attitudes toward the character and proper treatment of Asians and lesser breeds, as in this statement by Representative Tom DeLay:

> While the bombing of the embassy is an unfortunate example of collateral damage during Mr. Clinton's war, the prestige of the United States has been harmed more by the constant apologies and groveling of the President in its aftermath. It seems that every time the television is on, the President is apologizing to Communist China...No wonder the PRC government thinks it can walk all over the United States. Communist Chinese leaders do not understand weakness in leadership. They respect unquestioned power, firmness of purpose and unquestioned shows of strength.[159]

This instinctive belligerence has been much in evidence since 9/11, and in ways very damaging to the conduct of the struggle against Islamist terrorism. President Bush himself was careful to avoid this, and to speak of Islam and Muslim peoples with respect. But on the American nationalist Right, there was an explosion of aggressive chauvinism, not just against Al Qaeda and the Taliban, and even Saddam Hussein, but against Islam and the Muslim world in general.[160]

As disagreement between the United States and parts of Western Europe (and most of the rest of the world) over war with Iraq intensified in 2002–2003, the bitter hostility of American nationalists was extended to any country that refused to follow the United States into war.[161] This spirit led to the U.S. House of Representatives voting to change the designation of "French Fries" in its restaurant to "Freedom Fries," but it also affected even some normally moderate and intelligent American analysts.[162]

Even usually moderate figures succumbed to the hysteria, with Thomas Friedman declaring in the New York Times that "France is not just our annoying ally. It is not just our jealous rival. France is becoming our enemy." French opinions were, moreover, worthless in any case because "France has never been interested in promoting democracy in the modern Arab world."

Friedman therefore adopted, in essence, a mild version of the same position taken up by Charles Krauthammer and others: because other countries hate us, and for ignoble, wicked, and illegitimate reasons, their opinions do not count, and we are free to do whatever we like. These words were written in September 2003, by which time France's warnings about the consequences of war had been shown to be amply justified. They are an example both of the degree to which even centrist Americans can become the captive of nationalist emotions, of a nationalist insistence that the only acceptable criticism of America is by Americans, and of a belief that in a time of war, even this right of criticism should be suspended.[163]

At the time of the Iraq War, not just extremist publications like the *Washington Times*, but the *Washington Post* and *New York Times* became vehicles for "a well-orchestrated campaign of innuendoes, distortions and lies aimed not only at discrediting French arguments but France itself."[164] Articles accused France of harboring fugitive Ba'ath officials, possessing banned stocks of biological weapons, and supplying Iraq with weapons—all charges that were later admitted to be completely groundless.[165]

This Jacksonian nationalist background has important implications for the future behavior of the Tea Parties and the groups that gave them birth. On the one hand, the leaders and members of the Tea Parties are even more indifferent to the details of foreign policy than they are to the details of domestic policy. Most hardly get beyond passionate but ritualistic commitments to defend Israel and resist terrorists and Islamists—and even when it comes to the latter, this is often more likely to be focused on the imagined threat of Islamisation *within* the United States rather than what might be happening in the Muslim world. In keeping with the Jacksonian tradition, there is absolutely no desire for more U.S.-led "nation-building" exercises in the Muslim world or anywhere else.

This is, however, extremely unlikely to lead to any serious or consistent movement on the part of the Tea Party constituencies for U.S. strategic withdrawal. The Republican foreign and security establishment, the U.S. security establishment, and the U.S. military are all utterly opposed to this. Not merely are the leaders of the Tea Parties simply not intellectually equipped to argue with them, but the Tea Parties are nationalist to the core, and as described in the last chapter, a sense of America's global mission is deeply and permanently bound up with that nationalism, even if it often takes a back seat in response to particular reversals and disappointments. Thus Sarah Palin quotes approvingly a passage from *National Review*:

> Our country has always been exceptional. It is freer, more individualistic, more democratic, and more open and dynamic than any other nation on earth. These qualities are the bequest of our founding and of our cultural heritage. They have always marked America as special, with a unique role and mission in the world: as a model of ordered liberty and self-government and as an exemplar of freedom and a vindicator of it, through persuasion when possible and force of arms when absolutely necessary.[166]

In addition, to judge by the works of Sarah Palin and others, a consistent sentiment that extends across the Tea Parties as far as security politics is concerned is a deep love of and reverence for the U.S. armed forces, in which so many of their relatives serve or have served (including Palin's son, an Iraq War veteran).[167]

Palin's chapter "Why They Serve" makes no attempt to analyze, understand, or justify the Iraq War or any other recent U.S. operations, but is absolutely, passionately convinced that whenever and wherever American soldiers are fighting they are "defending freedom." The nearest she comes to a policy prescription in this chapter is the following quote from a country song by Toby Keith, *Courtesy of the Red White and Blue*:

> And you'll be sorry that you messed with
> The US of A,
> 'Cause we'll put a boot in your ass
> It's the American Way.[168]

This sentiment means that if a U.S. administration can get America into a war, or if an expansive U.S. strategy (with which most Tea Party members might actually disagree) leads to any kind of attack on U.S. troops, this section of the U.S. population can be relied on, for a while at least, to support a ferocious military response.

The only consistent isolationists among the prominent figures of the Tea Parties are Senator Rand Paul and his father Ron Paul, and they have been subjected to relentless attacks for this by much of the liberal media as well as the Republican establishment. As one of Paul's supporters wrote of the Tea Parties in an article entitled gloomily "Prepare to be Betrayed,"[169]

> just as with old-time conservatives, there are many issues on which the Tea Party tends toward inconsistency. The military and the issue of war is a major one. Many have bought into the line that the greatest threat this country faces domestically is the influx of adherents of Islam; in international politics, they tend to favor belligerence toward any regime that is not a captive of U.S. political control.

This view is endorsed from a different angle by Walter Russell Mead, who sees the Tea Parties as overwhelmingly Jacksonian in their basic attitudes to security and foreign affairs: "The contest in the Tea Party between what might be called its Palinite and Paulite wings will likely end in a victory for the Palinites... Although both wings share, for example, a visceral hostility to anything that smacks of "world government," Paul and his supporters look for ways to avoid contact with the world, whereas such contemporary Jacksonians as Sarah Palin and the Fox News host Bill O'Reilly would rather win than withdraw. 'We don't need to be the world's policeman,' says Paul. Palin might say something similar, but she would be quick to add that we also do not want to give the bad guys any room."[170]

In certain respects, however, the Tea Parties are operating in a more dangerous world than their McCarthyite predecessors, and pose a more dangerous threat to peace. McCarthyism took root at a time when white middle class and working class living standards and opportunities were improving at a faster rate than at any other time in American history. This socioeconomic context was crucial to the speed with which the McCarthyite movement receded again. China is a vastly more formidable opponent than the former Soviet Union, with a very prickly nationalism of its own. Finally, America has become embroiled in the Middle East in ways that expose the United States to terrorist attacks and risk drawing America into clashes with local states.

Finally, in the late 1940s and early 1950s fundamentalist religion, though a very important force in American life, played a very limited overt role in U.S. politics. Today, fundamentalist religion plays a vital role in conservative politics and an important one in the Tea Parties. In both domestic politics and attitudes toward foreign policy, some strands of this religion are helping to drive disastrously irrational and paranoid responses to America's problems. This aspect of the American nationalist antithesis is the subject of the next chapter.

Four

Antithesis Part II: Fundamentalists and Great Fears

Our God is marching on.

—Julia Ward Howe, *Battle Hymn of the Republic*

A vital though informal part of the American Creed has long been the belief that the United States epitomizes the triumph of modernity in economics, technology, and culture as well as in its democratic arrangements. This successful modernity, with the economic opportunities, the material culture, and the consumerism that it generates, is also at the heart of what has been called the "American Dream." This is, above all, true of consumer culture and mass entertainment. In East Asia, for example, Europe is hardly present as a trendsetter in these fields. This image of the United States has been undermined by the economic recession that has continued since 2008, the decline of U.S. industry, and the rise of China, but it remains extremely strong.

America is also seen as the country that has tended to undergo the fastest economic and cultural changes of any country in the developed world, and the one that is the most open to change. Closely connected to this is the fact that the United States is exceptionally open to immigration, and consequently has experienced the most radical demographic changes of any country in the Western world. It is still generally believed that "there has from the start been a marriage of true minds between the American and the type-man of the modern era, the New World Man."[1]

Yet amidst all this change, America is also home to by far the largest and most powerful forces of fundamentalist religion in the developed world. The attitude of these forces toward key aspects of modernity as this is usually understood was summed up in the 1960s by the leading Pentecostalist preacher A. A. Allen: "The most treacherous foe in America isn't Communism (as perilous as it may be), Nazism, Fascism or any alien ideology, but MODERNISM [capitals in the original]." This call to arms appeared in a booklet entitled *My Vision of the Destruction of America.* This title in itself brings out the contrast between the optimism of the American Creed and the profound pessimism of Protestant fundamentalism as far as progress in this world is concerned.[2]

As Samuel Huntington has observed, "those countries that are more religious tend to be more nationalist." Looking at the contrast between the United States and the rest of the developed world, Huntington and others have explained early twenty-first century America's greater nationalism partly in terms of its greater religiosity. As will be seen, this is especially true of American fundamentalist Protestantism, which, as described in chapter 3, has particular roots in the nationalist culture of the white South.[3]

American conservative evangelicalism and fundamentalism have not remained unchanged over the years; indeed, much of their modern history and growth has been produced precisely by *reaction* to change, and also by adaptation to change. Evangelicalism is "a religious persuasion that has repeatedly adapted to the changing tones and rhythms of modernity," especially of course when it comes to the employment of modern mass media and modern techniques of mass mobilization.[4] Furthermore, across large parts of America, the eighteenth- and nineteenth-century churches played a central part in civilizing—and therefore to a great extent modernizing—what might otherwise have remained semimedieval frontier societies.

By no means all evangelicals are either fundamentalist in religion (though evangelicalism and fundamentalism share most core beliefs) or right-wing nationalist in politics. For example, belief in the literal truth of the whole of the Bible (known as inerrancy) is critical to fundamentalist belief, but many members of the broader evangelical tradition take a more nuanced position. They are also less conservative in politics. Moreover, blacks make up a very considerable proportion of the evangelical population in the United States and the American South; for obvious historical reasons, they are not often led by their religious beliefs into right-wing political positions.[5]

The fundamentalist wing of the evangelical tradition is nonetheless a very powerful ideological force in large parts of the United States. Christian fundamentalism does not dominate the Tea Parties, but is certainly strongly present in them, and seems to play an important part in shaping the Tea Parties' view of America and its government. Republican Congresswoman, Tea Party leader, and 2012 presidential candidate Michele Bachmann's faith and views were strongly influenced by the fundamentalist thinker Francis Schaeffer, who preached that the Renaissance and the Enlightenment both represented dangerous turns away from the "total truth" of the Bible. Schaeffer represented the "Dominionist" strand of fundamentalist theology, which draws on the phrase in Genesis about God giving to man "dominion over the fish of the sea, and over the fowl of the air, and over the cattle, and over all the earth, and over every creeping thing that creepeth upon the earth."[6] This appears linked in the minds of many fundamentalists with instinctive hostility toward belief in climate change and any action to ameliorate it, and also with faith in technological progress and rightful and righteous American power.

Thus, according to CNN, 57 percent of Tea Party supporters polled agreed with the statement that "America is and always has been a Christian nation." On issues like gay marriage and abortion, majorities of between 59 and 64 percent of Tea Party supporters agreed with conservative religious positions, while 44 percent of self-declared conservative Christians polled agreed with the Tea Parties, against only 4 percent who disagreed. Both Sarah Palin and Michele Bachmann are deeply committed evangelical and fundamentalist Christians whose faith has profoundly shaped not only their politics, but their personal lives.

However, there is also a libertarian streak in a fair number of Tea Party supporters, which opposes government regulation of morality. This tendency is represented by Ron Paul, who is also at odds with most of the Tea Parties on military spending and America's superpower role.[7]

American fundamentalist Protestantism retains elements of thought that have come down with relatively few changes from much earlier eras. Its origins are pre-Enlightenment, and its mentality to a very great extent is anti-Enlightenment. It has also retained a strong element of geographical continuity. While many new adherents to these religious groups are from the heterogeneous ethnic and cultural worlds of newly growing cities in the Southwest and California, the heart of their support remains what it has long been, the white South and its outlying regions.[8]

A Pew survey of U.S. religious belief in 2011 still shows an unbroken belt of Southern Baptist majority counties stretching from central Virginia to eastern Texas, and taking in northern Florida and much of Kentucky and Missouri. Much of the remaining white population adheres to other evangelical and/or fundamentalist churches like the Pentecostalists.[9] As already explained, this area is not just religious, but is also home to some very tough, strongly held, and ancient social and cultural traditions, the roots of which predate not just the nation's independence, but the first white settlements in North America. A particular form of nationalism is one of the most important of these traditions.

The greater religiosity of the United States compared to Europe at the start of the twenty-first century, and the strength of Southern-based fundamentalist churches in particular, is rooted in key differences between European and North American history over the past 200 years or so. This involved not only the explosion of American Protestantism into a multiplicity of churches and sects (which at the same time were very homogeneous in their basic beliefs and cultural attitudes), but also the role played by those sects in the development of society on the frontier and in the backcountry of the Greater South.

The formation of these churches followed the old American tradition of settlers in the wilderness spontaneously creating their own churches. Although church membership was voluntary, it involved taking on serious duties in the church and the community as a whole. And since the church often in effect embraced the entire community, membership was often not truly voluntary. Leaving the church was easy only in the sense that it was relatively easy to leave the local community itself, by moving westward.[10] While on the one hand the religious culture of these churches was derived from that of the Protestant sects of seventeenth- and eighteenth-century England and Scotland, each also presented itself as sprung directly from the Bible and the word of God, without historical precedent or intermediary.

The increase in the number of sects in the early and mid-nineteenth-century South was accompanied by a sharp decrease in cultural pluralism and a growing culture of orthodoxy, conservatism, and conformism in religion and in social and cultural life more generally. "By 1860, religious liberalism was virtually dead in the South."[11] The greatest beneficiaries of this religious wave were the Baptist churches, which have continued to predominate in the region to this day, followed by the Methodists. Of course, individualism of a kind has been a key part of Southern culture since its beginnings, but it is an individualism of action, not of thought.

In seeking to understand the deep cultural differences between much of the United States and Western Europe, a combination of the American frontier and the role of the American Protestant churches is of central importance. In both America and Europe, much of the rural population remained largely medieval in its thinking and behavior until the eighteenth and even the nineteenth century (the last burning of a witch in France, with the apparent collusion of local officials, took place in 1835). In Europe, first the local upper classes, and then the state, often through those upper classes, played a leading role in civilizing these populations. The churches played only a subsidiary role, and by the later nineteenth century were in full retreat across much of Western Europe.

In the newly settled parts of the United States, neither a truly functioning state nor traditional upper classes existed. In these areas, it was above all the churches that prevented the settlers from lapsing into not only complete barbarism, but isolation—very often the church was literally the only social institution in the entire district, the only place where the local population met regularly; and it was also responsible for the local school. Without the Protestant churches, the societies of the American frontier would have remained much more backward, violent, and medieval than was the case. The churches therefore played an ambiguous role with regard to the modernization of large parts of the United States: on the one hand, they chastened frontier medievalism, and laid the basis for a modern social and economic order; on the other, they created a religious culture that has been in many ways at odds with modern culture as understood in the rest of the Western world.

And in the South and West, these were churches that local people had literally made themselves. As a result, these populations retained all the traditional European peasant fear and hatred of the state, without being exposed to the dense web of state influences, institutions, and benefits that in Europe later diminished this fear; or at least, not until the twentieth century, by which time some basic features of these American societies had long since been set.[12] This hatred of the state has remained strongly marked in portions of the U.S. population ever since, and forms the core ideological basis for the Tea Parties.

The power of religion in America also played a critical part in preventing the establishment of any strong mass socialist tradition. Thus William Jennings Bryan and the Populists of the 1890s were bitter critics of American capitalism; but Bryan's deeply held fundamentalist Protestantism made even the slightest tinge of ideological Marxism utterly alien to him.[13]

Hector St. Jean de Crevecoeur wrote more than two centuries ago that "the American is a new man who acts on new principles." Richard Hoftstadter wrote of America as "the country of those who fled from the past." In the 1960s, George Grant wrote that "the United States is the only society on earth that has no traditions from before the age of progress," and this was repeated approvingly by Seymour Martin Lipset in 1996.[14] They are all quite wrong as far as this section of Americans is concerned.

Hard-line evangelical Protestants in the United States coined the name "fundamentalists" for themselves in the 1920s because of their desire for a return to what they viewed as the "fundamentals" of Christianity, including a literal, word-for-word belief in the Bible. Their origins were "reactionary" in the strict sense; they were reacting against key aspects of twentieth-century modernity.[15] These religious elements form part of the wider world of American radical conservatism and radical nationalism, of which Richard Hofstadter wrote that "their political reactions express a profound if largely unconscious hatred of our society and its ways...The extreme right suffers not from the policies of this or that administration, but from what America has become in the 20th Century."[16]

There were indeed certain elements of this tendency even in the American revolt against Britain, which has been seen as motivated partly by the hostility of "a provincial people, [who] regarded their style of living as not only good but of God" toward cosmopolitan, latitudinarian, and modernizing British rule.[17] And from the very first days of the American colonies, the belief of the settlers that they were a people chosen by God was accompanied by an Old Testament belief that God was a "God of Warre." The image of the ancient Israelites and their battles with their neighbors was used to justify wars against latter day "Amelekites," whether Indians or French, and God was held to fight for the Americans in those wars.[18]

This body of belief is therefore one of the "huge political icebergs" of American life, which "move through time with massive stability, changing slowly and surviving in their essential form for many generations."[19] For several decades now, the evangelical and fundamentalist churches have been growing while the "mainline" Protestant churches have declined, a process symbolized in 1967 when membership in the churches of the Southern Baptist Convention overtook the Methodist Church, hitherto the largest Protestant church in the country.

Many American liberals have long been disappointed and also deeply puzzled by the Tea Parties and their antecedents; that is to say, by the way in which so many American workers and petty bourgeois have been led by conservative cultural affiliation to vote for right-wing Republicans. It is said, quite rightly, that the radical, unregulated capitalism espoused by these Republicans is often directly contrary to the economic interests of those same workers.[20]

To explain this political behavior, one must understand both the role of America's civic nationalist creed, as described in the second chapter, and the fact that these voters belong to coherent and immensely strong religious and cultural worlds that are genuinely under attack as a result of social and cultural change. Historically speaking, the political importance of the religious factor is not peculiar to the United States. As long as religious adherence remained of great importance in certain Western European societies, it also had an effect on political allegiances in those countries—sometimes, unfortunately, in extremist directions. The tragicomic aspect of the situation of politically conservative American religious believers is that the radically laissez-faire capitalism that they support is not only undermining their economic world, but through the mass media and entertainment industries is also playing a central role in biting away at their moral universe.

Godly Republicans

Conservative religiosity plays a very important part in U.S. politics, and especially in the Republican Party. Its growth has caused part of the "southernization" of that party in recent decades. According to the Christian Coalition, the leading grassroots political organization of the American Christian Right, 29 senators out of 100 and 125 House members out of 435 voted 100 percent of the time in accordance with the Christian Coalition's principles in 2001—in other words, more than one-quarter of the members of both houses of the U.S. Congress. Of these, 15 senators and 64 congressmen were from the Greater South, or just over half of the Christian conservative bloc in both cases (more than double the South's percentage of the U.S. population as a whole).[21]

The influence of this segment of the U.S. population on the Bush administration, and its link to American nationalism, was well expressed in a *Newsweek* article in early 2003:

> Every president invokes God and asks his blessing...But it has taken a war, and the prospect of more, to highlight a central fact: this president—this presidency—is the most resolutely "faith-based" in modern times, an enterprise founded, supported and guided by trust in the temporal and spiritual power of God. Money matters, as does military might. But the Bush administration is dedicated to the idea that there is an answer to societal problems here and to terrorism abroad: give everyone, everywhere, the freedom to find God, too ...
>
> Bible-believing Christians are Bush's strongest backers, and turning them out next year in even greater numbers is the top priority of the president's political adviser Karl Rove ...The base is returning the favor. They are, by far, the strongest supporters of a war—unilateral if need be—to remove Saddam.[22]

With a view to this constituency, but also apparently reflecting his own beliefs, President Bush repeatedly cast the struggle against terrorism and America's place in the world in explicitly religious terms. Not just the terrorists, but a range of other rivals of America were cast as "evil." A religiously inspired messianic spirit colored even those passages where Bush was ostensibly speaking of secular and universal values. Bush himself was reported as seeing himself as an instrument of divine providence.[23]

The statement that "if you are not with us you are against us," so endlessly repeated by the president and other officials, was originally Christ's, and has been repeated by American preachers and politicians down the centuries.[24] This religious element in Bush's thought fed into wider patterns of American moral absolutism, and produced statements like Bush's promise to "rid the world of evil," and the insane title of a book on terrorism by his former speechwriter, "An End to Evil."[25]

Addressing Congress, Bush declared that "the course of this war is not known, yet its outcome is certain. Freedom and fear, justice and cruelty, have always been at war, and we know that God is not neutral between them." The whole address was permeated with a form of religious nationalism. Bush took words from a hymn, "There's Power in the Blood," to refer to the "power, wonder-working power" of "the goodness and idealism and faith of the American people"—words that in the hymn are used of the lamb, Jesus Christ.[26] The identification of the nation with Christ himself (whether suffering or victorious) has a long tradition in the nationalism of Poland, Serbia, and certain other countries, but it is a striking image to find in the mouth of a president of the United States, the supposed embodiment of all that is modern, at the start of the twenty-first century.

The specifically Anglo-American lineage of this mode of thought, and its implications for views of the rest of the world, were well set out by a puritan minister during the English Civil War of the mid-seventeenth century: "All people are cursed or blessed according as they do or do not join their strength and give their best assistance to the Lord's people against their enemies."[27]

As the neoconservative intellectual Norman Podhoretz wrote before the Iraq War:

> One hears that Bush, who entered the White House without a clear sense of what he wanted to do there, now feels that there was a purpose behind his election all along; as a born-again Christian, it is said, he believes that he was chosen by God to eradicate the evil of terrorism from the world. I think it is a plausible rumor, and I would even guess that in his heart of hearts, Bush identifies more in this respect with Ronald Reagan—the President who rid the world of the "evil empire"—than with his own father, who never finished the job he started in taking on Saddam Hussein.[28]

An American patriotic artist best known for his popular "paintings of heroic firemen and policemen superimposed over images of Americana and faith" was encouraged by the White House to produce a painting of George Bush at prayer while leaning on a podium. At his side are Lincoln and Washington, each also praying, and with a hand on George Bush's shoulder.[29] Bush himself has written of his "belief in a divine plan that supersedes all human plans."[30]

According to Bob Woodward, "the President was casting his vision and that of the country in the grand vision of God's master plan."[31] As a sympathetic Christian writer, Stephen Manfield, notes, Bush was one of the very few American presidents "to have undergone a profound religious transformation as an adult":

> He was already engineering a religious renovation of the executive branch when the country suffered a traumatic terrorist attack that placed religion unashamedly at the center of American political and social life. The secular state seemed to recede for a time. Congressional leaders sang hymns on the Capitol steps and even introduced legislation to adopt "God Bless America" as the official national hymn.
>
> What followed was a freer rein for religion in American society. Bush seemed to embody it. He prayed publicly and spoke of faith, divine destiny, and the nation's religious heritage more than he ever had. Aides found him face down on the floor in prayer in the Oval Office. It became known that he refused to eat sweets while American troops were in Iraq, a partial fast seldom reported of an American president. And he framed America's challenges in nearly biblical language. Saddam is an evildoer. He has to go. There must be a new day in the Middle East. Isaac and Ishmael must shake hands in peace.[32]

At home, this tendency caused considerable alarm among secularist Americans and contributed to the growing cultural–political rift in American society. Fundamentalist religiosity has become an integral part of the radicalization of the Right in the United States, and the tendency to demonize political opponents as traitors and enemies of God and America.[33] In turn, the secularization of the American Left, and their espousal of a culturally progressive agenda, has destroyed the ability of economic progressives to appeal to a very large part of the American masses. This alienation of the Left from religion was not true in America before the 1940s. Had it been, American history would have been very different. For even in the depths of the Great Depression, Roosevelt could not have been elected on the basis of a party that espoused gay marriage and abortion. The assumption among American liberals is that like European societies, American society has been cul-turally transformed over the eight decades since. In fact, large parts of it have not been so transformed. Nor indeed has most of the world become less religious, even if forms of religion have changed. Increasingly, the "disenchantment of the world" appears to apply in fact mainly to Europe.

In the rest of the developed world, the strength of American fundamentalism has contributed a new element to fear and distrust of the United States. In the past, these feelings were concentrated mainly on the Left, and were concerned with American capitalism, imperialism, and militarism. But while these tenden-cies were often portrayed as wicked, they were not seen as inherently irrational, as far as the motives and interests of the American elites were concerned.

Moreover, outside the Left, a majority of Europeans looked on these tendencies with relative indifference, since none of them are alien to the history of modern Europe's relations with the rest of the world. Furthermore, most of the targets of American policy—Communists in the past, Muslim extremists more recently—were also seen by most Europeans as enemies. And of course, the populations of the developed world are becoming more and more dominated by a basically American popular culture.

But this was and is *secular* American popular culture. American fundamentalist Protestant missionaries have made considerable inroads among the poor of Latin America and Africa, but have gotten nowhere at all in the centers of the developed world, and among America's key allies. America as civilizational empire and America's thesis about itself and the world are represented by secular American culture: America as the embodiment of successful modernity. The radical religious element in American nationalism is something new, and deeply disquieting to many non-Americans.

Moral Panics

Although the Southern and Northern churches divided bitterly over slavery (with abolition becoming a great crusade for parts of northeastern Protestantism), after the Civil War the Southern churches were also closely associated with some of the northern and so-called mainline Protestant churches of the United States in certain moral crusades. These movements frequently reflected a desire to preserve the cultural dominance of the old "core" Protestant populations in the small towns and countryside over the new Catholic and Jewish populations of the great cities, and hostility to "aliens" in general.

The consequent anxieties often took the form of concern over sexual promiscuity, especially when linked to drugs, drunkenness, and venereal disease, and in the South, fed into perennial fears concerning the blacks.[34] Since the 1970s, this tradition has been revived in the Christian Right's crusade against abortion. As in the past, this is a real moral issue in itself, which has helped perpetuate the alliance between Southern and heartland Protestant conservatives and Catholic conservatives. It also acts both as a metaphor for wider anxieties and as a rallying cry for a wider political mobilization against a wider set of political and cultural enemies.

As with such past panics, it is also closely associated with fears of national decadence leading to national weakness. This is reflected most directly and traditionally in religious terms by the fear that if such wickedness continues, God will either abandon or smite America—a suggestion made directly by Christian Right leader Jerry Falwell after 9/11, which he attributed to God's punishment of America for its sins, including abortion and homosexuality. Michele Bachmann attributed Hurricane Irene in August 2011 to God's desire to send a message to the American people.

These recurrent cultural "panics" with ethnic and racial overtones have been chronicled by James A. Morone in his book, *Hellfire Nation*.[35] Thus starting in 1909, a panic swept Protestant America concerning a supposed huge growth in the number of brothels, with alien "white slavers" roaming the countryside to seduce and even abduct innocent white rural maidens.

Much of the language of this particular panic was anti-Semitic, with anti-Chinese, anti-Catholic ("Secrets of the Convent"), and anti-French feelings playing a secondary role: in the words of *McClure's* magazine, "Out of the racial scum of Europe has come for unnumbered years the Jewish *kaftan*, leading the miserable Jewish girl to her doom." Now, with the help of urban "Tammany Hall" Irish and other politicians, they had set their sights on American womanhood. In an effort to target two ethnoreligious enemies with one slur, it was alleged that sometimes these Jewish white-slavers dressed as Catholic priests! It was claimed as established fact that 60,000 American girls were lured or kidnapped into brothels every year, and that a similar number of prostitutes perished annually—a fantastic exaggeration.

These fears were closely linked to paranoia about the white race committing "race suicide" through decadence, birth control, and so on, and being overwhelmed by the yellow and brown tide. The result of this movement was the closure of most of America's red light districts, and the Mann Act on transporting women across state lines for immoral purposes, a means of harassment and oppression of blacks for decades thereafter.[36]

The most powerful of these movements was for the prohibition of alcohol. The passage of the Eighteenth Amendment in 1920 (greatly helped by wartime hysteria) was the greatest victory for the old core Protestant groups over the Catholic immigrants (Irish saloon keepers and German brewers); the decadent, cocktail-sipping East Coast elites; and the forces of social, cultural, and demographic change. Later, Prohibition became in practice—or rather lack of practice—their greatest defeat. It has been called "a Kulturkampf between two opposing religious-cultural lifestyles."[37]

Of course, it must be recognized that, as in the case of other such movements like the present one against drugs, Prohibition targeted a real problem of "inner city" alcoholism, leading in turn to unemployment, child abuse, and so on—and it may have had some real success in reducing these abuses.[38] This leads Michael Kazin to identify the Prohibition movement as in part at least a socially progressive movement.[39] It also marked a great difference between American and European populism in the strong role of women in its leadership—something that it shares with the contemporary Tea Parties.

Prohibition was also linked not only to anti-immigrant feeling, but also to concerns about social modernization as America emerged (according to the census of 1920) as an urban-majority country.

But such genuine concerns—then as now—have also been mixed up with much darker emotions. Morone quotes the temperance crusader Alphonse Ava

Hopkins, in words the anti-European tone of which have echoed down to our own day:

> Our boast has been that we are a Christian people, with Morality at the center of our civilization...Besodden Europe, worse bescourged than by war, famine and pestilence, sends here her drink-makers, her drunkard-makers, and her drunkards, or her more temperate and habitual drinkers, with all their un-American ideas of morality and government; they are absorbed into our national life but they are not assimilated; with no liberty whence they came, they demand unrestricted liberty among us, even to license what we loathe...they dominate our Sabbath, they have set up for us their own moral standards, which are grossly immoral; they govern our great cities...until foreign control or conquest could achieve little more through armies and fleets.[40]

Similar emotions and fears powered the appearance of the second Ku Klux Klan in the 1920s. Unlike its predecessor of the 1870s in the South, this short-lived but widespread movement was based chiefly in the Midwest and was devoted to anti-immigrant, anti-Semitic, anti-Catholic, and antimodernist sentiment, with negrophobia present but of lesser importance. It was deeply steeped in evangelical Protestantism and reflected among other things the agricultural depression of the 1920s and the pressure it was putting on the old farming communities and the old core populations (plus German Protestants).[41]

The end of open immigration in 1924 reduced the appeal of such movements.[42] This measure in turn owed a great deal to two episodes of public hysteria that were strongly fed by nativist and anti-immigrant sentiment: the wave of anti-German feeling that swept the country in 1917–1918 after America entered World War I, and the "Red Scare" of 1919–1920. During the first, the religious preacher Billy Sunday declared that "if you turn hell upside down, you will find 'made in Germany' stamped on the bottom."[43]

These two movements both saw the widespread use of the term "Americanism," or "one hundred percent Americanism," and demands that immigrants must be either rapidly assimilated or deported. Hysteria and even violence against German Americans was especially strong in Texas. Stanley Coben has written that the Red Scare drew on certain enduring tendencies among many Americans: "hostility towards certain minority groups, especially radicals and recent immigrants, fanatical patriotism, and a belief that internal enemies seriously threaten national security."[44]

Prohibition itself, of course, was later perceived to fail utterly even in its own terms; not merely to be rejected by so much of the population as to be unenforceable, but to have corrupted the police and judiciary, and given a critically important boost to the growth of organized crime. However, as Morone argues, even when such laws as the Volstead or Mann Acts failed, they left behind a new layer of federal bureaucracy, and above all, police—as in more recent times, the "war against drugs" and now the "war against terrorism." Far from being the work of ultimately irrelevant fringe groups, these movements mobilized millions of people, greatly influenced wider political behavior, and helped transform the American state.

Irish American Nationalism

So deep was the defeat of Prohibition and the humiliation of the controversy over evolution that for some 50 years after Congress (under pressure from President Roosevelt) repealed Prohibition in 1933, it was assumed that no extensive movement of this kind could ever again take place in America.[45] Thus Daniel Bell wrote in 1979 (just as the new Christian Right was about to make its appearance in response to the cultural, sexual, and black revolutions of the 1960s and defeat in Vietnam) that while this kind of "backlash" continued, it had been compelled to take a new form, that of nationalism, in the specific form of McCarthyite "Americanism" and anti-Communism.[46]

McCarthyism was indeed the classic example of a movement that brought together previously mutually hostile groups of white "middle class" Americans behind an essentially nationalist program strongly marked by traditions of Protestant cultural paranoia, but in ostensible defense of the American Creed of freedom, democracy, and law.[47] It succeeded in uniting ultranationalism, "Lockean absolutism" (in Louis Hartz's phrase), religious–cultural reaction, bitter class resentment, and (to a lesser and more veiled extent) anti-Semitism in one mass of hatred. McCarthyism was in some ways a precursor of the alliance between the white South and culturally conservative northern and midwestern white ethnic groups, which at the start of the twenty-first century forms a key foundation of the Republican Party, and of which nationalism is a vital element.

McCarthyism thus also symbolizes the way in which certain previously excluded ethnicities have been able to merge with the old core groups through militant nationalism. McCarthy was prefigured by the fascistic "radio priest," Father Charles Coughlin, in the mid-1930s, who similarly mixed anti-Communism and antielitism, though in his case—due to the Depression and the legacy of Catholic social thought—this also included explicit attacks on capitalism, and was also much more overtly anti-Semitic.[48]

McCarthy himself was a Catholic Irish petty bourgeois from a farming background in Wisconsin (with a German American mother). His alliance with white Anglo-Saxon Protestant reaction was created by a mixture of anti-Communism and bitter class resentment. Viewed in its own terms, McCarthyism seems like a modern version of the irrational "great fears" of peasant Europe (as the "witch hunt" analogy is of course meant to suggest). Viewed as a rather typical petty-bourgeois nationalist maneuver to displace existing WASP elites by accusing them of lack of patriotism, it becomes much more comprehensible, and even rational.[49]

As noted in the last chapter, one aspect of populist nationalism in the United States has always been a very strong element of class antagonism against the "East Coast elites." This is a hatred in which old "core" Protestant populations and newer immigrants can join, and has helped the populist nationalist tradition to become multiethnic. The origins of the strong strain of anti-intellectualism in this American tradition owe much to a fusion of class hostility to the educated elites and religious–cultural fear of their supposed culture of atheism.[50]

This anti-intellectual and antielitist sentiment is at the emotional heart not only of the Tea Parties, but of the widespread mass contempt on the Right for expert opinion on climate change. If it does not fuel belief in creationism (this, of course, has far older religious roots), it certainly contributes to a willingness among many Americans to accept creationism as a reasonable argument, and to react against attempts by the intellectual elites to keep it out of schools and universities. A Gallup survey of 2007 found 39 percent of Americans polled declaring that creationism (defined as a belief that "God created human beings pretty much in their present form sometime in the past 10,000 years) is "definitely true," and another 27 percent declaring it is "probably true." Only 18 percent declared that evolution is "definitely true"—though 35 percent declared it "probably true," indicating a considerable number of people who think that both creationism and evolution are "probably true."[51]

McCarthy can also be seen as in some ways the high—or low—point of a certain set of patterns in Irish America that had been developing for well over a century. Of course, his stance also reflected the strong anti-Communism of the Catholic Church at the time, in part because of the savage oppression to which it was being subjected by Stalinist rule in Eastern Europe.

Also of great importance, however, was bitter Irish American ethnic and class resentment of the old northeastern Protestant elites, stirred up by the quasi-racist contempt with which they were treated for so many years by those elites: the term "white nigger," the vicious racist cartoons portraying the Irish as subhuman monkeys, the notices reading "no Irish need apply," the continual, ostentatious social contempt—as well as, of course, wider anti-Catholic sentiments that in 1928 contributed to the humiliating defeat of Al Smith, the first Irish American candidate for president.

One way in which the Irish sought integration was by stressing their whiteness, to escape the hated "white nigger" epithet and join the ruling race. This established a pattern of cooperation in racial matters between the Irish and the white South during the Civil War—and especially in the New York conscription riots of 1863, posed a real threat to Union victory. Always present under the surface, it became of great political importance once again from the 1960s on, when many Irish and other white ethnic working class groups joined the white South in quitting the Democratic Party in protest at supposed Democrat pandering to the blacks.[52]

Class, however, was always almost as important as race. "From start to finish, McCarthy got his largest response from the New York Irish when he attacked the institutions of the White Anglo-Saxon Protestant Establishment."[53] This rhetorical appeal to the masses against the treacherous elites and intellectuals has of course been a characteristic of radical nationalist movements since their beginnings.[54] Rarely, however, has it been so explicit as in the United States. As a recent defender of McCarthy, Ann Coulter, has written, "[McCarthy's] appeal was directed to a sturdier set—the mass of ordinary Americans...From McCarthy to Richard Nixon to Ronald Reagan, it is conservatives who appeal to workers. When Republicans ignite the explosive power of the hardhats, liberals had better run for cover...McCarthy was beloved by workers. He had a gift for appealing to the great common sense of the American people."[55]

This hatred of the intellectual elites was strengthened by the failure of the Irish Catholics as a group to advance beyond a certain socioeconomic level—lower middle class and upper working class—even as a much more recent immigrant group, the Jews, went rocketing past them as the twentieth century progressed. It became strongly associated with a measure of anti-intellectualism, in part because for a long time the Irish of America—in striking contrast to their compatriots at home in Ireland—failed to produce an intellectual class in proportion to their numbers.[56]

McCarthyism also appeared at a time when the Irish Americans as a group had reached the maximum political power they were to achieve in America, and had begun to decline politically. John F. Kennedy's presidency and Tip O'Neill's speakership were both a number of years in the future, but at the local level in New York and the other great northern cities, the power of the old Irish Democratic machine was already in decline, whittled away by other immigrant groups.[57]

One other factor should be kept in mind, because it fits into wider American patterns of defeat and the embittered nationalism that they help produce: the Irish sense of historical defeat, oppression, and dispossession by England. For if the Confederate South's historical experience of defeat is unique among America's geographical sections, this is certainly not true of its ethnic sections: Irish, Poles, and other American immigrants all brought with them ethnic memories of defeats even more terrible than those of the South. Even the southern Italians had been conquered, despised, and exploited by northern Italians, while Jews and Armenians had suffered infinitely more horrendously. Indeed, in many cases it was precisely the attacks and oppression they had suffered that brought the immigrants to America's shores.

All these groups have had a certain tendency to compensate for past humiliation and suffering by glorying in American national power—and, of course, in many cases (the Irish included), seeking to harness that power to the achievement of their own national aims. Many have sought to overcome their exclusion from the centers of national power, wealth, and prestige by becoming "200 percent" American nationalists.[58]

The Irish American novelist and essayist Thomas Flanagan has attributed the contradictions in the character and work of John Ford (John Aloysius Feeney) to "his double sense of himself as both American and Irish...Like Eugene O'Neill, he believed that being Irish carried with it a burden of moods, stances, loyalties, quarrels with the world. Working with the most popular of American cultural forms, he was conscious of a majority culture, from which the Irish, despite their bellicose loyalty to it, stood somewhat apart."[59]

Ford's *Fort Apache* is a fascinating summary of some of these contradictions. The U.S. Army is portrayed as a kind of Irish clan, with a smattering of former Confederate soldiers and WASP officers. Toward the WASP upper classes, symbolized by Colonel Owen Thursday (Henry Fonda) and his daughter, there is a mixture of resentment, contempt, admiration, and desire for intermarriage.[60]

As shown in Ford's work, and in accordance with their self-image, cultural tradition, and economic status, the Irish Americans sought to overcome their exclusion not only through militant nationalism, but specifically through being "first in war."[61] They have sought with great success to turn the image of the fighting Irishman from a drunkard in a saloon to that of Colonel "Wild Bill" Donovan leading his regiment into the Argonne in 1918, and the Sullivan brothers dying to a man on the USS *Juneau* off Guadalcanal in 1942. This success was rooted in the fact that it reflected something real about the Irish Americans—as demonstrated by Ford himself, who though well overage for military service, showed conspicuous courage and determination as a documentary filmmaker for the U.S. Navy in World War II. In Hollywood, the Irish American actor, James Cagney, played both Irish criminals and Irish soldiers.[62]

In seeking prestige and national integration through bellicose nationalism, the Irish strongly resembled the white South after the Civil War—and according to Grady McWhiney, came from the same ultimate roots anyway.[63] John Ford's admiration for the military record of the Confederacy emerges both from some of his Westerns and from his biopic of "history's most decorated Marine," Lieutenant General Lewis B. "Chesty" Puller, whose grandfather was killed fighting for the Confederacy.[64]

For part of the twentieth century the Irish Americans, like other ethnic groups, had a particular need to assert their military nationalism because this had been made suspect by their stance in the early years of both World War I and II. In the run-up to both wars, hostility toward Britain had led many of them to take up positions of fierce isolationism, which led to accusations of treachery when America did go to war.

However, during the anti-Communist hysteria of the early 1950s "the Irish derived a strong temporary advantage from the McCarthy period...In the era of security clearances, to be an Irish Catholic became *prima facie* evidence of loyalty. Harvard men were to be checked; Fordham [a Catholic college in New York with mainly lower middle class Irish American students] men would do the checking."[65]

This image is still exploited by blowhard nationalist Irish American media figures like Sean Hannity and Bill O'Reilly, with their talk of America being "the greatest best country God ever gave man" [*sic*].[66] Although both are of middle class backgrounds, in an effort to appeal to their specific audience, both have adopted a proletarian style, and O'Reilly has even allegedly constructed a fake Irish American working class background for himself.[67]

For a long time the Irish-dominated American Catholic Church itself was thoroughly nationalist, a spirit that only increased in the first years of the cold war: "Irish, Catholic and American became almost identical in the Irish-American mind."[68] Since the 1960s, however, this nationalistic orientation of the American Catholic Church as a whole has changed somewhat.

First, Vatican II licensed the development of liberal and reformist tendencies that have survived through subsequent decades of reaction. Then these were mobilized by opposition to the Vietnam War. But equally important, the Catholic Church is, of course, a universal church. Its inevitable and instinctive tendency to a certain internationalism and respect for international institutions can be seriously at odds with American nationalism. This has become apparent since the end of the cold war, when Pope John Paul II, a great hero of anti-Communism, took positions on international affairs that seriously angered American nationalists, including Catholics, by strongly criticizing Israel and opposing the Iraq War. No such international inhibition has affected the American fundamentalist churches, which are indeed now the most purely national Christian churches outside the Orthodox world.

The Christian Right

From the end of Prohibition to the 1970s, however, these fundamentalist churches were largely absent from direct politics. They were almost in a form of "internal emigration," so completely did the dominant culture appear to have shifted against them. One book of essays on the new religious Right of the 1980s and 1990s is revealingly entitled *No Longer Exiles*, and a 1979 essay on the Jewish tradition in America described demands to define the United States as a Christian nation "local eccentricities." Max Lerner's monumental work of 1957, *American Civilization*, devotes only 14 pages (703–717) out of 950 to a systematic examination of Christianity in America.[69]

This process was encouraged by the waves of mockery that fell on fundamentalists after the so-called Monkey Trial in 1925, when a teacher, John Thomas Scopes, was prosecuted by the state of Tennessee for teaching Darwin's theory of evolution. The state won the case, but the arguments of the populist and evangelical leader, former Secretary of State William Jennings Bryan, who appeared for the prosecution, were made to appear utterly foolish by the defense and the media (with Mencken inspired to some of his most ferocious sallies). Bryan declared that "all the ills from which America suffers can be traced back to the teaching of evolution.

It would be better to destroy every other book ever written, and just save the first three verses of Genesis."[70]

It seemed for decades that such figures would never again be taken seriously in national politics; in other words, that the United States would in fact take much the same path as the rest of the industrialized world.[71] These decades strengthened still further the feeling among Protestant fundamentalists of being a persecuted minority, "strangers here, as in a foreign land," as the hymn has it. This feeling has old roots in the Christian tradition, but also fed into wider sentiments of defeat, alienation, and paranoia on the Right in America.[72]

Thus Lyndon Johnson, whose entire political career occurred in the decades between the repeal of Prohibition and the emergence of the new Christian Right, never had to deal with this particular kind of politics at a national level. In their standard textbook on U.S. history, published in 1969, Samuel Eliot Morison and his colleagues entitled the section on Prohibition, the Scopes Trial, and the revived Ku Klux Klan, "Nineteenth Century America's Last Stand."[73]

This, of course, has proved a grave mistake. Though "it would be almost a half century before large numbers of evangelicals again discovered an elite diabolic enough to make the building of their own mass movement seem both imperative and possible," the fundamentalist churches were not really undermined in their geographical and cultural heartlands, and in those areas, the insults and contempt of the metropolitan elites blended with other resentments to make their views, if anything, even more popular.[74] By the 1990s the fundamentalist counterattack against the teaching of evolution in schools was back with a vengeance.

Although the churches were largely absent from politics and government, they did not withdraw from society. On the contrary, these decades saw the evangelical churches spread both to new media—with the appearance of Billy Graham, and later the "televangelists"—and to new areas of the United States.[75] Although Graham himself was in most ways a political moderate, the world he represented also played a great part in McCarthyism.

The American churches, and especially the evangelical and fundamentalist ones, were able not just to retain, but in some respects expand their followings at a time when in the rest of the developed world religious belief and practice was in steep decline. One reason for this is that they have played a significant role in softening some of the harsher aspects of change for many Americans—especially migration from country to cities, and consequent social atomization.

Given the speed of socioeconomic change in America, the consequent atomization of society, and the lack of welfare and health safety nets comparable to those of other developed countries, this role has been all the more necessary and has helped them to retain their hold on important sections of society. Across much of America, churches have in a sense continued the formative role they played on the American frontier; and in doing so, they have helped maintain the cultural worlds that generate American populist nationalism.

It is important to recognize the immense amount of work and self-sacrifice that goes into these efforts, and the deep religious faith that inspires them. Liberals who mock conservative Christians as nothing more than bigoted hicks who swallow a religious opiate fed them by the capitalists are guilty of bad manners, bad politics, and bad analysis. They fail to understand both the tremendous importance of religion in much of American society, and the ways in which religion is a force for good—in some parts of America, perhaps the only organized force for good.

This is even true of some figures rightly seen by liberals as extreme and negative forces in American life, like Michele Bachmann and Sarah Palin. To understand both their appeal to so many people and the real force and drive of their personalities, it is necessary to understand—and respect—the religious faith that led Bachmann to foster (and apparently greatly help) 23 troubled teenage girls, and Sarah Palin's decision to give birth to and care for a child prenatally diagnosed with Down syndrome.

Many large American Protestant churches, with their associated web of schools; study groups; parents' groups; children's, adolescents', men's, women's, and seniors' clubs; marriage counseling services; excursions; sports activities; and even collective tourism (often to the Holy Land), form dense communities with a strong aspect of social welfare. They have in fact played a central role in bringing a sense of community to what would otherwise be the flat, arid social plains of many American suburbs—or in the words of Garrison Keillor, "if you want to meet single women in Minnesota, maybe you should join a church."[76]

In this sense, the churches resemble the Catholic Church of the nineteenth century (which played a related role among the new inhabitants of the great cities in Europe and America) much more than the anemic European churches of today.[77] And as with the Catholic Church in the past, this has also given conservative Protestant tendencies a formidable capacity for political mobilization and organization, both in the past and today in the "Christian Coalition" and associated movements.

The shift of the Southern Baptist Convention to de facto support for the Republican Party since the 1970s has stemmed from a general white Southern move in that direction, but has also reinforced that trend. It has left Democratic Southern Baptists like Bill Clinton and Al Gore in a decidedly minority position within their own church. In most of the South, their faith was of limited help to them among whites in either 1992 or 1996, and Gore's failure to carry the region in 2000 doomed his bid for the presidency.[78]

Also of great importance has been the replacement of urbanization with suburbanization. Urbanization around the world has generally marked a radical shift in environment and values from culturally homogeneous small towns and rural areas to heterogeneous, ethnically, culturally, and even racially mixed cities. A transformation in values, including most often a decline in religious faith, has been the general long-term result, stemming of course from the disintegration of small, relatively isolated communities.

Suburbanization is a rather different matter. It allows—and, in its American form, is often explicitly or implicitly *intended* to allow—the preservation of a "small-town" world as far as family life and culture are concerned: racially homogeneous, and also potentially at least culturally homogeneous, traditional, church-going, and patriotic.[79] The spread of (softened and modernized) forms of Southern culture, including country music, to much of the rest of the United States can be traced in part to the move of "middle class" whites away from urbanism and toward suburbanism.[80] Therefore, if American nationalism in 2004 sometimes resembles European nationalisms before 1914, that is because in some American regions, aspects of society and culture are closer to Europe in 1914 than Europe in 2004.[81]

In the preservation of this re-created small-town atmosphere, the evangelical Protestant churches have played a very important role, and as noted, this has helped not only preserve them in their traditional heartlands, but expand them to much of the rest of the United States.[82] Indeed, the strong recovery of religious belief and practice in the United States after World War II was contemporaneous with the astonishing growth of suburbia, and probably closely associated with it.[83]

The figures both for religious belief in the United States and for the strength within this sector of the "fundamentalist" element are somewhat disputed. A Gallup poll of 1993 showed 42 percent of Americans describing themselves as "born again." However, this figure includes both many members of the so-called mainline churches for whom this is more a formal statement of theological belief than a deeply felt personal statement, and black evangelicals, who with rare exceptions are not led by this belief to vote Republican. A study of 1996 by George Barna found 66 percent of Americans saying that they had made a "personal commitment to Jesus Christ," up from 60 percent in the 1980s. About one-third of the public attends church once a week, and another third at least once a month. The remaining third never attends.[84]

According to a survey published in 2011 by the University of Michigan, white evangelical Protestants (including churches defining themselves as "fundamentalist") made up 26.3 percent of the U.S. population in that year—an increase of almost 5 percent since 2000, which led to them overtaking the Catholics as America's largest religious grouping. Although the evangelicals have spread all over the United States, by far their greatest concentration of strength remains in the "Bible Belt" of the greater South and its outlying regions.

"Mainline Protestants" (Episcopalians, Methodists, Lutherans, and so on) declined to 18.1 percent, from 21.2 percent in 2000. This continued the historic shift in balance between the evangelicals and the mainline churches that began in the 1960s.[85] According to a Pew survey, in 2011 black Protestants were 6.9 percent, Jews 1.7 percent, and other non-Christians in general 3 percent. In a really striking divergence from Europe, only 10.3 percent of respondents described themselves as atheists, agnostics, or "secular unaffiliated."[86] As the term "Bible Belt" suggests, these figures include striking regional variations. In 1986, according to Gallup, 48

144

percent of southerners (more than twice the national average) described themselves as "born again" Christians, compared to 31 percent of midwesterners, and only 19 percent of northeasterners (the wicked, atheist "East Coast" again).

Determining how many of these possess truly "fundamentalist" beliefs, or support the agenda of the Christian Right in politics (closely associated in turn with nationalist attitudes and the Tea Parties) is a difficult question.[87] A Pew poll of March 2004 indicated that in that year 40 percent of Americans believed in the literal, word-for-word truth of the Bible, with another 42 percent declaring that it is the word of God, but not necessarily literally true.[88] Of course, most of these people do not actually even attempt to render their beliefs into real behavior, but nonetheless this does give the more determined minority a wide ocean of public acceptance in which to swim, something that simply does not exist elsewhere in the developed world. According to Gallup, 18 percent of Americans polled in 1993 believed that floods that year were a punishment by God for the sins of the people living on the Mississippi River.[89]

In Britain, even Tony Blair's far more moderate religious beliefs were toned down by his advisers for fear of public mockery and alienation. Advisers would never recommend this in the United States. By 1976, the overtly "born again" religious identity of presidential candidate Jimmy Carter of Georgia was already sufficiently appealing to the electorate that President Gerald Ford felt compelled to declare himself "born again"—though he was an Episcopalian![90]

With the exception of George Bush the elder, all subsequent U.S. presidents have also declared themselves "born again"—and in the case of Reagan and George Bush the younger, it would seem, quite sincerely. In a poll conducted in 1998, 56 percent of Americans declared that they would not vote for an atheist as president (admittedly a big change from 1958, when 82 percent said this).[91] Playing on this, George Bush the elder, like all Republican candidates over the past generation, declared in 1992 that "I believe with all my heart that one cannot be president without a belief in God." In 1996 more than one-fifth of registered members of the Republican Party described themselves as belonging to the Christian Right.[92] In the 2004 Democratic primary campaigns, several candidates declared, most improbably, that they had discovered religion while campaigning.[93]

It has been suggested that between one-third and one-half of the white evangelicals (including the fundamentalists), or about 7 percent to 12 percent of the entire population of the United States, support the Christian Right or at least share its ideology, with a large majority of these also supporting the Tea Parties.

However, the strength of the fundamentalists, like the strength of some ethnic minorities, lies not so much in numbers, but in relatively greater commitment—including high rates of turnout in elections—willingness to vote and agitate over particular issues, readiness to make personal sacrifices of time and money, and concentration in politically strategic regions. As in the Republican Party as a whole, this may have given the Christian Right an influence in the Tea Parties considerably greater than their proportion of the grass-roots membership—though not enough to turn the movement as a whole toward moral and cultural issues rather than tax cuts and the Constitution. In the words of former Republican House Majority Leader Dick Armey: "Government goes to those who show up."[94]

As Christian Coalition leader Ralph Reed has noted, concern over education and other local issues made Christian conservative activists over time into a formidable force in local politics (on school boards and so forth), laying the basis for their later success in national politics: "The advantage we have is that liberals and feminists don't generally go to church. They don't gather in one place three days before the election."[95] Christian conservative colleges have also proved a useful source of Republican campaign workers.[96] This has probably also given Christian Rightists in the Tea Parties an influence much greater than their actual proportion of the rank-and-file of that movement.

The power of the fundamentalists, like that of other highly motivated minority groups, has been greatly increased by the very low voter turnout in U.S. elections. Thus in the Congressional midterm elections of November 2010, the Republicans made extensive gains in the Senate and House of Representatives with the votes of barely 15 percent of those registered to vote in the districts concerned. Of a figure this small, the fundamentalists can obviously form a very large and powerful proportion.

The Christian Right of the 1970s arose above all as a reaction to the legalization of abortion. This was indeed a matter of deep concern to Christians, and one that united evangelical Protestants and Catholic conservatives like William Bennett. However, as in earlier periods, the fury over abortion also formed part of a much wider sentiment of fear and resentment that motivated both the Christian Right and the wider new Right of which it was part.[97]

The 1960s and 1970s saw defeats for the culture of the white South and the heartland that together were greater than anything experienced since the Civil War. The term "Negro socio-economic revolution," used by Kevin Phillips to describe aspects of the 1960s, is overdrawn, but certainly reflects the way many whites felt then, and even to a degree still do today.[98] Civil rights for blacks, coupled with inner-city rioting and pressure for concessions in education and housing, terrified and infuriated large portions of the white middle class, creating a new alliance between the white South and the Midwest along similar lines to the original "Jacksonian" alliance that for more than a century formed the foundation of the Democratic Party. The enforced "busing" of white children to black majority schools in order to encourage racial equality helped spread fear and hatred of government from the South to the white working classes of northern and midwestern cities. Not just that, but the more fashionably radical sections of the intelligentsia began actively to celebrate supposed "black" values, and sneer at "white" ones in ways that hit unfashionable, poor, small-town whites on the very rawest of nerves.[99] The legacy of this is still reflected in widespread hostility to Barack Obama, despite his stable marriage, public displays of religiosity, and complete espousal of respectable "white" values.

The sexual revolution, of which legalized abortion was part, struck at the very foundations of the conservative idea of the family. The sexualization of adolescence (which sits so oddly alongside savage laws against teenage sex in a number of states) became central to the marketing strategies of vast sectors of American capitalism. The appearance of open homosexuality was viewed by some fundamentalists as a sign of the impending end of the world. The reaction of conservative society to this became more, not less intense in the 1990s as homosexual and lesbian characters began to appear in positive roles on mainstream TV, and even have whole sitcoms like *Will and Grace* devoted to them and their society. This potentially brought gay influence to every American family with a television.[100] In 2003–2004, a push to legalize gay marriage provided a new stimulus to Christian Rightist mobilization in support of the Republicans. As of 2012, this continues to be a major theme of the Christian Right and of Republican presidential candidates close to the Right, though it played only a very small part in Tea Party rhetoric.

To conservative Christian America, the "counterculture" in general appeared as an unspeakably hateful, diabolical attack on its idea of society. Limited but vocal sections of American youth revolted against military service and patriotic values, and for the first time in its history, America was defeated in a war.[101] The Catholics had been hated in the past, but at least their ideas of family, sexual morality, and manly behavior were not significantly different from those of the hard-line evangelicals. To a traditional mind, the American culture that developed after the 1960s by contrast seemed like something out of Hieronymus Bosch, literally a pandemonium of scarcely credible monsters and abominations, and much of television constitutes nothing less than a daily assault on their world of faith and culture. Finally, beginning with the oil shock of 1973, the 1970s saw the end of the long postwar boom and the beginning of three decades of unprecedented decline in real incomes for the American middle classes, followed after 2007 by a very sharp downward plunge. The old white working and middle classes of the Midwest had got used to a world in which respectability and steady work guaranteed a steadily rising income and social status. The end of this world has been a dreadful blow to their "moral economy."[102] This combination of defeats provides much of the explanation for the embittered, mean-spirited, defensive, and aggressive edge to the contemporary American rightwing, and to the American nationalism that it espouses. Even when apparently in power, they still feel defeated. Its proponents have essentially spent many years trying to wipe out the defeats of the 1960s and early 1970s.

A hope exists—strongly reflected in the Republicans' 1994 "Contract with America" and in the Tea Parties—that given sufficient will, America can somehow be turned back to the perceived golden age of Eisenhower in the 1950s.[103] Since it cannot be admitted that American capitalist development itself is largely responsible for hated social and cultural change, the failure of this program must necessarily be explained by the "devil theory of politics": the resistance of wicked forces at home and abroad, notably the "liberal elites," especially in the media, their supposed allies in Europe, and the national enemies they supposedly pamper elsewhere in the world. President Obama has been only the latest in a series of such constructed "devils." And bizarre though it may seem in view of the power of conservative groups, if the standard for a healthy conservative society is the America of the 1950s, then of course the conservatives have been defeated, and always will be.

The context of the Vietnam War made the cultural changes of the 1960s and 1970s all the worse as far as many Americans were concerned. The perceived association with military defeat was indeed fatal to the chances of a successful progressive liberalism in appealing to wider sections of the American mainstream. The Christian Right, like the Right in general, was deeply committed to anti-Communism, opposing the second Strategic Arms Reduction Treaty (START II), demanding higher military spending and a tough antiradical strategy in Central America, supporting Ronald Reagan's "evil empire" rhetoric, and also supporting Taiwan against "Red China."[104] And this "anti-Communism" formed part of a wider complex of hardline nationalist attitudes; for politicians associated with the Christian Right, like my friends in Troy, Alabama, also bitterly opposed the abandonment of American rule over the Panama Canal Zone and demanded the toughest possible policies against Iran.[105] Since 9/11, the United States has not suffered a military defeat on the scale of Vietnam, but if, as seems likely, by 2025 China overtakes America to become the greatest economic power in the world, this could in its own way be an even more shattering blow to American middle class pride and self-confidence.

One of Jerry Falwell's most publicized campaigns was entitled "I Love America." The meetings, propaganda, and rhetoric of the Christian Right have always been suffused with nationalism and national symbolism. One evangelical pastor with an apocalyptic bent and considerable influence on the Right, retired Colonel Robert Thieme of Houston, became famous for wearing his old military uniform in the pulpit.[106] This tendency helps strengthen nationalist hatred of Europe in particular. According to conservative commentator Robert D. Novak, writing of Bush administration supporters in 2003, "these Bush backers see the President under worldwide attack as a Christian, particularly in a Europe where atheism is on the rise and religion in decline."[107]

The radical nationalism of the religious Right naturally emerged particularly strongly after 9/11 and fused with religious hostility to Islam as a religion. Bush himself was bitterly criticized by sections of the religious Right for his speech of September 17, 2001, at the Islamic Center in Washington, DC, praising Islam as a "religion of peace."[108] Franklin Graham, son of the Reverend Billy Graham, called Islam "very evil and wicked, violent and not of the same God." Jerry Falwell described Mohammed as a terrorist—remarks from which Bush officially distanced himself and the administration.[109] The influential millenarian Hal Lindsey (author of the best-selling book in American history after the Bible) produced a strikingly hate-filled work that combined Christian and radical Israeli sources to vilify Islam in general.[110] The effect of this on the outside world has been severe.[111] Given the violent edge to extreme Rightist thought and behavior (in Europe as well as the United States), there is real reason to fear that such propaganda could pave the way for pogroms against Muslims in parts of America, if—God forbid— the country should suffer another catastrophic terrorist attack.

In their identification of the Christian religion with the nation, the fundamentalist wings of the American evangelical churches are now unique in Western Christendom (except for Northern Ireland, from which much of their tradition is ultimately derived). The Catholic Church, as noted, is universal by nature. The national Protestant churches of Western Europe have, since 1945, been strongly committed to internationalism. Even in England, it is several decades since the Anglican Church was last described as "the Conservative Party at prayer"; whereas in Texas, according to Larry McMurtry, "a flavorless Protestantism seems to have yielded super-patriotism as a by-product."[112]

The American "mainline" Protestant churches, like their European equivalents, with which they are linked in the World Council of Churches and other international organizations, have come to adopt generally liberal and internationalist positions. To find a Western parallel for the instinctive nationalism of some of the evangelicals, one would once again have to go back to Europe before 1939, or even before 1914. In Eastern Christendom, the Orthodox churches are often very closely identified with their respective nationalisms, and often indeed with chauvinist positions, but quite unlike in America, these have historically been state churches.

Millenarians and Nationalists

Of the American evangelicals, significant numbers also hold millenarian beliefs that have frightening implications for their attitudes both to the outside world and to U.S. politics. In 1977 the number of American premillennialists alone was conservatively estimated at eight million. Premillennialists believe in Christ's bodily return *before* his thousand-year earthly reign; postmillennialists (a majority of the "mainline" Protestant churches) believe in his return only after the millennium has already been established by the power of God working through his people. This is a distinction with crucial implications for attitudes to politics, history, and the possibility and desirability of Christians seeking to bring about positive social change in this life.[113] The great majority of the leaders of the Christian Right have been premillennialists, and often from a more extreme variant of this belief known as dispensationalism. In 1987, 63 percent of Southern Baptist pastors declared themselves premillenarian.[114]

A very much larger number of Americans have some belief in "prophecy": that the Bible—and especially the book of Daniel and the Revelations of St John— provides accurate predictions of future events.[115] This is indicated by the popularity of millenarian religious fiction, such as Hal Lindsey's *Late Great Planet Earth* (28 million copies sold by 1990), or more recently, the "Rapture" series of Tim LaHaye and Jerry B. Jenkins. To date, this series has sold more than 40 million copies, putting Harry Potter to shame and making it by a long stretch the most successful series in the history of American print fiction. LaHaye was a cofounder (with Jerry Falwell) of the Moral Majority, the pioneering Christian Rightist group that laid the foundation for the later and much more successful Christian Coalition.[116]

These readership figures demonstrate once again a profound distance between a considerable part of the American population and modernity as the rest of the world understands it, as well as the rationalist and universalist principles of the American Creed. For not only is this tradition deeply and explicitly hostile to the Enlightenment and to any rational basis for human discourse or American national unity, it cultivates a form of insane paranoia toward much of the outside world in general. Thus *The End of the Age*, a novel by Pat Robertson, features a con-spiracy between a Hilary Clintonesque first lady and a Muslim billionaire to make the antichrist president of the United States. The antichrist has a French surname, and was possessed by Satan, in the form of the Hindu god Shiva, while serving with the Peace Corps in India.[117]

As China overtakes the United States, it can be expected that more and more such fantasies will focus on China as the new version of the beast from the apoc-alypse. Chinese observers of my acquaintance for their part look on American fundamentalism with a mixture of contempt, satisfaction, bewilderment, and fear. The contempt and satisfaction come from the fact that they see the antisci-entific and antirational elements in these religious ideologies as undermining America's educational, scientific, and economic lead, and helping China not just to overtake America economically, but to present itself to the world as the new image and standard of successful modernity. The bewilderment and fear come from an inability to understand how developments like those in America can be happening in a modern country, and a fear as to what policies the United States might adopt in the future if such forces become dominant in a U.S. administration.

American apocalyptic literature is not encouraging in regard to future atti-tudes toward China, since it is utterly, shockingly ruthless in its treatment of the unsaved—in other words, the vast mass of humanity. In accordance with one strand in prophetic belief, the "Rapture" series begins with God's selected being taken up to heaven in an instant, and dwells lovingly on the immense casualty rates that result as pilotless planes and driverless cars crash all over the world—with most of the victims presumably going to hell.[118]

The moral tone of such attitudes has real consequences for how these believ-ers think about the world today. Thus I remember the words of my "born again" landlady during a stay in Washington, DC, in 1996–1997. When challenged that the Bible cannot be literally God's word, for in this case sections of the books of Exodus and Joshua in particular would make God guilty of ordering genocide, she replied, in honey-sweet tones, "but don't you see, if those people had been wiped out 3,000 years ago as God ordered, we wouldn't have all these problems in the

Middle East today." Some millenarian language achieves a kind of pornography of hatred in its description of the fate of the damned, especially those from nations hostile to the United States.[119]

As these words suggest, one of the most important effects of millenarian thinking in the religious conservative camp in recent years has been to help cement the alliance of this camp with hard-liners in Israel—a subject that will be explored in chapter 6. This has become one of the most important practical connections between this sector of American culture and aspects of contemporary American nationalism. In the context of American nationalism, of particular interest is "dominion" or "reconstruction" theology—a relatively minor current in itself, but one that has been of great influence in the thinking of leading figures in the Christian Right like Pat Robertson and Michele Bachmann.

This theology is based on Genesis 1:26–29, in which God gives to Adam and Eve dominion over the Earth and all its plants and creatures. This has been taken as giving Christians dominion over the Earth, and has been used as an antienvironmentalist argument, since God has also given them the right of unlimited exploitation of the Earth's resources. Since America is, in the general evangelical view, the world's leading Christian nation, the implications for American power are also clear: "Our goal is world domination under Christ's lordship, a 'world takeover' if you will . . . We are the shapers of world history."[120]

These beliefs play their part in fuelling the tendency of the American Right to implacable nationalist moral absolutism, with a succession of foreign leaders from Hitler to Saddam Hussein identified as the antichrist or the antichrist's servant (earlier, of course, the Vatican had often played this role). Because Satan is supposed to be deceitful and alluring, these leaders do not even have to be actively hostile. In these circles, Mikhail Gorbachev was widely identified with the antichrist precisely because of his popularity in the West. Both millenarian belief itself and the tendency of its American exponents to link it to hard-line U.S. foreign and security policies were given a tremendous boost by the cold war and the much wider image of the Soviet Union as an "empire of evil." Since 9/11, the antichrist has naturally been identified as Muslim.[121]

Because the antichrist is supposed to extend his dominion over the whole earth, these beliefs fuse with nationalist ones in absolute, untrammeled American national sovereignty to produce a widespread and pathological hatred of the United Nations on the American Right, and the dark fantasies associated with these views—which are extraordinarily widespread in U.S. society, and by no means just in the Bible Belt.[122] The European Union (EU) too can be made to play this apocalyptic role, for example, in the pages of the millenarian journal *The Philadelphia Trumpet*, which sees the EU as a new "Holy Roman Empire" under German rule.[123] The Trilateral Commission and the Council on Foreign Relations have also frequently been portrayed as agencies of the antichrist for world unification and domination.

President Kennedy was cast in the role of the antichrist by some millenarians in the South, and according to a Harris poll of 2010, 14 percent of Americans polled and 24 per cent of registered Republicans said that President Obama was or might be the antichrist.[124] This poll has been widely criticized as exaggerated, but even if one were to halve the figure, it would still represent a significant proportion of (presumably) Republican voters. The belief in Obama as the antichrist has been linked to the constant rumors spread by Republicans that he is really Muslim.[125] As already noted, this talk is in part a code for racial hatreds that cannot now be publicly expressed, but it also taps into ancient beliefs and paranoias among fundamentalist Christians. Millenarian belief is not chiefly or even most probably largely responsible for the hysterical hatred directed at President Obama by the Right, but it does seem to contribute to its ferocity.[126]

Millenarian beliefs also feed into a wider American "ecology of fear," to use the phrase coined by Mike Davis for Los Angeles, and therefore a wider culture of national paranoia and aggression.[127] As Paul Boyer points out in his magisterial book on this subject, the strength of millenarian feelings among a minority of Americans means that it has also had an effect on wider culture, feeding into Hollywood films like the "Omen" series, science fiction novels, and pop music.[128]

Often these fantasies have a racial edge—as with the antichrist fantasies about Obama. Thus in 1999 Jerry Falwell, the influential televangelist, millenarian, and Christian Right politician, warned his followers to prepare for possible chaos as a result of computer meltdown (a consequence of the so-called Y2K or Millennium Bug problem) by stocking up on essential supplies. These, he said, should include arms and ammunition, to protect the well-provided (the "careful virgins," if you will) against the hungry and improvident others—and we can be pretty sure what colors he imagined those others were going to be. Drawing once again on "heartland" anti-immigrant and antiurban sentiments, much of apocalyptic literature is set amidst urban collapse and upheaval. Hal Lindsey, for his part, was possessed by pathological fear of the "Yellow Peril"—a fear that he has now transferred to Islam.[129]

Finally, in the context of American traditions of defeat and their link to paranoia and aggression, we must note the strong element of class resentment in the whole millenarian tradition. This was superbly analyzed by Norman Cohn in his famous book *The Pursuit of the Millennium*, in which he saw the millenarian cults of medieval and early modern Europe, with their dreams of an egalitarian kingdom of God and the obliteration of the unrighteous rulers and masters, as acting in some ways as precursors of Communism (and in some cases of modern anti-Semitism).[130]

Cohn and others failed to notice, however, that while they were analyzing 500-year-old cults, millenarian groups embodying the same tradition were still alive in the America of their own day. In the United States there is a very strong correlation between such beliefs and poverty, residence in the countryside and small towns, and, above all, lack of education.[131] This, of course, fed into wider Southern and heartland resentments of the "East Coast elites," and lower-class resentments of the elites in general, especially those widely identified as of "alien" origin, like bankers. Indeed, some historians have seen U.S. fundamentalism as a whole as a form of "opium of the people," a process that diverts socioeconomic resentments into a form that is hostile to the culture of the elites but does not threaten their actual power.[132]

Again and again in millenarian fiction, wealthy, educated, and prestigious figures perish and go to hell because of their wicked lifestyles, while simple, ordinary, God-fearing believers are saved. Millenarian writers equally regularly excoriate American hedonism and consumer culture. As throughout history, American millenarianism is to a great extent a "religion of the disinherited," a form of spiritual Socialism for people who are not able, for whatever reason, to be Socialist.[133] According to Billy Graham, "Let me tell you something: when God gets ready to shake America, he may not take the PhD and the DD. God may choose a country boy. God may choose a shoe salesman like He did D. L. Moody...God may choose the man that nobody knows, a little nobody to shake America for Jesus Christ in this day."[134]

Evangelical and especially millenarian preachers speak of the future kingdom of Christ on earth in terms that are strongly reminiscent of Karl Marx. It will be essentially a greatly improved America, stripped of poverty, sinfulness, and alien values: "much like the present life...but missing all the imperfections that have destroyed the full and true meaning of life." Christ's reign will bring "labor, adventure, excitement, employment and engagement." There is a very strong stress on the equality—including economic equality—of all believers in this future kingdom, in which all men will be kings.[135]

It would be quite wrong, though, to portray this segment of belief in America as purely the province of the poor and marginalized. On the contrary, as Paul Boyer, Grace Halsell, and other students of the subject have emphasized, it has considerable influence both among the regional elites of the South and West, and among the Republican national elites. The Pentecostalist faith, closely linked to millenarian belief, includes in its number John Ashcroft and a number of senior military officers. Pat Robertson, cofounder of the Christian Coalition, who has spoken of liberal America doing to evangelical Christians "what Nazi Germany did to the Jews," is the son of a U.S. Senator, from a patrician Virginia family.[136]

The link between millenarianism and radical nationalism was exemplified by Lieutenant General William G. "Jerry" Boykin, a Pentecostalist believer appointed in 2003 as deputy under-secretary of defense for intelligence. A minor scandal blew up in that year when the content of some talks that General Boykin had given to Evangelical church groups in the United States made their way into the national media (President Bush eventually condemned General Boykin's statements, but did not dismiss him from his post, one that, it may be noted, later involved a measure of responsibility for the intelligence-gathering strategy that contributed to the abuses at Abu Ghraib and elsewhere).

Among other things, General Boykin declared that America is a "Christian nation," and that George Bush had been elevated to the presidency by a miracle—an idea with which many Democrats would agree, but not quite as General Boykin meant it. Of judgments by the U.S. Supreme Court of which he disapproved, he said, "don't you worry about what these courts say. Our God reigns supreme." He informed his listeners that in examining photographs of Mogadishu, where he served as a special forces officer, he found an unexplained black mark, which he explained as a manifestation of evil; and that there were actually two more planes taken over by terrorists on 9/11, but they were "thwarted by the hand of God."[137]

America's enemy in the war against terrorism, he said, is Satan, and he will only be defeated "if we come against him in the name of Jesus." Most famously, General Boykin said of a Somali warlord, "I knew that my God was bigger than his. I knew that my God was a real God and his was an idol." This last was widely described as "crude machismo," which it may have been, but it was also a straight biblical reference to the victorious contests of Hebrew prophets with the priests of Baal.[138] Similar statements concerning Islam have emanated from several leaders of the Christian Right, including Franklin Graham (son of Billy), Jerry Falwell, and the Reverend Ted Haggard, president of the National Association of Evangelicals.[139]

Concerning the United States itself, leading officials of the Bush administration made no secret of their belief that the American state rests on essentially religious foundations, that "the source of freedom and human dignity is the Creator," in Ashcroft's words.[140] Even Vice President Dick Cheney sent a Christmas card in 2003 with a message asking, in the words of Benjamin Franklin, "And if a sparrow cannot fall to the ground without His notice, is it probable that an empire can rise without His aid?"[141]

General Boykin's remarks indicate once again two salient features of this sector of American society, as discussed above. The first is their intense nationalism. As for the English and Scottish Puritans of the seventeenth century, from whom they derive their religious culture—as indeed for the Israelites of the Old Testament—their God is essentially a tribal God, a Cromwellian "God of Warre" who fights for them against Amelekites, Irish papists, Red Indians, Mexicans, Spaniards, Germans, Japanese, Communists, Russians, Chinese, Vietnamese, Muslims, and any other enemy who comes along.

The second is that their religion-based culture is to a very great extent pre-modern and definitely pre-Enlightenment. A comparison of General Boykin with his equivalents in other armed forces is instructive. A great many French, British, and Russian officers would feel more comfortable in the nineteenth century, and some surviving aristocratic elements in the eighteenth century. British officers in particular sometimes have an affection for horses that trembles on the brink of impropriety. However, the golden ages they yearn for are still post-Enlightenment. Unlike General Boykin, they would not feel at home in Cromwell's New Model Army. The extent of this ideologically premodern sector in the United States is therefore greater than almost anywhere else in the developed world—except for Northern Ireland.

This kind of religious nationalism is fuelled both by religious moralism and by a paranoia fed in turn by a feeling of cultural embattlement. In the words of Richard Hofstadter:

> Since what is at stake is always a conflict between good and evil, the quality needed is not a willingness to compromise but the will to fight things out to the finish. Nothing but total victory will do. Since the enemy is thought of as being totally evil and utterly unappeasable, he must be totally eliminated...This demand for unqualified victories leads to the formulation of hopelessly demanding and unrealistic goals, and since these goals are not even remotely attainable, failure constantly heightens the paranoid's frustration.[142]

The implications of this belief system for the "war on terrorism" will be one of the subjects explored in the next two chapters.

Five

The Legacy of the Cold War

Where the hell is Cambodia? People see a headline, and suddenly we're in trou-
ble in Cambodia. It's got to be somebody's fault, so we start attacking somebody.
The news is too fast and too confusing. We see a headline, and we go over to the
atlas to find out where Cambodia is. Then we attack somebody about it. We do
more damn talking about things we don't know anything about than anybody
in history.

—Sam Bloom (Texan businessman, 1960s)[1]

The cold war perpetuated and strengthened long-standing messianic, paranoid, and Manichaean strands in American nationalism. However, it also added a new element, largely unknown in the United States before World War II, but very important in the history of nationalism elsewhere: a massive military–industrial and security complex with great influence and a stake in promoting armed rivalry with other states.

Since the Vietnam War, the impact of this new force in American affairs has been seen above all in what I have described as the American Nationalist Party, or Republicans. However, it has had a strong presence among the Democrats as well. No one should have been surprised that while the Obama administration took a much more restrained, pragmatic, and multilateral approach than the Bush administration to a number of key issues, it also deferred heavily to the military establishment and remained devoted to preserving American military superiority and American dominance in the world. In the 1990s, although Bill Clinton some-what reduced the military budget, he also presided over both a still greater exten-sion of the U.S. military presence in the world and a geopolitical campaign to "roll back" the influence of Russia within the former Soviet Union.

This legacy of the cold war had a very damaging effect on U.S. strategy after 9/11, by helping to direct U.S. attention away from the terrorist groups themselves. In the words of James Mann, the collective biographer of the George W. Bush for-eign and security policy team, "the Vulcans [the name Bush's senior foreign and defense policy team gave themselves] were fully prepared to deal with security threats of the sorts they had confronted in the past—major powers, rogue states, dictators and land armies, all entities that operated inside fixed territories and identifiable borders—but they were not as ready to combat a stateless, amorphous terrorist organization like Al Qaeda."[2]

Moreover, even in confronting threats from states, their approach was based on a simplistic right-wing cold war paradigm of building up ever stronger American military forces. "The Vulcans were far less active in developing new institutions, diplomacy or other approaches that could deal with these issues."[3]

The cold war essentially created all the leading members of the Bush administration's foreign and security staff. Many had already been senior officials in Republican administrations of the 1970s.[4] As the official White House photographer of the Ford administration remarked concerning the George W. Bush administration: "I feel like Rip van Winkle. It's like I woke up twenty-five years later, and not only are my friends still in power, they're more powerful than ever."[5]

The Neoconservatives

The cold war also produced the neoconservative academic and bureaucratic grouping, whose members between 2001 and 2003 critically influenced the Bush administration and acted as some of its leading officials and propagandists.[6] The neoconservatives had their ultimate origin in the "Vital Center" group set up by Reinhold Niebuhr and others in the late 1940s to rally American liberals against the threat of Stalinist Communism. The "Vital Center" split over the Vietnam War, with the future neoconservatives generally taking up stances in support of the war and of tough anti-Soviet policies. Via support for the hawkish Democrat Senator Henry "Scoop" Jackson, most ultimately moved to the Republicans (though some remain formally Democrats to this day).[7]

Also of central importance to their development was their reaction against the left-wing "counterculture" of the 1960s, and especially its romantic, pacifist, anti-intellectual, and hooligan elements, and against the increasing tendency of the Left to condemn Israel. However, just as many of the original neoconservatives like Irving Kristol had been Trotskyite Marxists, so some of the second generation were also 1960s radicals, like Stephen Schwartz (of the "Foundation for the Protection of Democracy"), who later moved to the radical Right. In both generations they brought with them from the Left a radical style, a taste for vicarious violence, and a certain sense of politics as theater. In this, they closely resembled an old pattern in Europe of members of the radical Left crossing over to the radical Right (Mussolini is the most famous example of this sort of movement).[8]

As Irving Kristol admitted in a candid moment, a desire for drama played a part in his shift to the radical Right. In the 1950s he had become "bored with my own sensibly moderate liberal ideas."[9] Like many of the cold war elites in general, they have proved incapable of dropping this style once the ostensible reason for it—the Communist threat—disappeared.

Over time, the original neoconservative grouping became highly fractured.[10] Some of those still occasionally described as neoconservatives, like Samuel Huntington, in fact came to differ radically from the remaining core group on key issues, such as the right and ability of the United States to spread its values in the world, especially by force of arms.[11] Others, like the late Daniel Patrick Moynihan, broke with their former comrades a generation ago.

The remaining neoconservatives are best described as a kind of parabureaucratic grouping that (as Jacob Weisberg has pointed out), given the level of intermarriage and hereditary descent among its members, also somewhat resembles a sort of clan.[12] This kind of grouping is made possible by the American system's blurring of the lines between government, academia, the media, and business, which I described in chapter 2. The self-image of this grouping was encouraged by the cold war tendency in the American security elites as a whole to see themselves as a version of Plato's Guardians, a closed, all-knowing, elect group guiding, protecting (like guard dogs), and when necessary deceiving an ignorant and flaccid populace for its own good in order to protect it from ruthless enemies.[13]

In the case of the neoconservatives, this tendency was also encouraged by certain secretive and conspiratorial tendencies in the thought of one of their founding intellects, Leo Strauss.[14] His thoroughly Platonic belief that it is both necessary and legitimate for the philosophical elite to feed the populace with religious and patriotic myths in which the elites themselves do not believe may have contributed to the remarkable facility with which the neoconservatives over the years have abandoned prior positions (e.g., on humanitarian and democratic interventionism, as described in chapter 2) and formed alliances with groups, like the Christian Right, that should be quite alien to them.

This inconsistency and opportunism is one reason why, despite their harshly ideological tone and radical nationalism and imperialism, I would hesitate to describe the neoconservatives today as a true ideological tradition. Another is that for all their noise, they have not in fact contributed anything truly new to American political culture. With the exception of Leo Strauss and Allan Bloom, their works are characteristic of many radical nationalist movements in that they often combine fanaticism with dullness and banality. Most indeed are little more than collages of newspaper op-eds.

Rather, what they have done is to take some of the existing traditions described in this book and given them a radical and extremist twist. Thus they have turned sympathy for Israel into support for Likud, and they have taken beliefs in America's role as a democratic model and the need for American national security and turned them into arguments for interventionist war. The triumph of the neoconservative program under Bush was only possible in the context of a wider feeling of national emergency existing at times during the cold war, and in a more dramatic form after 9/11. However, because they tap into and seek to build upon the deep strains of American nationalism described in this book, the neoconservatives have a future even after the disasters of the Bush administration. In Justin Vaisse's words,

> Seeing neoconservatism as a form of nationalism only strengthens the likelihood that it will remain an intellectual force of some importance on the American scene and that it will someday make its influence felt once more, even though its fortunes now seem on the decline. Although it will always remain a minority school of thought, it resonates with certain deep currents in the American psyche, has a simple and powerful message, and is borne by a historical vision that justifies it in the eyes of those who want to believe. In short, neoconservatism has a future.[15]

Present Dangers, a book of essays by leading neoconservatives and other right-wing hard-liners, edited by Robert Kagan and William Kristol and published in 2000, provides evidence of how Bush administration policy might have developed had 9/11 not intervened. Its title intentionally recalled the "Committee on the Present Danger," a group of hard-line cold warriors that grossly exaggerated Soviet power and threats in the early 1980s. Such works remain worrying in the context of growing U.S. fears of China.

In keeping with the pre-9/11 realist tradition, the authors were indifferent to terrorism and issues of violence and stability within societies; of 15 essays, not one was devoted to terrorism as such (with the partial exception of one on Israel). Instead, they were obsessed with the threat to the United States from a range of supposedly powerful rival states, all of which must be approached with the maximum degree of toughness. "Appeasement" was a constant theme. The last essay of *Present Dangers*, for example, was a paranoid attempt to suggest that the U.S. position vis-à-vis China resembles that of Britain vis-à-vis Germany in the early 1930s.[16]

The former British diplomat Jonathan Clarke described the tendency the authors represent:

> Far from looking for ways to take the toxicity out of international problems, the authors purposefully seek out trouble spots (the Taiwan Strait, North Korea, Iraq) and then reach for the gas can…"Steely resolve" is the watchword, with the emphasis on steel. Indeed, it is hardly an exaggeration to say that if the book's combined recommendations were implemented all at once, the U.S. would risk unilaterally fighting at least a five-front war…
>
> There is a curious flavor of Nietzschean "will" running through this book. There is a constant appeal to the need to mobilize the people to war. The "present dangers" of the title turn out to be not external threats, but the possibility that the American people will not be sufficiently ready to lift up arms. There is a fascination with history's strong men, as if the "Triumph des Willen" was an admirable trait, albeit expressed as evil in certain of them. Whether this is really compatible with American ideals of limited, constitutional government by laws rather than men is a subject for another essay.[17]

This widespread and sinister obsession with national "will" among the neocon-servatives is brought out in a striking passage by Charles Krauthammer: "America is no mere international citizen. It is the dominant power in the world, more domi-nant than any since Rome. Accordingly, America is in a position to reshape norms, alter expectations and create new realities. How? By unapologetic and implacable demonstrations of will."[18]

And once again, these words were not written after 9/11, calling for a tough response to savage terrorism. They appeared in March 2001, and were pegged to what the author at that stage celebrated as a tough new Bush approach to dealing with Russia, a state which since 1991 had posed no direct threat whatsoever to the United States.

In such circles, neither 9/11 nor the bloody occupation of Iraq had much effect on this underlying psychological stance. If anything, it only widened the circle of enemies and intensified demands for America to display its will and toughness by deliberately standing alone. Thus the book *An End to Evil*, by Richard Perle and former Bush speechwriter David Frum (2003), expressed a greater or lesser degree of embittered hostility not just to the Muslim world, but to Russia, China, the United Nations, and every country or institution that had in any way questioned or resisted the United States over war with Iraq.

In this book the United States is advised to oppose European unity. Most of Western Europe is said to be affected by "the same jealousy and resentment that animate the terrorists"—an astonishingly extreme and provocative statement to come from a man still serving as a senior government advisor at the time he wrote it. No exception whatsoever was to be made for different terrorist movements, or between their political and military wings—except in the case of Russia, which is accused of having invented its terrorist threat and fabricated its terrorist attacks. The only country treated positively is Britain—whose views and interests are then treated with dismissive contempt.[19]

Despite public disillusionment with military interventions and state-build-ing programs, in 2012 neoconservatives remained of great importance in the Republican Party, dominating the foreign and security policy side of leading con-servative think tanks and journals, and continuing to contribute heavily to suppos-edly "mainstream" papers, including the *Washington Post*. In 2009 Bill Kristol, Robert Kagan, and Dan Senor launched a new organization, the Foreign Policy Initiative, with a wholly neoconservative agenda.[20]

Moreover, growing tension between a declining America and a rising China could give a new impetus to American beliefs in America's mission to lead "the free world" against "dictatorship," thereby giving neoconservatism a new lease on life. Neoconservatism therefore seems likely to play an important part in shaping the policy of any future Republican administration—unless, perhaps, that admin-istration is headed by a president who is a retired general, for in senior military circles there is far less admiration for this movement.

Confirmation of Myths

The development of a program of containment of China justified in terms of a "defense of democracy" would continue that of the cold war against Communism in general and the Soviet Union in particular. Ideologically speaking, the U.S. struggle against the Soviet Union was expressed above all in terms of defending democracy and freedom, though the theme of defending religion against Communist atheism was also present. The American struggle against first Nazism and then Communism naturally gave a tremendous new strength to messianic feelings stemming from the American Creed. These feelings stressed America's role as the exemplar, leader, protector, and savior of the "free world" in the battle against the evil Communist "enemies of freedom." Indeed, for a number of years these sentiments were justified, at least as far as Western Europe and (to a lesser extent) northeast Asia were concerned.

The successful democratization of Germany and Japan under U.S. occupation created a fatally alluring image of liberation by force that was to be trotted out later from Vietnam to Iraq. The historical, economic, geographical, cultural, and social positions and experiences of these countries bore no relation whatsoever to those of Germany and Japan, but no matter. The image of the U.S. soldier as conqueror, liberator, and modernizer rolled into one was already firmly established during the Spanish-American War and World War I, and drew on still older roots.[21]

As a result of a combination of old American myths and developments in the mid-twentieth century, this image achieved a power in the American mind that survived what should have been the shattering counterlesson of Vietnam, and which has offset to some extent fears of imperial involvements and military quagmires. The role of America as "guardian of freedom" was played on incessantly by official propaganda, political rhetoric, the media, and indeed much of American society. It achieved its most eloquent expression in the speeches of John F. Kennedy and Ronald Reagan—the first a Democrat, the second a Republican, but in this regard not easily distinguishable.

This image was used continuously by Bush and other officials after 9/11, and was of tremendous importance in the mobilization of support for the Iraq War. Even in the case of Afghanistan, the simple and justifiable arguments for war in self-defense against Al Qaeda were accompanied by surreal statements about turning that country into a "beachhead of democracy and progress in the Muslim world" (in the words of a U.S. senator at a conference I attended in 2002). As the aftermath of the Taliban's defeat has amply demonstrated, it bore no resemblance whatsoever to Afghan reality, and displayed a complete ignorance of modern Afghan history, society, and culture.[22]

But if the cold war strengthened the messianic aspects of the American Creed, then it poured new sustenance into the maw of America's demons and the "paranoid style" of American politics: an obsession with domestic subversion, a belief in an outside world dominated by enemies and potential traitors, a reliance on military force, and a contempt for many of America's leading allies. The cold war also strengthened messianic nationalism, expressed not only in the quasi-religious terms of adherence to the creed, but in the explicitly religious ones of belief in America as a nation chosen by God to lead the struggle against the enemies of God. These of course included "Godless Communism" and any forces associated with it, but by extension meant any enemies of America.

Coming right after the war against the Nazis, the cold war thus strengthened and indeed institutionalized the Manichean elements in the American view of the outside world, a belief in absolute powers of light led by America fighting against absolute forces of darkness. The struggle against a revolutionary and conspiratorial enemy also attracted a certain personality type on the U.S. side, people who saw themselves as a kind of anti-Communist revolutionary elite dedicated to fighting the Communist: self-described "Bolsheviks of the Right" like David Stockman, or the curious figure of Grover Norquist, a radical Rightist who reportedly admires Lenin's "iron dedication" and keeps his portrait in his living room—not behavior characteristic of your traditional conservative.[23]

This Manichaean tendency in the American right-wing and nationalist intellectual world at the start of the twenty-first century was perfectly summed up in a passage about the American Enterprise Institute (AEI) in 2003 by a horrified British observer, Mark Almond:

> Acting as the ideological enforcers of the Bush administration, the American Enterprise Institute is a kind of Cominform of the new world order. Its so-called scholars are the inquisitors of a global regime. Minutes of their foreign seminars are more like sitting in on a hate session from China's cultural revolution than a political science class at Yale. Participants rise to denounce the hate figure of the day or to endorse a visiting dignitary favored by the regime. There is an overwhelming stench of ideological conformity. Washington think-tanks promote not pluralism, but a Stalinist-style dogmatism with eulogized conformists and excommunicated heretics. This show-trial mentality is hardly surprising, as the American Enterprise Institute brings the ideological successors of McCarthy and renegade leftists together with émigrés educated in the Soviet bloc.[24]

This portrait is still true of the AEI in 2012. The extraordinary rigidity, narrowness, and authoritarianism of that institution was demonstrated in March 2010 when they dismissed David Frum, the neoconservative speechwriter allegedly responsible for Bush's "axis of evil" phrase. He was sacked for daring to criticize the Republican position on health care reform and warn the party against the closeness of its links to Fox News and figures like Rush Limbaugh. Frum's sacking followed a bitter attack on him by the *Wall Street Journal*. He was quoted by the *Washington Post* as saying that AEI staffers "had been ordered not to speak to the media" about health care "because they agreed with too much of what Obama was trying to do...The donor community is only interested in financing organizations that parrot the party line."[25]

The cold war both contributed to and legitimated the drives to hysterical hatred in radical conservative circles. In part precisely because these roots are so deep, this tendency outlived the disappearance of Communism in the early 1990s and was then directed both against new enemies abroad and "liberals" at home. These were people for whom the cold war atmosphere had become an addiction, irrespective of any intellectually serious analysis of real threats. Or as Irving Kristol wrote in 1993, "there is no 'after the Cold War' for me. So far from having ended, my Cold War has increased in intensity, as sector after sector has been corrupted by the liberal ethos. Now that the other 'Cold War' is over, the real Cold War has begun. We are far less prepared for this Cold War, far more vulnerable to our enemy, than was the case with our victorious war against a global communist threat."[26]

Domestic threats preoccupied the American radical Right for much of the cold war, often strangely eclipsing the Soviet Union as a menace in their minds.[27] This redirection of an ostensibly national struggle toward attacks on domestic enemies is also a much older and wider pattern in nationalism. As Alfred Cobban remarks of the French nationalists before 1914, "Though the nationalists of the early years of the 20th Century often used bellicose language and were xenophobic, their aggression was directed more against their compatriots than against foreigners."[28]

As Kristol's statement suggests, wars are always morally corrupting, and the cold war after all went on for a very long time compared to most "hot" wars. They are corrupting no less in their idealization of their own side than in their demonization of the enemy, and as noted, in their deliberate and systematic cultivation of hatred, including toward rival compatriots guilty of alleged weakness or treason in the face of the enemy. This has been a staple of American right-wing attacks on liberals throughout the cold war and post–cold war periods, taken to lunatic heights in works such as Ann Coulter's *Treason*, and the broadcasts of Glenn Beck.[29] It is important to note though that this is not the work of an impotent lunatic fringe, but of very powerful forces within the Republican Party. One of the most extreme books attacking Obama, by Pam Geller, has a foreword by Bush's ambassador to the United Nations, John Bolton.[30]

Wars are also corrupting in their encouragement of the belief that "the truth has to be protected by a bodyguard of lies," in Churchill's phrase: that public lying is morally and patriotically justified for the higher good of victory, and that enemy propaganda is to be met not with the truth, but with counterpropaganda. Conscious or unconscious falsification of facts and evidence has become a staple of much of the discussion of international affairs in the United States—as demonstrated, for example, in the 2003 media campaign against France. This is the spirit in which publicly funded institutions like Radio Free Europe and Radio Free Asia were founded and have continued, even after the end of the cold war.

The cold war allowed institutions like the upper class Public Affairs Luncheon Club of Dallas in the 1960s to weave different paranoias into one seamless web, with speeches on themes like, "the UN is the springboard from which the great Communist movements are coming"; "international socialists still control the

State Department"; and "the internationalists have all but destroyed U.S. national independence."[31] The fear of Communism taking over a defeatist United States seems strongly to have affected even so apparently sober a bureaucratic figure as Dick Cheney.[32] Far from the end of the cold war liberating the United States from this malign discourse, the victory of 1989–1991 sealed it in place. All of these tendencies continued (albeit at a diminished level) during the 1990s, and gained a new and frightening strength after 9/11. Fears of Sharia law taking over the United States with the help of a covertly Muslim U.S. president are even crazier than their cold war predecessors, but stand in the same tradition. The content of some of the conspiracy theories concerning President Obama is directly linked to cold war paranoias. Aaron Klein's *The Manchurian President: Barack Obama's Ties to Communists, Socialists and Other Anti-American Extremists* is probably the most lurid example of this approach.[33]

Permanent Mobilization

The cold war therefore perpetuated and intensified already existing tendencies in American political culture. Coming on top of World War II, however, it also introduced something quite new: a state system of permanent semi-mobilization for war, institutionalized in the military–industrial–academic complex and the academic bodies linked to it. As the radical U.S. critic and historian C. Wright Mills wrote in 1959:

> For the first time in American history, men in authority are talking about an "emergency" without a foreseeable end...the American elite does not have any real image of peace—other than as an uneasy interlude existing precariously by virtue of the balance of mutual fright. The only seriously accepted plan for "peace" is the fully loaded pistol. In short, war or a high state of war preparedness is felt to be the normal and seemingly permanent condition of the United States.[34]

In typical fashion for security elites of this kind, they became deeply conditioned over the decades to see themselves not just as tougher, braver, wiser, and more knowledgeable than their ignorant, innocent compatriots, but as the only force standing between their country and destruction. They are therefore entitled if necessary to deceive their compatriots for their own good, because, after all—so the wisdom goes—if the American people had been left to their own instincts, America would have been left almost defenseless in the face of German and Japanese aggression in the 1940s and Soviet aggression at the start of the cold war. And, be it said, there are historical grounds for a limited and prudent form of this attitude. General George Marshall—not a man given to hysterical exaggeration—described the reduction of the armed forces after 1945 as "not demobilization, but a rout."[35]

This "emergency without end" has now been repeated in an intensified form in the "war against terrorism," but the nature of the security establishment and military–industrial–academic complex created by the cold war also left the United States poorly equipped to fight against terrorists. Instead, this complex of institutions and attitudes requires states as enemies—and if such enemies are not readily apparent, it will instinctively seek to conjure them up, at least in the American public mind.[36]

As military spending and the military–industrial sector grew during World War II and the cold war—with space exploration as a minor adjunct—they have become fundamental to the U.S. economy, U.S. economic growth, and above all U.S. technological development. Despite its often almost incredible wastefulness and corruption, it must be admitted that this was also in some ways a kind of unacknowledged but rather successful state industrial development strategy, in a country whose free market ideology meant that it could not formally adopt or admit to such a strategy.

The growing importance of the military and associated institutions and interests was quite unlike anything that had ever existed before in U.S. history. Hostility to standing armies—involving both high taxes and the threat of royal tyranny—was a central part of the motivation for the American revolt against Britain. This sentiment helped fuel the belief in popular militias as a free and democratic alternative—which, as written into the Second Amendment to the Constitution, constitutes today the main constitutional defense of the right to bear arms and the U.S. gun lobby, and has been adopted as one of the ideological planks by the Tea Parties.[37] Three times before the cold war, the United States resorted to conscription in order to fight wars—in the Civil War, World War I, and World War II—but each time, victory was followed by very rapid demobilization. Only with the cold war did the notion of permanent readiness for war become an integral part of the American system. This was doubtless unavoidable, given the permanent (if often exaggerated) nature of the threat from a permanently mobilized and nuclear-armed Soviet Union; but just because it was unavoidable does not make its consequences any less dangerous.

While new to the United States, this kind of system and atmosphere have been all too widespread in world history. In the decades before 1914, all the major European powers, with the partial exception of Britain, lived in this state of permanent semimobilization. This reflected the objective security circumstances of the European continent at the time; but as in the United States during the cold war, it also first created and was then itself fed by great military, bureaucratic, and industrial blocs with a strong vested interest in the maintenance of a mood of national paranoia, fear and hatred of other countries, and international tension. A classic example is the German Navy League, backed by the great steel and armaments interests, allied to the old military aristocracy, and dedicated to the creation of an arms race with Britain.[38] Such groups contributed a good deal to the competing aggressive nationalisms that eventually clashed between 1914 and 1918.

Every country had its version of the "Committee on the Present Danger," which mobilized fear of the Soviet Union in the early 1980s. Every European country before 1914 had its own repeated and carefully stoked panics concerning the enemy's military capabilities, like the "missile gap" scare that the Democrats created as a weapon against Eisenhower with the help of intellectual allies like Edward Teller.[39]

In the United States, one of the first employers of this tactic was Senator Lyndon Johnson as chairman of the "Preparedness Subcommittee" of the Senate during the Korean War, and since then it has become a fixed and recurring feature of American political theatre.[40] Such moves can be used either by the opposition to discredit the government in power, or by the government to whip up patriotic support and discredit the opposition. Lord Salisbury, several times British premier at the height of the British Empire, once remarked sourly that if British generals and their political allies had their way, he would have to pay to "fortify the Moon against an attack from Mars."[41]

Indeed, in 1897, a British magazine published a story with a title that could have been written by Charles Krauthammer—"How Britain Fought the World in 1899"—in which France and Russia invade Britain. In the words of its publisher, this story was "no wild dream of the imaginative novelist, this threat of an invasion of our beloved shore. It is solidly discussed in French and Russian, aye and in German newspapers ... The Frenchman and the educated Russian talk of such a thing as coolly as we talk of sending out a punitive expedition to the Soudan or up to the hills of North-West India."

This bizarre fantasy was praised as realistic by senior British officers, and was part of a very extensive genre of such stories in Europe at the time.[42] In the United States, such fictional "scares" concerning invasion of the United States by the Soviet Union, China, Cuba, and even Nicaragua became a staple of thrillers during the cold war, recalling nineteenth-century Protestant fears of a Catholic army invading America by balloon.[43] More and more American novels are now being produced on the subject of future war with China—invariably, of course, brought about by Chinese aggression.[44]

These old cultural and historical roots of American paranoia helped anti-Communist hysteria become part of American political culture—a matter of assumptions and fears that exist and operate below the level of political discussion, and which are not indeed really open to rational argument.[45] Such wild fantasies did not just appear in fictional works, but in those of highly influential and respected officials and commentators. In his book *The Present Danger*, of 1980, neoconservative Norman Podhoretz warned of the imminent "Finlandization" of America, the political and economic subordination of the United States to superior Soviet power, and asked if a point had come at which "surrender or war are the only choices."[46]

After what became obvious about the real condition of the Soviet economy and military at that time, one would have thought that Podhoretz and his colleagues would have become at least somewhat chastened and modest in their judgments, or that their public would have lost confidence in that judgment. But no. Long after the Soviet collapse, Podhoretz was still there, editor in chief of *Commentary*, a regular pundit on television, now warning of the Muslim threat to the United States and advising on "how to win World War IV."[47]

Bismarck on occasions used such scares as a tactic in his struggle to control the German parliament, co-opt or emasculate the liberal parties, and maintain royal control over the executive. Under his successors, it became a repeated practice.[48] In the United States, such scares concerning Soviet power continued even as the Soviet Union was manifestly collapsing, and were then immediately revived in the form of paranoia about Russian "revanche," even as the Russian armed forces were similarly rotting before our eyes.[49]

I came to Washington on a visiting fellowship in 1996, fresh from covering the immense retreat of Russia from empire—with the partial exception of Britain, by far the greatest peaceful abandonment of empire in all history. I had also covered both the Russian military defeat in the first Chechen war (a war not for empire, but against the secession of part of the Russian Federation itself), and the mixture of corruption, cynicism, materialism, and political apathy that gripped Russian society after the fall of Communism.[50]

On arrival, I was first astonished, and then horrified, to find large portions of the American elites—serving officials as well as unofficial commentators—dedicated to creating an image of Russia in the minds of the American people that bore only a tangential relation to reality; and this line was swallowed by large portions of the American media and public opinion.[51] As far as many members of the U.S. establishment were concerned, the fall of Communism and the end of the Soviet Union hardly changed at all their hostility toward Russia as a state—unless that state adopted a position of complete subservience to American wishes not only in the world as a whole, but in Russia's own region. With this experience behind me, I was not too surprised by the success of the Bush administration and its media allies in conflating Al Qaeda and Saddam Hussein, and of the Israel lobby in conflating Al Qaeda and the Palestinians.[52]

A mixture of exaggerated fear of Russia and rhetoric of America's duty to spread freedom and democracy was used to justify the expansion of the North Atlantic Treaty Organization (NATO) into the former Soviet Union, something that Russians found deeply threatening. Here was another case where the language of American civic nationalism was used to shut down internal debate—since anyone who opposed this expansion was likely to be accused of lacking in commitment to freedom and democracy, and faith in America's mission.[53]

American Nationalism and the Rise of China

This past history has worrying implications for the U.S. handling of by far the biggest challenge for U.S. foreign and security policy—and indeed for the entire American nation—over the coming decades: the rise of Chinese power relative to that of the United States. The appearance of new great powers has always created an extra potential for conflict. In the case of China, this risk is heightened by China's own prickly nationalism, which contains both strong historical resentments and a strong sense of historical entitlement to hegemony within China's own region.

More pessimistic observers have compared China's rise to that of imperial Germany in the decades before World War I and have argued that the probable resulting tensions between China, China's neighbors, and the United States pose a comparable threat to world peace.[54] The question for the present book is what role American nationalism will play in shaping U.S. policy toward China, and the answer does not seem a very encouraging one.

In these circumstances of China's rise, U.S. policy toward China will need to be guided by a cool head and an iron nerve. At home, if the United States is to revive its economy in ways that will allow it to compete successfully with China, it may need a capacity for radical new thinking and the junking of old shibboleths comparable to that displayed by Deng Xiaoping and the Chinese leadership when they jettisoned Maoism and adopted capitalism after 1979.

In the past, the United States has proved capable of such transformations. If, however, the analysis of different aspects of American nationalism presented in this book is correct, then today they point in the opposite direction: toward a combination of outbursts of paranoia and a hysterical desire to return to a vanished past. It must also be said that while, in the past, American statesmen have often displayed cool heads and iron nerves, they have equally often had to do so in the teeth of some of the popular impulses described in this book.

If American elites decide that only fury and fear at China's overtaking the United States can mobilize the white middle class behind a program of radical domestic reform and self-sacrifice, they may find themselves in the same position as the Truman administration when it sought to overcome U.S. isolationism and mobilize support for the Marshall Plan and NATO by stirring up anti-Communism. The result was a wave of hysterical chauvinism that threatened the Truman administration at home and risked nuclear war abroad.[55]

Some fascinating insights into the difficulties that America will face in dealing with China's rise are to be found in an article by the neoconservative Irwin Stelzer in the right-wing *Weekly Standard* of January 2011, "Our Broken China Policy."[56] After an acute examination of the brilliant success to date of China's industrial policy (albeit qualified by routine praise of the risk of Chinese political upheaval and the superiority of American democracy), Stelzer presents his ideas for how the United States should respond. Two of his key recommendations are the following:

> Recast trade and tax policy so that the incentives facing the private sector coincide more closely with the broader public interest. Recognize that private corporations, charged with maximizing shareholder value, cannot factor into their operations all of the externalities, most especially national security considerations, that China's state-managed companies are required to consider.

Get our economic house in order and reduce dependence on our creditor in chief. If that means some tax increases, well, the Tea Party will just have to live with it. If that means some reductions in entitlements and other programs, well, the liberals will just have to live with it. And if that means an end to—let's be realistic, a reduction in—corporate welfare, well the corpocracy will just have to live with it.

The point is of course that there is no way that the Tea Parties or a Republican Party heavily influenced by them would "live with" tax increases and a state-directed program of economic change. Nor indeed would the Tea Parties live with sharply reduced middle class entitlements or the Republican elites live with reduced corporate subsidies. For reasons set out in this book, Americans' nationalist belief in the innate superiority of their own system will make such radical change extremely difficult.

If the Republican Party remains in its present form, and is also able to block Democratic administrations from adopting such policies, then all that will be left of Stelzer's recommendations are those arguing that America should stop "apologizing" and "bending the knee" to China, and that America must "do whatever is needed to maintain superiority in the Asia-Pacific region, as our allies and potential allies are urging us to do." If, however, the United States attempts to contain China militarily and diplomatically, and attacks her rhetorically, while all the while America gets relatively weaker economically, well, the dangers of this course should be obvious.

If a future Republican administration does adopt a strategy of confronting China, it will be building on a previous Republican approach that was partially derailed by 9/11 but never quite disappeared even in the depths of the wars in Iraq and Afghanistan.[57] The hope of hard-line Republican analysts—and some Democrats—in the later 1990s was to create a U.S. security strategy of "containing" China, modeled on the "containment" of the Soviet Union during the cold war; to attempt to bankrupt the Chinese state by forcing it into an unsustainable arms race; and to undermine the Chinese state from within by encouraging movements for democratic revolution and ethnic secession. Meanwhile, the Chinese nuclear deterrent was to be neutralized by an American system of missile defense.

These views were pushed especially hard by the so-called Blue Team, an informal grouping of anti-Chinese junior officials, think-tank members, and Congressional staffers, and had considerable impact in Congress, though much less within the official community. The Blue Team was a conscious attempt to imitate the success of the so-called B Team, a similar (but more senior) group of officials and propagandists of the 1980s who set out to dramatize the supposed extent of Soviet power. The curious thing is, of course, that virtually every proposition advanced by the B Team concerning the Soviet Union has since been proved to be false.

Some of the anti-Chinese agenda of the Blue Team appears to have been embodied in the Project 2049 Institute, a Washington think tank with strong Taiwanese links founded in 2008.[58] This group is also strongly committed to containing China and maintaining U.S. primacy in East Asia.

In 1999 Republicans in Congress mounted a classic scare of the "missile gap" type, with the "Cox Committee" accusing China of having spied so successfully on the United States as to be able in a short space of time to match American nuclear technology and threaten the U.S. mainland. The report also declared that "essentially all Chinese visitors to the US are potential spies."[59] The report set off an orchestrated Republican media campaign attacking the Clinton administration for "weakness" and pushing for tougher policies against China. It was replete with phrases like "the greatest nuclear theft since the Rosenbergs" and "every nuclear weapon in the US arsenal has been compromised." Former United Nations Ambassador Jeanne Kirkpatrick declared—incredibly—that "it renders us immediately a great deal more vulnerable than we have ever been in our history." Former House Speaker Newt Gingrich called it "the largest espionage success against the United States since the Soviet Union in the 1940s."[60]

Echoing "yellow peril" racist stereotypes that long predated the cold war, the *Washington Times* reported that "both Mrs. Kirkpatrick and Mr. Gingrich believe the Chinese are capable of launching a missile at American troops, allied targets, and even American cities. Mrs. Kirkpatrick said the Chinese do not value human life and might be willing to suffer retaliatory consequences for the psychological benefit of striking American soil with a missile."[61]

Among many right-wing politicians, such attitudes toward China continued unabated even after 9/11, with House Majority Leader Tom DeLay in June 2003 publicly calling China "a backward, corrupt anachronism, run by decrepit tyrants, old apparatchiks clinging to a dying regime."[62]

In the first months of the Bush administration it seemed that this anti-Chinese approach, like their anti-Russian approach, might be adopted as official U.S. policy. Given the ferocious views of the Chinese system that he had expressed in the media, the appointment of John Bolton to the State Department could have been taken in itself as an anti-Chinese act.[63] Like Condoleezza Rice, Bush repeatedly called China a "strategic competitor," and called for a range of tougher U.S. policies.[64] Rice called on the United States to build up India as a strategic counter to China, and to take a more firmly pro-Taiwan stance in its relations with Beijing.[65] *Time* magazine reported the Bush administration in its first weeks in office as "hosing down China with acid."[66]

The approach consisted of a familiar cold war mixture of exaggerating China's military capabilities (at that stage still very limited) and calling for tougher condemnation of China over democracy and human rights. In effect, China was to be cast as the new cold war enemy, along the lines of the former Soviet Union.[67] Richard Clarke and others alleged that the Bush administration's obsession with China and Russia helped blind them to the threat from Islamist terrorism before 9/11, despite warnings from counterterrorism officials like himself.[68]

After 9/11 the Bush administration pursued a much more diplomatic and pragmatic policy toward China—which included backing away from confrontation with North Korea, even when that country conducted nuclear tests. The Obama administration in effect continued this policy. It should be noted, however, that the Democratic foreign and security elites have also contained their share of hawks with regard to China. One senior Clinton administration defense official quoted by Chalmers Johnson actively celebrated the fact in government departments dealing with China that experts on China were being pushed aside by a "new strategic class" of generalists from strategic studies and international relations, who might not know much about China but would be watchful "for signs of China's capacity for menace"—a most revealing statement.[69]

Above all, while the language of Democrats may be less aggressive and their approach more sophisticated, they are equally determined to maintain American "leadership" in East Asia and to prevent China from achieving parity, let alone superiority. Both President Obama and Secretary of State Hillary Clinton made clear their commitment to American leadership in Asia and continued U.S. military superiority.[70] There is almost no understanding in U.S. policy circles that other countries might not see absolute American military superiority as a given, or that the Pacific Ocean is by nature "an American lake."

This American goal of primacy is not in itself illegitimate, since many states in East and Southeast Asia do in fact prefer U.S. hegemony to that of China. However, it is something that China is bound to oppose, particularly if China's economy does indeed overtake that of the United States. A strong form of containment, as advocated by many Republicans, would mean essentially a return to the U.S. strategy of the 1950s—but under circumstances where China is vastly richer and more powerful. The probable Chinese response was summarized by Xu Yunhong, writing in a journal of the Communist Party Central Committee, *Qiushi*, in early 2011:

> The U.S. seems highly interested in forming a very strong anti-China alliance. It not only made a high-profile announcement of its return to East Asia but also claimed to lead in Asia...What is especially unbearable is how the U.S. blatantly encourages China's neighbouring countries to go against China...
>
> Countries like Japan, India, Vietnam, Australia, the Philippines, Indonesia, and Korea are trying to join the anti-China group because they either had a war or another conflict of interest with China...Our wishes to persuade the imperialists and those who are against China to be kind-hearted and repent are fruitless. The only way is to organise forces to fight against them...If friends come, treat them with wine; if jackals come, we have shotguns for them.[71]

In these circumstances, for America to lead regional states in balancing against China without this leading to conflict will require American diplomacy of the highest order. This will require an accurate assessment of what constitutes vital as opposed to secondary U.S. interests, an avoidance of unnecessary points of conflict, a wariness of the agendas and ambitions of local allies, and an ability to carry out tactical retreats when necessary. Ideally Washington should pursue a strategy outlined by Hugh White, that of drawing China into a "concert of powers" in East and Southeast Asia, that would accommodate Chinese interests without yielding to Chinese hegemony.

A wise U.S. strategy with regard to China is threatened by aspects of American nationalism. As with Russia after the end of the cold war, this threat comes partly from chauvinism. The United States does not contain the anti-Russian ethnic lobbies whose national agendas bedeviled U.S.–Russian relations, but if the white middle class comes to blame China for their economic decline, that will provide an even more potent source of hatred.

Equally dangerous, however, could be some of the civic nationalist impulses analyzed in the second chapter of this book. If both the past and the present language of the Republicans is anything to go by, any strategy of creating a new alliance to contain China is bound to be accompanied by a great flood of rhetoric justifying this in terms of "defending freedom" in the region. This stems from both conviction and the need to co-opt the support of American liberal intellectuals (as in the case of the Iraq War) and convince American public opinion to support what would be an extremely expensive (not to say dangerous) project, which would have to be pushed through amidst cuts to domestic services and programs.[72]

To ideologize an alliance against China would bring with it two great dangers. The first is that it would most probably be accompanied by increased rhetoric in support of democracy within China. The Chinese authorities would be likely to see this as an existential threat—and as the following very frank passage by Max Boot makes clear, they would not be wrong to do so:

> Beyond containment, deterrence, and economic integration lies a strategy that the British never employed against either Germany or Japan—internal subversion. Sorry, the polite euphemisms are "democracy promotion" and "human rights protection," but these amount to the same thing: The freer China becomes, the less power the Communist oligarchy will enjoy. The United States should aim to "Taiwanize" the mainland—to spread democracy through such steps as increased radio broadcasts and Internet postings...In general, the U.S. government should elevate the issue of human rights in our dealings with China. The State Department wrote in its most recent human rights report that the Chinese government's "human rights record remained poor, and the Government continued to commit numerous and serious abuses." The U.S. government should do much more to publicize and denounce such abuses. We need to champion Chinese dissidents, intellectuals, and political prisoners, and help make them as famous as Andrei Sakharov, Václav Havel, and Lech Walesa.[73]

In response, not only would the Chinese establishment adopt a much stronger anti-American strategy abroad, but (like the Russian, Iranian, Cuban, and other regimes) they would seek to neutralize domestic threats by stirring up Chinese nationalism and seeking to brand members of the opposition as American agents. In turn, a new upsurge of mass nationalism in China would make it even more difficult for the Chinese leadership on its side to seek pragmatic accommodations with the United States on points of difference.

Equally dangerous might be the befuddlement on the American side that would result from ideologizing the rivalry with China and turning it in American eyes into another crusade of the kind described in chapter 2, for this would make it even more difficult for Americans to conduct the pragmatic accommodations and tactical retreats that would be essential if this rivalry were not to lead to conflict.

A melancholy precedent for this would be set by U.S. policy toward Russia after the end of the cold war, and especially the plan to expand NATO to take in Georgia and Ukraine. Attempts to discuss in practical terms the dangers and costs of this strategy, and to question whether specific aspects were in America's interest, were liable to be drowned in a flood of words about America's duty to support "nations struggling to be free" and to defend their sovereignty.

As a result, the United States got itself into a position where U.S. administrations were seriously proposing to risk war with Russia for a Georgian South Ossetia and a Ukrainian Sevastopol, without the wisdom of this ever being seriously debated in the mainstream U.S. media, let alone its more extreme elements. In particular, there was no serious attempt to assess relative U.S. interests and ask if it made sense to pick a fight with Russia over these countries at a time when China's rapid rise relative to America was already apparent.

Nor was sufficient attention paid to the internal nature of Georgia and Ukraine. The wishes of ordinary Ukrainians themselves regarding NATO membership were ignored and the internal state of Georgia was either ignored or absurdly characterized in the U.S. media—all in the name of supporting "democracy."[74] In the end, when Georgia and Russia went to war in August 2008, the Bush administration backed away from defending Georgia—but it would not have been nearly so easy to do so if the United States had already entered into a formal alliance with that country.

The various territorial disputes between China and some of its neighbors make the idea of an American military alliance with them a very serious matter, which the American public needs to be aware of and to think clearly about. Such clarity will not occur if the Vietnamese and Filipino claims to the Paracel and Spratly Islands and India's claims to the McMahon Line in the Himalayas have become bound up in American minds with America's mission to defend freedom and spread democracy in the world.

This is not to say that such a development is certain. If American civic nationalism contains strong impulses to messianism, it is also true that both the American people and the American establishment contain strong tendencies toward pragmatism. Indeed, it might almost be said that while thanks to the dominant civic nationalist discourse, nationalist idealism has generally won the public arguments, in private it is pragmatism that has actually shaped policy.

One central reason why this is so comes from an unlikely source: the U.S. military, and the military–industrial complex to which it is linked. At least since

Vietnam, it is not the uniformed military that has driven American military adventures abroad. For example, I have been told by former Bush administration officials that Vice President Dick Cheney's desire to send U.S. troops to Georgia in August 2008 was blocked by Admiral Mullen and the Joint Chiefs of Staff. If the U.S. population and some of its representatives harbor strong traditions of instinctive bellicosity, but are not imperialists, much of the American military and officials close to them might, in contrast, be described as imperialist but not bellicose.

Under Bush, leading generals were notoriously lukewarm about the Iraq adventure, for the U.S. uniformed military remains more profoundly influenced by the debacle of Vietnam than perhaps any other portion of American society.[75] It was not the uniformed military that pressed for war with Iraq in 2002, but a small group of politically appointed and harshly ideological civilian officials in the Pentagon. Indeed, the Army chief of staff, General Eric Shinseki, warned publicly, and numerous other officers privately, of exactly the bloody and troop-consuming war of occupation that followed—with the result that he was publicly humiliated by Paul Wolfowitz and other Rumsfeld allies.[76]

But when it comes to the real possibility of conflict with the major powers, it is also worth remembering that Rumsfeld's own plans when he took office called for a smaller, lighter U.S. military with a more expeditionary focus and capability. This was seemingly predicated on the belief that there would be no land war with another serious military power for a generation at least.[77] Beneath all the talk of Russian and Chinese threats, very few Americans indeed have wished for actual conflict with these states. The desire, and need, are for tension, not conflict; for large-scale military spending, not full-scale war. Of course, the issue of Taiwanese independence may all too easily bring America and China into conflict, but this will almost certainly be the result of a combination of actions by a third party, with miscalculations in Beijing and Washington, rather than a conscious decision for war by an American administration.[78]

Thus in the case of China, Bush personally recommitted America very strongly to oppose Taiwanese independence.[79] Despite continuing bursts of unilateralist rhetoric from hawks like John Bolton, on the issue of preventing North Korea's development of nuclear weapons, the U.S. administration tacitly recognized the bankruptcy of its previous unilateralist strategy, and the practical impossibility of following the "Bush Doctrine" of preventive war in East Asia.

In consequence, while still refusing to negotiate with Pyongyang directly, it was forced willy-nilly toward a strategy of relying heavily on China to help in restraining and influencing Pyongyang. This recognized not only the impossibility of waging war against North Korea, but also the power of the other regional states—South Korea, Japan, and above all China—all of them vastly more formidable countries in their different ways than the feeble dictatorships of the Middle East.

Perhaps partly because of shame at having failed to stand up to the Bush administration over Iraq, during Bush's last year in office, two senior U.S. officers, Admiral William Fallon, commander of CENTCOM (U.S. Central Command),

and Admiral Mick Mullen, Chairman of the Joint Chiefs of Staff, played a key part in blocking moves by neoconservatives and others within the administration for a U.S. or Israeli strike against Iran's nuclear program. Admiral Fallon was forced to resign for publicizing his opposition to an attack.

Thanks to military opposition and the sheer impact of what was happening in Iraq, by the end of 2003 the Bush administration had in effect abandoned some more extreme elements of the neoconservative program. Some commentators were writing of a neoconservative moment that had really only lasted from September 11, 2001, to late 2003, or barely two years—though this judgment may be premature given their continued power within the Republican Party.[80]

This more pragmatic approach adopted toward a number of issues in the last months of 2003 was seen as a limited victory for the vision and strategy of Secretary of State Colin Powell and the State Department. However, it also reflected the "realism" of Dick Cheney, Donald Rumsfeld, and the institutions and traditions they represent. For if this brand of realism suffers from the faults described above, it nonetheless operates on the basis of rational calculations about power, interests, and risks, and derives from ways of looking at the world characteristic of diplomats and strategists since the seventeenth century.

The policy toward China adopted by the Bush administration after 9/11 fits admirably into this tradition. At bottom, it remained strongly distrustful of China's motives and plans. Equally, it recognized that it was not in the interest of the United States to seek confrontation, and that to risk war with China would be catastrophic. Washington therefore sought good, cooperative relations, without itself giving too much away.[81]

Such realists can, of course, make terrible mistakes, like the occupation of Iraq. They are also hopelessly at sea when faced with challenges that fall outside traditional realist frames of reference: Metternich when faced with rising ideological nationalism, Cheney and Rumsfeld when confronted with the threat of global warming. Nonetheless, they can be rather clearly distinguished from ideologues of the neoconservative type, let alone the Christian Right, and because their views also reflect the views and interests of the complex of institutions and corporations they represent, they have a tremendous weight in the U.S. establishment that the neoconservatives lack. The triumph of the realist approach in later 2003 caused deep anguish in hard-line neoconservative circles, and the hysteria of some of their language reflected the depth of their sense of defeat.[82]

This relative caution reflects in part the nature and interests of the U.S. military–industrial and security elites. These elites are obviously interested in the maintenance and expansion of U.S. global military power, if only because their own jobs and profits depend on it. Jobs and patronage also ensure the support of much of the U.S. Congress, which often lards defense spending bills with weapons systems the Pentagon does not want and has not even asked for, so as to help some group of senators and congressmen whose states produce these systems.[83] And as already noted, to maintain a measure of wider support in the U.S. media and public, it is also necessary to maintain the perception of certain foreign nations as threats to the United States, and a certain minimum and permanent level of international tension.

But a desire for permanent international tension is a different matter from a desire for war, and least of all a major international war that might bring ruin to the international economy. The American generals of the Clinton era have been described as "aggressive only about their budgets."[84] The American ruling system therefore is not a Napoleonic or Moghul one. It does not actively desire major wars, because it does not depend on major victorious wars for its own survival, and would indeed be threatened by them even if they were victorious.

Since the experiences of Iraq and Afghanistan, the military has also become much more cautious about supposedly "small" wars. When Secretary of Defense Robert Gates told West Point cadets in February 2011 that "any future defense secretary who advises the president to again send a big American land army into Asia or into the Middle East or Africa should have his head examined," he was undoubtedly speaking for most of the High Command in general. There was no protest from senior officers against President Obama's decision to keep U.S. military involvement in the NATO campaign against Colonel Gadhafi of Libya to an absolute minimum.

For that matter, even in the last decades of the cold war, under the roiling waves of public anxiety, continually whipped into spray by the winds of political propaganda, the feelings of the security establishment were often actually relatively complacent. As the U.S. National Security Strategy of 2002 admits, "in the Cold War, and especially following the Cuban Missile Crisis, we faced a generally status-quo, risk-averse adversary. Deterrence was an effective defense."[85] As Chalmers Johnson remarks bitterly, it is a pity we were not told this by U.S. official analysts while the cold war was still on.[86] Indeed, George Kennan's famous telegram and essay of 1947–1948, which formulated the intellectual basis for America's cold war stance against Soviet expansionism, also stated clearly that a direct military challenge to the West was unlikely.[87]

Of course, the military are absolutely committed to maintain America's superpower status, and the global network of bases that underpin it. They will certainly resist any overt attempt by China or any other power to overthrow American hegemony. If the military find themselves in a war like Iraq or Afghanistan, they are determined to win it—or perhaps it would be more accurate to say that they are determined not to be seen to lose it. This may well be a mistaken approach in the case of Afghanistan, but it is a natural one for soldiers, and should not be seen as the same as a desire to embroil the country in any more wars.

In the past, the military was also committed to high military spending, at whatever cost to the American economy. This may be changing, however, as far as more intelligent U.S. soldiers are concerned. Mr. Gates and Admiral Mullen have both echoed Eisenhower in speaking of America's fiscal stability as of equal or greater importance to its security than its military power, and in calling for a downgrading of the role of the military in U.S. external relations in favor of diplomacy and aid. Admiral Mullen also encouraged a rather visionary essay on a national strategic narrative, written by Captain Wayne Porter (USN) and Colonel Mark Mykleby (USMC) in 2011 under the name "Mr. Y"—a reference to George Kennan's famous "X" essay of 1947. Part of this essay reads as follows:

> In this strategic environment, it is competition that will determine how we evolve, and Americans must have the tools and confidence required to suc-cessfully compete. This begins at home with quality health care and education, with a vital economy and low rates of unemployment, with thriving urban centers and carefully planned rural communities, with low crime, and a sense of common purpose underwritten by personal responsibility. We often hear the term "smart power" applied to the tools of development and diplomacy abroad empowering people all over the world to improve their own lives and to help establish the stability needed to sustain security and prosperity on a global scale. But we can not export "smart power" until we practice "smart growth" at home.[88]

The authors call for a National Prosperity and Security Act that would "inte-grate policy across agencies and departments of the Federal government and provide for more effective public/private partnerships; increase the capacity of appropriate government departments and agencies; align Federal policies, taxa-tion, research and development expenditures and regulations to coincide with the goals of sustainability; and converge domestic and foreign policies toward a com-mon purpose."[89]

All this makes a rather striking contrast with the prevailing mood in the Republican Party leadership, especially since the officers concerned empha-size climate change as a threat—something that most Republicans deny is even happening.

This raises a future possibility with roots in the past that go back to George Washington: namely, that if the Republican Party has become radicalized to the point where it cannot provide rational government, and that the U.S. Constitution allows the Republicans to block effective government by a Democratic adminis-tration, it may be that only a successful retired general will have the mixture of rationality, patriotism, independence, and prestige to lead the Republicans back to rationality and lead an effective and sensible Republican administration. This happened under Eisenhower in 1951. Ike is now an almost forgotten figure in the Republican Party—but he may not remain so forever. Such a new approach would also be able to draw on the basic pragmatism that continues to govern most areas of U.S. foreign policy, despite the irrational impulses examined in this book.

However, there is one great exception to this rule of the ultimate realist domi-nation of U.S. policy: namely U.S. attitudes to Israel. Here, U.S. behavior is colored by nationalist and religious passion to a degree that is not remotely the case in East Asia, for example. Here, the terrible memory of the Holocaust has combined with the long struggle with the Palestinians and Arab states to produce an inflamed nationalism not only among Jewish Americans, but in much wider segments of the U.S. population. The resulting influences on American thinking and policy often stand quite outside any realist—or indeed rational—framework of thought. The role of these influences in shaping U.S. foreign policy and American nationalism is the subject of the next and last chapter.

Six

American Nationalism, Israel, and the Middle East

> *When we look at you from a distance, maybe a little sketchily, we see in you a*
> *dangerous threat to what is dear and sacred to us... you threaten to boot Israel*
> *out of the union between Jewish tradition and western humanism. As far as I*
> *am concerned, you threaten to push Judaism back through history, back to the*
> *Book of Joshua, to the days of the Judges, to the extreme of tribal fanaticism,*
> *brutal and closed.*

—Amos Oz[1]

In the fall of 2003 there were two votes in the United Nations (UN) General Assembly concerning Israel's policy toward the Palestinians. The resolution of September 19, 2003, demanded that Israel not deport or harm Yasser Arafat. The resolution of October 27, 2003, while condemning Palestinian suicide bombings and calling on both parties to implement the U.S.-designed "Road Map," demanded that Israel cease construction of its "security fence" within the West Bank. The first vote was 133–4; the second was 141–4. The minority view, rejecting the resolutions, was represented by Israel itself, the United States, and two tiny Pacific island states and dependencies of the United States, Micronesia and the Marshall Islands.[2]

The countries that voted for the resolutions criticizing Israel included some of America's oldest and closest allies, like Britain; countries that have recently begun to seek close relations with both the United States and Israel, like India; and of course the whole of the Arab and Muslim worlds. In their absolutely overwhelming nature, these votes find their mirror in resolutions of the U.S. Congress pledging unconditional support for Israel—with the difference that whereas these UN votes condemning Israeli behavior also denounced Palestinian terrorism, votes in the U.S. Congress are almost always completely one-sided.

This was true, for example, of the U.S. Senate resolution of May 6, 2002, at the height of Israeli–Palestinian violence, which attacked Palestinian terrorism and declared that "the Senate stands in solidarity with Israel, a frontline state in the

179

war against terrorism, as it takes necessary steps to provide security to its people by dismantling the terrorist infrastructure in the Palestinian areas." Not one clause of the resolution contained even the slightest hint of criticism of any Israeli action. The resolution passed the Senate by a vote of 92–2.[3] Israel's invasion of Lebanon in July 2006 was backed unanimously by the U.S. Senate, once again in the face of criticism from the overwhelming majority of the international community.

In the face of all evidence to the contrary, and reports by U.S. and international human rights groups, the House resolution supporting the invasion recognized "Israel's longstanding commitment to minimizing civilian loss and welcomes Israel's continued efforts to prevent civilian casualties." On January 9, 2009, during the Israeli intervention in Gaza, the House of Representatives voted 390–5 to "reaffirm the United States' strong support for Israel in its battle with Hamas." And so on, and on.

These votes were overwhelmingly bipartisan. Strikingly, while Republicans in Congress under George Bush were supporting the unconditionally pro-Israel stance of a Republican administration, support by Democrats in Congress has not changed even when the Democratic administration of Barack Obama has sought to bring some pressure to bear on Israel to compromise. Especially emblematic in this regard were the 29 standing ovations that members of both houses of Congress, from both parties, gave to Israeli Prime Minister Benjamin Netanyahu on May 24, 2011, when he gave an address explicitly opposing the stance of the Obama administration that a peace settlement between Israel and the Palestinians should be based on the borders of 1967.[4]

Largely in consequence of this support for Israel within the U.S. political establishment, President Obama's attempts to bring about a settlement between Israel and the Palestinians between 2009 and 2012 got precisely nowhere. And while no serious pressure was applied to Israel to comply with official U.S. policy, the Obama administration brought great diplomatic pressure to bear on other countries to prevent them from voting in the UN to recognize Palestinian independence. On the basis of this experience, there seem no serious grounds for belief that as long as the U.S. domestic political order retains its present shape, the United States— whether under Democratic or Republican administrations—will ever be able to bring about peace between Israel and the Palestinians. If change is to come, it will have to come from within Israel itself, and the Israeli political order seems too fragmented to be able to generate a consensus behind the necessary concessions.

The U.S. relationship with Israel, in the form that it has taken from the 1960s to the present day, has two highly negative effects on the United States (as well as highly negative effects on Israel, but these are the subject for a different book). The first relates to the U.S. position in the Muslim world, and threats to the United States from Islamist terrorism. The second relates to the subject of this book, and how the character of American nationalism is affected by the link to Israel.

Since 9/11, U.S. relations with the Muslim world have become central to American strategy and American security. At the time of this writing, the United States was fighting a war in one Muslim country, remained heavily involved in several more, and was deeply engaged in the entire Middle East. Most importantly, through Sunni Islamist terrorism, Muslim societies are generating the only truly serious threat now existing of a catastrophic attack on the American mainland. Success or failure in the struggle against this terrorism may also therefore be of existential importance for the survival of Western liberal and pluralist democracy. Given certain tendencies observable in the wake of 9/11, it is not difficult to imagine how even worse attacks in the future could push Western political cultures in a much harsher, more chauvinist, and authoritarian direction in America, away from the creed and toward its various antitheses.

As repeated polls and surveys have indicated, the Israeli–Palestinian conflict is also central to how Muslims perceive the United States, and how Europeans and others view U.S. strategy in the Middle East. Large majorities in every Arab country view the Palestinian issue as "the most" or a "very important" issue facing the Arab world today.[5] This has remained true after the "Arab Spring" of 2011. In November 2011, a poll in Arab countries by the Saban Center in Washington asked what two steps by the U.S. administration would most help improve the respondents' attitude toward America. Of those polled, 55 percent said that this would be a U.S.-sponsored Israeli–Palestinian peace agreement, and 42 percent said an end to U.S. aid to Israel.

This poll did show an increase in positive views of the United States (though only from 10 percent to 26 percent), perhaps as a result of America's endorsement of the democratic revolutions and failure to back President Mubarak of Egypt. However, it made clear that Israel continued to be the biggest reason for Arab hostility toward the United States. President Obama received a relatively high popularity rating of 34 percent, thanks to his rhetorical support for a peace settlement; but 43 percent had a negative view, above all because of his failure to actually achieve one.[6]

In 2011, hostility toward the United States in Turkey reached an all-time high, with only 10 percent of the population expressing a favorable view. This was in large part because of the way in which the U.S. administration had supported Israel over the incident on May 10, 2010, when Israeli commandos stormed a Turkish ship attempting to break the Israeli blockade of Gaza, killing nine.[7] Turkey was long regarded as a U.S. ally in the Middle East, second only to Israel itself. The fact that the U.S. political elites have watched with indifference as this alliance has collapsed says a great deal about the supremacy of the link to Israel over every other U.S. interest in the region.

According to the Bush administration's most important international ally, British prime minister Tony Blair, "there is no other issue with the same power to reunite the world community than progress on the issues of Israel and Palestine." Blair also declared that "this terrorism will not be defeated without peace in the Middle East between Israel and Palestine. Here it is that the poison is incubated. Here it is that the extremist is able to confuse, in the mind of a frighteningly large number of people, the case for a Palestinian state and the destruction of Israel; and to translate this moreover into a battle between East and West; Muslim, Jew and Christian."[8]

The European Union's (EU's) security strategy of December 2003 declares that "resolution of the Arab/Israeli conflict is a strategic priority for Europe. Without this, there will be little chance of dealing successfully with other problems in the Middle East."[9] It also goes without saying that if China ever decides to challenge the U.S. position in the Middle East, Beijing will find unconditional American support for Israel to be by far China's greatest political asset.

Unfortunately, as the above votes indicate, of all important world issues, this is probably the one on which the United States is most completely isolated from the rest of the international community. It has thereby contributed significantly to weakening the U.S. capacity for leadership by persuasion and consent. America's position, and isolation, on this issue has fed the spirit of unilateralist nationalism in the United States and helped draw large sections of the U.S. liberal intelligentsia (not just Jewish Americans, but sympathizers with Israel in general) away from previously held internationalist positions. For if on this critical issue it is believed that America need not and should not listen even when the whole of the international community tells it something, how long can any genuine sense of internationalism or "decent respect to the opinion of mankind" (in the words of the Declaration of Independence) survive with regard to other issues?

This is the second evil effect of the "love affair" between Israel and the United States: the boost it has given to American chauvinism in general. The effort to explain how the United States can be correct or justified in the face of such a unanimous weight of world opinion against it has encouraged a view of the international community in general as irredeemably malignant, anti-Semitic, and by extension anti-American. This has fed into much older hatreds and paranoias on the Right in the United States concerning the outside world in general and international institutions in particular. It has contributed to the kind of vicious attitudes toward "the world" displayed by people like Charles Krauthammer and Phyllis Schlafly in the passages quoted in the introduction and elsewhere.

In the view of the British scholar and journalist Timothy Garton Ash, the new split between the United States and Western Europe after the unity created by 9/11 began with the escalation of the Israeli–Palestinian conflict in early 2002:

> The Middle East is both a source and a catalyst of what threatens to become a downward spiral of burgeoning European anti-Americanism and nascent American anti-Europeanism, each reinforcing the other. Anti-Semitism in Europe, and its alleged connection to European criticism of the Sharon government, has been the subject of the most acid anti-European commentaries from conservative American columnists and politicians. Some of these critics are themselves not just strongly pro-Israel but also "natural Likudites"...pro-Palestinian Europeans, infuriated by the way criticism of Sharon is labeled anti-Semitism, talk about the power of a "Jewish lobby" in the US, which then confirms American Likudites' worst suspicions of European anti-Semitism, and so it goes on, and on.[10]

The Israeli–Palestinian conflict in turn contributes to wider tendencies on the American Right toward national autism, an inability either to listen to others or to understand their reactions to U.S. behavior. This is, of course, especially true of the views of Muslims, and of U.S. officials who are viewed as too friendly to Muslims. The resulting prejudice against "Arabists" in the State Department and Central Intelligence Agency (CIA) on the part of supporters of Israel has done immense damage to the ability of the American government to develop accurate analyses of the Middle East.[11]

As noted, this is a strange feeling to encounter in a country as powerful, wealthy, and open as America. It is, however, very characteristic of small and embattled nations, especially when their populations have in the past been subjected to ferocious massacre and persecution—as in the case of Israel. The aggrieved and embattled sentiments of Israel have spread back to the United States, strengthening the already existing tendencies toward paranoia, resentment, and chauvinism that were examined earlier.

For this and other reasons, contemporary U.S. policies toward Israel and toward the Middle East in general fit all too well into the thesis–antithesis duality set out in this book, and are perceived to do so by Muslims and Europeans. On the one hand, President Bush committed the United States to what he called "a forward strategy of freedom in the Middle East," a strategy solidly rooted in the universalist values of the American Creed: the encouragement of liberty, democracy, free speech, the rule of law, and "healthy civic institutions." The Obama administration followed this with a public commitment to support the democratic revolutions of the "Arab Spring" (even if that support was often qualified and hesitant).[12]

On the other hand, the U.S. Congress, and to a very considerable extent successive U.S. administrations as well, have pursued policies of largely unconditional support for Israel, irrespective of Israeli behavior in the "Occupied Territories"— behavior that is often completely incompatible with the ideals the United States professes and the standards it demands elsewhere. The reasons for this almost unanimous stance by U.S. politicians in support of Israel are rooted partly in genuine identification with that country, and in some cases sympathy with Israeli ideologies. Thus the dominant elements of the Bush administration proved especially close to the Likud-led government of Ariel Sharon.[13] There is also, however, a strong element of political calculation, opportunism, and indeed fear related to the real or perceived strength of the Israel lobby. In the words of M. J. Rosenberg of the Israel Policy Forum:

> The fact is that both Democrats and Republicans are very adept at this game and sometimes the sheer effrontery of it is astonishing. Democrats attack a Republican for "selling out" Israel even though the policy advocated by the Republican is the same one they supported when a Democrat advanced it. And Republicans do the exact same thing. Is it any wonder that candidates seem to go to great lengths to avoid saying anything remotely substantive on

the Middle East?...Knowing that any substantive statement could be used against them, candidates just play it safe. And segments of the pro-Israel community encourage them by criticizing constructive suggestions as anti-Israel, and by giving ovations to candidates who tell them what the candidates think they want to hear.[14]

The conservative commentator Robert D. Novak summed up the domestic political factor in American policy very cogently in May 2003, describing

> serious GOP [i.e., Republican] efforts to end absolute Democratic domination over the small but important Jewish constituency. The question is whether that constrains President Bush's pursuit of Israeli–Palestinian peace. The private assessment by important Republicans is that it should and that it does...
>
> [Republican leaders]...argue that social and economic liberalism now runs a poor second to support for Israel and that they have for the first time outdone Democrats in cheering the Jewish state. There is no more unyielding supporter of Israeli Prime Minister Ariel Sharon's policies than House Majority Leader Tom DeLay, the exemplar of muscular Republicanism.
>
> But what about Bush's advocacy of the Road Map [for Israeli–Palestinian peace]? He surely had to embrace it to retain Britain in the Iraq War coalition and to keep moderate Arab states friendly. The question is whether he will risk Jewish votes by pressing for Middle East peace.
>
> Republican activists leave no doubt about their views. Delay has called the Road Map "a confluence of deluded thinking" between European elites, the State Department bureaucracy and American intellectuals. Former House Speaker Newt Gingrich, an intimate adviser of Defense Secretary Donald H. Rumsfeld, called the Road Map a conspiracy by the State Department and foreign powers to work against US policies...
>
> This confronts Bush with a classic presidential decision that may forge his place in history. Should he follow Powell's advice that American leadership on creating a Palestinian state is essential for peace in the Middle East? Or should he follow the path urged by his party's leaders to guarantee his re-election?[15]

This Republican strategy can be seen as a continuation of Reagan's strategy of the 1980s in trying to draw away the votes of "Reagan Democrats," described by Joseph Harsch as comprising mainly "Southern [white] evangelicals, Northern 'blue collar' workers and pro-Zionist Jews."[16] This Republican bloc was based on thoroughly Jacksonian principles of conservative populism at home and aggressive nationalism abroad (though under Reagan, as noted, this nationalism was to some degree more rhetorical than real).

That is not to say, of course, that this Republican strategy has necessarily been successful after Reagan left the scene. In general, voting patterns and surveys suggest that when it comes to elections, most Jewish Americans remain true to their liberal traditions. In the 2008 elections 78 percent of American Jewish voters voted for Obama, though by 2010 according to some polls support for him among Jews had dropped to only 51 percent, largely because of the way in which he had been portrayed as hostile to Israel.[17] The alliance with Christian fundamentalists does often make Jewish American liberals very uneasy, for as Roberta Feuerlicht has written, "in Jewish history, when fundamentalists came, Cossacks were not far behind."[18] However, Jewish voters punished Carter very severely in 1980 for his moves toward dialogue with the Palestinian Liberation Organization (PLO), and there were fears among Democrats and hopes among Republicans that the same might happen to Obama in the elections of 2012.

If Bush had wished his administration to be taken seriously as a force for peace in the Middle East, he would have had to fire those of his own senior officials who in the course of the 1990s had opposed the Oslo peace process and advised the Israeli government to abandon it.[19] In their policy paper of 1996, "A Clean Break," Richard Perle (later chairman of the Defense Advisory Board in the Bush administration), Douglas Feith (later deputy under-secretary of defense in the Bush administration), and other members of the "Project for the New American Century" (PNAC) advised the Israeli government of Benjamin Netanyahu to abandon both the Oslo process and the whole idea of land for peace in favor of insistence on permanent control of the occupied territories: "Our claim to the land—to which we have clung for hope for 2000 years is legitimate and noble...Only the unconditional acceptance by Arabs of our rights, *especially* in their territorial dimension, *"peace for peace,"* is a solid basis for the future [italics in the original]." The use of the word "our" in this context is especially striking.

The paper makes clear that it rules out the "peace for land" idea on which the whole "two state" solution is based, describing this as "cultural, economic, political, military and diplomatic retreat"; and what it means by "peace for peace" is to go on attacking Arab regimes until they accept Israeli rule over the whole of Palestine. The authors were thereby opposing, in the name of "our" claim to the whole of Palestine, not only the then policy of the Clinton administration, but that of all previous U.S. administrations, and that formally adopted later by the Bush administration, in which some of them were to be officials.[20] Elliott Abrams, appointed by Bush in 2003 as chief official for the Middle East at the National Security Council, had also argued—before the collapse of talks in 2000 and the second Intifada—that Oslo should essentially be abandoned in favor of a new crackdown on the Palestinians.[21] By 2012, the vast majority of both Democrats and Republicans in Congress had in effect abandoned all opposition to Israeli settlements and all concrete support for a Palestinian state.

It is true that, on the one hand, U.S. policy, and the U.S. public discourse concerning the Palestinians, has improved greatly since the 1970s, when Washington essentially echoed Israel in declaring that no such separate people existed.[22] A critical moment in this regard was the Sadat peace initiative, when, for the first time, an American poll showed more Americans approving of an Arab leader's policy than that of the Israeli government, by 57 percent to 34 percent.[23]

Since the Iraq War, public figures like Zbigniew Brzezinski and General Anthony Zinni have argued strongly that the new U.S. role in the Middle East demands a serious change of emphasis in dealing with the Israeli–Palestinian conflict. On the other hand, 9/11, and the link made between anti-American and anti-Israeli terrorism, means that much of the American political class and public opinion have once again become strongly anti-Palestinian, and are willing to see Israeli actions simply as part of the "war against terrorism." As a result of this and the iron grip of the Israeli lobby on the U.S. Congress, American support for Israel, including its occupation of the Palestinian territories, has continued unchanged—with all that this means for the image of the United States in the Muslim world, and therefore for U.S. chances of success in the struggle against Islamist terrorism.

Israel and the American Antithesis

One of the principal arguments made in defense of unconditional U.S. support for Israel over the past generation is rooted in the American Creed: namely, that Israel is a fellow democracy, and the "only democracy in the Middle East," and therefore deserves American support. This is repeated incessantly by Israeli spokesmen, including Benjamin Netanyahu in his address to Congress of May 2011.[24] But as this becomes more and more difficult to square with Israeli actions—most especially, the occupation of the West Bank and Gaza Strip and the planting of Jewish settlements there—other arguments, which have always been present, may gain greater prominence.

These arguments are closely related to the values and beliefs that I have described as forming part of the "American antithesis." A resort to this value system—rather than liberal democracy—to provide arguments in favor of Israel may also be encouraged by the revolutions of the "Arab Spring," which seem likely to bring to power a number of democratically elected Arab governments that at the same time are strongly hostile to Israel. This has already been true of Turkey since the election of a moderate Islamist government there.

Indeed, even the argument that Israel is a "bastion of democracy" is often paired with the spoken or unspoken view, more reminiscent of the nineteenth century, that it is also "an island of Western civilization in a sea of savagery." Indeed, the use of "democracy" in this context sometimes seems more a contemporary version of the nineteenth century use of the word "civilization" than a reference to actual behavior.[25]

Arguments rooted in the American antithesis were admirably summarized in a speech to the U.S. Senate in March 2002 by Senator James Inhofe (R-OK) setting out seven reasons why "Israel alone is entitled to possess the Holy Land," including the Palestinian territories. These views are widely shared among the other members of the Christian Right in the U.S. Congress. As described earlier, these make up a significant proportion of senators and congressmen, and a very powerful proportion of the Republicans. Their numbers include both of former Republican leaders in the House, Dick Armey and Tom DeLay, both of them very strong supporters of Israel. Thus, in May 2002, Armey, then House majority leader, called during a television interview for the deportation of the Palestinians from the Occupied Territories.[26] Tom DeLay has also expressed unconditional support for Israel, without reference to Palestinian rights.[27]

Democracy was not among the arguments set out by Senator Inhofe; indeed, the only one that is compatible with U.S. official public values as presently understood, let alone with the official policies toward the issue in every U.S. administration, was that of "humanitarian concern" for the Jewish survivors of the Holocaust. Instead, the senator set out archaeological and historical arguments proving that the Jewish claim "predates any claims that other peoples in the region may have"— the same arguments so often used by nationalist intellectuals in the Balkans and Caucasus. In contrast, the Senator claimed that in 1913, "Palestinians were not there." Two of Senator Inhofe's reasons were realist ones: that Israel is a "strategic ally of the United States" and "a roadblock to terrorism."

Other of his arguments concerned civilizational superiority: the idea that Israel took desert land that "nobody really wanted" from its supposedly nomadic native inhabitants, and made it bloom. Despite all the years since the conquest of the West, this is still an idea with great resonance for Americans from the Jacksonian tradition, or influenced by it. After all, both this belief and the explicit parallel between the American settlement of the New World and the Israelites' occupation of Canaan go back to the first days of white settlement in North America.[28] In the words of T. R. Fehrenbach concerning the Texan consciousness of Texan history (and remembering that Oklahoma borders Texas and was largely settled from there):

> The Texan did not shed his history in the 20th century; he clung to it. Texas history was taught in Texas schools before the study of the United States began...This Anglo history was shot through with the national myths all such histories have; it had its share of hypocrisy and arrogance. Parts of its mythology made both ethnic Mexicans and Negroes writhe. But in essence, it rang true. *We chose this land; we took it; we made it bear fruit,* the Texan child is taught.[29]

Or in the words of John Wayne, "I don't feel that we did wrong in taking this great country away from them [the Indians]...Our so-called stealing of this country from them was just a matter of survival. There were great numbers of people who needed new land, and the Indians were selfishly trying to keep it for themselves."[30] Leo Strauss, one of the intellectual fathers of the neoconservatives, made "theft of land" the basis for *all* states, while arguing that this unpleasant truth should veiled from the masses.[31]

In this vein, like so many American supporters of Israel over the decades, Senator Inhofe quoted a passage from Mark Twain about his travels through a desolate Palestine; and long-held views of Palestine's backwardness before the start of Jewish settlement, and therefore the Palestinians' inferiority, hark back directly to nineteenth-century attitudes.[32]

Senator Inhofe's final argument also stems directly from another key strand in the American antithesis, set out at length in chapter 3. In his words,

> this is the most important reason; because God said so. As I said a minute ago, look it up in the book of Genesis. It is right up there on the desk...The Bible says that Abram removed his tent and came and dwelt in the plain of Mamre, which is in Hebron, and built an altar there before the Lord. Hebron is in the West Bank. It is at this place where God appeared to Abram and said "I am giving you this land"—the West Bank. This is not a political battle at all. It is a contest over whether the world of God is true.[33]

Such an argument not only removes this critical issue from the sphere of negotiation, it removes it from any possibility of rational discussion based on universally accepted criteria. This argument in fact rejects the Enlightenment as a basis for political culture, and in doing so also rejects modern Western civilization. The rejection of the Enlightenment tradition is especially true of the millenarian Christians in the United States, who believe that the restoration of Israeli rule over the entire biblical Kingdom of David is an essential precondition of the apocalypse (a very old belief among Protestant fundamentalists, shared by Oliver Cromwell).[34]

As recorded by Donald Wagner, Grace Halsell, Gabriel Almond, and other leading students of this tradition, especially sinister are the links between these forces in the United States and the powerful mixture of fundamentalist and ultra-nationalist forces on the Israeli radical Right. The latter share the moral absolutism of their American Christian counterparts without necessarily sharing their commitment to democracy. Such Israelis are, of course, especially strongly represented among the settlers on the West Bank.

Israeli radical fundamentalists and nationalists are implacably opposed to a state for the Palestinians, and in many cases are committed to the most radical of all solutions to the Israeli–Palestinian conflict, the ethnic cleansing ("transfer") of the Palestinians from the occupied territories. According to opinion polls, in 2003 some 46 percent of the Jewish population of Israel in general also believed in this solution, with 33 percent calling for the deportation of even Arab citizens of Israel.[35] In 2003 the possibility of future deportation was raised by a leading Israeli liberal historian, Benny Morris.[36] Such a move would indeed mark a definitive break with "the democratic West" as this has been defined in recent decades, and a return to previous Western behavior of which Jews were among the greatest victims. If America were to support such a move, it would mark a historic triumph for the forces of the American antithesis over the American Creed.

Ian Lustick has written of this fundamentalist element in Israel—with fundamentalism defined as "political action to radically transform society according to cosmically ordained imperatives"—as forming "a key element on the Israeli side of the Middle Eastern equation."[37] In 1991 Ehud Sprinzak described how

> one of the great successes of the [Israeli] radical right has been its ability to penetrate the Likud and the National Religious Party. Thus, approximately

a quarter of the leaders and members of the Likud look at the world today through the ideological and symbolic prism of the radical right. The most outstanding example is cabinet member Ariel Sharon, a person with great charisma and a large following, who thinks and talks like the ideologues of the extreme right.[38]

Or in the simple words of the Reverend Jerry Falwell, "to stand against Israel is to stand against God."[39] Over the past decade unconditional support for Israel has become increasingly strong on the Republican Right, in tandem with the rise of the Christian Right "from an irrelevant fringe into a centerpiece of the conservative movement." This is a very marked change from the days of Eisenhower, and indeed of George H. W. Bush.[40] As Inhofe's and Falwell's words indicate, the origins of this lie by no means only in the political opportunism analyzed by Novak, but also in profound religious, ideological, and cultural identification.

Hal Lindsey, the millenarian author whose *Late Great Planet Earth* still exceeds any other in sales in the United States (apart from the Bible itself) produced a book after 9/11 on Arabs and Muslims that repeats the same biblical and pseudohistorical arguments as those of Inhofe (quoting extensively from a work by Joan Peters purporting to "prove" that Arabs actually immigrated to Palestine in the nineteenth century). Lindsey adds a strong element of hatred and contempt for Islam and for "the nature and genetic characteristics of Ishmael and his descendants, the Arabs." These he identifies with "the donkeys of the wilderness" mentioned by God in the Book of Job—in other words, rootless nomads with no attachment to place. He speaks of hate as a Muslim "religious doctrine."[41]

A symposium of the Christian Coalition on Islam in Washington, DC, on February 15, 2003, which I attended (Daniel Pipes was among the speakers) was a phantasmagoria of hatred. One speaker declared that the reason why there would always be conflict between Christians and Muslims was that Muslims denied the truth of the resurrection. Don Feder said that "Islam is not a religion of peace. It is a religion which, throughout its 1,400-year history, has lent itself well to fanaticism, terrorism, mass murder, oppression and conversion by the sword."[42] By 2012 such language extended across the U.S. religious Right and permeated considerable portions of the Tea Parties.

Of course, such views represent a distinctly minority opinion in the United States as a whole concerning the Israeli–Palestinian issue. But the rise of the Christian Right within the Republican Party means that in this wing of U.S. politics, they are views that are becoming more and more significant. The Israeli Fundamentalist Right is even developing a closer relationship with more moderate sections of the Christian Right in the United States.[43] Indeed, it would seem that since the mid-1990s Likud governments have come to rely more on the Christian Right than on "unreliable" liberal Jewish Americans in their attempts to mobilize support in the United States for its policies.[44] Thus the *Washington Times* reported a series of visits to the United States by the Israeli tourism minister in 2003: "Israeli tourism minister Benyamin Elon has embarked on a 'Bible Belt tour' to exploit evangelical Christian enthusiasm for Israel, to lure Christian tourists back to Israel and to derail President Bush's 'road map' to Middle East peace... 'We either have to oppose the road map or oppose the Bible,' says Mike Evans, founder of the Jerusalem Prayer Team, a coalition of 1,700 churches."[45]

In almost any other truly vital area of U.S. international policy, such views would have few consequences for policy.[46] But in the case of Israel, a variety of factors have made this impossible. These include the depth of American historical and cultural sympathy for Israel, the power of the Israeli lobby (which includes by no means just Jewish Americans, but the Christian Right and other forces as well), and the particular limitations on the discussion of Israel in the political arena and mass media.

Together these factions have made it impossible for liberal or realist forces in the United States—including portions of Jewish America—to isolate and overcome such ideas politically, however much they may argue against them in the educated media.[47] It is not that the extremist ideas held by Inhofe, DeLay, and others are shared by anything resembling a majority of Americans. Rather, in the case of Israel, both the Democratic Party and the liberal intelligentsia have been disabled from presenting strong and coherent opposition to them, whether by sincere identification with Israel, or fear of being attacked by the Israeli lobby. As a result, there is in effect no real political alternative or opposition in the United States concerning the Israeli–Palestinian conflict and U.S. policies toward it.

In 2008 J Street was founded, a political action committee representing liberal Jews who support Israel, but oppose the Israeli occupation of the Palestinian territories, and call for a peace settlement on the basis of the borders of 1967. J Street is supported by numerous leading Jewish intellectuals and rabbis in both the United States and Israel, and it has gained some presence in portions of the educated media. J Street demonstrates that the hard-line Israel lobby cannot claim to speak for all American Jews, and that many Jewish liberals—while deeply and rightly committed to Israel's survival as a state—reject Israel's occupation of land beyond the borders of 1967 and support Israeli reconciliation with the Arab states. Compared to the unconditionally pro-Israel groups, however, as of 2012 J Street's impact on politics, and especially Congress, remains minimal—as is all too clear from the latest congressional votes on Israel.[48]

Over the past four decades U.S. policy has become bogged down in a glaring contradiction between American public ideals and U.S.-financed Israeli behavior. On the one hand, America preaches to Arabs contemporary civic ideals of democracy, modernity, and the peaceful resolution of disputes. On the other, it subsidizes not only a brutal military occupation, but the seizure of land from an established population on the basis of ethnoreligious claims that in any other circumstances would be regarded by the U.S. government and a majority of public opinion as utterly illegitimate.[49]

The most truly tragic aspect of all this, as more and more Israelis and Jewish Americans have begun to argue, is that this kind of unconditional U.S. support, coupled with continued Israeli occupation of Palestinian territory, is also proving disastrous for Israel itself, and for the noble ideals that motivated the best elements in the Zionist enterprise. These critics include not just liberals, but senior retired military and security officials, like the four former directors of the Shin Bet domestic security service who, in November 2003, warned the Sharon government that if Israel does not withdraw from the West Bank and Gaza Strip, Israel's very existence will ultimately be endangered. They also said that this withdrawal is necessary even if this leads to a clash with Jewish settlers.

According to one of the four, Avraham Shalom, "we must once and for all admit that there is another side, that it has feelings and is suffering, and that we are behaving disgracefully... We have turned into a people of petty fighters using the wrong tools."[50] In April 2011, a group of former Israeli generals and chiefs of the security services drafted a proposed peace settlement based on the principles set out in the Arab peace initiative of 2002. The Israeli generals' plan backed President Obama's call for a settlement based on the borders of 1967. It was rejected by the Israeli government and received no backing in the U.S. Congress.

In the words of former Knesset Speaker Avraham Burg:

> The Zionist revolution has always rested on two pillars: a just path and an ethical leadership. Neither of these is operative any longer. The Israeli nation today rests on a scaffolding of corruption, and on foundations of oppression and injustice. As such, the end of the Zionist enterprise is already on our doorstep. There is a real chance that ours will be the last Zionist generation. There may yet be a Jewish state in the Middle East, but it will be a different sort, strange and ugly... We cannot keep a Palestinian majority under an Israeli boot and at the same time think ourselves the only democracy in the Middle East.

The Israeli lobby in the United States is well aware that the settlements—which have been condemned in principle by successive U.S. administrations—are by far the weakest element in its entire argument. Determined attempts have therefore been made to distract attention from this issue, described in one advisory paper as "our Achilles heel" in terms of wooing U.S. public support.[51]

Because of the way in which America and Israel are entwined—spiritually, politically, and socially—and because the Israeli–U.S. relationship is treated by so many other people in the world as a litmus test of U.S. behavior, the choices that Israel makes will have very grave implications not only for the security of the United States and its Western allies like Britain, and for America's role in the world, but also perhaps for the political culture of the United States itself.[52]

From an American point of view, Israel cannot be compared with Russia, China, or other authoritarian states that have waged even crueler wars against national secessionist movements. This comparison is made repeatedly by the Israeli lobby in an effort to prove that demands for U.S. pressure on Israel are hypocritical and/ or anti-Semitic, since the authors of these demands do not ask that the United States apply similar pressure to states like Russia or China.

This argument, however, fails in both ethical and realist terms. What most U.S. and European critics of the U.S. relationship with Israel are asking is not that the United States should impose trade sanctions against Israel, or expel it from international bodies, but only that the United States should use its aid and support for Israel as a powerful lever to influence Israeli behavior, as these other states do not receive massive subsidies, military support, and diplomatic protection from the United States. Israel as of 2012 received more than one-quarter of the entire U.S. aid budget (excluding that for the reconstruction of Afghanistan). The figure for U.S. aid to Israel in 2012 was more than five times that provided to the entire desperately impoverished continent of Africa.

This radical imbalance clearly makes Israel a special case. It makes the United States morally complicit in Israel's crimes, not only in the eyes of the world, but in reality, and it gives Americans both the right and the duty to put pressure on Israel to end the occupation of the Palestinian territories.

The United States' need to bring about an end to the Israeli–Palestinian conflict is also dictated on purely realist grounds, especially in the context of the "war against terrorism." Israeli strategies and tactics in that conflict, and U.S. support for Israel, are central to how a large majority of Muslims view the United States and U.S. policies in the Muslim world. This fact has been attested to by an almost endless procession of opinion polls and media reports, including surveys by the State Department, and is not and should not be open to serious question.[53]

This combination of factors also critically affects how Europeans view U.S. strategy in the region, and contribute enormously to European doubts about the wisdom and sanity of American leadership. The refusal among many Americans to recognize this, and the vilification by many of European motives for unease at Israel's behavior, also help to drive a deeper wedge between the United States and Europe. One of the greatest hopes that Europeans invested in President Obama was that he would bring about peace between Israel and the Palestinians. He still receives credit for having tried, but his administration's complete failure—as of 2012—to actually achieve anything has only increased European concerns about the U.S. political system as a whole.

Thus the debate in Europe in 2003–2004 on Bush's plan for developing the Middle East, the role of Israel, and unconditional U.S. support for Israel featured prominently as reasons for skepticism. This factor was barely mentioned in many U.S. reports and analyses of the difficulties over the issue between the United States and Europe—leaving the impression that European resistance was motivated chiefly by "petulance" or "anti-Americanism."[54]

The "Love Affair"

The widespread failure in the United States to address these issues has become especially striking and especially dangerous since 9/11 emphasized with dreadful force the threat to the United States and the West from terrorist groups based within Muslim societies. To most outside observers, including ones in countries and governments closely allied with the United States, it is apparent—as implied by Tony Blair in the remark quoted earlier in this chapter—that Israel has ceased to be the "vital strategic ally" of the United States that it was during the cold war.[55] It has become instead a very serious strategic liability to the United States and its allies in their effort to fight Islamist and Arab nationalist terrorism.

This is indeed demonstrated by Israel's role, or rather non-role, in the Iraq wars of 1991 and 2003, in which Israeli forces did not participate. They were, of course, begged by Washington not to participate openly, so as not to infuriate the Arab world and risk disastrously spreading these conflicts. Strategic allies are, after all, supposed to come into their own when there is a conflict in their region. It is a funny kind of ally that has to be asked to go away and keep quiet so as not to cause greater trouble.

An even more astonishing insight into the nature of the relationship between Israel and the United States—and Israeli assumptions about that relationship—is to be found in the memoirs of Dov Zakheim, under-secretary and chief financial officer at the Department of Defense in the Bush administration from 2001 to 2004. Zakheim is an Orthodox Jew and a passionate supporter of Israel, but records the following exchange in 2003:

> The Israelis did offer to provide materiel support for the U.S. efforts in Iraq and Afghanistan and did not insist on taking credit for it publicly. Initially I was delighted by the offer on two counts. First, the Israeli military was reputed to be among the world's best, and its systems would be a welcome addition to our own. And second, the United States provided Israel with billions of dollars worth of military assistance, and it seemed appropriate, at least to me, that Israel should offer to help America in its own time of need. But then the Israelis told me that the U.S. government would "of course" have to buy whatever it was that Israel made available. I was not amused, and told them "thanks, but no thanks."[56]

Before 1991, the major U.S. military intervention in the Middle East was that in Lebanon in 1983—a debacle that was made necessary by Israel's prior invasion of Lebanon. This intervention led to hundreds of unnecessary American dead, and increased hostility toward America in the region, while bringing the United States no strategic or political gain whatsoever. The terms of the U.S.–Israeli alliance are not a case of the tail wagging the dog, they represent the tail whirling the unfortunate dog around the room and banging its head against a wall.

In the context of either a realist or an ethical international tradition, there is of course nothing wrong in a U.S. commitment to Israel based on a sense of cultural and ethnic kinship, nor in U.S. willingness to make geopolitical sacrifices for the sake of defending Israel. This, after all, was the position of Britain vis-à-vis its former white colonies long after they had become politically independent from Britain, and even when some had ceased to be real strategic assets.[57]

In the case of Israel's role in the U.S.–Israel alliance, alas, a darker historical parallel suggests itself. If anything, the U.S.–Israel alliance is beginning to take on some of the same mutually calamitous aspects of Russia's commitment to Serbia in 1914—a great power guarantee that encouraged parts of the Serbian leadership to behave with criminal irresponsibility in their encouragement of irredentist claims against Austria, leading to a war that was ruinous for Russia, Serbia, and the world.[58]

One might almost say that as a result of the way in which the terms of the U.S.–Israel alliance have been set, the United States and Israel have changed places. The United States, which should feel protected both by the oceans and by matchless military superiority, is cast instead in the role of an endangered Middle Eastern state that is under severe threat from terrorism, and which also believes itself to be in mortal danger from countries with a tiny fraction of its power. Meanwhile, thanks largely to support from the United States, Israel has become a kind of superpower, able to defy its entire region, and Europe as well. This is not only bad for the United States, it is terribly bad for Israel itself, for reasons that will be set out later in this chapter. For Israel is not a superpower. It is rich and powerful, but it is still a small Middle Eastern country that will have to seek accommodations with its neighbors if it is ever to live in peace. Blind and largely unconditional U.S. support has enabled Israeli governments to avoid facing this fact, with consequences that are likely to prove utterly disastrous for Israel itself in the long run.

As in the case of Serbia and powerful Pan-Slavist sections of pre-1914 Russian public and official opinion, so in the case of Israel have important portions of U.S. opinion (by no means only Jewish) over the past half century come to view the United States and Israel as almost one country, so tightly identified with each other as to transcend America's own identity and interests. They genuinely believe in an "identity of interests between the Jewish state and the United States."[59] The relationship has been described as a "love affair," or in the words of Governor Jerry Brown of California, "I love Israel. If you would show me a map and ask me to identify Israel, I probably wouldn't find it. But Israel is in my heart."[60]

The roots of this "love affair" long precede the foundation not only of Israel, but of the United States itself, and lie ultimately in the Old Testament–centered religion of the American Protestant tradition. The acknowledgement (conscious or subconscious) of Israel as a form of chosen nation was closely related to the long tradition in American thought examined in chapter 2, and dating back to the first settlers, that identifies America as "God's new Israel." In the words of a sermon by the Reverend Abiel Abbot in 1799, "it has often been remarked that the people of the United States come nearer to a parallel with Ancient Israel, than any other nation upon the globe. Hence *Our American Israel* is a term frequently used; and common consent allows it apt and proper."[61]

This affinity has continued down the generations and must be set against the snobbish WASP anti-Semitism (directed mainly against the East European Jewish immigrants who arrived in the United States from the 1880s on, rather than the longer-established Germans and Sephardim). To it was added a strong liberal iden-tification with the Western democratic culture of Israel's founding generation.[62]

Less openly acknowledged, but immensely important, has been a "Jacksonian" respect for Israel's tough, militarist society and its repeated victories in war, and for the military achievements and the macho personal style of Israeli soldiers-turned politician, like Ariel Sharon. This became especially important after 1967, when Israel's crushing victory over superior odds in a morally justified war of self-defense provided a measure of psychological compensation for America's own defeat in Vietnam.[63]

There is, however, a darker side to this, recalled by T. R. Fehrenbach's words on Texan memory. The conquest of land from savage enemy peoples remains central to most of the history of white North America. Gordon Welty, among others, sees a strong affinity between the "muscular theology" of the Israeli Fundamentalist Right and that of the American pioneer tradition: "Since the 'frontier' of America is gone, they seek to re-create it elsewhere."[64] This tradition is reflected in Donald Rumsfeld's notorious remark of 2002 concerning the Jewish settlements on the West Bank: "Focusing on settlements at the present time misses the point... Settlements in various parts of the so-called occupied area... were the result of a war, which they [the Israelis] won."[65]

The circumstances of the Israeli–Palestinian conflict since the 1930s, and the creation of Jewish settlements in the occupied territories since 1967, have also created a parallel between the situation of Israel and that of the American Indian frontier. In such cases, soldiers and civilians are mixed up together and fight, and the distinction between them often becomes blurred. Media attention has been focused on terrorism by Palestinians, but this takes place against a backdrop of con-tinual low-level civilian violence on both sides: stone throwing and other attacks on settlers by Palestinian youths, and vigilante-style behavior by the settlers.[66]

Thus Amos Elon described Meir Har-Zion, the famous paratrooper who com-bined his official military service in the 1950s with private freelance raids and reprisals against the Arabs: "Unsparing of himself and others, he was brutally indiscriminate in inflicting punishment upon his adversaries. He began to person-ify an Israeli version of the Indian Fighters in the American Wild West. Laconically killing Arab soldiers, peasants and townspeople in a kind of fury without hatred, he remained cold-blooded and thoroughly efficient, simply doing a job and doing it well."[67]

Of course, in this case as in that of the American frontier, to recall the ferocity of the Israeli fighters does not involve in any way glossing over the barbarity of their Palestinian and Arab opponents. These were and are savage wars on both sides. However, the chance to end the conditions that exacerbated such conflicts has been passed up by Israel through the settlement policy, as well as by Palestinian groups through their continued pursuit of terrorism.

Israel's development since 1967 into what Meron Benvenisti has called a *herrenvolk* Democracy, with power and status held by a ruling ethnicity, also corresponded to a core part of the "Jacksonian" ethos in the United States, at least until the 1960s.[68] Such beliefs formed a strong subtext to works like Leon Uris's fantastically popular novel *Exodus* (20 million copies sold by the 1990s, placing it in the same top category of success as the millenarian novels of Hal Lindsey and Tim LaHaye) and the film based on it.[69]

This identification with Israel would not matter much to U.S. and Western security, except that over the same period the wider Arab (and to a lesser extent Muslim) worlds have come equally to identify with the Palestinians in their struggle with the Israelis. The United States has a separate hegemonic agenda in the region, which is focused on control of access to oil, the deterrence or removal of hostile states, and the attempt to develop states and societies so as to ward off state failure, anti-Western revolution, or both.

This task would be difficult enough in itself, but it is made immeasurably more difficult by the embroilment of the United States in an essentially national conflict with the Palestinians and their Arab backers. The overthrow of pro-U.S. regimes in Egypt and Tunisia, and the electoral victories of Islamist parties in those countries, seems likely to worsen the U.S. position still further. This is especially true of Egypt, which because it borders on Israel and the Gaza Strip, may find itself drawn into new clashes with Israel even if its government would prudently wish to avoid these.

So as a result of a combination of Israel and oil, the United States finds itself pinned to a conflict-ridden and bitterly anti-American region in a way without precedent in its history. In all other regions of the world, the United States has been able to either help stabilize regional situations in a way that broadly conforms to its interests (Europe, Northeast Asia, Central America), or, if regional hostility is too great and the security situation too intractable, to withdraw (as from Mexico in 1917 and Indochina in the early 1970s).

If the result of U.S. entanglement in the Middle East is unprecedented embroilment in a series of conflicts, then this is likely to severely damage not only U.S. global leadership, but the character of U.S. nationalism, and even perhaps U.S. democracy. As the period of the Vietnam War indicated, prolonged war can bitterly divide American society and create severe problems for public order, and it may also help push the American government in the direction of secretive, paranoid, authoritarian, and illegal behavior.

America's regional position is not only worsened by the increased hostility that its support for Israel arouses among Muslims and in the former colonial world generally, equally important perhaps is that the violent nationalist passions that this conflict has engendered within U.S. society have made it much more difficult for that society to think clearly about its strategy in the Middle East and its relations with a range of countries around the world. The Obama administration attempted to rethink U.S. strategy in 2008–2012, and did manage to withdraw U.S. troops from Iraq. However, elsewhere in the Middle East, it has found itself stuck with many of the same policies as the Bush administration—above all, because the attachment of the U.S. political elites to Israel made any wider and deeper rethink extremely difficult. As with Pan-Slavism's role in Russian nationalism before 1914, the nature of the identification with Israel has become an integral part of the entire U.S. nationalist mixture and has helped influence U.S. nationalism in the direction of more radical and chauvinist positions.

Once again, this is not to criticize the principle of American identification with and support for Israel, which is, in itself, entirely legitimate, just as it is in the case of Armenia, Poland, or other countries with which large numbers of Americans retain close ethnic ties.[70] It is the combination of the unconditional terms of this commitment with Israeli policies that are so dangerous.[71] Compare this issue with the role of other ethnic lobbies: partly as a result of the influence of the Polish lobby in the United States, the United States strongly supported the accession of Poland and other Central European countries to NATO and the European Union. A condition of these accessions, however, was that the countries concerned should be fully democratic, should give fair and equal treatment to their ethnic minorities, and should have no unresolved territorial disputes with their neighbors.

A Tragic Imperative

The above propositions would be assented to by the overwhelming majority of the educated populations of Britain and America's other key allies in the world, and indeed by the great majority of people in the world who observe the Israeli–Palestinian conflict. They are very difficult to refute from the standpoint of the American Creed, at least as this has been defined during the decades since World War II.

It may well be the difficulty of defending their position within the scope of basic liberal principles that explains in part the hysteria among Israeli partisans that too often surrounds—and suppresses—attempts at frank discussion of these issues in America, and which is one of the most worrying aspects of the U.S. foreign policy scene. Of course, the principal reason for this atmosphere is the appalling crime and the terrible memory of the Holocaust, and its effects in deterring criticism of Israel and creating a belief in the legitimacy of Israeli demands for absolute security. The image of the Holocaust has been used deliberately by the Israeli lobby to consolidate support for Israel in the United States and elsewhere, but it also emerges quite naturally and spontaneously from Jewish and Jewish American consciousness.

However, whatever the natural, legitimate, and understandable roots of unconditional loyalty to Israel, the effects it must be said often resemble wider patterns of nationalism in the world. One of the saddest experiences of visits to countries experiencing national disputes and heightened moods of nationalism is to meet with highly intelligent, civilized, and moderate individuals whose capacity for reason and moderation vanishes as soon as the conversation touches on conflicts involving their own nation or ethnicity. Otherwise universally accepted standards of behavior, argument, and evidence are suspended, facts are conjured from thin air, critics are demonized, wild accusations are leveled, and rational argument becomes impossible.

I observed this as a journalist in the southern Caucasus in the run-up to the wars there in the early 1990s, and more than a decade earlier when visiting the then Yugoslavia as a student. It was therefore with dismay that I found exactly the same pattern repeating itself at dinner parties in Washington, DC, and New York as soon as the conversation touched on the Israeli–Palestinian conflict. Also immensely sad and troubling is to see ethical principles and intellectual standards crumble at the touch of national allegiance among scholars and thinkers whose work you deeply admire.[72]

Any condemnation of the pro-Israeli liberal intelligentsia of the United States, both Jewish and non-Jewish, must be tempered not only by the terrible impact of the Holocaust, but by an awareness of the extremely difficult ideological and ethical position in which they have found themselves since 1945, a position that is nothing short of a tragic dilemma. This stems in origin from the fact that for equally valid and legitimate reasons, Western Europe and the liberal intelligentsia of the United States on the one hand, and the greater part of the world's Jewish population on the other, drew opposing conclusions from the catastrophe of Nazism. And this split ran straight through the individual consciousness of most of the Jewish diaspora intelligentsia. This is not an enviable situation to be in.

The Western European elites, and the liberal intelligentsia of the United States, essentially decided that the correct response to Nazism, and to the hideous national conflicts that preceded, engendered, and accompanied Nazism, was to seek to limit, transcend, and overcome nationalism. Hence the creation of common European institutions leading to the European Union, and the great respect paid in Europe, and by many liberal Americans, to the UN and to developing institutions of international law and cooperation. Given the strong past connections between chauvinist nationalism and anti-Semitism (even to a degree in the United States), and the role of nationalism in Fascism, most of the Jewish diaspora intelligentsia naturally also identify with these attempts to overcome nationalism around the world.

However, given the failure of the Western world (including the United States) in the 1930s and 1940s to prevent genocide, or even—shamefully—to offer refuge to Jews fleeing the Nazis, it is entirely natural that a great many Jews decided that guarantees from the international community were not remotely sufficient to protect them against further attempts at massacre. They felt that, in addition, a Jewish national state was required, backed by a strong Jewish nationalism. This nationalism embodied strong and genuine elements of national liberation and social progressivism, akin to those of other oppressed peoples in the world, and it was from this that Zionism drew its powerful elements of moral nobility, as represented by figures like Ahad Ha'am, Martin Buber, and Nahum Goldmann.[73]

Israel also developed a central importance for Jewish diaspora communities because of the decline of religious belief and practice, of ethnic traditions, and of the Yiddish language, concurrent with the steep rise in intermarriage. These trends meant that these communities themselves feared that they might be in the process of dissolution.[74] Judaism had always been what Heinrich Heine called "the portable Fatherland of the Jews"; its eclipse threatened a form of soft extinction, unless a substitute could be found.[75]

Jacques Torczyner of the Zionist Organization of America declared during the Carter administration that "whatever the administration will want to do...the Jews in America will fight for Israel. It is the only thing we have to sustain our Jewish identity."[76] Or according to religious historian Martin Marty, "as other bases of Jewish identity continued to dwindle... Israel progressively became the spiritual center of the American Jewish experience."[77]

But although the bases for this sacralization of the nation were specifically and tragically Jewish, the advancement of nationalism as a substitute for fading religion and the transmogrification of religious passions into nationalist ones also forms part of a wider pattern in nationalist history, and one that in the past has contributed to national and international catastrophes: "Our most blooming life for Thy most withered tree, Germany!"[78]

Unlike most other national senses of martyrdom, the Jewish one was truly justified—unlike that of France after 1871, or Germany after 1918. But that has not saved many Jews from the pernicious results of such a sense of martyrdom in terms of nationalist extremism and self-justification—any more than it has the Armenians, for example. It has produced an atmosphere that has shaded into and tolerated the religious–nationalist fundamentalism of Israeli extremist groups and different groups of ideological settlers in the occupied territories, and crude hatred of Arabs and Muslims.[79]

Furthermore, while Zionism originated in the late nineteenth century and is a classic example of the modern "construction" of a nation, the Jewish ethnoreligious basis on which it did so represents the oldest and deepest "primordial" national identity in the world. As demonstrated by a series of clashes within Israel over the definition of who is a Jew, who can become a Jew, and who has the right to decide these questions, this is a basis for nationalism that, if not necessarily completely antithetical to notions of civic nationalism based on the American Creed, certainly has a complex and uneasy relationship to them, and this too is perceived by Muslim peoples to whom the United States wishes to spread its version of civic nationalism.

An appeal to religious and quasi-religious nationalist justifications for rule over Palestine was also implicit in the entire Zionist enterprise. Given the large majority of Palestinian Arabs throughout Palestine—even at the moment of the declaration of Israeli statehood in 1948—the claim to create a Jewish state in Palestine could not easily be justified on grounds of national liberation alone. It needed also to be backed by appeals to ancient ethnic claims and religious scripts, and by civilizational arguments of superiority to the backward Arabs and "making the desert bloom." These could not easily be assented to by other peoples around the world, and indeed made even many Western liberals think uneasily of their own nationalist and imperialist pasts.[80]

Following one original strand of Zionism, great Zionist leaders and thinkers like Nahum Goldmann originally dreamed that Israel would, like other civilized states, also be anchored in international institutions, and might even form part of a multiethnic federation with the Arab states of the Middle East, thereby resolving the dilemma in which Jewish diaspora liberalism found itself.[81]

Tragically, the circumstances in which Israel was created made any such resolution of the Jewish intellectual and moral dilemma exceptionally difficult, and would have done so for any group in this position. The intention here is not to condemn or vilify, but simply to point out the nature of the dilemma and the sad and dangerous consequences that have stemmed from it.

Amos Oz has written of the Israeli–Palestinian conflict that

> Zionism is a movement of national liberation, which has no need of any "consent" or "agreement" from the Arabs. But it must recognize that the conflict between us and the Palestinians is not a cheap Western in which civilized "goodies" are fighting against native "baddies." It is more like a Greek tragedy. It represents a clash between two conflicting rights. The Palestinian Arabs have a strong and legitimate claim, and the Israelis must recognize this, without this recognition leading us into self-denial or feelings of guilt. We are bound to accept a painful compromise, and admit that the land of Israel is the homeland of two nations, and we must accept its partition in one form or another.[82]

It cannot be emphasized too strongly that if the Palestinian Arabs in the 1930s and 1940s had agreed that a large part of Palestine—where they were still a large majority and had until recently been an overwhelming one—should be given up to form the state of Israel, they would have been acting in a way that, as far as I am aware, would have had no precedent in all of human history. And it is not as if intelligent and objective observers did not point this out at the time. As Hannah Arendt wrote in 1945, three years before Israeli independence, the war with the Arabs, and the expulsion of the Palestinians:

> American Zionists from left to right adopted unanimously, at their last annual convention held in Atlantic City in October 1944, the demand for a "free and democratic Jewish commonwealth...[which] shall embrace the whole of Palestine, undivided and undiminished"...The Atlantic City Resolution goes even a step further than the Biltmore Program (1942) in which the Jewish minority had granted minority rights to the Arab majority. This time the Arabs were simply not mentioned in the resolution, which obviously leaves them the choice between voluntary emigration or second-class citizenship. It seems to admit that only opportunist reasons had previously prevented

the Zionist movement from stating its final aims. These aims now seem to be completely identical with those of the extremists as far as the future political constitution of Palestine is concerned…By stating it with such bluntness in what seemed to them an appropriate moment, Zionists have forfeited for a long time any chance of *pourparlers* with Arabs; for whatever Zionists may offer, they will not be trusted.[83]

Throughout history, even the great assimilating religious–nationalist movements and empires were only rarely able to incorporate new peoples without some violence, and—despite the dreams of Herzl and others concerning a multiethnic Jewish state—Zionism is very explicitly *not* a force for the assimilation of non-Jews. In other words, whatever one's condemnation of the Palestinians and Arabs for their long delay in coming to terms with the reality of Israel, to blame them for initially resisting that reality is to engage in moral and historical idiocy. While condemning the Arabs as demons, it suggests that they should have acted as saints. The tragedy of 1948 is therefore not only of a clash of valid rights, but also that neither side in this conflict could have acted otherwise. Abba Eban said just as much, years later:

> The Palestine Arabs, were it not for the Balfour Declaration and the League of Nations Mandate, could have counted on eventual independence either as a separate state or in an Arab context acceptable to them…It was impossible for us to avoid struggling for Jewish statehood and equally impossible for them to grant us what we asked. If they had submitted to Zionism with docility, they would have been the first people in history to have voluntarily renounced their majority status.[84]

Thus it is surprising that self-styled Western liberals, scholars, and intellectuals among Israel's partisans go on using the Palestinian rejection of partition in 1948 as a form of permanently damning original sin. The reasons why most Americans have had such difficulty recognizing this, however, go beyond the desire to support Israel and edit out anything that might qualify that support or give any ammunition to the enemies of Israel. They are also related to features of American culture well summed up by T. R. Fehrenbach concerning the deep unwillingness of Americans to look seriously at the fate of the Native Americans: "The culmination of the Indian wars was a tragedy, with all the classic inevitability of tragedy, and against true tragedy the North American soul revolts."[85]

Thus to his great credit, Saul Bellow, in the 1970s, joined Walter Laqueur, Leonard Bernstein, and other leading Jewish American cultural and intellectual figures in publicly opposing the establishment of settlements in the Occupied Territories (the then senator Abraham Ribicoff took the same line).[86] In his memoir *To Jerusalem and Back*, Bellow acknowledged that "a sweeping denial of Arab grievances is an obstacle to peace." At the same time, he agrees with Laqueur in saying of the Zionists that in seeking to establish a state "their sin was that they behaved like other peoples. Nation states have never come into existence peace-fully and without injustices."[87]

Yet these writers did not follow up with the obvious corollary, which is that the Palestinians too "behaved like other peoples" in fighting to hold on to their ances-tral land where they were a large majority. Even Norman Mailer, while strongly criticizing present Israeli policies, has suggested that the Palestinians are at fault for not having welcomed Jewish refugees in the 1940s.

Instead, self-described liberals like Alan Dershowitz have explicitly used argu-ments of collective Arab and Palestinian guilt as a justification. This is not only false historically, but is also incompatible with contemporary liberal values, and feeds into American chauvinism toward Muslims and Arabs. According to Dershowitz, "the Arabs bore sufficient guilt for the Holocaust and for supporting the wrong side during World War II to justify their contribution, as part of the losing side, in the rearrangement of territory and demography that inevitably follows a cataclys-mic world conflict."[88]

Saul Bellow, for his part, in the passage cited above, immediately slips into familiar tropes about Arab hostility to Israel being akin to German cruelty toward the Jews, both of them reflecting a kind of "insanity," and ends on a plangent note that simply sweeps away concrete issues of Israeli behavior and Palestinian suffer-ing: "Israel must reckon with the world, and with the madness of the world, and to a most grotesque extent. And all because the Israelis wished to lead Jewish lives in a Jewish state." Such statements, which in one form or another I have heard repeated again and again in conversations in the United States, laid the founda-tions for a view of "the world" itself as the mad and evil enemy of Israel and the United States.

In contrast, David Ben Gurion himself is reported (by Nahum Goldmann) to have asked in private:

> Why should the Arabs make peace? If I were an Arab leader I would never make terms with Israel. That is natural: we have taken their country. Sure, God promised it to us, but what does that matter to them? Our God is not theirs. We came from Israel, it's true, but two thousand years ago, and what is that to them? There has been anti-Semitism, the Nazis, Hitler, Auschwitz, but was that their fault? They only see one thing: we have come here and stolen their country. Why should they accept that?[89]

Together with the establishment of the Jewish state came the war of 1948 and the expulsion of most of the Arab population of Palestine from the territories of the new Jewish state. So intolerable to the liberal conscience was this action, and so deeply did it seem to call into question the legitimacy of the new state, that for two generations it had to be denied, with absurd arguments being advanced instead—in the face of logic and both Palestinian and Jewish testimony—that the Palestinians had somehow fled voluntarily on the orders of the Arab governments and their own leaders. Indeed, some leading Israeli partisans in the United States are in essence still arguing this.[90]

For my own part, though, I deeply regret the human suffering caused by the expulsions of 1948, but I have never been especially shocked by them—if only because the facts were largely available, from Israeli sources quoted in various books, long before Israeli revisionist historians "revealed" from the late 1980s on that the expulsion of the Palestinians was in large part a process deliberately planned by the Israeli leadership and accompanied by numerous atrocities.[91] And with regret—and without in any way endorsing the infamous collective guilt argument advanced by Dershowitz and others—I must on the whole accept Morris's recent arguments that this cruel process was necessary if the state of Israel was to be established and its Jewish population was to avoid renewed extermination or exile:

> Ben-Gurion was a transferist. He understood that there could be no Jewish state with a large and hostile Arab minority in its midst. There would be no such state. It would not be able to exist...Ben-Gurion was right. If he had not done what he did, a state would not have come into being. That has to be clear. It is impossible to evade it. Without the uprooting of the Palestinians, a Jewish state would not have arisen here...There are circumstances in history that justify ethnic cleansing. I know that this term is completely negative in the discourse of the 21st century, but when the choice is between ethnic cleansing and genocide—the annihilation of your people—I prefer ethnic cleansing.[92]

This was, after all, the 1940s. At the end of World War II, some 12 million Germans were expelled from eastern Germany when those lands were annexed to Poland and Russia, and three million from Czechoslovakia, amidst immense suffering, atrocity, and loss of life. Hungarians were deported from Czechoslovakia and Rumania. And allied peoples also suffered. As Poles moved westward into former German lands, so millions were deported by Stalin into Poland from the Soviet Union to create more ethnically homogeneous populations in Soviet Lithuania, Byelorussia, and Ukraine. In 1947, a year before the creation of Israel and the expulsion of the Palestinians, more than 10 million Hindus, Sikhs, and Muslims fled from their homes as a result of the partition of the British Indian Empire, amidst horrendous bloodshed. A generation earlier, Greece and Turkey had conducted a great exchange of populations after repeated national conflicts involving great atrocities on both sides.

Horrible though these events were, they did in some ways lay the ground for a future absence of war, which is difficult to imagine if these populations had remained mixed up together. Certainly it is difficult to imagine how a Jewish state could possibly have been established and consolidated with such a huge and understandably hostile Palestinian minority.[93] Finally, Israel does have a legitimate case that the subsequent expulsion to Israel of hundreds of thousands of Jews from Arab countries did create a kind of rough justice between Israel and the Arab world.

Today it should also be quite clear that if one of the absolute preconditions for peace between Israel and the Palestinians is Israeli abandonment of many settlements in the Occupied Territories, the other is Palestinian abandonment of the "right of return" for those Palestinians who were expelled in 1948.[94] I should add that I strongly support the Jewish "right of return" to Israel within the borders of 1967 as an ultimate fallback line in the event of a real return of anti-Semitism elsewhere in the world.

But while the expulsions may have been necessary for Israel's survival, the lies that they have generated over the succeeding generations, and which continue to this day, have been extremely dangerous for both Israel and the United States. It would have been far better if Israel, and partisans of Israel in the United States, had—like Ben Gurion in private—accepted the truth of what happened in 1948 and then used it as the basis for thinking seriously about compensation and laying the foundations for future peace. Instead, the pro-Israel camp committed itself to an interlocking set of moral and historical falsehoods.[95] Over time, the intellectual consequences of these positions have spread like a forest of aquatic weeds until they have entangled and choked a significant part of the U.S. national debate concerning relations not only with the Muslim world, but with the outside world in general, and have thereby fed certain strains of American nationalism.

To the refusal to consider the Palestinian case before 1948, and to acknowledge the expulsions of that year, was added for several decades a widespread refusal to admit the existence of the Palestinians as a people, with consequent national rights, summed up in Golda Meir's notorious statement (echoed by innumerable Israeli partisans in the United States): "It was not as though there was a Palestinian people and in Palestine considering itself a Palestinian people and we came and threw them out and took their country away from them. They did not exist."[96]

Thus in 1978 Hyman H. Bookbinder of the American Jewish Committee denounced the Carter administration for even using the words "homeland" or "legitimate rights" with reference to the Palestinians.[97] This meant, in turn, that the real bases of Arab grievances against Israel could not be considered, and Arab hostility had to be explained away either by inveterate hatred and malignity (anti-Semitism) or the sinister and cynical machinations of Arab regimes.[98]

Of course, both these elements have indeed been present among Arab and Muslim enemies of Israel. But the necessity of making them the *only* real explanations for Arab and Muslim hostility led inexorably to the demonization of Arab and Muslim societies and culture—and later, by extension, of sympathizers with the Palestinians in Europe and elsewhere. Such demonization was by no means always a deliberate strategy of Israeli partisans. In many cases, the sin was rather one of omission. By keeping silent on the subject of what had happened to the Palestinians, and the roots of the Israeli–Palestinian and Israeli–Arab conflicts, intellectual supporters of Israel left irrational, cynical, and implacable hostility as the only available explanations of Arab behavior. Or as Edward Said has written, "to criticize Zionism...is to criticize not so much an idea or a theory but rather a wall of denials."[99]

The position of the pro-Israeli liberal intelligentsia in the United States toward the Israeli–Palestinian conflict came somewhat to resemble the position of many enlightened nineteenth-century Americans toward the clash between slavery and the American Creed, as described 100 years ago by Herbert Croly: "The thing to do was to shut your eyes to the inconsistency, denounce anyone who insisted on it as unpatriotic, and then hold on tight to both horns of the dilemma. Men of high intelligence, who really loved their country, persisted in this attitude."[100]

One result of this uneasy moral situation has been a tendency to launch especially vituperative attacks on anyone who draws attention to the radical inconsistencies between the stances of many American liberals on the Israel–Palestine conflict and the attitudes of the same people toward other such conflicts. Backed by the tremendous institutional power of the Israeli lobby, this has had the effect of severely limiting discussion of this conflict in the United States. The reporting of the conflict is generally fair enough, but it tends to lack all historical context, thereby allowing Palestinians to be portrayed simply as terrorists with no explanation of why they are fighting (unlike the U.S. coverage of the Chechen wars, for example). Much more serious, however, is the general bias of the editorial pages toward partisans of Israel. Unconditional, hard-line partisans of Israel are given regular space even in the *New York Times* (which emerged as a moderate critic of Likud policies and Bush administration support for them). Hard-line critics of Israel, in contrast, never appear. Such criticism as is permitted is by moderates, and is highly qualified and restrained.[101]

As Arnaud de Borchgrave (himself a hard-line conservative, and, in part, of Jewish descent) has written bitterly, "for many American Jews, anyone who writes disapprovingly of the policies of Israeli Prime Minister Ariel Sharon and of his Dionysian neo-conservative backers in Washington is evidence of 'classic anti-Semitism.' The mere reference to 'neo-cons' is interpreted to mean an attack against a 'Jewish cabal'...Israeli newspapers—particularly Ha'aretz, the New York Times of Israel—make our own critiques tame by comparison."[102]

With time, freedom of debate in the United States might have increased, and indeed it did improve markedly in the 1990s, until the collapse of the Israeli–Palestinian peace process, the resumption of Palestinian terrorism, and 9/11 turned the clock back again. Over time, Israeli military victories and technological advances have assured it of security against invasion, and Israel has become a more and more firmly established and indeed brilliantly successful state and society. These successes should have diminished fears that by discussing the circumstances of its birth one would somehow be calling its legitimate existence into question. Despite the hateful rhetoric of the Iranian regime, a large majority of Arab countries remain supportive of a peace settlement with Israel, assuming that Israel withdraws from the lands occupied in 1967 and is willing to reach some form of compromise over Jerusalem and refugee return.

Ever since 9/11 the editorial pages of the *New York Times* and a number of other American journals have taken a more fair and balanced view of the Israel–Palestinian conflict than they did 20 years ago. Very few mainstream writers, however, have gone from criticism of Israel to adopt the logical consequence of their criticisms and call for pressure on Israel and withdrawal of U.S. support—which they would certainly have done in the case of any other state that received massive U.S. aid and defied U.S. wishes. As a result, their criticisms are deficient in both political and moral content.[103] Even the State Department each year produces a human rights report on Israel and the Occupied Territories that is often very critical of Israeli behavior. The problem is that the United States takes no action as a result.[104]

Starting with President Anwar Sadat of Egypt in 1977, more and more of the Arab world has admitted that Israel is here to stay, and ideas of driving it into the sea are an empty fantasy. This process culminated in the peace plan drawn up by Prince Abdullah of Saudi Arabia in 2002, and approved by an overwhelming majority of the Arab League, offering to recognize Israel within the borders of 1967.

In the meantime, however, successive Israeli governments made the fateful decision to encourage the creation of Jewish settlements in the territories conquered in the Six Day War.[105] This decision necessitated a continued denial of the national existence of the Palestinians, long after it had become obvious that the Palestinians had in fact developed a coherent national consciousness separate from that of other Arab peoples. Indeed, one of the tragicomic aspects of the Israeli hard-line camp is that it might be described as Pan-Arabist, since it professes to believe that the Arabs are all one people and therefore that Palestinians have no homeland of their own and might as well live anywhere in the Arab world.

The issue of the settlements helped add another thick layer of evasion and chauvinism to the politics and rhetoric of the Israeli lobby in the United States, and not just to the rhetoric, but to the reasoning of U.S. politicians who support Israel, because as a result of their creation and the need to defend their presence, Arab states and individuals could not be admitted to be moderate and reasonable *even if* they offered to sign a peace treaty with Israel within the borders of 1967. Any such offers had to be either ignored, or their authors demonized as inherently mendacious, untrustworthy, and devoted to Israel's destruction. Discussions with Arab and Palestinian moderates had to be either prevented, or drowned in a torrent of denunciation. Offers like that of Prince Abdullah had to be first brushed aside, and then their authors discredited by a flood of attacks on Arab countries in general and Saudi Arabia in particular as regressive, barbarous, dictatorial, and therefore inherently untrustworthy.[106]

The question of Israeli occupation of the West Bank and Gaza Strip had to be presented as vital to Israel's very survival. This in turn required a constant exaggeration of existential threats to Israel, and hence of the power and malignity of Israel's (and America's) Muslim enemies. The result has been a paranoid discourse of permanent emergency and existential crisis with all too many precedents in the history of militarist nationalism. And too much of this discourse is not focused where it should be, on the real terrorist threat to Israel, and the need to reduce this by ending settlement construction and withdrawing from the West Bank and Gaza Strip. Nor is it focused on the equally real demographic threat to Israel if it continues to rule over huge numbers of Palestinians. On the contrary, it portrays a quite unreal military threat to Israel from Arab states, and is used as a means of diverting public debate away from the real issues of settlements and occupation. Thus, in February 2003, Daniel Pipes wrote that "the existence of Israel appeared imperiled as it had not been for decades." Yaacov Lozowick, of the Israeli Holocaust Museum, has written a book in which all Israel's conflicts, whether of genuine self-defense and survival or of invasion and occupation, are subsumed under "Israel's right to exist."[107] In June 2011, Newt Gingrich declared that "Israel and America are at a dangerous crossroads in which the survival of Israel and the safety of the United States both hang in the balance."[108]

Remarks like this deliberately feed the paranoia of American nationalism as well, and they go to the heart of what has gone wrong with Israeli strategy and U.S. support for that strategy in recent decades. During that period, Israel was repeatedly attacked, but in consequence won a series of great victories, first military, then political. For most of its early history Israel was threatened by militarily powerful Arab rejectionist states backed and armed by the Soviet Union. However, these states were crushingly defeated by Israel in 1967, and to a lesser extent in 1973.

Thereafter, the defection of Egypt from the anti-Israel bloc, and the Egyptian regime's adoption of the United States as supplier and protector, made any further serious conventional military threat to Israel inconceivable for the foreseeable future. The victory of Islamist parties in Egyptian elections following the revolution of 2011 will increase the danger that Palestinian terrorists will receive help from Egypt. However, in view of the crushing defeats suffered by Egypt in the past, it is extremely unlikely that an Islamist government would push this to the point of war, or that the Egyptian army—which at the time of writing retain ultimate control of Egypt—would permit them to do so.

An additional reason why another attack on Israel similar to 1967 or 1973 is highly unlikely is that Israel has developed a powerful nuclear deterrent as an ultimate and effective guarantee against any threat to its existence from Muslim states (though not, of course, against catastrophic terrorist attack). After 1989, the collapse of the Soviet Union not only reduced the threat to Israel still further by depriving the remaining Arab "rejectionist" states of their superpower backer, it released a huge flood of Soviet Jewish emigrants, securing Israel's demographic position within the borders of 1967.

If the occupied territories are kept in a "Greater Israel," of course, the demographic picture looks utterly different, and Israel really will be in terrible danger either as a Jewish state, or as a democracy, or both. Henry Siegman has written of the Palestinian demographic threat, in words that also remind us of the falsity of claims concerning continued existential threats to Israel within the borders of 1967:

> Morris's account points to the sorry fact that there is not much that distinguishes how Jews behaved in 1948 in their struggle to achieve statehood from Palestinian behavior today. At the very least, this sobering truth should lead to a shedding of the moral smugness of too many Israelis and to a reexamination of their demonization of the Palestinian national cause.
>
> The implication of the above for the territorial issue is that it would be irrational for Palestinians *not* to believe that the goal of Sharon's fence is anything other than their confinement in a series of Bantustans, if not a prelude to a second transfer...
>
> Unless Israelis are willing to preserve their majority status by imposing a South African–style apartheid regime, or to complete the transfer begun in 1948, as Morris believes they will—policies which one hopes a majority of Israelis will never accept—it is only a matter of time before the emerging majority of Arabs in Greater Israel will reshape the country's national identity. That would be a tragedy of historic proportions for the Zionist enterprise and for the Jewish people.
>
> What will make the tragedy doubly painful is that it will be happening at a time when changes in the Arab world and beyond...are removing virtually every strategic threat that for so long endangered Israel's existence. That existence is now threatened by the greed of the settlers and the political blindness of Israel's leaders.[109]

Abba Eban's famous line that the Palestinians have "never missed an opportunity to miss an opportunity" to seek peace or gain political advantage has all too often been proved true. Certainly the PLO's record has often been both politically lamentable and morally revolting, and the same is true of leading Arab regimes. Palestinian leadership has been generally abysmal. Palestinian terrorism has been disastrous and unjustifiable from every possible point of view. But this does not excuse the policies of successive Israeli governments toward the Palestinians. In the words of Amos Elon, "it does not condone terror and murder to say that the Palestinians have a case."[110] Until the 1990s most Arab governments refused to recognize Israel under any circumstances, and Israel similarly refused to recognize the existence of the Palestinians as a separate people enjoying rights of self-determination and genuine self-government.

If Israel had respected the Geneva Convention, and maintained a military occupation of the West Bank and Gaza Strip pending a peace treaty without planting illegal settlements there, then it could have responded positively to later Arab offers to recognize and make peace with Israel within the borders of 1967—like those of King Hussein in the 1970s and Prince Abdullah of Saudi Arabia in 2003.[111] Israel would also have been in a position to negotiate both quickly and sincerely on the basis of Oslo, focusing on the establishment of international guarantees for Israeli security and Palestinian abandonment of the right of return.

Instead, Oslo was frittered away in endless haggling while the settlements expanded further—giving the Palestinians the feeling that the whole process was only a delaying tactic to allow more land to be stolen from under their feet. This eventually contributed greatly to the disastrous Palestinian decision to reject Barak's peace offer of July 2000 and Clinton's of January 2001, and to the catastrophe of the second Intifada.[112]

"Anti-Semitism" and Hatred of the World

Closely linked to systematic exaggeration of the degree of contemporary geopolitical threat to Israel by the Israeli lobby in the United States has been the recent campaign in both the United States and Israel alleging that criticism of Israel is overwhelmingly anti-Semitic in motivation. It is also stated that this reflects a great wave of new anti-Semitism in Europe and around the world, which is closely linked to hatred of America. Or in the simple title of an essay by Manfred Gerstenfeld: "Anti-Semitism: Integral to European Culture."[113] This too feeds into wider American chauvinism vis-à-vis Europe and the outside world in general. It increases the tendency in the American antithesis to see the entire world outside America (except for Israel) as irredeemably wicked and hostile, and the belief that the values and institutions of the American Creed can be truly held only by Americans and Israelis.

The savage history of anti-Semitism culminating in the Holocaust makes this subject one of unparalleled moral gravity, and the accusation of anti-Semitism one that should carry crushing moral weight. And indeed, the very grave consequences that can occur for an academic or public figure in the United States who is accused of anti-Semitism also make this matter an extremely serious one.

Unfortunately, all too often in the United States today it is not being treated seriously. For example, this book was attacked as "anti-Semitic" in a review by Jonathan Tepperman that appeared in the New York Times. Readers can judge for themselves from this chapter whether there is the slightest truth in this allegation.[114]

The slur of "anti-Semitism" was used on a very large scale against the most important book on the U.S. relationship with Israel to have appeared over the past decade, The Israel Lobby, by Stephen Walt and John Mearsheimer.[115] The original essay on which the book was based was commissioned but then rejected by the Atlantic Monthly, and was published instead in the London Review of Books. The facts that the book was published in America, was widely reviewed there (quite often positively, at least compared to previous works on the same subject), and, that unlike previous works on the same subject (like Feuerlicht's brilliant work The Fate of the Jews), it was not subsequently shunted into oblivion, are all encouraging signs for the state of the U.S. debate on Israeli policy and the U.S. relationship with Israel. Mearsheimer and Walt benefited by association from a book published in the same year by former President Jimmy Carter (the architect of the Camp

David Accords between Israel and Egypt), *Palestine: Peace Not Apartheid*, which, while not focusing on the Israel lobby as such, made many of the same criticisms of Israeli policy.[116] As a result, the debate on this subject in America has opened up to some extent compared to the situation a generation ago.

Other aspects of the Mearsheimer–Walt controversy have however been a good deal less encouraging. All too many American establishment liberals, instead of taking a clear stand on Mearsheimer and Walt's central argument, resorted to nitpicking criticisms of alleged minor historical inaccuracies, which in other circumstances they would have ignored. Mearsheimer and Walt showed great moral courage in writing a book that they knew well would attract bitter unpopularity in important circles (something that I was also warned of when I first presented the theses of this book in Washington, DC). However, it has to be said that as senior tenured professors at the University of Chicago and Harvard, respectively, their jobs at least were fairly safe—something that is emphatically not true of junior untenured academics or members of think tanks, let alone aspiring politicians or government officials. Finally, while works such as theirs and Jimmy Carter's may perhaps have strengthened to some degree the desire of President Obama for an Israeli–Palestinian settlement, as of 2012 it is alas all too clear that they have had no effect whatsoever on the behavior of the U.S. Congress or the overwhelming majority of U.S. political elites.

Accusations that authors like Mearsheimer, Walt, and myself are guilty of "anti-Semitism" have formed part of a much wider campaign suggesting that the threat from anti-Semitism in the world is greater than at any time since the 1930s—or even as bad as then. Thus Abraham Foxman of the Anti-Defamation League states, "I am convinced we currently face as great a threat to the safety and security of the Jewish people as the one we faced in the 1930s—if not a greater one."[117] Phyllis Chesler wrote that "I fear that the Jews may again be sacrificed to a world gone mad and in search of a sacred scapegoat."[118] Representatives of the Christian Right in the United States joined in these warnings.

This language is itself more than a little mad. Despite the rise of China, America as of 2012 remains the world's only superpower and a stable liberal democracy. It is committed to support and defend Israel. Unlike the situation of the defenseless Jews of Europe under Nazi rule, Israel not only exists as a haven for Jews fleeing persecution, but possesses nuclear weapons and has repeatedly shown its willingness and ability successfully to defend itself against attack. Unlike in the 1930s, the American political classes are overwhelmingly opposed to anti-Semitism in any form. The major European states are also stable and successful democracies, in which Jews enjoy the same rights as all other citizens. With very rare exceptions like Austria, anti-Semitic parties are tiny, marginal, or even illegal. Among the larger extreme right-wing parties, like the National Front in France and the Liberal Democrats in Russia, anti-Semitic feeling is now dwarfed by hatred of Muslims. In fact, Muslim minorities seem to have pretty definitively taken on the role of the alien and disliked "other" in European right-wing thinking. It is overwhelmingly thugs from these Muslim minorities who are carrying out physical attacks on Jews in Europe, while these communities are themselves being targeted by right-wing thugs from the majority European populations. This is worrying, and disgraceful, but it is not the 1930s.

The leaders and main political parties in these countries for their part have repeatedly denounced anti-Semitism, and their programs or ideologies bear no resemblance whatsoever to those of the Nazis or the other extreme Rightist movements before 1945. Indeed, the entire European project, including the enlargement of the EU to the former Soviet bloc, has been explicitly based on a repudiation of those past crimes and errors. Although there is a historical strain of anti-Semitism in certain sections of the European Left, the absolutely overwhelming majority of mainstream left-wing critics of Israel in Europe—among whom are many Jewish Europeans— would never contemplate the introduction into their own states of even the mildest of the anti-Semitic measures of the past. Such steps as restrictions on entry into universities, exclusion from leading social institutions, or banning from the civil service and officer corps would be utterly alien to their traditions and ideology, which stress openness and equality for people of all races, ethnicities, and religions.

Thus in the course of vilifying the contemporary French Left as anti-Semitic, American critics have forgotten that it was the Left that defended Dreyfus, that three Socialist premiers of France have been Jewish, and that though there certainly were anti-Semites on the Left, the defining hostility of the French Left historically was not anti-Semitism, but anticlericalism. Whatever writers like Gabriel Schoenfeld may allege, there is in fact *no* "clear fit between…anti-Jewish hatred and the general ideological predispositions of the contemporary European Left."[119]

Russia, of course, is not a stable democracy, but even there the government has condemned anti-Semitism and sought good relations with Israel (leading to excellent relations between Vladimir Putin and Natan Sharansky, for example), and Jews hold leading positions in the state and economy. Since the fall of the Soviet Union, no less than three Russians of Jewish origin have been prime minister of Russia: Sergei Kiriyenko, Yevgeny Primakov, and Mikhail Fradkov. How on earth can this situation be rationally compared to the world of Hitler, Mussolini, Stalin, and Antonescu?

Such charges are in part natural and spontaneous, stemming from the ghastly history of Jewish persecution culminating in the Holocaust. Seymour Lipset notes that in 1985, according to a poll, a majority of Jewish Americans in San Francisco were sincerely convinced that no Jew could be elected to the U.S. Congress from San Francisco—when in fact all three members of Congress were Jewish Americans, plus the two state senators and the mayor![120]

In the words of Irving Howe, which also have relevance for the wider feelings of hereditary defeat and persecution among many Americans described in chapter 3:

> Haunted by the demons of modern history, most of the immigrants and many of their children kept a fear, somewhere in their minds, that anti-Semitism might again become a serious problem in America. By mid-century, it was

often less an actual fear than a persuasion that they *should* keep this fear, all past experience warranting alertness even if there was no immediate reason for anxiety…It is crucial to note here that even in the mid-twentieth century many American Jews, certainly a good many of those who came out of the east European immigrant world, still *felt* like losers. Being able to buy a home, or move into a suburb, or send kids to college could not quickly dissolve that feeling. Black antagonism…was linked in their minds with a possible resurgence of global anti-Semitism and the visible enmity of Arabs towards Israel. And who could easily separate, in such reactions, justified alarm from "paranoid" excess?[121]

Accusations of anti-Semitism are also being used consciously and deliberately as part of a strategy to try to silence critics of Israel. This was in effect admitted in a backhanded way by Norman Podhoretz, Nathan Perlmutter, and Irving Kristol, who urged that anti-Semitic statements on the part of Christian conservatives like Pat Robertson should be forgiven because they are supporters of Israel: "After all, why should Jews care about the theology of a fundamentalist preacher when they do not for a moment believe that he speaks with any authority on the question of God's attentiveness to human prayer? And what do such theological abstractions matter as against the mundane fact that the same preacher is vigorously pro-Israel?"[122] Or in the words of Perlmutter: "Is it good for the Jews? This question satisfied, I proceed to the secondary issues…Jews can live with all the domestic priorities of the Christian Right on which liberal Jews differ so radically because none of these concerns is as important as Israel."[123]

The Israeli lobby, like the American nationalist Right, pays special attention to U.S. academia, which is the one major portion of U.S. society where a genuine debate on this subject does take place.[124] Now it should be noted that, as in Europe, left-wing and Arab groups on campus do all too frequently engage in rhetoric and actions that are not only excessively anti-Israeli but also on occasions anti-Semitic.[125] As David Friedman accurately writes of this wing of American academic politics, "many of the speeches have a mindless quality which repels the listener. The speakers are loud in their denunciations of American and Israeli policy, but they lose moral force and political effectiveness by maintaining a tight-lipped silence about terrorism and dictatorship in the Middle East and elsewhere."[126]

American teachers and administrators on campuses where such propaganda is prevalent have a duty to combat it and where appropriate to suppress it. However, it should be noted that however revolting, the forces guilty of these rhetorical excesses are utterly powerless beyond the narrow confines of some U.S. university campuses, and of course not dominant even there. In the world of politics, lobbying, and think tanks in Washington, DC, they are, in my experience, virtually nonexistent. They do not even remotely begin to compare in influence on American society, politics, and government with the Israel lobby.[127] Moreover, it must be emphatically stated that Mearsheimer and Walt are certainly *not* guilty of whitewashing Muslim crimes in order to attack Israel.

Indeed, it often seems that their most important role is to be used by partisans of Israel in the West as "straw men" whose extremist arguments can be both easily demolished and used as a diversionary tactic to avoid engaging with the serious arguments of Israeli liberals and patriots like Avraham Burg, Amos Oz, Yossi Beilin, or General Shlomo Gazit.[128] For in the words of Akiva Eldar, in the Israeli newspaper *Ha'aretz*:

> It is much easier to claim the whole world is against us than to admit that the State of Israel, which rose as a refuge and source of pride for Jews, has not only turned into a place less Jewish and less safe for its citizens, but has become a genuine source of danger and a source of shameful embarrassment to Jews who choose to live beyond its borders. Arguing that it takes an anti-Semite to call the Israeli government's policies of 2003 a danger to world peace is a contemptible cheapening of the term anti-Semitism.[129]

The campaign to brand critics of Israel as anti-Semites, and to portray a monstrous and terrifying wave of anti-Semitism in Europe and the world, has effects on the United States that go far beyond the specific issues concerned, effects that directly strengthen the forces of the "American nationalist antithesis" described and analyzed in this book. This campaign contributes to wider American hostility toward the outside world, made worse by the levels of ignorance described in chapter 2. To judge by the comments of university teachers with whom I have spoken, for all too many American students the entire history of France has been reduced to the Dreyfus Case and Vichy, the whole history of Germany before 1945 to the Holocaust, and the whole history of Tsarist Russia to Cossacks and pogroms.

In the Muslim world and among Muslim immigrant groups in Europe, hatred of Israel certainly has spilled over into hatred of Jews in general, and this hatred is being fed by recycled anti-Semitic myths from the darkest pages of Europe's past. This tendency must be combated as part of general efforts to bring peace to the region, to improve its level of education and public discourse, and to lay the foundations for democracy and help it develop in other ways—and in Europe, to help integrate Muslim immigrants into Western society.[130]

However, to use these vile beliefs as a means of absolving Israel of any responsibility for its actions is just as wrong—and just as bad for Israel—as to suggest that the existence of anti-Americanism in the world means that it does not matter what the United States does. All the evidence suggests, for example, that the flare-up in anti-Semitic violence by Muslims in France stemmed directly from what they saw as Israeli atrocities against the Palestinians. Granted, their views of these atrocities were exaggerated, but equally, their criminal response was a response to events as well as the product of a warped intellectual background.

It is entirely clear that while Muslim prejudice against Jewish and Christian "infidels" (though to a much lesser extent than against Hindu and other "heathens") existed historically, modern anti-Semitism in the Muslim world stems overwhelmingly from the creation of Israel and its real or perceived crimes against the Palestinians. In answer to charges by Dershowitz and others that it was the other way around, and that Muslim anti-Semitism led to anti-Israeli feeling, Brian Klug has proposed the simple counterfactual question: What if a state had been established in Palestine by Christian European settlers, as in French Algeria? Would the Muslim world not have opposed it just as fiercely? And in these circumstances, would there have been any strong degree of anti-Semitism in the Muslim world?[131]

Equally, if as a matter of just compensation for the Holocaust Germany east of the Oder-Neisse line had been given to Jews for a state in 1945 rather than being divided between Poland and the Soviet Union, would Muslims or anyone else in the world (other than Germans and some Poles) have denounced this as unjust or a Jewish crime? In this case, could there conceivably have been a wave of anti-Semitism among Muslims?

As Klug argues, hostility toward Israel in the developing and former colonial world (leading to repeated votes in the UN condemning Israel, and the infamous—and later reversed—equation of Zionism with racism), although it is colored by anti-Semitism, stems fundamentally from anticolonial feeling related to hostility toward Western colonists and the circumstances of Israel's gestation under British imperial rule.

Of course, much of this left-wing anticolonial attitude toward Israel may well be wrong, cynical, and even wicked. For that matter, this is true of a good part of "anticolonial" politics and rhetoric in general, both in the past and today. But the repellent and cynical use of such rhetoric by Robert Mugabe or the rulers of Burma is not generally held to compromise the positive, enlightened, state-building anticolonialism of a Nehru or a Mandela; and the failure in the U.S. mainstream to understand the anticolonial roots of hostility toward Israel in much of the world has wider effects in fuelling a contempt for world public opinion. It also contributes to an American blindness to the reasons why many former colonies and dependencies around the world that are by no means instinctively anti-American are nonetheless deeply hostile to the idea of American (or Western) military intervention in other states, and to any hint of new Western "civilizing missions."

But the damage done by much of the present discourse in the United States concerning anti-Semitism goes beyond its results in terms of increasing hostility toward Muslims, Europeans, and others, and thereby undermining the "war against terrorism." It also corrodes American political culture in general, by increasing nationalist paranoia, arrogance, hatred, and irrationality. When people can be anti-Semites without even knowing it and without proposing or believing anything that would have been regarded historically as anti-Semitic, when highly decorated Israeli soldiers become traitors and "self-hating Jews," when anti-Semitism itself loses all historical or cultural context and becomes a kind of free-floating miasma, drifting unchanged down the centuries, when it is argued that "Arab pre-Islamic persecution of the Jews began as early as the third century BCE," then rational debate is at an end.[132] This discourse has contributed to the atmosphere on the American Right as part of which—as described in previous chapters—President Obama has been accused of being a Muslim, a traitor, a non-American, and a sympathizer with terrorists.

In the words of Arendt in 1945, which remain entirely true in 2012: "The Zionists likewise fled the field of actual conflicts into a doctrine of eternal anti-Semitism governing the relations of Jews and Gentiles everywhere and always, and mainly responsible for the survival of the Jewish people. Thus both sides [i.e., the Zionists and the Assimilationists] relieved themselves of the arduous tasks of fighting anti-Semitism on its own grounds, which were political, and even of the unpleasant task of analyzing its true causes."[133]

Because by their nature such charges of anti-Semitism, unbacked by concrete evidence, can be neither proved nor disproved, they lead discussion away from the clearly lit arena of rational public discussion and toward the dark corridors of paranoia and conspiracy theories, evil spirits, and demonic possession—regions of the mind that in the past have been precisely the breeding grounds of anti-Semitic madness. In this way, parts of the U.S. discourse on Israel feed into the irrational and fanatical elements of the American nationalist antithesis in ways that endanger the United States, Israel, and indeed the world.

Conclusion

Gnothi Seauton ("Know Thyself")

—Epigraph in the Temple of Delphi

The American Creed, American civic nationalism, and the American democratic system they sustain have been a great force for civilization in the world. Within the United States they have, in the past, provided what might be called America's self-correcting mechanism, which has saved the United States from falling into either authoritarian rule or a permanent state of militant chauvinism.

Periods of intense nationalism, such as the panic leading to the passage of the Alien and Sedition Acts in the 1790s, the Know-Nothings of the 1840s, the anti-German hysteria of World War I, the anti-Japanese chauvinism of World War II, and McCarthyism in the 1950s, have been followed by a return to a more tolerant and pluralist equilibrium. Chauvinist and bellicose nationalism, though always present, has not become the U.S. norm and has not led to democratic institutions being replaced by authoritarian ones. Moreover, imperialist tendencies in the United States have been restrained by the belief, stemming from the creed, that America does not have and should not have an empire, as well as by isolationism and an unwillingness to make the sacrifices required.

Given the power of the American Creed in American society, there are good grounds to hope that this self-correcting mechanism will continue to operate in future. Indeed, even by the middle of 2004 the wilder ambitions of the Bush administration had already been considerably reduced as a result of public disquiet over the aftermath of the war in Iraq, and of the fundamental rationality of the greater part of the American establishment; and the Bush administration was succeeded in 2008 by that of President Obama, who, while he certainly sought to maintain U.S. predominance in the world, did so by far more restrained, multilateral, and intelligent means than those of Bush and his team.

However, there are also grounds for concern that in the future this self-correcting mechanism may fail and America may be drawn in a more and more chauvinist direction. The reasons for this can be summed up by saying that in the past the

216

United States went out to shape the world, while being itself protected from the world. Militarily, it was protected by the oceans; economically, it was protected by the immense strength and dominance of the American economy. This combination led in no small part to the unique American combination of power, omnipresence, innocence, and ignorance vis-à-vis the rest of humanity.

The first change is obviously that like most other countries in the twentieth century, the American heartland is now at risk of terrible attack with no precedents since the French-backed Indian menace disappeared after 1763. The Soviet nuclear menace was obviously a terrifying one, and had a seriously disturbing effect on U.S. politics, but no attack ever actually occurred. Throughout the cold war, not one American was ever killed by Communism on American soil. In contrast, a monstrous terrorist attack on the U.S. mainland occurred on September 11, 2001. It whipped aspects of American nationalism into a fury, and this fury was then directed by a U.S. administration and its domestic supporters against quite different targets.

Contrary to fears in the aftermath of 9/11, terrorist attacks on the American mainland have not become a pattern, thanks both to the weakness of the terrorists and effective security measures put in place by the Bush and Obama administrations. As a result, efforts by the Right in America to whip up a permanent state of anti-Muslim hysteria have had only limited success. However, the danger of further terrorist attacks has not gone away. Plans to carry out such attacks have been made, and in other parts of the world they have succeeded: in Madrid, London, Moscow, and many parts of the Muslim world.

If, God forbid, more large-scale acts of terrorism within the United States do occur, the mood of the American population could become one of a permanent "state of siege" and atmosphere of war, with civil liberties restricted and chauvinist politicians fishing assiduously for opportunities in the stew. In this context, it should be remembered that vigilantism and racial justice on the U.S. frontier ended only with the frontier itself, and the atmosphere of racial fear and a belief in potential conflict in the South also lasted for by far the greater part of American history, and ended only when the Southern racist system was overthrown by intervention from the rest of the United States in the mid-twentieth century. September 11 knocked U.S. pluralist democracy off balance. Further terrorist attacks might increase the list and make it permanent.

Closely connected with this new threat is the fact that the United States is involved in the greater Middle East in a way with no real precedent in U.S. history. In the case of all the other U.S. international military involvements throughout history, the United States was able to either pacify an area or withdraw from it, or both. In the case of Europe, Japan, and South Korea after World War II, the U.S. military remained present, but in peaceful countries that accepted the U.S. presence. In Vietnam, once it became clear that pacification was impossible, the United States was able to make a completely clean break and withdraw. This was, of course, very humiliating, but in the end it proved politically acceptable within the United States, and led to no truly harmful results for the nation's security.

In the Middle East, in contrast, the United States appears hopelessly and permanently bound to an unstable, violent, and hostile region by two immensely strong ties. The first is the defense of the "American way of life" as presently defined, insofar as this has come to be associated with the gas-consuming automobile. This requires continued American access to cheap and guaranteed supplies of oil. Less and less of America's oil comes from the Middle East, but that region has a critical effect on the international price of oil, and is therefore vital to U.S. energy needs. The second tie is the American attachment to Israel, which involves the United States in a national struggle with Arab nationalism and Muslim radicalism—also, so it would seem, for the foreseeable future.

Further terrorist attacks on the United States are a potential danger. After the first edition of this book appeared in 2004, the second great threat that I described became an actual and acute danger. This is the fading of the "American dream" as far as large portions of the American middle and working classes are concerned, due to economic change and the effects of globalization. Over the past 30 years, this central part of American society has seen incomes stagnate or even fall, with the skilled and semiskilled working classes suffering particularly badly. Meanwhile, incomes at the lower end of the scale have been held down by the resumption of mass immigration, both legal and illegal. This combination of factors has undermined the "moral economy," which prevailed for most of American history, whereby a man who worked hard, was honest, and did not drink or take drugs could be assured of a steadily rising income, enough to support himself and his wife in their old age, and to give his children a head start in social advancement through education. The decline of the middle class has worsened drastically as a result of the recession that began in 2008.

Although America will no doubt recover sooner or later from the present recession, the overall trend is likely to continue, for it is rooted not only in global economic trends that are beyond America's control, but in the growing inability of American governments to take the kinds of actions that could make a real difference. This it seems would require not just a new consensus for economic reform among the American people, but quite far-reaching changes to the U.S. Constitution. Tragically, much of the evidence that I have examined for this book suggests that both these outcomes may be unlikely, in part because of various aspects of American nationalism.[1] Instead, civic nationalism is helping to ossify the Constitution and justify what risks becoming a political system more and more blatantly skewed to the advantage of a shrinking proportion of conservative white Americans—above all, through the composition, powers, and rules of the Senate.

If, as seems all too probable, secure working class jobs continue to become rarer and rarer as a result of economic change and globalization, the resulting economic suffering and anxiety concerning social status and security will be gravely worsened by the lack of state-funded safety nets. The danger to the ability of the American economy to serve a majority of the American people is increased both by the expense of America's international hegemony, and by the apparently insatiable nature of American free-market capitalism.

If the middle classes continue to crumble, they will take with them one of the essential pillars of American political stability and moderation. As in European countries in the past, this would be the perfect breeding ground for radical nationalist groups and for even wilder dreams of "taking back" America at home and restoring the old moral, cultural, and possibly racial order. Such developments might lead to unrestrained strikes against America's enemies abroad, or they might lead to isolationism. Or, if past patterns are anything to go by, it might lead to first one and then the other.

Such a combination would be especially dangerous because of a quite new historical factor: the decline of the United States on the world stage and the rapid rise of China, to the point where if present trends continue, China will overtake America as the world's largest economy sometime in the 2020s. The precise impact of this on the American psyche cannot be foreseen, but is unlikely to be pleasant. Not since the mid-nineteenth century has the United States faced a geopolitical rival that at the same time was economically more powerful than itself.

Nothing in the U.S. experience of the past century has equipped the U.S. elites and people to work out how to respond to this new situation, or to play second fiddle in the world. Even Americans who are at heart deeply hostile to an expansive and expensive U.S. role in the world are likely to find this new position psychologically very hard to bear.

Meanwhile, as this book has argued, strong forces in the U.S. establishment will go on pushing for a confrontational strategy toward China, modeled on the cold war and justified in the civic nationalist terms of America's mission and duty to lead "democracies" against the "threat of dictatorship." And as Chinese power grows, the Chinese too cannot be relied on to stick to their "peaceful rise," or to respond peacefully to anything they see as an American provocation. In these circumstances, a combination of an overall tendency toward U.S. withdrawal into isolationism with periodic outbursts of chauvinist reaction could have truly catastrophic consequences.

America's immunity from the world clearly no longer exists, and as the twenty-first century progresses, it will be more and more vulnerable to a variety of international infections. The dangers posed to America and the world by America joining the world in this way are greatly increased by certain features of American nationalism that I have described in this book: not only the strength of this nationalism, and its alternation between messianic idealism and chauvinism, but also its highly unreflective character. In the past, because America was so victorious, so isolated, and so protected, even American intellectuals never had to reflect on their own nationalism to the extent that was forced on Europeans by the disasters of the twentieth century. It is now urgently necessary that they begin to do so, and I hope that this book has provided a small impetus toward such reflection.

To examine their own nationalism in this way, it will be necessary for Americans to be willing to learn from the often terrible example of other nationalisms in modern history and around the world. This requires an ability to step outside

American national myths and look at America with detachment, not as an exceptional "city on a hill," but as a mortal nation among other nations, better than most, no doubt, but also subject to the moral hazards, temptations, and crimes to which many peoples have been exposed.[2]

American intellectuals have a special responsibility in this regard, given the rise of irrational hatred on the Right, the spinelessness of all too many establishment liberals in Washington, and the tendency of progressives either to adopt unrealistically dogmatic positions (as witness some of the attacks on Obama from the Left) or to retire from public debate into narcissistic conversations among themselves. Stephen M. Walt has described his own decision to become involved in public debate in words with which I am glad to associate myself. Reacting to the growth of hysterical Islamaphobia on the Right, he wrote of how as a student he attended lectures on Weimar Germany by the historian Gordon Craig: "The lesson I took from Craig's lecture was that when intellectuals abandon liberal principles, disengage from politics, and generally abdicate their role as 'truth-tellers' for society at large, it is easy for demagogues to play upon human fears and lead a society over the brink to disaster."[3]

The disastrous outcomes for America that I have sketched are certainly not inevitable, given the tremendous resilience and dynamism of American society, American values, and the American democratic tradition, but to prevent them will require not just thought, but serious action by the American political class. At home, this means action to restrain the excesses of capitalism and reshape the American economy so as to serve the American people. Abroad, it requires action to make America once again a leader by consent, concerned for the health, stability, and longevity of the present international system, and dedicated to working with other responsible states so as to achieve these goals.

Most important of all, the American elites should show more concern for the example their country sets to the world, through their institutions, their values, and the visible well-being of ordinary Americans. This example remains of critical importance to democracy in the world as a whole, as the rise of China may present, for the first time in many years, a model of authoritarian development to rival America's democratic model.

It is America's example that forms the basis of America's "soft power," and which thereby makes possible a form of U.S. hegemony by consent. It is these institutions and values that constitute America's "civilizational empire," heir to that of Rome, and which, like the values of Rome, will endure long after the American empire, and even the United States itself, has disappeared. The image of America as an economically successful pluralist democracy, open to all races, and basically peaceful and nonaggressive, has been so powerful in the past because it has largely been true. Americans must make sure it goes on being true.

Notes

Introduction

1. See Anatol Lieven, "China is the Quiet Big Winner in War on Terror," *The Australian*, August 29, 2011; Timothy Garton Ash, "The Years Since 9/11," *The Guardian*, September 8, 2011.
2. For books on the Tea Parties by supporters of the movement, see John M. O'Hara and Michelle Malkin, *A New American Tea Party: The Counterrevolution Against Bailouts, Handouts, Reckless Spending and More Taxes* (New York: John Wiley & Sons, 2011); Joseph Farah, *The Tea Party Manifesto* (New York: WND Books, 2010); Dick Armey and Matt Kibbe, *Give Us Liberty: A Tea Party Manifesto* (New York: William Morrow, 2010).
3. Louis Hartz, *The Liberal Tradition in America* (1955; repr., New York: Harcourt Brace and Co., 1991).
4. Don Siegel (director), *The Shootist*, starring John Wayne, 1976.
5. Sarah Palin, *America By Heart: Reflections on Family, Faith and Flag* (London: Harper Collins, 2010), 69.
6. Cf. Steven Kull, "Americans on Foreign Aid and World Hunger: A Study of US Public Attitudes," Program on International Policy Attitudes, February 2, 2001; Robert Bellah, in his foreword to Richard Hughes, *Myths America Lives By* (Champaign: University of Illinois Press, 2003), x.
7. Erik Erikson, *Childhood and Society*, quoted in Robert Bellah, *The Broken Covenant: American Civil Religion in a Time of Trial* (New York: Seabury Press, 1975), 63.
8. Figures in the public opinion survey "Evenly Divided and Increasingly Polarized: 2004 Political Landscape," Pew Research Center for the People and the Press, Washington, DC, November 5, 2003, at http://www.people-press.org/files/legacy-pdf/196.pdf.
9. For profiles of "Jacksonian nationalism," see Walter Russell Mead, *Special Providence: American Foreign Policy and How It Changed the World* (New York: Routledge, 2002), 218–263; Michael Kazin, *The Populist Persuasion: An American History* (New York: Harper Collins, 1995), 21–22, 166; Samuel Eliot Morison, Henry Steele Commager, and William E. Leuchtenburg, *The Growth of the American Republic* (New York: Oxford University Press, 1969), 419–443; Robert V. Remini, *The Life of Andrew Jackson* (New York: Harper Collins, 2001).
10. Irving Kristol, *Reflections of a Neo-conservative* (New York: Basic Books, 1983), xiii. See also Kristol, *Neo-Conservatism, Autobiography of an Idea* (New York: Free Press, 1994), 365; and Shadia B. Drury, *Leo Strauss and the American Right* (New York: St. Martin's Press, 1997), 149–153.
11. Kenneth Minogue, *Nationalism* (New York: Basic Books, 1997).
12. Richard Hofstadter, *The Age of Reform* (New York: Vintage Books, 1955), 15.

13. Figures in "Global Attitudes 2002: 44-Nation Major Survey," Pew Research Center for the People and the Press, Washington, DC, November 5, 2003, at http://people-press. org/http://people-press.org/files/legacy-pdf/185.pdf.

14. Gunnar Myrdal, *An American Dilemma: The Negro Problem and Modern Democracy* (Piscataway, NJ: Transaction Publishers, 1996), xlviii.

15. Cf. David H. Bennett, *The Party of Fear: From Nativist Movements to the New Right in American History* (Chapel Hill: University of North Carolina Press, 1989), 7–8; for a succinct recent statement of the nativist position on the creed from a leading conservative intellectual, see Samuel Huntington, "The Hispanic Challenge," *Foreign Policy*, March/April (2004) at http://www.foreignpolicy.com/articles/2004/03/01/the_ hispanic_challenge; and "Dead Souls: The Denationalization of the American Elite," *National Interest* 75 (Spring 2004) at http://nationalinterest.org/article/dead-souls-the-denationalization-of-the-american-elite-620.

16. Ralph Reed, "Separation of Church and State: 'Christian Nation' and Other Heresies" in *God's New Israel: Religious Interpretations of American Destiny*, ed. Conrad Cherry (Chapel Hill: University of North Carolina Press, 1998), 373–379.

17. Alexis de Tocqueville, *Democracy in America*, Vol. I (New York: Bantam Classics, 2000), 51; for the decline of religious belief in Germany before 1914, see Hans-Ulrich Wehler, *The German Empire 1871–1918* (Leamington Spa: Berg Publishers, 1997), 115.

18. "Among Wealthy Nations, the US Stands Alone in its Embrace of Religion," Global Attitudes Project report, December 19, 2002, Pew Research Center for the People and the Press, Washington, DC, November 5, 2003, at http://www.pewglobal. org/2002/12/19/among-wealthy-nations/.

19. Cf. Richard Hofstadter, *The Paranoid Style in American Politics and Other Essays* (1952; repr., Cambridge, MA: Harvard University Press, 1996); Kevin Phillips, *The Emerging Republican Majority* (New York: Arlington House, 1969), 614ff; Michael Lind, *The Next American Nation: The New Nationalism and the Fourth American Revolution* (New York: Simon & Schuster, 1995), 99.

20. D. G. Hart, "Mainstream Protestantism, 'Conservative' Religion, and Civil Society," in *Religion Returns to the Public Square: Faith and Policy in America*, ed. Hugh Heclo and Wilfred M. McClay (Washington, DC: Woodrow Wilson Center Press, 2003), 197.

21. Speaking of House Speaker Sam Rayburn of Texas. Quoted in Robert A. Caro, *The Years of Lyndon Johnson: Master of the Senate*, vol. 3 (New York: Vintage Books, 2003) and *The Years of Lyndon Johnson: The Path to Power*, vol. 1 (New York: Vintage Books, 1990), 759.

22. Hofstadter, *The Paranoid Style*, 3.

23. Clinton Rossiter, *Conservatism in America* (New York: Random House, 1962), 206.

24. Sheldon Hackney, "The Contradictory South," *Southern Culture* (Winter 2001): 77; cf. also Jerome L. Himmelstein, "The New Right," in *The New Christian Right: Mobilization and Legitimation*, ed. Robert C. Liebman and Robert Wuthnow (New York: Aldine, 1983), 21–24.

25. Garry Wills, *Reagan's America: Innocents at home* (New York: Doubleday, 1987), 382.

26. Karl Marx and Friedrich Engels, *The Communist Manifesto*, trans. Samuel Morse (London: Penguin Books, 1967), 222–223.

27. Sacvan Bercovitch, *The Puritan Origins of the American Self* (New Haven, CT: Yale University Press, 1975), 185.

28. For Rick Perry's indebtedness for foreign policy advice to former members of the Bush administration, see Josh Rogan, "Rick Perry, the Hawk Internationalist," *Foreign Policy*

(online), August 20, 2011, at http://thecable.foreignpolicy.com/posts/2011/08/10/ rick_perry_the_hawk_internationalist.

29. I am indebted for this comparison to Dr. David Chambers of the Middle East Institute in Washington.

30. Fouad Ajami, "The Falseness of Anti-Americanism," *Foreign Policy* September/ October (2003) at http://www.foreignpolicy.com/articles/2003/09/01/the_falseness _of_anti_americanism.

31. Charles Krauthammer, "To Hell With Sympathy," *Time*, November 17 (2003), at http:// www.time.com/time/nation/article/0,8599,557638,00.html.; or see Dinesh D'Souza, *What's So Great About America* (Washington, DC: Regnery Books, 2002) by another American right-wing nationalist intellectual of recent immigrant origins.

32. On *The O'Reilly Factor*, Fox News Channel, January 17, 2003

33. Brian Klug, "The Collective Jew: Israel and the New Anti-Semitism," *Patterns of Prejudice* 37, no. 2 (2003).

Chapter One

1. Reinhold Niebuhr, *The Irony of American History* (New York: Charles Scribner's Sons, 1952), 42.

2. The phrase is that of Seymour Martin Lipset, *American Exceptionalism: A Double-edged Sword* (New York: W. W. Norton, 1976); see also Minxin Pei, "The Paradoxes of American Nationalism," *Foreign Policy* May–June (2003): 30–37.

3. Michael Lind, *The Next American Nation: The New Nationalism and the Fourth American Revolution* (New York: Simon & Schuster, 1995), 100–102, 140–161, 215–216.

4. "The Elusive 90 Percent Solution," Pew Research Center for the People and the Press, March 11, 2011, http://pewresearch.org/pubs/1925/elusive-90-percent-solution-gas-prices.

5. William R. Brock, "Americanism," in *The United States: A Companion to American Studies*, ed. Dennis Welland (London: Methuen, 1974), 58.

6. Jim Brosseau, ed. *A Celebration of America: Your Helpful Guide to America's Greatness* (Des Moines, IA: Meredith Publications, 2002).

7. Lynne Cheney and illus. Robin Preiss Glasser, *America: A Patriotic Primer* (New York: Simon and Schuster Children's Publishing, 2002); cf. also George Grant, *The Patriot's Handbook* (Nashville, TN: Cumberland House Publishing, 1996).

8. *Washington Post*, Parade section, November 9 and December 20, 2003.

9. Cf. Michael Paris, *Warrior Nation: Images of War in British Popular Culture, 1850–2000* (London: Reaktion Books, 2000).

10. Cf. Conrad Cherry, ed. "Introduction," in *God's New Israel: Religious Interpretations of American Destiny* (Chapel Hill: University of North Carolina Press, 1998); Conrad Cherry, "American Sacred Ceremonies," in *Social Patterns of Religion in the United States*, ed. Phillip E. Hammond and Benton Johnson (New York: Random House, 1970), 303–316; W. Lloyd Warner, "An American Sacred Ceremony," in *American Civil Religion*, ed. Russell E. Richey and Donald G. Jones (New York: Harper and Row, 1974).

11. Max Lerner, *American Civilization: Life and Thought in the US Today* (New York: Simon & Schuster 1957), 903.

12. Alexis de Tocqueville, *Democracy in America*, vol. I, trans. Henry Reeve (1835; repr., New York: Bantam Classics, 2000), 281, 704, 764–766.

13. Cf. Eugen Weber, *Peasants into Frenchmen: The Modernisation of Rural France, 1870–1914* (Stanford, CA: Stanford University Press), 19; cf. also Theodore Zeldin, *France 1848–1945: Intellect and Pride* (New York: Oxford University Press, 1980), 3ff.

14. For the formation of a British identity and patriotism in the 18th century out of the different Protestant nationalities of the British isles, see Linda Colley, *Britons: Forging the Nation, 1707–1837* (London: Yale University Press, 1992). For the ideology of the law as a state-supporting force in 18th-century England, cf. Douglas Hay et al., *Albion's Fatal Tree: Crime and Society in 18th Century England* (New York: Random House, 1975), 32–39.

15. Louis Hartz, *The Liberal Tradition in America* (1955; repr., New York: Harcourt Brace and Co., 1991), 9, 307.

16. Herbert Croly, *The Promise of American Life* (1909; repr., Boston: Northeastern University Press, 1989), 1.

17. Andrew Bacevich, *American Empire: The Realities and Consequences of US Diplomacy* (Cambridge, MA:, Mass., Harvard University Press 2004), 237; Bill Maher, "Introduction," in *When You Drive Alone You Drive With Bin Laden: What the Government Should Be Telling Us to Help Fight the War on Terrorism* (Beverly Hills, CA: Phoenix Books, 2003).

18. Cf. Joe Galloway, "Thanks to Rumsfeld, Iraq is Still America's to Lose," military.com, December 17, 2003; Max Boot, "Washington Needs a Colonial Office," *Financial Times*, July 3, 2003; Hendrik Hertzberg, "Building Nations," *New Yorker*, June 9, 2003.

19. Polls at http://www.ropercenter.uconn.edu.

20. "Presidential Debate Clouds Voters' Choice," Pew Research Center for the People and the Press, October 10, 2000, http://www.people-press.org/2000/10/10/presidential-debate-clouds-voters-choice/.

21. *New York Times*, August 10, 2000.

22. Niall Ferguson, *Empire: The Rise and Demise of the British World Order and the Lessons for Global Power* (New York: Basic Books, 2003).

23. Cf. Sebastian Balfour, *Deadly Embrace: Morocco and the Road to the Spanish Civil War* (Oxford: Oxford University Press, 2002); for an attempt to place the Russian disaster in Chechnya in this historical perspective, see Anatol Lieven, *Chechnya: Tombstone of Russian Power?* (New Haven, CT: Yale University Press, 1997), 150–151, and passim.

24. Bacevich, *American Empire* 141–166.

25. Cf. Weber, *Peasants into Frenchmen*, 292–302. For the unpopularity of North African service, see the popular song of 1891 by Aristide Bruant, "A Biribi," in *Anthologie de la Chanson Francaise: Soldats, Conscrits et Deserteurs*: Paris, EPM Musique, 1996).

26. Quoted in Roger Magraw, *France 1815–1914: The Bourgeois Century* (London: Fontana, 1983), 261.

27. Douglas Porch, *The Conquest of Morocco* (New York: Alfred A. Knopf, 1983), 187–188, 293–294.

28. Jean-Jacques Becker, *1914* (Paris: Presses de la Fondation Nationale des Sciences Politiques, 1977); Alfred Cobban, *A History of Modern France, 1871–1962* (London: Penguin, 1990), 105.

29. Cf. Perry Anderson, "Force and Consent," *New Left Review* September/October (2002), pp. 5–30.

30. Transcript of televised debate with Al Gore, Winston Salem, NC, October 11, 2000.

31. Cf. William Pfaff, *Barbarian Sentiments: America in the New Century* (New York: Farrar, Strauss and Giroux, 2000), 9.

32. Max Weber, quoted in Clifford Geertz, *The Interpretation of Cultures* (London: Fontana, 1993), 5.

33. For works on the history of Wilhelmine Germany that have corrected both the traditional approach based on *primat der aussenpolitik* (the dominance of external relations) and simplistic Marxian versions of elite manipulation, see Geoff Eley, "The Wilhelmine Right: How It Changed," in *Society and Politics in Wilhelmine Germany*, ed. Richard J. Evans (London: Croom Helm, 1978), 112–135; Wolfgang J. Mommsen, *Imperial Germany 1867–1918: Politics, Culture and Society in an Authoritarian State*, trans. Richard Deveson (New York: Arnold, 1995), 166ff; David Blackbourn, "Introduction," in *The Long Nineteenth Century: A History of Germany, 1780–1918* (Oxford: Oxford University Press, 1997); Klaus Epstein, *The Genesis of German Conservatism* (Princeton, NJ: Princeton University Press, 1966).

34. Sean Hannity, "The Battle over Competing Visions of the Family and Family Values" (speech, United Families International Conference, November 21–22, 2003), http://www.unitedfamilies.org.

35. Cf. also Robert Bork, *Slouching Towards Gomorrah: Modern Liberalism and American Decline* (New York: Regan Books, 1997); Dinesh D'Souza, *What's So Great About America* (Washington, DC: Regnery Publishing, 2002), also raises the question of whether "an open society, where such criticisms are permitted and even encouraged, has the fortitude and will to resist external assault."

36. Richard Rorty, *Achieving Our Country: Leftist Thought in Twentieth Century America* (Cambridge, MA: Harvard University Press, 1998), 35.

37. Gordon Alexander Craig, *Germany 1866–1945* (New York: Oxford University Press, 1978), 206.

38. George Kennan, quoted in John Hellmann, *American Myth and the Legacy of Vietnam* (New York: Columbia University Press, 1986), 42–43.

39. Quoted in David Brock, *Blinded by the Right: The Conscience of an Ex-Conservative* (New York: Three Rivers Press, 2002), 75.

40. George L. Mosse, *Nationalism and Sexuality: Middle Class Morality and Sexual Norms in Modern Europe* (Madison: University of Wisconsin Press, 1988); cf. also Fritz Stern, *The Politics of Cultural Despair* (Berkeley: University of California Press, 1974); for an American right-wing nationalist linkage of homosexuality with national weakness and decline, see Norman Podhoretz, "The Culture of Appeasement," *Harper's* October (1977); for a work linking Clinton's sexual "decadence" with his foreign policy "weakness," see Lt. Colonel (Ret.) Robert "Buzz" Patterson, *Dereliction of Duty: The Eyewitness Account of How Bill Clinton Compromised America's National Security* (Washington, DC: Regnery Publishing, 2003).

41. Lee Harris, *Civilization and Its Enemies: The Next Stage of History* (New York: Free Press, 2004), 69–84; Robert D. Kaplan, *Warrior Politics: Why Leadership Requires a Pagan Ethos* (New York: Vintage Books, 2003).

42. Timothy Garton Ash, "Anti-Europeanism in America," *New York Review of Books* 50, no. 2 (2003). For a sophisticated neo-conservative view of the underlying differences between the United States and Europe, see Robert Kagan, *Of Paradise and Power: America and Europe in the New World Order* (New York: Alfred A. Knopf, 2002).

43. Cf. John W. Whitehead and Steven H. Aden, *Forfeiting "Enduring Freedom" for "Homeland Security": A Constitutional Analysis of the USA Patriot Act of 2001 and the Justice Department's Anti-Terrorism Measures* (Charlottesville, VA: Rutherford Institute, 2002); Ann Beeson and Jameel Jaffer, *Unpatriotic Acts: The FBI's Power to*

Rifle Through Your Records and Personal Belongings Without Telling You (New York: American Civil Liberties Union, July 2003); Muzaffar A. Chishti et al., *America's Challenge: Domestic Security, Civil Liberties and National Unity after September 11* (Washington, DC: Migration Policy Institute, 2003).

44. Cf. Eric Alterman, *What Liberal Media? The Truth About Bias and the News* (New York: Basic Books, 2003), 277.

45. Jerry L. Martin and Anne D. Neal, *Defending Civilisation: How Our Universities are Failing America and What Can Be Done About It* (Washington, DC: American Council of Trustees and Alumni, November 2001).

46. David Frum, "Unpatriotic Conservatives: A War Against America," *National Review*, April 7, 2003.

47. Sean Hannity, *Deliver Us From Evil: Defeating Terrorism, Despotism and Liberalism* (New York: Simon & Schuster, 2004).

48. Saul Padover, ed., *The Complete Jefferson* (New York: Irvington Publishers, 1943), 385–386.

49. Cf. Edward Shils, "Ideology and Civility: On the Politics of the Intellectual," *Sewanee Review* 66, no. 3 (1958): 450–480.

50. William J. Bennett, *Why We Fight: Moral Clarity and the War on Terrorism* (New York: Doubleday, 2002), 132–133.

51. Mission statement and principles are to be found at the Project's website, http://the912-project.com.

52. John Hellmann, *American Myth and the Legacy of Vietnam* (New York: Columbia University Press, 1986), 5–7.

53. Quoted in James H. Moorhead, "The American Israel: Protestant Tribalism and Universal Mission," in William R. Hutchison and Hartmut Lehmann, *Many are Chosen* (Harrisburg, PA: Trinity Press International, 1998), 163; for how this belief was reflected in American textbooks of the 1940s and 1950s, see Frances FitzGerald, *America Revised: What History Textbooks Have Taught Our Children About Their Country, and How and Why Those Textbooks Have Changed in Different Decades* (New York: Vintage Books, 1980), 116–117.

54. Cf. Hartz, *Liberal Tradition*, 35–38.

55. Cf. Conor Cruise O'Brien, *God Land: Reflections on Religion and Nationalism* (Cambridge, MA: Harvard University Press, 1987); Lind, *Next American Nation*, 227–234.

56. Cf. Paul Johnson, "God and the Americans," *Commentary* January 1995.

57. Herman Melville, *White-Jacket* (New York: Holt, Rhinehart & Winston, 1967), 150.

58. Cherry, "American Sacred Ceremonies," 111; Walter A. McDougall, *Promised Land, Crusader State: American Encounters with the World since 1776* (New York: Houghton Mifflin, 1997), 204ff.

59. J. G. Fichte, *Addresses to the German Nation* (1806) (Chicago: Open Court Publishing Company, 1922), quoted in Lind, *Next American Nation*, 227.

60. Quoted in Lind, *Next American Nation*, 230.

61. Cf. Niebuhr, *Irony of American History*, 68–69.

62. Jules Michelet, *The People*, trans. John P. McKay (Champlain: University of Illinois Press, 1973), p.27.

63. For French influence on the American Bill of Rights, see Mark Hulliung, *Citizens and Citoyens: Republicans and Liberals in America and France* (Cambridge, MA: Harvard University Press, 2002), 19ff.

64. "Il existe un pacte, vingt fois seculaire, entre la grandeur de la France et la liberté du monde."

65. Reported in the *Financial Times*, January 28, 2004.

66. Quoted in Zeldin, *France 1848–1945*, 9; cf. also Jules Michelet, *The People*, 93–94.

67. Karl Kaiser, quoted in Ash, "Anti-Europeanism in America,".

68. Cf. Hulliung, *Citizens and Citoyens*, 162ff.

69. Cf. Brubaker, *Citizenship in France*, 7–8, 13–14, 35–49.

70. Cf. Johannes Willms, "France Unveiled: Making Muslims into Citizens," *Open Democracy*, February 26, 2004.

71. Hans J. Rogger and Eugen Weber, *European Right: A Historical Profile* (Berkeley: University of California Press, 1965), 579.

72. Brock, *Blinded by the Right*, 59.

73. Ernest Barker, quoted in Sidney E. Mead, *The Nation with the Soul of a Church* (Macon, GA: Mercer University Press, 1985), 51.

74. Weber, *Peasants into Frenchmen*, 24.

75. Cf. Magraw, *France 1815–1914*, 255–284; Cobban, *A History of Modern France*, 48–57, 86–91; Anthony D. Smith, *Nationalism* (Oxford: Blackwell, 2001), 128–129.

76. "Je m'écriais avec Schiller:/Je suis citoyen du monde…/De mes tendresses détournées/Je me suis enfin repenti./Ces tendresses je les ramene/étroitement sur mon pays/Sur les hommes que j'ai trahis/Par amour de l'espéce humaine." Sully Prudhomme, extract in Raoul Girardet, *Le Nationalisme Français* (Paris, Points, 1983), 50.

77. For the strength of such feeling in the Indian diaspora in the West, see the furious attacks on Western historians of India for allegedly "denigrating" Hinduism and the Hindu role in Indian history, reported by Shankar Vedantam, "Wrath Over A Hindu God," *Washington Post*, April 10, 2004.

78. For a comparison from the 1950s, see Lerner, *American Civilization*, 934–938.

79. Quoted in Hans Kohn, *American Nationalism: An Interpretative Essay* (New York: Macmillan, 1957), 133.

80. McDougall, *Promised Land*, 126.

81. Reinhold Niebuhr, "Anglo Saxon Destiny and Responsibility," *Christianity and Crisis*, October 4, 1943; reprinted in Cherry, *God's New Israel*, 296–300; Gunnar Myrdal, *An American Dilemma: The Negro Problem and Modern Democracy* (Piscataway, NJ: Transaction Publishers, 1996), 1018–1024; cf. also Eric Foner, *Who Owns History? Rethinking the Past in a Changing World* (New York: Farrar, Straus and Giroux, 2002), 65–68.

82. Lind, *Next American Nation*, 105ff; Francis Butler Simkins and Charles Pierce Roland, *A History of the South* (New York: Alfred A. Knopf, 1972), 588ff.

83. Foner, *Who Owns History*, 61.

84. Cf. Arthur Cooper, trans. and ed., *Li Po and Tu Fu* (London: Penguin, 1973), 24–26. The Chinese, like the Russian Empire, admittedly also possessed ethnic groups of licensed semi-outcasts with strictly defined social roles. These people were often employed in the entertainment and sex industries: in Russia the Gypsies, in T'ang China the Tanka, a former tribal people of the southern coastal fringes. The Jews in Russia too were assigned particular socioeconomic roles, and attempts were made to repress them when they broke out of those roles and out of the geographical limits to which the state had tried to restrict them.

85. For the difference between the rigid separation and subordination of the American "one drop of blood" system and the relatively more complex and tolerant racial

shadings of Brazil, see George M. Fredrickson, "The Strange Death of Segregation," *New York Review of Books* 46, no. 8 (1999).

86. Robert J. Blendon et al., "America's Changing Political and Moral Values," in *What's God Got to Do with the American Experiment?*, ed. E. J. Dionne and John J. Dilulio (Washington, DC: Brookings Institution Press, 2000), 26, 29; figures for attitudes toward interracial "dating" can be found in the public opinion survey "The 2004 Political Landscape: Evenly Divided and Increasingly Polarized," Pew Research Center for the People and the Press, November 5, 2003, 45–50, http://www.people-press.org/2003/11/05/the-2004-political-landscape/.

87. Cf. Adam Clymer, "Divisive Words: GOP's 40 Years of Juggling on Race," *New York Times*, December 13, 2002; David von Drehle and Dan Balz, "For GOP, South's Past Rises in Tangle of Pride, Shame," *Washington Post*, December 15, 2002.

88. For the continuation of racist attitudes in new forms, see David K. Shipler, *A Country of Strangers: Blacks and Whites in America* (New York: Alfred A. Knopf, 1998), especially its discussion of the University of Chicago study of 1990; Orlando Patterson, *The Ordeal of Integration: Progress and Resentment in America's "Racial" Crisis* (New York: Basic Civitas, 1997); see also George M. Fredrickson, "America's Caste System: Will It Change?" *New York Review of Books* 44, no. 16 (1997).

89. Sara Diamond, *Not By Politics Alone: The Enduring Influence of the Christian Right* (New York: Guilford Press, 1998), 220–228.

90. Cf. Ronald R. Stockton, "The Evangelical Phenomenon: A Falwell–Graham Typology," in *Contemporary Political Involvement: An Analysis and Assessment*, ed. Corwin E. Smidt (Lanham, MD: University Press of America, 1989), 45–69.

91. Peter W. Williams, *America's Religions From Their Origins to the 21st Century* (Chicago: University of Illinois Press, 2002), 378.

92. Cf. Howard Elinson, "The Implications of Pentecostalist Religion for Intellectualism, Politics and Race Relations," *American Journal of Sociology* 70, no. 4 (1965).

93. Cf. Walter Russell Mead, *Special Providence: American Foreign Policy and How it Shaped the World* (New York: Routledge, 2002), 260–261.

94. Cf. C. Vann Woodward, *The Strange Career of Jim Crow* (New York: Oxford University Press, 2002), 134–139.

95. Lind, *Next American Nation*, 105–106.

96. Cf. Joseph McBride, *Searching for John Ford* (New York: St. Martin's Press, 2001), 452–455, 560–572, 603–611.

97. Cf. Lind, *Next American Nation*, 81.

98. Cf. Michelle Cottle, "Color TV: How Soaps Are Integrating America," *New Republic*, August 27, 2001.

99. Cf. Clint Eastwood's *Unforgiven* (1992), co-starring Morgan Freeman.

100. Cf. *In the Heat of the Night* (1967) and *A Soldier's Story* (1984) directed by Norman Jewison, and *Remember the Titans* (2000), starring Denzel Washington.

101. See Shanto Iyengar, Kyu Hahn, Christopher Dial, and Mahzarin R. Banaj, "Understanding Explicit and Implicit Attitudes: A Comparison of Racial Group and Candidate Preferences in the 2008 Election," http://pcl.stanford.edu/research/2010/iyengar-understanding.pdf.

102. Glenn Beck, cited in Andrew Edgecliffe-Johnson and David Gelles, "Vanquished by Vitriol," *Financial Times*, January 12, 2011.

103. Nicholas D. Kristof, "The Push to 'Otherize' Obama," *New York Times*, September 20, 2008.

104. The American National Election Study Evaluations of Government and Society Survey (EGSS), October 2010, cited in Alan I. Abramowitz, "The Race Factor: White Racial

Attitudes and Opinions of Obama," May 12, 2011, "Sabato's Crystal Ball," http://www.centerforpolitics.org/crystalball/articles/AIA2011051201/.

105. See Jon Cohen and Michael D. Shear, "Poll Shows More Americans Believe that Obama Is a Muslim," *Washington Post*, August 19, 2010, http://www.washingtonpost.com/wp-dyn/content/article/2010/08/18/AR2010081806913.html.

106. See ANES 2010–2012 Evaluations of Government and Society Study, October 2010 survey, http://www.electionstudies.org/studypages/2010_2012EGSS/2009EGSS1Documentation_preliminary_release.pdf.

107. Clyde Prestowitz, *Rogue Nation: American Unilateralism and the Failure of Good Intentions* (New York: Basic Books, 2003), 42.

108. Cf. Loren Baritz, *Backfire: A History of How American Culture Led Us Into Vietnam and Made Us Fight the Way We Did* (New York: William Morrow, 1985), 40.

109. Lerner, *American Civilization*, 921.

Chapter Two

1. Louis Hartz, *The Liberal Tradition in America* (1955; repr., New York: Harcourt Brace and Co., 1991), 175.

2. Cf. Gunnar Myrdal, *An American Dilemma: The Negro Problem and Modern Democracy* (Piscataway, NJ: Transaction Publishers, 1996), 1–25. For the original use of the term "American Creed," see G. K. Chesterton, *What I Saw in America* (New York: Dodd, Mead and Co., 1922), quoted in Seymour Martin Lipset, *American Exceptionalism: A Double-Edged Sword* (New York: W. W. Norton, 1976), 31.

3. Frances FitzGerald, *Fire in the Lake: The Vietnamese and the Americans in Vietnam* (New York: Vintage Books, 1973), 9.

4. Cf. Michael Lind, *The Next American Nation: The New Nationalism and the Fourth American Revolution* (New York: Simon & Schuster, 1995), 1–18.

5. David Frum, *Dead Right* (New York: Basic Books, 1994), 130.

6. Walt Whitman, *Democratic Vistas* (Charleston, SC: BiblioBazaar, 2009), quoted in Sacvan Bercovitch, *The Puritan Origins of the American Self* (New Haven, CT: Yale University Press, 1975), 183.

7. Quoted in Hans Kohn, *American Nationalism: An Interpretative Essay* (New York: Macmillan, 1957), 13.

8. Cf. Michael H. Hunt, *Ideology and U.S. Foreign Policy* (New Haven, CT: Yale University Press, 1987), especially 125–170.

9. Cf. Alexis de Tocqueville, *Democracy in America*, Vol. I, trans. by Henry Reeve (1835; repr., New York: Bantam Classics, 2000), 544ff and passim; cf. also the definitions of the creed in Lipset, *American Exceptionalism*, 19; in Michael Lind, *The Next American Nation*, 90–91, 219–233; and in Herbert McClosky, "Consensus and Ideology in American Politics," *American Political Science Review* 58, no. 2 (1964). For "the American Proposition," see *USA: The Permanent Revolution* (New York: Prentice-Hall, 1951), by the editors of *Fortune* magazine, quoted in Hartz, *Liberal Tradition*, 305.

10. For the quasi-religious nature of American capitalist ideology, see Robert Bellah, *The Broken Covenant: American Civil Religion in a Time of Trial* (New York: Seabury Press, 1975), xiii.

11. Hartz, *Liberal Tradition*, 9, 15, 175, 225–237.

12. Reinhold Niebuhr, *The Irony of American History* (New York: Charles Scribner's Sons, 1952), 4.

13. Samuel Huntington, *American Politics: The Promise of Disharmony* (Cambridge, MA: Harvard University Press, 1981), 2–3, 25.

14. Bercovitch, *Puritan Origins*, quoted in Lipset, *American Exceptionalism*, 291.

15. Cf. Andrei K. Sitov, "America: Back in the USSR?" ITAR-TASS, Washington, DC, August 4, 2003.

16. Russel Nye, *This Almost Chosen People: Essays in the History of American Ideas* (East Lansing: Michigan State University Press, 1966), quoted in William J. Cobb, Jr., *The American Foundation Myth in Vietnam: Reigning Paradigms and Raining Bombs* (New York: University Press of America, 1998), 4.

17. Samuel P. Huntington, *Political Order in Changing Societies* (New Haven, CT: Yale University Press, 1968), 96–98; see also R. A. Humphreys, "The Rule of Law and the American Revolution," in *The Role of Ideology in the American Revolution*, ed. John R. Howe (New York: Holt, Rinehart and Winston, 1970), 20–27.

18. Quoted in Lind, *The Next American Nation*, 225ff.

19. Huntington, *American Politics*, 104.

20. Bellah, *The Broken Covenant*, 5–8; Cobb, *American Foundation Myth*, 21.

21. Speech in James Melvin Washington, ed., *A Testament of Hope: The Essential Writings of Martin Luther King, Jr.* (New York: Harper & Row, 1986), 217–220.

22. Cf. Lind, *The Next American Nation*, 90.

23. Lind, *The Next American Nation*, vii, 133.

24. Lind, *The Next American Nation*, 69ff.

25. Cf. Richard Hughes, *Myths America Lives By* (Champaign: University of Illinois Press, 2003), 6–8, 153–186; Bellah, *The Broken Covenant*.

26. Quoted in "This is a Different Kind of War," *Los Angeles Times*, October 12, 2001.

27. The White House, *The National Security Strategy of the United States of America* (Washington, DC: U.S. Government Printing Office, 2002), prologue.

28. Garry Wills, *Reagan's America: Innocents at Home* (New York: Doubleday, 1987), 378–388.

29. Cf. Rabbi Isaac M. Wise, quoted in Bellah, *The Broken Covenant*, 40–41; see also Bellah, *The Broken Covenant*, 5–8; Cobb, *American Foundation Myth*, 7–10.

30. Hector St. Jean de Crevecoeur, *Letters From an American Farmer* (repr., New York: Dutton, 1926), 40–44; see also Gordon S. Wood, "Republicanism as a Revolutionary Ideology," in *Role of Ideology in the American Revolution*, ed. John R. Howe (Toronto: Holt, Rinehart and Winston, 1970), 83–91.

31. Cf. Randall Bennett Woods, "Dixie's Dove: J. William Fulbright, the Vietnam War and the American South," *Journal of Southern History* 60, no. 3 (August 1994): 533–552; for Fulbright's condemnation of American messianism, see his *Arrogance of Power* (New York: Random House, 2004), passim.

32. Richard Cohen, "Blame, Blindness...," *Washington Post*, February 3, 2004.

33. Conor Cruise O'Brien, "Purely American: Innocent Nation, Wicked World," *Harper's* (April 1980).

34. Fulbright, *Arrogance of Power*, 27.

35. Hartz, *Liberal Tradition*, 11.

36. Alexis de Tocqueville, *Democracy in America*, trans. Joseph Reeve with an introduction by Joseph Epstein (New York: Bantam Classics, 2000), 305.

37. Robert Bellah et al., *Habits of the Heart: Middle America Observed* (Berkeley: University of California Press, 1985), 206.

38. John Higham, "Hanging Together: Divergent Unities in American History," *Journal of American History* 61, no. 1 (June 1974): 5–28; see also Sidney E. Mead, *The Nation With the Soul of a Church* (Macon, GA: Mercer University Press, 1985), 71–77.

39. Quoted in Mead, *Nation With the Soul of a Church*, 25.

40. Hughes, *Myths America Lives By*, 171.

41. Cf. Will Herberg, "America's Civil Religion: What It Is and Whence It Comes," in *American Civil Religion*, ed. Russell E. Richey and Donald G Jones (New York: Harper & Row, 1974); Robert N. Bellah, "Civil Religion in America," *Daedalus* 96, no. 1 (1967): 1–21; and Bellah, *Broken Covenant, passim*.

42. Adam Gamoran, "Civil Religion in American Schools," *Sociological Analysis* 51, no. 3 (1990): 235–256, quoting Fay Adams and Ernest W. Tiegs, *Our People* (Lexington, MA: Ginn).

43. Each of Hughes' chapters in *Myths America Lives By* is followed by a coda commenting on the theme he has just explored from a black point of view; see also Richard Rorty, *Achieving Our Country: Leftist Thought in Twentieth Century America* (Cambridge, MA: Harvard University Press, 1998), 31–32.

44. Hartz, *Liberal Tradition*, 58–59.

45. Cf. Eric Alterman, *What Liberal Media? The Truth About Bias and the News* (New York: Basic Books, 2003), 268–292.

46. Cf. Alterman, *What Liberal Media?*, 268–292.

47. W. H. Auden, "To Keep the Human Spirit Breathing," speech upon acceptance of the 1967 Medal for Literature, Smithsonian Institution, Washington, DC, November 30, 1967. Speech reproduced in the *Washington Post Book World*, December 24, 1967.

48. Quoted in Conrad Cherry, ed., *God's New Israel: Religious Interpretations of American Destiny* (Chapel Hill: University of North Carolina Press, 1998), 304.

49. Reinhold Niebuhr, "The Children of Light and the Children of Darkness," in *The Essential Reinhold Niebuhr: Selected Essays and Addresses*, ed. Robert McAfee Brown (New Haven, CT: Yale University Press, 1986), 160–181; for Melville's later disillusionment, see Bercovitch, *Puritan Origins*, 180–181.

50. C. Vann Woodward, *The Burden of Southern History* (Baton Rouge: Louisiana State University Press, 1968), 218.

51. For an analysis of *Apocalypse Now*, see John Hellmann, *American Myth and the Legacy of Vietnam* (New York: Columbia University Press, 1986), 188–204.

52. Loren Baritz, *Backfire: A History of How American Culture Led Us Into Vietnam and Made Us Fight the Way We Did* (New York: William Morrow, 1985), 349–350.

53. Cf. Stanley Hoffmann, "The High and the Mighty," *American Prospect*, January 13, 2003.

54. Cf. Richard Slotkin, *Gunfighter Nation: The Myth of the Frontier in Twentieth Century America* (Norman: University of Oklahoma Press, 1998), 643–654.

55. Stanley Hoffmann, "The Great Pretender," *New York Review of Books* 34, no. 9 (May 28, 1987): see also Hoffmann, "The Vicar's Revenge," *New York Review of Books* vol. 31, no.9 (May 31, 1984).

56. Lou Cannon, *President Reagan: The Role of a Lifetime* (New York: Simon & Schuster, 1991), 793.

57. Wills, *Reagan's America*, 94.

58. William H. McNeill, "The Care and Repair of Public Myth," *Foreign Affairs* (Fall 1982), reprinted in McNeill, *Mythistory and Other Essays* (Chicago: University of Chicago Press, 1986). For a critique of this essay, see Slotkin, *Gunfighter Nation*, 626–628.

59. Cf. Cobb, *American Foundation Myth*, 196–198.

60. Hellmann, *American Myth*, 222.

61. Hellmann, *American Myth*, 135–136. See also Cobb, *American Foundation Myth*, 151–192.

62. Cf. Baritz, *Backfire*, 341.

63. Cf. Slotkin, *Gunfighter Nation*, 632–633.

64. Cf. Eric Foner, *The Story of American Freedom* (New York: W. W. Norton, 1998), xxi.

65. Frances FitzGerald, *America Revised: What History Textbooks Have Taught Our Children About Their Country, and How and Why Those Textbooks Have Changed in Different Decades* (New York: Vintage Books, 1980), 100–101, 218.

66. Diane Ravitch, *The Language Police: How Pressure Groups Restrict What Students Learn* (New York: Alfred A. Knopf, 2003), 101; for a choice selection of some of the more idiotic words and actions by proponents of political correctness, see David E. Bernstein, *You Can't Say That: The Growing Threat to Civil Liberties from Anti-Discrimination Laws* (Washington, DC: Cato Institute, 2003).

67. Gary B. Nash, Charlotte Crabtree, and Ross E. Dunn, *History on Trial: Culture Wars and the Teaching of the Past* (New York: Alfred A. Knopf, 1997), 124–126, 149–277.

68. Lind, *The Next American Nation*, 273.

69. Andrew Gumbel, "What Americans Know," *The Independent* (London), September 8, 2003, The passages quoted are from the original unpublished draft of the article, kindly supplied by the author.

70. For the continuing sanitization of the American Civil War, and the elimination of blacks and slavery from presentations of the conflict, see Eric Foner, *Who Owns History? Rethinking the Past in a Changing World* (New York: Farrar, Straus and Giroux, 2002), 189–204.

71. National Center for Education Statistics, *National Assessment of Educational Progress* (Washington, DC: U.S. Department of Education, 2001); see also Brian Friel, "Don't Know Much About History," August 2, 2003; Cheryl Wetzstein, "Seniors' History Scores Abysmal," *Washington Times*, June 10, 2002; Georgie Anne Geyer, "What happened to Geography—And Just Where is Iraq?," *Tulsa World*, November 27, 2002; for a comparison to levels of knowledge in the 1940s, see Scott Fornek, "What We Don't Know Hasn't Hurt Us," *Chicago Sun-Times*, July 31, 2003.

72. Lind, *The Next American Nation*, 139–188.

73. Lynne Cheney and illus. Robin Preiss Glasser, *America: A Patriotic Primer* (New York: Simon & Schuster Children's Publishing, 2002).

74. Ernest Renan, *What Is a Nation?* (1882), transl. Martin Thom, in *Becoming National: A Reader*, ed. Geoff Eley and Ronald Grigor Suny (New York: Oxford University Press, 1996), 45.

75. Hunt, *Ideology and U.S. Foreign Policy*, 189.

76. Hunt, *Ideology and U.S. Foreign Policy*, 189.

77. Henry Kissinger, *Diplomacy* (New York: Simon & Schuster, 1994), 833.

78. Lipset, *American Exceptionalism*, 20; see also Clyde Prestowitz, *Rogue Nation: American Unilateralism and the Failure of Good Intentions* (New York: Basic Books, 2003), 23; for a comparison with U.S. official language during the Vietnam War, see Woodward, *Burden of Southern History*, 219–220.

79. The full text of Bush's speech is to be found at http://www.washingtonpost.com/wp-srv/nation/specials/attacked/transcripts/bushaddress_092001.html.

80. The White House, *National Security Strategy 2002*, prologue.

81. Full text at http://georgewbush-whitehouse.archives.gov/news/releases/2002/06/20020601–3.html http://www.whitehouse.gov for June 1, 2002.

82. Cf. Edmund Pelligrino et al. *The Teaching of Values and the Successor Generation* (Washington, DC: Atlantic Council of the United States, 1983).

83. From George Bush's speech, "A Distinctly American Internationalism," delivered at the Reagan Presidential Library, November 19, 1999, quoted in Bercovitch, *Puritan Origins*, 201; see also James W. Ceaser, "Providence and the President: George W. Bush's Theory of History," *Weekly Standard*, March 10, 2003.

84. Cf. Max Boot, "George W. Bush: The "W" Stands for Woodrow," *Wall Street Journal*, July 1, 2002, ; David Ignatius, "Wilsonian Course for War," *Washington Post*, August 30, 2002; William Safire, "Post-Oslo Mideast," *New York Times*, June 27, 2002; "Bush the Crusader," editorial, *Christian Science Monitor*, August 30, 2002, Walter LaFeber, "Alliance with the Option to Act Alone," *The Washington Post*, October 6, 2002; for postwar justifications along these lines, see George Melloan, "Protecting Human Rights Is a Valid Foreign Policy Goal," *Wall Street Journal*, June 10, 2003; Jim Hoagland, "Clarity: The Best Weapon," *Washington Post*, June 1, 2003; and Thomas L. Friedman, "Because We Could," *Washington Post*, June 4, 2003.

85. Cf. Lars-Erik Nelson, "Military-Industrial Man," *New York Review of Books* 47, no. 20 (December 21, 2000).

86. Cf. Hughes, *Myths America Lives By*, 106–108.

87. Transcript of the second presidential debate, Wake Forest University, Winston-Salem, North Carolina, October 11, 2000, at www.presidency.ucsb.edu/debates.php.

88. John Quincy Adams, presidential speech on July 4, 1821, quoted in Mead, *Special Providence*, 185.

89. Hunt, *Ideology and U.S. Foreign Policy*, 92ff; cf. Fulbright, *Arrogance of Power*, 21ff.

90. George Kennan, "America and the Russian Future," *Foreign Affairs* 29, no. 3 (April 1951).

91. Johnson and Keehn, ibid; for the quasi-religious nature of American capitalist ideology, see Bellah, *Broken Covenant*, xiii.

92. Cf. Stephen M. Walt, "Rigor or Rigor Mortis? Rational Choice and Security Studies," *International Security* 23, no. 4 (Spring 1999): 5–48.

93. Edward Shils, "Ideology and Civility: On the Politics of the Intellectual," *Sewanee Review* 66, no. 3 (1958): 450–480.

94. Text of President Obama's inaugural address, at http://news.bbc.co.uk/1/hi/world/americas/obama_inauguration/7840646.stmh.

95. Newt Gingrich, "The Failure of US Diplomacy," *Foreign Policy* (July/August 2003): 42–48. For his speech, "Transforming the State Department," of April 22, 2003, see the website of the American Enterprise Institute at http://www.aei.org/search/Gingrich+the+failure+of+US+diplomacy. In support of Gingrich and against the "Road Map," see also Frank J. Gaffney, Jr., "Mideast Road Trap," *Washington Times*, May 6, 2003.

96. Elie Kedourie, *Nationalism* (London: Hutchinson, 1979), 15–16; cf. also Raoul Girardet, *Le Nationalisme Francais* (Paris: Points, 1983), 13.

97. Woodward, *Burden of Southern History*, 205–207.

98. Cf. Alterman, *What Liberal Media?*, 270.

99. Cf. Adrian Karatnycky, "The 30th Anniversary Freedom House Survey," *Journal of Democracy* 14, no. 1 (January 2003); for Freedom House's "methodology" and mission statement, see http://freedomhouse.org/research/freeworld/2000/methodology.htm.

100. Cf. FitzGerald, *America Revised*, 119ff; Edward S. Herman and Noam Chomsky, *Manufacturing Consent: The Political Economy of the Mass Media* (New York: Pantheon Books, 1988), 26–28, 211–228.

101. Jacqueline Newmyer, "Will the Space Race Move East?," *New York Times*, October 20, 2003.

102. Cf. Foner, *Story of American Freedom*, 263.

103. Cf. Lind, *The Next American Nation*, 3.

104. Kirkpatrick, quoted in Tony Smith, *America's Mission: The United States and the Worldwide Struggle for Democracy in the Twentieth Century* (Princeton, NJ: Princeton University Press, 1994), 286.

105. Irving Kristol, "'Moral Dilemmas' in Foreign Policy" (1980), reprinted in Kristol, *Reflections of a Neoconservative: Looking Back, Looking Ahead*, ed. Irving Kristol (New York: Basic Books, 1983), 261–265; for a neoconservative attack on just this line of argument, see James W. Ceasar, "The Great Divide: American Interventionism and Its Opponents," in *Present Dangers: Crisis and Opportunity in American Foreign and Defense Policy*, ed. Robert Kagan and William Kristol (San Francisco: Encounter Books, 2000), 25–43.

106. Irving Kristol, "The 'Human Rights' Muddle," in *Reflections of a Neoconservative: Looking Back, Looking Ahead*, ed. Irving Kristol (New York: Basic Books, 1983), 266–269; for an almost identical statement by one of the greatest targets of neoconservative abuse, George Kennan, see his "Morality and Foreign Policy," *Foreign Affairs* (1985). For the long-standing neoconservative hostility toward humanitarian intervention-ism, see John Ehrman, *The Rise of Neoconservatism: Intellectuals and Foreign Affairs, 1945–94* (New Haven, CT: Yale University Press, 1996), 50ff.

107. Cf. Joshua Muravchik, *Exporting Democracy: Fulfilling America's Destiny* (Washington, DC: American Enterprise Institute, 1991), 19–38, 64–81; William Kristol and Robert Kagan, "Towards a neo-Reaganite Foreign Policy," *Foreign Affairs* (July–August 1996).

108. Cf. Jeane J. Kirkpatrick, *Dictatorships and Double Standards* (Washington, DC: American Enterprise Institute, 1982).

109. http://whoisrichhand.blogspot.com/.

110. Philip Rucker and Chrissah Thomson, "Two new rules will give Constitution a star role in GOP-controlled House," *Washington Post*, December 20, 2011.

111. Quoted in "The Perils of Constitution-Worship," *The Economist*, September 23, 2010.

112. http://www.nccsstore.com/5000-Year-Leap/productinfo/5000YL.

113. John Eidsmoe, *Christianity and the Constitution: The Faith of Our Founding Fathers* (Ada, MO: Baker Academic Publishers, 1995). See also David Barton, *Original Intent: The Courts, the Constitution and Religion* (Aledo, TX: Wallbuilder Press, 2008); and Glenn Beck, *The Original Argument: The Federalists' Case for the Constitution, Adapted for the Twenty-First Century* (New York: Threshold Editions, 2011).

114. Phyllis Schlafly, "Beware of Clinton's 'web' of Treaties," speech to the Christian Coalition, Washington, DC, September 18, 1998, at http://www.eagleforum.org.

115. Jeff Sharlet, "Is the Tea Party becoming a religious movement?" CNN, October 27, 2010, at http://edition.cnn.com/2010/OPINION/10/27/sharlet.tea.party.evangelical/index.html; Scott Clement and John C. Green, "The Tea Party, Religion and Social Issues," Pew Forum on Religion and Public Life, February 2, 2011, at http://pewre-search.org/pubs/1903/tea-party-movement-religion-social-issues-conservative-christian. See also Amy Gardner, "Gauging the Scope of the Tea Party Movement in America," *Washington Post*, October 24, 2011.

116. http://www.themountvernonstatement.com.

117. Michael Lind, "Let's Stop Pretending the Constitution Is Sacred," April 4, 2011, at http://www.salon.com/news/politics/war_room/2011/01/04/lind_tea_party_constitution. See also Elizabeth Wydra and David Gans, "Setting the Record Straight: The Tea Party and the Constitutional Powers of the Federal Government," Issue Brief No. 4, July 16, 2010, at http://www.theusconstitution.org. For a critique of the Tea Parties' understanding of the history of the American Revolution, see Jill Lepore, *The Whites of Their Eyes: The Tea Party's Revolution and the Battle Over American History* (Princeton, NJ: Princeton University Press, 2011).

118. See Jane Mayer, "Covert Operations: The Billionaire Brothers Who Are Waging a War Against Obama," *New Yorker*, August 30, 2010; Frank Rich, "The Billionaires Bankrolling the Tea Party," *New York Times*, August 28, 2010. For earlier background on capitalism's funding of populism, see Kim Phillips-Fein, *Invisible Hands: The Making of the Conservative Movement From the New Deal to Reagan* (New York: W. W. Norton, 2009).

119. Cf. Kate Zernicke, *Boiling Mad: Inside Tea Party America* (New York: Henry Holt, 2010), 135.

120. Ezra Klein, "After Health Care, We Need Senate Reform," *Washington Post*, December 27, 2009.

121. For the U.S. Census overview, see http://www.census.gov/prod/cen2010/briefs/c2010. See also William H. Frey, "Immigration and the Coming 'Majority Minority'," Brookings Institution, September 18, 2009, at http://www.brookings.edu/opinions/2009/1218_immigration_frey.

122. For racial anxiety in the Tea Parties, see Zernicke, *Boiling Mad*, 59.

Chapter Three

1. Vachel Lindsay, *Selected Poems*, ed. Mark Harris (New York: Macmillan, 1963), 124.

2. Cf. David Blackbourn, *History of Germany, 1780–1918: The Long Nineteenth Century* (Oxford: Blackwell, 2003), 37–68.

3. Cf. Hans J. Rogger and Eugen Weber, eds., *European Right: A Historical Profile* (Berkeley: University of California Press, 1965).

4. Cf. Klaus Epstein, *The Genesis of German Conservatism* (Princeton, NJ: Princeton University Press, 1966).

5. Daniel Bell, "The Dispossessed," in *The Radical Right*, ed. Daniel Bell (New York: Doubleday, 1963), 12; see also Richard Hofstadter, "The Pseudo-Conservative Revolt-1955," in *The Radical Right*, 64–86.

6. Samuel Huntington, "The Hispanic Challenge," *Foreign Policy* (March/April 2004); Samuel Huntington, *The Clash of Civilizations and the Remaking of World Order* (London: Simon & Schuster, 1996), map, 205; see also his essay "Dead Souls: The Denationalization of the American Elite," *National Interest* 75 (Spring 2004).

7. Cf. Jean Hardisty, *Mobilizing Resentment: Conservative Resurgence from the John Birch Society to the Promise Keepers* (Boston: Beacon Press, 1999), 30–35.

8. Cf. Joseph Farah, *Taking America Back: A Radical Plan to Revive Freedom, Morality and Justice* (Nashville, TN: Thomas Nelson, 2003).

9. Quoted in Garry Wills, "The Born Again Republicans," *New York Review of Books* 39, no. 15 (September 24, 1992).

10. Rick Perlstein, *Before the Storm: Barry Goldwater and the Unmaking of the American Consensus* (New York: Hill and Wang, 2001), 474.

11. Sarah Palin, *Going Rogue: An American Life* (New York: Harper Collins, 2009); and *America By Heart: Reflections on Family, Faith and Flag* (New York: Harper Collins, 2010).

12. For the immense importance of ethnic and regional origins in shaping different strands of American political culture, see Kevin Phillips, *The Cousins' Wars: Religion, Politics and the Triumph of Anglo-America* (New York: Basic Books, 1999), 117ff.

13. Cf. David H. Bennett, *The Party of Fear: From Nativist Movements to the New Right in American History* (Chapel Hill: University of North Carolina Press, 1989), 27–182; Richard Hofstadter, *The Paranoid Style in American Politics and Other Essays* (1952; repr., Cambridge, MA: Harvard University Press, 1996), 19–23.

14. Hardisty, *Mobilizing Resentment*, 32.

15. See John Weiss, *Conservatism in Europe, 1770–1945: Tradition, Reaction and Counter-Revolution* (London: Thames and Hudson, 1977), 71–89. For the role of the small-town *mittelstand* and the effects on later German nationalism of the destruction of their ancient social and political order by the modern state, see Mack Walker, *German Home Towns: Community, State and General Estate, 1648–1817* (Ithaca, NY: Cornell University Press, 1998), especially 405–431.

16. Cf. Geoff Eley, "The Wilhelmine Right: How It Changed," in *Society and Politics in Wilhelmine Germany*, ed. Richard J. Evans (London: Croom Helm, 1978), 112–135.

17. Alan Brinkley, *Voices of Protest* (New York: Alfred A. Knopf, 1982), quoted in Kevin Phillips, *Boiling Point: Republicans, Democrats and the Decline of Middle Class Prosperity* (New York: Harper Perennial, 1994), 233.

18. Daniel Bell, *The Cultural Contradictions of Capitalism* (New York: Basic Books, 1976), 79; cf. also Bennett, *Party of Fear*; Michael Kazin, "The Right's Unsung Prophets," *The Nation*, February 20, 1989; Richard Hofstadter, *The Age of Reform: From Bryan to F.D.R.* (New York: Alfred A. Knopf, 1956), 135, 175.

19. Quoted by Larry McMurtry, in "Separate and Unequal," *New York Review of Books* 48, no. 4 (March 8, 2001). See also Hans Kohn, *American Nationalism: An Interpretative Essay* (New York: Macmillan, 1957), 143–144.

20. Cf. Liah Greenfield, *Nationalism: Five Roads to Modernity* (Cambridge, MA: Harvard University Press, 1992); Anthony D. Smith, *Nationalism* (Oxford: Blackwell, 2001), 97.

21. David Morris Potter, *The Impending Crisis, 1848–1861* (New York: Perennial, 1976), 243; Bennett, *Party of Fear*, 17–20.

22. Reinhold Niebuhr, "A Note on Pluralism," quoted in Sidney Mead, *The Nation With the Soul of a Church* (Macon, GA: Mercer University Press, 1985), 31.

23. A. James Reichley, "Faith in Politics," in *Religion Returns to the Public Square: Faith and Policy in America*, ed. Hugh Heclo and Wilfred M. McClay (Baltimore: Johns Hopkins University Press, 2003), 175; cf. also Robert Bellah, *The Broken Covenant: American Civil Religion in a Time of Trial* (New York: Seabury Press, 1975), 91ff; Daniel Bell, ed., *The Radical Right* (New York: Transaction Publishers, 1963), 1–38.

24. Hofstadter, *The Paranoid Style*, 3–40.

25. Walter Russell Mead, *Special Providence: American Foreign Policy and How It Shaped the World* (New York: Routledge, 2002), 241; see also Kevin Phillips, *The Emerging Republican Majority* (New York: Arlington House, 1969), especially 290–392 (on the Midwest).

26. Nathan Glazer and Daniel P. Moynihan, *Beyond the Melting Pot: The Negroes, Puerto Ricans, Jews, Italians and Irish of New York City* (Cambridge, MA: MIT Press, 1979), 222.

27. See Gary Gerstle, *American Crucible: Race and Nation in the Twentieth Century* (Princeton, NJ: Princeton University Press, 2001); and Alan Wolfe, "Strangled by Roots," *The New Republic*, May 28, 2001.

28. Chris Stirewalt, "Newt's Jacksonian Revolution," FoxNews.com, January 23, 2012, at http://www.foxnews.com/politics/2012/01/23/newts-jacksonian-revolution/#ixzz1kNIfFP8Y.

29. For the role of the experience and portrayal of the frontier in American culture, see the three-part work by Richard Slotkin, *Regeneration Through Violence: The Mythology of the American Frontier, 1600–1800*; *The Fatal Environment: The Myth of the Frontier in the Age of Industrialization*; and *Gunfighter Nation: The Myth of the Frontier in Twentieth Century America* (Norman: University of Oklahoma Press, 1973, 1985, and 1998, respectively).

30. Quoted in David Hackett Fischer, *Albion's Seed: Four British Folkways in America* (New York: Oxford University Press, 1989), 781–782; for this trait in the Scots-Irish, see also James G. Leyburn, *The Scots-Irish: A Social History* (Chapel Hill: University of North Carolina Press, 1962), especially 68–71, 290–291.

31. Cf. Robert V. Remini, *Andrew Jackson and His Indian Wars* (New York: Penguin, 2001); Samuel Eliot Morison, Henry Steele Commager, and William E. Leuchtenburg, *The Growth of the American Republic*, vols. 1 and 2 (New York: Oxford University Press, 1969), 402–404, 419–443. For Jackson's Scotch-Irish roots and character, see Fischer, *Albion's Seed*, 643–644, 685–688, 755–776.

32. Cf. Remini, *Andrew Jackson and His Indian Wars*, 254–271. See also John Ehle, *Trail of Tears: The Rise and Fall of the Cherokee Nation* (New York: Anchor Books, 1988), 230–264; and Theda Perdue, "Cherokee Women and the Trail of Tears," in *American Encounters: Natives and Newcomers from European Contact to Indian Removal, 1500–1850*, ed. Peter C. Mancall and James H. Merrell (New York: Routledge, 2000), 526–540.

33. For some of the history of this tradition, see Robert Kelley, *The Cultural Pattern in American Politics: The First Century* (Alfred A. Knopf, New York, 1979); and Lee Benson, *The Concept of Jacksonian Democracy: New York as a Test Case* (Princeton, NJ: Princeton University Press, 1961).

34. Cf. Walter Russell Mead, "The Tea Party and American Foreign Policy: What Populism Means for Globalism," *Foreign Affairs* 90, no. 2 (March/April 2011.

35. Cf. Lisa McGirr, *Suburban Warriors: The Origins of the New American Right* (Princeton, NJ: Princeton University Press, 2002), 27.

36. Richard Hofstadter, *Anti-Intellectualism in American Life* (New York: Vintage Books, 1963), 57; and Richard Niebuhr, *The Social Sources of Denominationalism* (Cleveland, OH: Meridian Books, 1957), 30.

37. For the ideas of Thomas Jefferson as a basis for Jacksonianism, see Michael Lind, *The Next American Nation: The New Nationalism and the Fourth American Revolution* (New York: Simon & Schuster, 1995), 45–46, 370; Bellah, *Broken Covenant*, 116–119; for the "agrarian myth" as a basis for both Jacksonianism and the later Progressive movement, see Hofstadter, *Age of Reform*, 23–59.

38. Cf. Paul Krugman, "True Blue Americans," *New York Times*, May 7, 2002,.

39. Phillips, *The Emerging Republican Majority*, 65.

40. Hofstadter, *Anti-Intellectualism*, 146–151.

41. Cited on the BBC, at http://www.bbc.co.uk/news/world-us-canada-16549624.

42. Samuel Eliot Morison, *The Oxford History of the American People*, vol. 2 (New York: Penguin Books, 1994), 76–81.

43. Frances FitzGerald, *America Revised: What History Textbooks Have Taught Our Children About Their Country, and How and Why Those Textbooks Have Changed in Different Decades* (New York: Vintage Books, 1980), 74–75.

44. Dinesh D'Souza, *What's Great About America*, quoted in Louis Menand, "Faith, Hope and Clarity: September 11th and the American Soul," *The New Yorker* (September 16, 2002).

45. Michael Kazin, *The Populist Persuasion: An American History* (New York: Basic Books, 1995), 19–22; see also Robert V. Remini, *The Life of Andrew Jackson* (New York: Harper Collins, 1988), 157–162.

46. Cf. Phillips, *The Emerging Republican Majority*, especially 37–40, 187–289, 315, 407–411, 461–474. For books setting the American populist tradition in the context of populist movements worldwide, see Ghita Ionescu and Ernest Gellner, eds., *Populism: Its Meanings and National Characteristics* (London: Weidenfeld and Nicholson, 1969); and Paul Taggart, *Populism* (Philadelphia: Open University Press, 2000).

47. Morison, Commager, and Leuchtenburg, *The Growth of the American Republic*, 419–443; Kazin, *The Populist Persuasion*, 19.

48. Gunnar Myrdal, *An American Dilemma: The Negro Problem and Modern Democracy* (Piscataway, NJ: Transaction Publishers, 1996), 459.

49. Michael Lind, *Made in Texas: George Bush and the Southern Takeover of American Politics* (New York: Basic Books, 2003), 25.

50. W. J. Cash, *The Mind of the South* (repr., New York: Vintage Books, 1991), 134–141; C. Vann Woodward, *The Burden of Southern History* (Baton Rouge: Louisiana State University Press, 1968), 197–203.

51. Gingrich's remarks during the debate can be seen on YouTube at "Newt's Plan for America's Enemies.", at http://www.youtube.com/watch?v=50WYM-1SjQQ.

52. T. R. Fehrenbach, *Lone Star: A History of Texas and the Texans* (New York: MacMillan, 1968), 643.

53. See T. R. Fehrenbach, *Comanches: The Destruction of a People* (New York: Alfred A. Knopf, 1974), 270–271.

54. For contemporary English Protestant portrayals of atrocities and massacres by the native Irish in the 1640s against Protestant settlers (looking forward to similar accounts of atrocities by the Indians), see William Lamont and Sybil Oldfield, *Politics, Religion and Literature in the Seventeenth Century* (London: J. M. Dent and Sons, 1975), 65–69; for the experiences of Jackson's own family at Indian hands, and his later campaigns, see Robert V. Remini, *The Life of Andrew Jackson* (New York: Harper Collins, 2001); for frontier warfare in the South, see Armstrong Starkey, *European and Native American Warfare 1675–1815* (Norman: University of Oklahoma Press, 1998), 90–92, 158–161.

55. Grady McWhiney, *Cracker Culture: Celtic Ways in the Old South* (Tuscaloosa: University of Alabama Press, 1988).

56. For a vivid picture of the class element in one of the battles over the teaching of evolution that have taken place over the past generation, see Paul Cowan, *The Tribes of America: Journalistic Discoveries of Our People and Their Cultures* (New York: Doubleday, 1979), 77–92.

57. See Paul Boyer, *When Time Shall Be No More: Prophesy Belief in Modern American Culture* (Cambridge, MA: Harvard University Press, 1992), 275, 342, note 9.

58. See Ian Gentles, *The New Model Army in England, Ireland and Scotland, 1645–1653* (Oxford: Blackwell, 1992), 361–367, 371–372; and J. G. Simms, *War and Politics in Ireland, 1649–1730* (London: Hambledon Press, 1986), 1–23. For the Irish clearances, see Margaret MacCurtain, *Tudor and Stuart Ireland* (Dublin: Gill and Macmillan, 1972), 51–61, 89–113, 154–166, 188–192. For the history and ideology of the Scots-Irish, see Kevin Phillips, *The Cousins' Wars*, 177–190.

59. J. T. Cliffe, *The World of the Country House in Seventeenth Century England* (New Haven, CT: Yale University Press, 1999), 182; see also Fischer, *Albion's Seed*, 765–771.

60. Lawrence Stone, *The Crisis of the Aristocracy, 1558–1641* (Oxford: Oxford University Press, 1965), 223. See also J. A. Sharpe, *Crime in Early Modern England, 1550–1750* (New York: Longman, 1984), 95–99.

61. Bertram Wyatt-Brown, *Honor and Violence in the Old South* (New York: Oxford University Press, 1986); McWhiney, *Cracker Culture*, 146–170; see also Joel Williamson, *William Faulkner and Southern History* (New York: Oxford University Press, 1993), 20ff.

62. Warren Leslie, *Dallas, Public and Private: Aspects of an American City* (Dallas, TX: Southern Methodist University Press, 1998), 98–99; see also Lind, *Made in Texas*, 30–31.

63. Wyatt-Brown, *Honor and Violence in the Old South*, 1–15, 187–213, 237–245; John Shelton Reed, *The Enduring South* (Lexington, MA: Lexington Books, 1972), 45–55; and by the same author, "Below the Smith and Wesson Line," in *One South: An Ethnic Approach to Regional Culture* (Baton Rouge: Louisiana State University Press, 1982), 143, 146; Edmund S. Morgan, "The Price of Honor," *New York Review of Books* 48, no. 9 (May 31, 2001).

64. Cash, *The Mind of the South*, 43.

65. Cf. Francis Carney, "A State of Catastrophe," *New York Review of Books* 17, no. 5 (October 7, 1971); Phillips, *The Emerging Republican Majority*, 443–452.

66. Robert A. Caro, *The Years of Lyndon Johnson: The Path to Power*, Vol. 1 (New York: Vintage Books, 1990), 8–32. For wider studies of social violence and vigilantism in the United States beyond the South, see the essays in Hugh Davis Graham and Ted Gurr, eds., *Violence in America: Historical and Comparative Perspectives* (New York: Bantam Books, 1969).

67. Frederick Merk, *History of the Westward Movement* (New York: Alfred A. Knopf, 1978), 474ff; Robert V. Hine and John Mack Faragher, *The American West: A New Interpretive History* (New Haven, CT: Yale University Press, 2000), 337–341.

68. For a brief portrait of rural defeat in one part of the Midwest, see Larry McMurtry, "The 35 from Duluth to Oklahoma City," in *Roads: Driving America's Great Highways* (New York: Simon & Schuster, 2000), 24–47.

69. For populism in the Texas Hill Country and its impact on Lyndon Johnson's family, see Caro, *The Years of Lyndon Johnson*, Vol. 1, 33–49, 79–85; Lind, *Made in Texas*, 35–36.

70. Ursula K. Le Guin, "Malheur County," in *The Compass Rose* (London: Grafton Books, 1984), 230.

71. Christopher Bigsby, notes on Arthur Miller's *The Last Yankee*, quoted in William R. Hutchison and Hartmut Lehmann, *Many are Chosen* (Harrisburg, PA: Trinity Press International, 1998), 10; cf. also Robert K. Merton, *Social Theory and Social Structure* (Glencoe, IL: Free Press, 1957), 167–169; Seymour Martin Lipset, *American Exceptionalism: A Double-Edged Sword* (New York: W. W. Norton, 1976), 47; Louis

Hartz, *The Liberal Tradition in America* (1955; repr., New York: Harcourt Brace and Co., 1991), 224.

72. Francis Butler Simkins and Charles Pierce Roland, *History of the South* (New York: Alfred A. Knopf, 1972), 11.

73. Cf. Rhodes Cook, "The Solid South Turns Around," *Congressional Quarterly Weekly* (October 2, 1992).

74. 2010 census figures, at http://www.census.gov. See also Peter Applebome, *Dixie Rising: How the South is Shaping American Values* (New York: Times Books, 1996), 8–9.

75. Michael Lind, *Up From Conservatism: Why the Right Is Wrong for America* (New York: Simon & Schuster, 1996), 121–137; Lind, *Made in Texas*; see also Applebome, *Dixie Rising*; Kevin Phillips, *American Dynasty: Aristocracy, Fortune and the Politics of Deceit in the House of Bush* (New York: Viking, 2004). For the impact of the Southern Baptists on the Republican Party since the 1960s, see Oran P. Smith, *The Rise of Baptist Republicanism* (New York: New York University Press, 1997); Jonathan Knuckey, "Religious Conservatives, the Republican Party, and Evolving Party Coalitions in the United States," *Party Politics* 5, no. 4 (1999); John F. Persinos, "Has the Christian Right taken over the Republican party?" *Campaigns and Elections* 15, no. 9 (September 1994).

76. Cf. Zell Miller, *A National Party No More: The Conscience of a Conservative Democrat* (Atlanta: Stroud and Hall, 2003); see also the extracts in the *Washington Times* of November 3, 4, and 5, 2003; for the catastrophic Democratic decline among Southern whites, see Thomas F. Schaller, "A Route for 2004 That Doesn't Go Through Dixie," *Washington Post*, November 16, 2003; and James Taranto, "Why Do Dems Lose in the South? Don't Blame Civil Rights," *Wall Street Journal*, March 8, 2004.

77. For the Southern grip on Congress, see, e.g., Phillips, *The Emerging Republican Majority*, 311, and Robert A. Caro, *The Years of Lyndon Johnson: Master of the Senate*, Vol. 3 (New York: Vintage Books, 2003), 32, 89–97, 104.

78. See Earl Black and Merle Black, *The Vital South: How Presidents Are Elected* (Cambridge, MA: Harvard University Press, 1992), 344.

79. Richard E. Cohen, "How They Measured Up," *National Journal*, no. 9 (February 28, 2004); for the impact of conservative religious belief on voting patterns in Congress, see Chris Fastnow, J. Tobin Grant, and Thomas J. Rudolph, "Holy Roll Calls: Religious Tradition and Voting Behavior in the US House," *Social Science Quarterly* 80, no. 4 (December 1999).

80. Cf. Wyatt-Brown, *Honor and Violence in the Old South*; Mead, *Special Providence*, 250–259; Applebome, *Dixie Rising*, 10.

81. Peter W. Williams, *America's Religions From Their Origins to the 21st Century* (Champaign: University of Illinois Press, 2002), 283.

82. Cf. *Churches and Church Membership in the United States, 2000: An Enumeration by Region, State and County Based on Data for 133 Church Groupings* (Atlanta: Glenmary Research Center, 2002). See especially the attached map.

83. Cash, *The Mind of the South*, xlviii.

84. See Reed, *One South*. For a review of Reed's work, see Larry J. Griffin, "The Promise of a Sociology of the South," *Southern Cultures* 7, no. 1 (Spring 2001): 50–75.

85. For a classic statement of the argument that modern nationalisms are "invented," see the essays by Eric Hobsbawm in Eric Hobsbawm and Terence Ranger, eds., *The Invention of Tradition* (Cambridge: Cambridge University Press, 1983). For the "constructivist" theory of nationalism, see Ernest Gellner, *Encounters with Nationalism*

(Oxford: Blackwell, 1984); for nations as "imagined communities," see the classic work by Benedict Anderson, *Imagined Communities: Reflections on the Origin and Spread of Nationalism* (New York: Verso, 1991); for an overview of the study of nationalism from the point of view of a believer in nations as the product of a combination of modern processes with much older elements (a view I generally share), see Anthony D. Smith, *Nationalism* (Oxford: Blackwell, 2001).

86. Cf. Eugene D. Genovese, *The Southern Tradition: The Achievement and Limitations of an American Conservatism* (Cambridge, MA: Harvard University Press 1994).

87. Fehrenbach, *Lone Star*, 712.

88. For the genesis of this South–North opposition in literature, see William R. Taylor, *Cavalier and Yankee: The Old South and American National Character* (New York: Anchor Books, 1963), especially 72–119; for a reexamination of this issue, see David L. Carlton, "Rethinking Southern History," *Southern Cultures* 7, no. 1 (Spring 2001): 38–49.

89. Morison, Commager, and Leuchtenburg, *The Growth of the American Republic*, 426.

90. Cf. Slotkin, *The Fatal Environment: The Myth of the Frontier in the Age of Industrialization* (Norman: University of Oklahoma Press, 1985), 303; cf. also Bennett, *Party of Fear*, 163–164, 181–182.

91. Quoted in Slotkin, *Gunfighter Nation*, 97.

92. Cf. James G. Leyburn, *The Scotch-Irish: A Social History* (Chapel Hill: University of North Carolina Press, 1962), 108–153; Fischer, *Albion's Seed*, 605–782; Phillips, *The Cousin's Wars*, 177–190.

93. Fischer, *Albion's Seed*, 775.

94. For the creation of modern national myths in the Baltic region, see Anatol Lieven, *The Baltic Revolution: Estonia, Latvia, Lithuania and the Path to Independence* (New Haven, CT: Yale University Press, 1983), 118–123; William A. Wilson, *Folklore and Nationalism in Modern Finland* (Bloomington: Indiana University Press, 1990); for the epics themselves, see Elias Lonnrot, *The Kalevala: An Epic Poem After Oral Tradition*, translated with an introduction by Keith Bosley (New York: Oxford University Press, 1989); and Andrejs Pumpurs, *Lacplesis, A Latvian National Epic* (Riga: Writers Union, 1988).

95. Bernard Quinn et al., *Churches and Church Membership in the United States, 1980: An Enumeration by Region, State and County Based on Data Reported by 111 Church Bodies* (Atlanta: Glenmary Research Center, 1982), 32; Dale E. Jones et al., *Churches and Church Membership in the United States, 1980: An Enumeration by Region, State and County Based on Data Reported by 149 Religious Bodies* (Atlanta: Glenmary Research Center, 2000), 47.

96. Smith, *The Rise of Baptist Republicanism*, 17, 43; for a fictional portrait of small-town Texas from the 1950s to the 1990s, reflecting this homogeneity, conservatism, and isolation, see Larry McMurtry's series on the town of Thalia: *The Last Picture Show* (1966), *Texasville* (1987), *Duane's Depressed* (1999) (New York: Simon & Schuster).

97. For the thesis that the black–white split in America as a whole now resembles an "ethnic" division, see Orlando Patterson, *The Ordeal of Integration: Progress and Resentment in America's "Racial" Crisis* (New York: Basic Civitas, 1997); see also Reed, *Enduring South One South*, 173–175, 182–183.

98. See, e.g., the *Financial Times* special report on the region, "Southern Exposure," September 24, 2003.

99. Quoted in Thomas A. Tweed, "Our Lady of Guadeloupe Visits the Confederate Memorial," *Southern Cultures*, 8, no.2 (Summer 2002), 72–93.

100. For some aspects of the systematic and murderous oppression and exploitation that formed the background to this migration, see John M. Barry, *Rising Tide: The Great Mississippi Flood of 1927 and How It Changed America* (New York: Simon & Schuster, 1997), especially 308–335. See the 1880 census figures, at http://fisher.lib.virginia.edu/census/.

101. Morison, Commager, and Leuchtenburg, *Growth of the American Republic*, vol. 1, 482; Myrdal, *American Dilemma*, 1012; cf. also Simkins and Roland, *History of the South*, 161ff.

102. Woodward, *The Burden of Southern History*, 201–202; Cash, *The Mind of the South*, 134–135.

103. Cf. Eric Foner, *Reconstruction: America's Unfinished Revolution, 1863–1877* (New York: Harper and Row, 1988), 124–129; Morison, Commager, and Leuchtenburg, *The Growth of the American Republic*, 726–729; Simkins and Roland, *History of the South*, 241–245.

104. Simkins and Roland, *History of the South*, 558.

105. See Foner, *Reconstruction*; for an expression of the Southern view, see Claude G. Bowers, *The Tragic Era: The Revolution After Lincoln* (New York: Blue Ribbon Books, 1929), especially 45–64, 198–220, 348–371. On the creation of the legend, see Kenneth M. Stampp, *The Era of Reconstruction, 1865–1877* (New York: Alfred A. Knopf, 1965), especially 3–23.

106. Cf. C. Vann Woodward, *The Strange Career of Jim Crow* (repr., New York: Oxford University Press, 2003), 31–109.

107. Quoted in Paul Robinson, "Sword of Honour," *The Spectator* (London) 26 July 2003, at http://www.spectator.co.uk/essays/all/11323/sword-of-honour.thtml.

108. Quoted in Black and Black, *The Vital South*, 165.

109. Zell Miller, "How Democrats Lost the South," *Washington Times*, November 3, 2003.

110. See Diane Roberts, "Reynolds Rap," *Oxford American* (Winter 2002): 142–145.

111. As I wrote this, yet another remake in the "Texas Chainsaw Massacre" film tradition had just appeared, featuring deranged and debased small-town Texas rednecks attacking travelling students. This is close to the bottom of the barrel in the genre of Hollywood Southern horror, with *Deliverance* and *Easy Rider* at the top.

112. For suppressed religious guilt over the evils of slavery, see Eugene D. Genovese, *A Consuming Fire: The Fall of the Confederacy in the Mind of the White Christian South* (Athens: University of Georgia Press, 1998). For the beginnings of unease over the race question in the post–Civil War literature of the South, see Edmund Wilson, *Patriotic Gore: Studies in the Literature of the American Civil War* (New York: Farrar, Straus and Giroux, 1977), 548–604 (on George Washington Cable).

113. Woodward, *The Burden of Southern History*, 187ff.

114. Cf. FitzGerald, *America Revised*, 83–89.

115. Cf. Eric Foner, *Who Owns History? Rethinking the Past in a Changing World* (New York: Farrar, Straus and Giroux, 2002), 189–204.

116. See C. Vann Woodward, "A Southern Critique for the Gilded Age," in *The Burden of Southern History*, 109–140; for the classic statement of Southern agrarian conservatism, see the essays by Allen Tate et al., *I'll Take My Stand: The South and the Agrarian Tradition* (New York: Harper, 1930).

117. John Sheldon Reed, "The Banner That Won't Stay Furled," *Southern Cultures* 8, no. 1 (Spring 2002), 76–100. For a black perspective on the flag question, see Franklin Forts, "Living with Confederate Symbols," *Southern Cultures* 8, no. 1 (Spring 2002), pp.60–75.

118. One of the finest short portraits of redneck culture has been written by—of all people—V. S. Naipaul, in *A Turn in the South* (London: Viking, 1989), especially 204–214; for an equally sensitive portrait of the spirit of country music, see pp. 223–233. For the original literary redneck, Sut Lovingood (the creation of George Washington Harris), see Wilson, *Patriotic Gore*, 507–519.

119. For the enduring prestige of the Confederate soldier even for a Southerner who was bitterly critical of most aspects of his own tradition, see Cash, *The Mind of the South*, 44, 428.

120. See, e.g., Reed, *One South*, 166–167.

121. Weber, *European Right*, 15–16.

122. For example, the dangerous hysteria surrounding General MacArthur's return from Korea after having been dismissed by Truman. See Caro, *The Years of Lyndon Johnson*, vol. 3, 367–382.

123. Hartz, *Liberal Tradition*, 59, 209.

124. Jean-Jacques Rousseau, *The Social Contract*, translated with an introduction by Maurice Cranston (London: Penguin, 1978), 70–83, 149–151, 176–187.

125. J. L. Talmon, *The Origins of Totalitarian Democracy* (New York: Frederick A. Praeger, 1960), 40–49; for the debate on this question, see Talmon, ed., *Totalitarian Democracy and After* (New York: Frank Cass and Co., 2002).

126. Ralph Reed, "Separation of Church and State: 'Christian Nation' and Other Heresies," in Conrad Cherry, *God's New Israel: Religious Interpretations of American Destiny* (Chapel Hill: University of North Carolina Press, 1998), 373–379.

127. Quoted in Mark Hulliung, *Citizens and Citoyens: Republicans and Liberals in America and France* (Cambridge, MA: Harvard University Press, 2002), 6–9; see also Kelley, *Cultural Pattern in American Politics*, 39ff.

128. Cf. Walter Russell Mead, "The Jacksonian Tradition," *National Interest* 58 (Winter 1999/2000); and Mead, *Special Providence*, chapter 7 and passim; Lind, *Made in Texas*; Lee Harris, *Civilization and Its Enemies: The Next Stage of History* (New York: Free Press, 2004), 115–135.

129. Cf. Eric Foner, *The Story of American Freedom* (New York: W. W. Norton, 1999), 307–332.

130. "We don't smoke marijuana in Muskogee;
    We don't take our trips on LSD
    We don't burn our draft cards down on Main Street;
    We like livin' right, and bein' free.
    I'm proud to be an Okie from Muskogee,
    A place where even squares can have a ball
    We still wave Old Glory down at the courthouse,
    And white lightnin's still the biggest thrill of all."

    (Merle Haggard, *Okie from Muskogee*).

    It should be said that given Haggard's own hell-raising past, this song has ironic and even mocking overtones that (as with Springsteen's *Born in the USA*) have been completely lost on most of the people who sing it.

131. Cf. Myrdal, *American Dilemma*, 558–569.

132. Helen Lee Turner and James L. Guth, "The Politics of Armageddon: Dispensationalism Among Southern Baptist Ministers," in *Religion and Political Behavior in the United States*, ed. Ted G. Jelen (New York: Praeger, 1989), 203.

133. Mead, *Special Providence*, 236, 245.

134. For an account of the abuses by the journalist who broke the story, see Seymour Hersh, "Torture at Abu Ghraib," *New Yorker*, May 10, 2004; and "The Gray Zone:

How a Secret Pentagon Program Came to Abu Ghraib," May 24, 2004; see also Scott Wilson, "An Iraqi Detainee Tells of Anguishing Treatment at Iraq Prison," *Washington Post,* May 5, 2004; Scott Wilson and Sewell Chan, "As Insurgency Grew, So Did Prison Abuse," *Washington Post,* May 9, 2004; Dana Priest and Joe Stephens, "Secret World of U.S. Interrogation," *Washington Post,* May 11, 2004; Ian Fisher, "Iraqi Recounts Hours of Abuse by U.S. Troops," *New York Times,* May 4, 2004; Ian Fisher, "Iraqi Tells of U.S. Abuse," *New York Times,* May 13, 2004. For a discussion of the abuse and the background in Bush administration thinking, see Mark Danner, "Torture and Truth," *New York Review of Books,* June 10, 2004; and "The Logic of Torture," *New York Review of Books,* June 24, 2004.

135. For a recent new account of atrocities by U.S. forces in Vietnam, see the *Toledo Blade's* series on the killing of civilians by the "Tiger Force" in 1967: Michael D. Sallah and Mitch Weiss, "Rogue GIs Unleashed Wave of Terror in Central Highlands," *Toledo Blade,* October 22, 2003; and Nicholas Turse, "The Doctrine of Atrocity," *Village Voice,* May 11, 2004.

136. Poll by the Roper Center, University of Connecticut, May 27, 2004, at abcnews.go.com/sections/US/Polls/torture.

137. For the Gonzales memo and Powell's dissent, see Michael Isikoff, "Memos Reveal War Crimes Warnings," *Newsweek,* May 18, 2004. For the other memos, see Dana Priest and R. Jeffrey Smith, "Memo Offered Justification for Use of Torture," *Washington Post,* June 8, 2004; and Edward Alden and James Harding, "U.S. Lawyers Said Interrogators Could Violate Torture Laws Abroad," *Financial Times* (London), June 8, 2004, and "Bush Team Accused of Sanctioning Torture," *Financial Times* (London), June 9, 2004.

138. Quoted by Charles Babington, "Senator Critical of Focus on Prisoner Abuse," *Washington Post,* May 12, 2004.

139. Lott quoted in "Media Notes," *Washington Post,* June 4, 2004; see also Zoe Heller, "How Quickly America Forgot Its Outrage," *Daily Telegraph* (London), May 15, 2004; for attempts in the right-wing media to defend what happened at Abu Ghraib or play down its importance, see, for example, Wesley Pruden, editor in chief, "He Said the Word. Who's Sorry Now?" *Washington Times,* May 7, 2004; James D. Zirin, "The Objective . . . and a Metaphor Too Far," *Washington Times,* May 17, 2004; Victor Davis Hanson, "Abu Ghraib," *Wall Street Journal,* May 3, 2004; Mark Alexander, "The Abu Ghraib Feeding Frenzy," *The Federalist,* May 7, 2004; Deroy Murdock, "Kinder, Gentler War on Terror: Are We Overreacting?" *National Review Online,* May 17, 2004; Reuel Marc Gerecht, "Who's Afraid of Abu Ghraib," *Weekly Standard,* May 24, 2004.

140. Rush Limbaugh, on May 6, 2004, http://americanassembler.com/ newsblog.

141. Michael Savage, on *Savage Nation* (radio show), May 12, 2004 at http:// mediamatters.org.

142. Figures at www.wjno.com/hosts/rush and www.talkradionetwork.com.

143. "Red Double Cross," *Wall Street Journal* editorial, May 14, 2004.

144. John McCain, "In Praise of Do-Gooders: The Red Cross Is Right to Criticize the U.S. Military When It Steps Out of Line," *Wall Street Journal,* June 1, 2004.

145. Mead, "The Tea Party and American Foreign Policy."

146. Kazin, *The Populist Persuasion,* 12.

147. David Brooks, "The Mother of All No Brainers," *New York Times,* July 4, 2011.

148. Matt Kennard, "Times grow hard for working man as unions lose grip," *Financial Times,* September 23, 2011.

149. U.S. Census Bureau, "The Changing Shape of the Nation's Income Distribution 1947–1968," http://www.census.org/prod/2000pubs/p60–204.

150. Emily Beller and Michael Hout, "Intergenerational Social Mobility: The United States in Comparative Perspective," http://futureofchildren.org/futureofchildren/publications/docs/16_02_02.pdf.

151. Tom Hertz, "Understanding Mobility in America," Center for American Progress, 2006, http://www.americanprogress.org/kf/hertz_mobility_analysis.pdf; and Isabel Sawhill and John E. Morton, "Economic Mobility: Is the American Dream Alive and Well?" Economic Mobility Project of the Pew Charitable Trusts, http://www.economicmobility.org/assets/pdfs/EMP%20American%20Dream%20Report.pdf.

152. See "The Middle Class Squeeze 2008," the Drum Major Institute for Public Policy, http://www.drummajorinstitute.org/library/report.php?ID=74.

153. Merle Haggard, America First, from his album *Chicago Wind* (Capitol Records, Nashville, Tennessee, 2005).

154. Cf. Max Lerner, *American Civilization: Life and Thought in the US Today* (New York: Simon & Schuster, 1957), 907ff.

155. Niall Ferguson, "American Terminator," *Newsweek* (January 2004).

156. Cf. Max Boot, "American Imperialism? No Need to Run Away from Label," *USA Today*, May 6, 2003.

157. Kazin, *The Populist Persuasion*, 69.

158. Irving Kristol quoted in Michael Lind, "A Tragedy of Errors," *The Nation* 278, no. 7, (February 23, 2004).

159. Tom DeLay, "Power and Principle," *Washington Times*, May 26, 1999.

160. Cf. Phillips, *American Dynasty*, 236; Meyrav Wurmser, "No More Excuses: Anti-American Leaders Stand to be Accused," *Washington Times*, September 17, 2001; Zev Chafets, "Arab Americans have to Choose," *Daily News* (New York), September 16, 2001.

161. Cf. Senator Trent Lott, "New World, New Friends," official press statement, March 21, 2003, http://www.lott.senate.gov; Helle Dale, "The World According to Chirac," *Washington Times*, June 4, 2003; Editorial, "Thanks, but No Thanks, France," *Washington Times*, March 19, 2003; Paul Johnson, "Au Revoir, Petite France," *Wall Street Journal*, March 18, 2003; Holman Jenkins, "A War for France's Oil," *Wall Street Journal*, March 19, 2003.

162. Cf. the extraordinarily bitter and mendacious attack on France by David Frum and Richard Perle in *An End to Evil: How to Win the War on Terror* (New York: Random House, 2003), 238–253; and "David Frum's Diary" in the *National Review Online* of February 19 and March 11, 2003. For French reporting of these charges, see, e.g., Denis Lacorne, "Les dessous de la francophobie," *Le Nouvel Observateur* (Paris), February 27–March 5, 2003.

163. Thomas L. Friedman, "Our War With France," *New York Times*, September 18, 2003; Justin Vaisse, "Bringing Out the Animal in Us," *Financial Times*, March 15, 2003.

164. Stanley Hoffmann, "France, the United States and Iraq," *The Nation*, February 16, 2004.

165. For the weapons charge, see William Safire "The French Connection,"*New York Times*, March 13, 2003; Bill Gertz, "Iraq Strengthens Air Force With French Parts", *Washington Times*, March 7, 2003. For the biological weapons charge, see "Four Nations Thought to Possess Smallpox," *Washington Post*, November 5, 2002. For an official French rebuttal of all these accusations, see the Fact Sheet issued by the French Embassy in Washington on May 14, 2003, and published in the *Washington Post* on May 15, 2003.

166. Richard Lowry and Ramesh Ponnuru, quoted by Sarah Palin, *America by Heart: Reflections on Family, Faith and Flag* (New York: Harper Collins, 2010), 63–64.

167. Palin, *America by Heart*, 35–60.

168. Quoted in Palin, *America by Heart*, 44.

169. Llewellyn H. Rockwell, Jr., "Prepare to be Betrayed," http://www.lewrockwell.com/rockwell/prepare-for-betrayal155.html.

170. Mead, "The Tea Party and American Foreign Policy."

Chapter Four

1. Max Lerner, *America as a Civilization: Life and Thought in the US Today* (New York: Simon & Schuster, 1957).

2. Quoted in Howard Elinson, "The Implications of Pentecostal Religion for Intellectualism, Politics, and Race Relations," *American Journal of Sociology* 70, no. 4 (January 1965).

3. Samuel Huntington, "Dead Souls: The Denationalization of the American Elite," *National Interest* 75 (Spring 2004): see also Adrian Hastings, *The Construction of Nationhood: Ethnicity, Religion and Nationalism* (New York: Cambridge University Press, 1997).

4. Joel Carpenter, *Revive Us Again: The Reawakening of American Fundamentalism* (New York: Oxford University Press, 1997), 234–235.

5. Cf. Corwin Smidt, "Evangelicals within Contemporary American Politics: Differentiating between Fundamentalist and Non-Fundamentalist Evangelicals," *Western Political Quarterly* 41, no. 3 (September 1988).

6. Ryan Lizza, "Leap of Faith: The Making of a Republican Front-Runner," *New Yorker*, August 15, 2011.

7. Jeff Sharlet, "Is the Tea Party becoming a religious movement?" CNN, October 27, 2010, at http://edition.cnn.com/2010/OPINION/10/27/sharlet.tea.party.evangelical/index.html; Scott Clement and John C. Green, "The Tea Party, Religion and Social Issues," Pew Forum on Religion and Public Life, February 23, 2011, http://pewresearch.org/pubs/1903/tea-party-movement-religion-social-issues-conservative-christian. See also Amy Gardner, "Gauging the Scope of the Tea Party Movement in America," *Washington Post*, October 10, 2011.

8. For individual motivations for new converts to the fundamentalist churches, see Robert R. Monaghan, "Three Faces of the True Believer: Motivations for Attending a Fundamentalist Church," in *American Mosaic: Social Patterns of Religion in the United States*, ed. Phillip E. Hammond and Benton Johnson (New York: Random House, 1970), 65–79.

9. The Pew Forum on Religion and Public Life, "US Religious Landscape Survey 2011," http://religions.pewforum.org/reports. For the situation in 2000, see *Churches and Church Membership in the United States, 2000: An Enumeration by Region, State and County Based on Data for 133 Church Groupings* (Atlanta: Glenmary Research Center, 2002). See especially the attached map.

10. Cf. Kenneth D. Wald, *Religion and Politics in the United States* (New York: Rowman and Littlefield, 2003), 49.

11. See Francis Butler Simkins and Charles Pierce Roland, *History of the South* (New York: Alfred A. Knopf, 1972), 152–175; Eugene D. Genovese, *The Southern Tradition: The*

Achievement and Limitations of an American Conservatism (Cambridge, MA: Harvard University Press, 1994), 27.

12. James G. Leyburn, *The Scotch-Irish: A Social History* (Chapel Hill: University of North Carolina Press, 1962), 71–79, 143ff, 282ff.

13. Cf. Robert Bellah, *The Broken Covenant: American Civil Religion in a Time of Trial* (New York: Seabury Press, 1975), 113–124.

14. George Grant, quoted in Seymour Martin Lipset, *American Exceptionalism: A Double-Edged Sword* (New York: W. W. Norton, 1976), 37; Richard Hofstadter, *Anti-Intellectualism in American Life* (New York: Vintage Books, 1963), 238.

15. Cf. Gabriel A. Almond, R. Scott Appleby, and Emmanuel Sivan, *Strong Religion: The Rise of Fundamentalism Around the World* (Chicago: University of Chicago Press, 2003), 106ff.

16. Richard Hofstadter, "The Pseudo-Conservative Revolt-1955," in *The Radical Right*, ed. Daniel Bell (New York: Doubleday, 1963), 64, 85.

17. Robert Kelley, *The Cultural Pattern in American Politics: The First Century* (New York: Alfred A. Knopf, 1979), 39.

18. Cf. Kenneth D. Wald, *Religion and Politics in the United States* (New York: Rowman and Littlefield, 2003), 200ff.

19. See Dean M. Kelley, *Why Conservative Churches Are Growing* (Macon, GA: Mercer University Press, 1986), 4.

20. Cf. Thomas Frank, *What's the Matter with Kansas? How Conservatives Won the Heart of America* (New York: Metropolitan Books, 2004).

21. Cf. the Christian Coalition's "2001 Senate Score Card" and "2001 House Scorecard" at http://www.cc.org.

22. Howard Fineman, "Bush and God," *Newsweek* (March 10, 2003).

23. Cf. Kevin Phillips, *American Dynasty: Aristocracy, Fortune and the Politics of Deceit in the House of Bush* (New York: Viking, 2004), 233.

24. Matthew 12:30, cited in Henry Ward Beecher's sermon at the start of the Civil War, "The Battle Set in Array," in *God's New Israel: Religious Interpretations of American Destiny*, ed. Conrad Cherry (Chapel Hill: University of North Carolina Press, 1998), 169–183.

25. David Frum and Richard Perle, *An End to Evil: How to Win the War on Terror* (New York: Random House, 2003); see also the critique of Bush's religion in Phillips, *American Dynasty*, 228–244.

26. The provenance of the president's phrase was pointed out by Reverend Fritz Ritsch in his article "Of God, and Man, in the White House", *Washington Post*, March 2, 2003.

27. Stephen Marshall, quoted in Michael Walzer, *Exodus and Revolution* (New York: Basic Books, 1985), 147.

28. Norman Podhoretz, "How to Win World War IV," *Commentary* 113, no. 2 (February 2002).

29. Stephen Mansfield, *The Faith of George W. Bush* (Lake Mary, FL: Charisma House, 2003), 174.

30. George W. Bush, *A Charge to Keep* (New York: William Morrow, 1999), 6; David Gergen, quoted in "A President Puts His Faith in Providence," *New York Times*, February 9, 2003; see also Elizabeth Bumiller, "Talk of Religion Provokes Amens as well as Anxiety," *New York Times*, April 22, 2002; for Bush's religion and its political uses, see Phillips, *American Dynasty*, 211–244. See also Bob Woodward, *Bush at War* (New York: Simon & Schuster, 2002), 75.

31. Woodward, *Bush at War*, 67.

32. Mansfield, *The Faith of George W. Bush*, 172–173.

33. Cf. Phillips, *American Dynasty*, 211–244.

34. Cf. Gunnar Myrdal, *An American Dilemma: The Negro Problem and Modern Democracy* (Piscataway, NJ: Transaction Publishers, 1996), 457, 523–558.

35. James A. Morone, *Hellfire Nation: The Politics of Sin in American History* (New Haven, CT: Yale University Press, 2003).

36. Morone, *Hellfire Nation*, 260–273.

37. Ira M. Wasserman, "Prohibition and Ethnocultural Conflict: The Missouri Prohibition Referendum of 1918," *Social Science Quarterly* 70, no. 4 (December 1989).

38. For a reasoned argument in favor of Prohibition and its partial success, see Norman H. Clark, *Deliver Us From Evil: An Interpretation of American Prohibition* (New York: W. W. Norton, 1976), especially 145–153.

39. Michael Kazin, *The Populist Persuasion: An American History* (New York: Harper Collins, 1995), 79–106.

40. Morone, *Hellfire Nation*, 304.

41. Cf. David H. Bennett, *The Party of Fear: From Nativist Movements to the New Right in American History* (Chapel Hill: University of North Carolina Press, 1989), 208–237.

42. Michael Lind, *The Next American Nation: The New Nationalism and the Fourth American Revolution* (New York: Simon & Schuster, 1995), 88.

43. Quoted in Cherry, *God's New Israel*, 269.

44. Stanley Coben, "A Study in Nativism: The Red Scare of 1919–20," *Political Science Quarterly* 79, no. 1 (March 1964). For a description of the two scares, see Bennett, *Party of Fear*, 183–198; Samuel Eliot Morison, *The Oxford History of the American People*, vol. 3 (New York: Penguin, 1994), 206–219. For the World War I hysteria in Texas, see T. R. Fehrenbach, *Lone Star: A History of Texas and the Texans* (New York: MacMillan, 1968), 643–648; Robert A. Caro, *The Years of Lyndon Johnson: The Path to Power*, V vol. 1 (New York: Vintage Books, 1990), 80–81. For pressure on the (traditionally pro-German) Yiddish press during World War I, see Irving Howe, *World of Our Fathers: The Journey of the East European Jews to America and the Life They Found and Made* (New York: Harcourt Brace Jovanovich, 1976), 538–540.

45. Cf. George Marsden, "The Religious Right: A Historical Overview," in *No Longer Exiles: The Religious New Right and American Politics*, ed. Michael Cromartie (Washington, DC: Ethics and Public Policy Center, 1993), 1; Martin Marty, *Pilgrims in Their Own Land: 500 Years of Religion in America* (New York: Penguin, 1985), 410.

46. Daniel Bell, ed., *The Radical Right* (New York: Transaction Publishers, 1963), 79.

47. Cf. Seymour Martin Lipset and Earl Raab, *The Politics of Unreason: Right Wing Extremism in America, 1790–1970* (New York: Harper and Row, 1970), 209–247.

48. Kazin, *The Populist Persuasion*, 109–133; Bennett, *Party of Fear*, 253–266.

49. This argument for the sources of McCarthyism is set out in the essays by Richard Hofstadter, Peter Viereck, and others in Daniel Bell, ed., *The Radical Right*; see also Bennett, *Party of Fear*, 310–315.

50. See Hofstadter, *Anti-Intellectualism in American Life*, 55.

51. Gallup, "Evolution, Creationism, Intelligent Design," http://www/gallup.com/poll/21814/evolution-creationism-intelligent design.aspx.

52. For the mid-nineteenth century, see Noel Ignatiev, *How the Irish Became White* (New York: Routledge, 1995).

53. Nathan Glazer and Daniel P. Moynihan, *Beyond the Melting Pot: The Negroes, Puerto Ricans, Jews, Italians and Irish of New York City* (Cambridge, MA: MIT Press, 1979), 270.

54. See David Schoenbaum, *Hitler's Social Revolution: Class and Status in Nazi Germany, 1933–1939* (New York: W. W. Norton, 1980).

55. Ann Coulter, *Treason: Liberal Treachery from the Cold War to the War Against Terrorism* (New York: Crown Forum, 2003), 69.

56. Cf. Dorothy Doren, *Nationalism and Catholic Americanism* (New York: Sheed and Ward, 1967); Glazer and Moynihan, *Beyond the Melting Pot*, 230–231, 247–250.

57. Glazer and Moynihan, *Beyond the Melting Pot*, 262, 270–274.

58. Lerner, *American Civilization*, 904.

59. Quoted in Joseph McBride, *Searching for John Ford* (New York: St. Martin's Press, 2001), 6; see also Thomas Flanagan's essays on John Ford in "Western Star," *New York Review of Books* 48, no.19 (November 29, 2001); and no. 20 (December 20, 2001).

60. Cf. Richard Slotkin, *Gunfighter Nation; The Myth of the Frontier in Twentieth Century America* (Norman: University of Oklahoma Press, 1998), 334–343; McBride, *Searching for John Ford*, 446–458.

61. Doren, *Nationalism and Catholic Americanism*, 134–162.

62. Including at least one Irish American character who is first a soldier and then a gangster, the protagonist of *The Roaring Twenties*.

63. Grady McWhiney, *Cracker Culture: Celtic Ways in the Old South* (Tuscaloosa: University of Alabama Press, 1988), xxi–xliii. I should perhaps place on record that I am of German Irish ethnicity myself, with a mother whose maiden name was Monahan, and I have nothing against pugnacity in a good cause.

64. McBride, *Searching for John Ford*, 698.

65. Glazer and Moynihan, *Beyond the Melting Pot*, 271.

66. Sean Hannity, *Let Freedom Ring: Winning the War of Liberty Over Liberalism* (New York: Regan Books, 2002), 127.

67. Cf. Eric Alterman, *What Liberal Media? The Truth About Bias and the News* (New York: Basic Books, 2003), 35; Michael Kinsley, "O'Reilly Among the Snobs," *Washington Post*, March 2, 2001; Noam Scheiber, "Class Act: Chris Mathews and Bill O'Reilly v. The Working Man," *New Republic* (June 25, 2001); for John Ford's assumption of an Irish macho style at odds with aspects of his real nature, see McBride, *Searching for John Ford*, 298; for Ford on the Vietnam War, see McBride, *Searching for John Ford*, 691–692.

68. Will Herberg, *Protestant, Catholic, Jew: An Essay in American Religious Sociology* (New York: Doubleday, 1956), 146–147.

69. Cromartie, *No Longer Exiles*; Oscar Handlin, "American Jewry" in *The Jewish World: Revelation, Prophecy and History*, ed. Elie Kedourie (London: Thames and Hudson, 1979), 281–282; Lerner, *America as a Civilization*, 703–717.

70. Quoted in Hofstadter, *Anti-Intellectualism*, 125.

71. Cf. Daniel J. Kevles, "Darwin in Dayton," *New York Review of Books* 45, no. 18 (November 19, 1998); Robert C. Liebman and Robert Wuthnow, *The New Christian Right* (Hawthorne, NY: Aldine Transaction, 1983), 1.

72. Gabriel A. Almond, R. Scott Appleby, and Emmanuel Sivan, *Strong Religion: The Rise of Fundamentalism Around the World* (Chicago: University of Chicago Press, 2003), 26–27.

73. Samuel Eliot Morison, Henry Steele Commager, and William E. Leuchtenburg, *The Growth of the American Republic*, vol. 1 (New York: Oxford University Press, 1969), 435–436; see also Marty, *Pilgrims in Their Own Land*, 380–381.

74. Kazin, *The Populist Persuasion*, 106.

75. Marty, *Pilgrims in Their Own Land*, 410–415; Joel Carpenter, *Revive Us Again: The Reawakening of American Fundamentalism* (New York: Oxford University Press, 1997), 211–229.

76. *The Prairie Home Companion*, National Public Radio, October 26, 2003.

77. Cf. Kenneth Wald, Dennis E. Owen, and Samuel S. Hill, Jr., "Churches as Political Communities," *American Political Science Review* 82, no. 2 (1988), 531–548.

78. Oran P. Smith, *The Rise of Baptist Republicanism* (New York: New York University Press, 1997), 46–67, 98–112, 191–212.

79. See Bill Bishop, *The Big Sort: Why the Clustering of Like-Minded America Is Tearing Us Apart* (New York: Mariner Books, 2009); and Lisa McGirr, *Suburban Warriors: The Origins of the New American Right* (Princeton, NJ: Princeton University Press, 2002).

80. Cf. Peter Applebome, *Dixie Rising: How the South Is Shaping American Values* (New York: Times Books, 1996), 241ff.

81. Cf. Lerner, *America as a Civilization*, 172–182.

82. Cf. Robert Bellah et al., *Habits of the Heart: Middle America Observed* (Berkeley: University of California Press, 1985), 196, 204–206, 251.

83. For this recovery, see Herberg, *Protestant, Catholic, Jew*, 59–84.

84. Figures quoted in Sara Diamond, *Not By Politics Alone: The Enduring Influence of the Christian Right* (New York: Guilford Press, 1998), 9–10.

85. Diamond, *Not By Politics Alone*, 9–10.

86. The Pew Forum on Religion and Public Life, "US Religious Landscape Survey 2011," http://religions.pewforum.org/reports. For the 2000 figures, see American National Election Studies (ANES), Center for Political Studies, University of Michigan, quoted in Wald, *Religion and Politics in the United States*, 160–162.

87. For the impact of the Southern Baptists on the Republican Party since the 1960s, see Smith, *The Rise of Baptist Republicanism* (New York: New York University Press, 1997).

88. Pew telephone survey commissioned by *Newsweek* and cited in David Gates, "The Pop Populists," *Newsweek* (May 24, 2004).

89. Cited in Lipset, *American Exceptionalism*, 268–269.

90. Peter W. Williams, *America's Religions From Their Origins to the 21st Century* (Champaign: University of Illinois Press, 2002), 379.

91. See Robert J. Blendon et al., "America's Changing Political and Moral Values," in *What's God Got to Do With the American Experiment*, ed. E. J. Dionne and John J. Dilulio (Washington, DC: Brookings Institution Press, 2000), 26.

92. Almond et al., *Strong Religion*, 227.

93. Cf. Colbert I. King, "Dean's Faith-Based Folly," *Washington Post*, January 10, 2004; and Steven Waldman, "When Piety Takes Centre Stage," *Washington Post*, January 11, 2004.

94. For the importance of fundamentalist Christianity to Michele Bachmann and to Tea Party activists in Iowa, see Stephanie Jirchgaessner, "Meet Michele," *Financial Times* magazine, July 2–3, 2011.

95. Ralph Reed, "The Future of the Religious Right," in *Christian Political Activism at the Crossroads*, ed. William R. Stevenson, Jr. (Lanham, MD: University Press of America, 1994), 81–86; see also Reed quoted in Wald, *Religion and Politics in the United States*, 200; for a survey of Christian Rightist activism and organization building, see Mark J. Rozell and Clyde Wilcox, "Second Coming: Strategies of the New Christian Right," *Political Science Quarterly* 111, no. 2 (Summer 1996); and Kimberley H. Conger and

John C. Green, "Spreading Out and Digging In: Christian Conservatives and State Republican Parties," *Campaigns and Elections*, February 2002, http://www.theocracy-watch.org/campaigns_Elections_study.htm.

96. Cf. Rosalind S. Helderman, "Outfitted with Placards and Prayer: Students from Virginia's New Patrick Henry College Planting Political Seeds," *Washington Post*, October 20, 2003.

97. Diamond, *Not By Politics Alone*, 63–66, 131–155; Alan I. Abramowitz, "It's Abortion, Stupid: Policy Voting in the 1992 Presidential Election," *Journal of Politics* 57, no. 1 (February 1995); Richard Hughes, *Myths America Lives By* (Champaign: University of Illinois Press, 2003), 85–89.

98. Kevin Phillips, *The Emerging Republican Majority* (New York: Arlington House, 1969), 25, 33, 37.

99. Cf. Bellah, *The Broken Covenant*, 105–106.

100. Cf. Tracy L. Scott, "Gay Characters Gaining TV Popularity," *Washington Post TV Week*, November 30–December 6, 2003.

101. Maurice Isserman and Michael Kazin, *America Divided: The Civil War of the 1960s* (New York: Oxford University Press, 2000), 205–220.

102. For the correlation between relative poverty and lack of education and fundamentalist belief, see Corwin Smidt, "Born Again Politics" in *Religion and Politics in the South: Mass and Elite Perspectives*, ed. Tod A. Baker, Robert B. Steed, and Laurence W. Moreland (New York: Praeger, 1983), 27–56.

103. This spirit breathes, for example, from Newt Gingrich's book *To Renew America* (New York: Harper Collins, 1995).

104. For the correlation between evangelical belief and opposition to nuclear reduction treaties, see Corwin E. Smidt, ed., *Contemporary Evangelical Political Involvement: An Analysis and Assessment* (Lanham, MD: University Press of America, 1989), 85–96.

105. Robert C. Liebman, "Mobilizing the Moral Majority," in Liebman and Wuthnow, *The New Christian Right*, 69; Almond et al., *Strong Religion*, 45ff; Bennett, *Party of Fear*, 375–377, 396–398.

106. Cf. an early call for the war against terrorism to be extended from Afghanistan to Iraq and elsewhere; Lt Colonel (retd.) Robert L. Maginnis, "Hunting Down Backers of Terrorism," *LA Daily Journal*, October 22, 2001. The link in the minds of this conservative religious group between their pro-family, anti-abortion beliefs and a hardline strategy in the fight against terrorism may not be intellectually apparent, but is entirely culturally coherent.

107. Robert D. Novak, "Bush's Gay Marriage Test," *Washington Post*, December 1, 2003.

108. Speech at the Islamic Center of Washington, DC, September 17, 2001, http://www.youtube.com/watch?v=w0phxuzQ7sE www.whitehouse.gov.

109. Mansfield, *The Faith of George W. Bush*, 139–142.

110. Hal Lindsey, *The Everlasting Hatred: The Roots of Jihad* (Murrietta, CA: Oracle House, 2002), especially 58–124.

111. Phillips, *American Dynasty*, 235; see also the attack on these figures by Fareed Zakaria, "Time to Take On America's Haters," *Newsweek* (October 21, 2002).

112. Larry McMurtry, *In a Shallow Grave: Essays on Texas* (New York: Touchstone Books, 2001), 155; and Warren Leslie, *Dallas, Public and Private: Aspects of an American City* (Dallas, TX: Southern Methodist University Press, 1998), 89, 95, 167.

113. For a sketch of millenarian beliefs, see Carpenter, *Revive Us Again*, 247–249; Paul Boyer, *When Time Shall Be No More: Prophesy Belief in Modern American Culture* (Cambridge, MA: Harvard University Press, 1992), 21–45; for the origins of American

beliefs in seventeenth-century England, see Richard Niebuhr, *The Social Sources of Denominationalism* (Cleveland, OH: Meridian Books, 1957), 46–49.

114. Helen Lee Turner and James L. Guth, "The Politics of Armageddon: Dispensationalism Among Southern Baptist Ministers," in *Religion and Political Behavior in the United States*, ed. Ted G. Jelen (New York: Praeger, 1989), 187–190. For a useful chart of the relationship between the different schools of millennialism, see Timothy P. Weber, *Living in the Shadow of the Second Coming: American Premillennialism, 1875–1925* (New York: Oxford University Press, 1979), 10.

115. See Boyer, *When Time Shall Be No More*, 1–7.

116. Hal Lindsey, *The Late Great Planet Earth* (repr., Murrietta, CA: Oracle House, 2002); Tim LaHaye and Jerry B. Jenkins, *Left Behind: A Novel of the Earth's Last Days* (Wheaton, IL: Tyndale House, 1995).

117. Pat Robertson, *The End of the Age* (Dallas, TX: Word Publishing, 1996). This sketch is from Diamond, *Not By Politics Alone*, 198.

118. LaHaye and Jenkins, *Left Behind*, 25–76.

119. Cf. the passages by Jerry Falwell, Hal Lindsey, and others quoted in Grace Halsell, *Prophecy and Politics: Militant Evangelists on the Road to Nuclear War* (Westport, CT: Lawrence Hill & Co., 1986), 28–35.

120. Boyer, *When Time Shall Be No More*, 303, note 29.

121. For the Muslim antichrist theme, see, e.g., Joel Richardson, *The Islamic Antichrist: The Shocking Truth About the Real Nature of the Beast* (Los Angeles: WND Books, 2010); and Glenn Beck's broadcast on Fox News, February 17, 2011, http://www.youtube.com/watch?v=nNzel6tPrFk.

122. Cf. Bennett, *Party of Fear*, 409–475.

123. Cf. Gerald Flurry, "Continue to Watch Stoiber," *Philadelphia Trumpet*, November 2002, http://www.thetrumpet.com; Boyer, *When Time Shall Be No More*, 111, 121, 148, 277.

124. "'Wingnuts' and President Obama," Harris Interactive, March 24, 2010, http://www.harrisinteractive.com/NewsRoom/HarrisPolls/tabid/447/ctl/ReadCustom%20Default/mid/1508/ArticleId/223/Default.aspx.http://www.harrisinteractive.com/vault/Harris_Interactive_Poll_Tea_Party_Opposition.

125. For a book arguing that Obama is the antichrist, see Stephen Kirk, *Satan as Barack Obama* (Bloomington, IN: AuthorHouse Publishing, 2011). For websites arguing that Obama is or may be the antichrist, see "Obama Antichrist," http://www.obamaantichrist.org/category/obama-antichrist/; and the website of Landover Baptist Church, http://www.landover-baptist.net ("Final Proof! Obama is the Antichrist"). For the Bible Nation Society's dissemination of this idea, see Sarah Posner, "Group Behind King James Bible Congressional Resolution thinks Obama might be Antichrist," *Religion Dispatches*, September 11, 2011, at http://www.religiondispatches.org/dispatches/sarahposner/4539/group_behind_king_james_bible_congressional_resolution_thinks_obama_might_be_antichrist/.

126. Mathew Avery Sutton, "Is Obama the Antichrist? Why Armageddon Stands Between the President and the Evangelical Vote," http://www.religiondispatches.org/archive/politics/1671/.

127. Mike Davis, *Ecology of Fear: Los Angeles and the Imagination of Disaster* (New York: Metropolitan Books, 1998), 355.

128. Boyer, *When Time Shall Be No More*, 10.

129. Boyer, *When Time Shall Be No More*, 257–260. For the racial element in American apocalyptic fears, see Davis, *Ecology of Fear*, 281–300, 325–344; for Lindsey's new anti-Muslim hysteria, see Lindsey, *The Everlasting Hatred*.

130. Norman Cohn, *The Pursuit of the Millennium: Revolutionary Millenarians and Mystical Anarchists of the Middle Ages* (New York: Oxford University Press, 1990), 58–74, 309–310; cf. also Edward Shils, "Ideology and Civility: On the Politics of the Intellectual," *Sewanee Review* 66, no. 3 (1958): 450–480.

131. Turner and Guth, "The Politics of Armageddon," 191–192, 208.

132. See R. Laurence Moore, *Religious Outsiders and the Making of Americans* (New York: Oxford University Press, 1986).

133. Niebuhr, *The Social Sources of Denominationalism*, 30–31.

134. Quoted in Carpenter, *Revive Us Again*, 224.

135. Billy Graham, quoted in Boyer, *When Time Shall Be No More*, 320.

136. In an interview with Molly Ivins, *Fort Worth Star-Telegram*, September 14, 1993, http://www.christianforums.com/t2013475-3/.

137. See "Wrong and Divisive", editorial in the *Washington Post*, October 21, 2003.

138. Cf. Kings 1:18, 20–40. I am indebted to Professor Charles King of Georgetown University for this reference.

139. See Michelle Cottle, "Bible Brigade," *New Republic* (April 21, 2003) and (April 28, 2003); Alan Cooperman, "Bush's Remark about God Assailed," *Washington Post*, November 22, 2003.

140. Peter Beinart, "Bad Faith," *New Republic* (March 25, 2002); for more such statements, see *The Religious Right: The Assault on Tolerance and Pluralism in America* (New York: Anti-Defamation League, 1994), 5.

141. Cf. Molly Ivins, "Cheney's Card: The Empire Writes Back," *Washington Post*, December 30, 2003.

142. Richard Hofstadter, *The Paranoid Style in American Politics and Other Essays* (1952; repr., Cambridge, MA: Harvard University Press, 1996), 31.

Chapter Five

1. Quoted in Warren Leslie, *Dallas, Public and Private: Aspects of an American City* (Dallas, TX: Southern Methodist University Press, 1998), 222.

2. James Mann, *Rise of the Vulcans: The History of Bush's War Cabinet* (New York: Viking, 2004), 293.

3. Mann, *Rise of the Vulcans*, 246.

4. Cf. Joshua Micah Marshall, "Vice Grip," *Washington Monthly* (January/February 2003); and Nicholas Lemann, "The Quiet Man" (profile of Dick Cheney), *New Yorker* (May 7, 2001); for the importance of the cold war as a moral and political paradigm among the radical Right, see David H. Bennett, *The Party of Fear: From Nativist Movements to the New Right in American History* (Chapel Hill: University of North Carolina Press, 1989), 469–470.

5. David Hume Kennerly, quoted in Kevin Phillips, *American Dynasty: Aristocracy, Fortune and the Politics of Deceit in the House of Bush* (New York: Viking, 2004), 93; see also Derek Leebaert, *The Fifty Year Wound: How America's Cold War Victory Shapes Our World* (New York: Little, Brown and Co., 2002); Chalmers Johnson, *Blowback: The Costs and Consequences of American Empire* (New York: Holt/Owl Books, 2003).

6. The best book on the neoconservatives is Justin Vaisse, *Neoconservatism: The Biography of a Movement* (Cambridge, MA: Harvard University Press, 2010). See also Joshua Micah Marshall, "Remaking the World: Bush and the Neoconservatives," *Foreign Affairs* (November/December 2003).

7. Cf. Lars-Erik Nelson, "Military-Industrial Man," *New York Review of Books* 47, no. 20 (December 21, 2000).

8. Cf. Michael Lind, *Up From Conservatism: Why the Right is Wrong for America* (New York: Simon & Schuster, 1996), 69.

9. Quoted in John Ehrman, *The Rise of Neoconservatism: Intellectuals and Foreign Affairs, 1945–94* (New Haven, CT: Yale University Press, 1996), 42.

10. Ehrman, *The Rise of Neoconservatism*, 45–46.

11. Samuel Huntington, *Clash of Civilizations: And the Remaking of World Order* (London: Simon & Schuster, 1996), 301–321.

12. Jacob Weisberg, "The Family Way: How Irving Kristol, Gertrude Himelfarb, and Bill Kristol became the family that liberals love to hate," *New Yorker* (October 21, 1996); and (October 28, 1996).

13. Plato, *The Republic*, trans. Desmond Lee (London: Penguin, 1976), 181–182, 316–325.

14. Stephen Holmes, *The Anatomy of Antiliberalism* (Cambridge, MA: Harvard University Press, 1996), 61–87.

15. Justin Vaisse, *Neoconservatism: The Biography of a Movement* (Cambridge, MA: Harvard University Press, 2010), 279.

16. Robert Kagan and William Kristol, eds., *Present Dangers: Crisis and Opportunity in American Foreign and Defense Policy* (San Francisco: Encounter Books, 2000).

17. Jonathan Clarke, "The Guns of 17th Street," *National Interest* 63 (Spring 2001).

18. Charles Krauthammer, "The Bush Doctrine," *Time* 157, no. 9 (March 5, 2001).

19. David Frum and Richard Perle, *An End to Evil: How to Win the War on Terror* (New York: Random House, 2003), 235–273.

20. Vaisse, *Neoconservatism*, 267–268.

21. Bacevich, *American Empire*, 167; Michael H. Hunt, *Ideology and U.S. Foreign Policy* (New Haven, CT: Yale University Press, 1987), 29–45.

22. In the words of a U.S. senator (from the Democratic Party) to me in January 2002.

23. See David Stockman, *The Triumph of Politics: Why the Reagan Revolution Failed* (New York: Harper Collins, 1986); David Brock, *Blinded by the Right: The Conscience of an Ex-Conservative* (New York: Three Rivers Press, 2002), 71; see also the profile in the *Washington Post*, "Zealous Norquist Plans Conservative Golden Era," January 12, 2004.

24. Mark Almond, "Your Tyrant or Ours?" *New Statesman* (London), November 17, 2003.

25. See Howard Kurtz, "Conservative David Frum Loses Think Tank Job After Criticizing GOP," *Washington Post*, March 26, 2010. For the attack on Frum in the *Wall Street Journal*, see "The GOP and Obama Care," *Wall Street Journal*, March 23, 2010.

26. Irving Kristol, "My Cold War," *National Interest* (Spring 1993).

27. Daniel Bell, "The Dispossessed—1962," in *The Radical Right* (New York: Transaction Publishers, 1963), 8–12.

28. Alfred Cobban, *A History of Modern France* (London: Penguin, 1990), 48.

29. Ann Coulter, *Treason: Liberal Treachery from the Cold War to the War Against Terrorism* (New York: Crown Forum, 2003).

30. Pamela Geller, Robert Spencer, and John Bolton, *The Post-American Presidency: The Obama Administration's War on America* (New York: Threshold Editions, 2010).

31. John Bainbridge, *The Super-Americans: A picture of life in the United States, as brought into focus, bigger than life, in the land of the millionaires—Texas* (New York: Holt, Rinehart and Winston, 1972), 237.

32. Cf. Nicholas Lemann, "The Quiet Man" (profile of Dick Cheney), *New Yorker* (May 7, 2001), 69.

33. Aaron Klein, *The Manchurian President: Barack Obama's Ties to Communists, Socialists and Other Anti-American Extremists* (New York: WND Books, 2010).

34. C. Wright Mills, *The Power Elite* (New York: Oxford University Press, 1959), 184.

35. Quoted in Samuel Eliot Morison, *The Oxford History of the American People* (New York: Penguin Books, 1994), 417.

36. Cf. Michael T. Klare, "America's Military Revolution: Cold War Government with No War to Fight," *Le Monde Diplomatique* (English edition), July 2001.

37. Quoted in Chalmers Johnson, *The Sorrows of Empire: Militarism, Secrecy and the End of the Republic* (New York: Metropolitan Books, 2004), 44–45.

38. Cf. Gordon Alexander Craig, *Germany 1866–1945* (New York: Oxford University Press, 1978), 288, 293–296, 307–308; Eckart Kehr, *Economic Interest, Militarism and Foreign Policy* (Berkeley: University of California Press, 1977), 75ff; Richard Owen, "Military Industrial Relations: Krupp and the Imperial Navy Office," in *Society and Politics in Wilhelmine Germany*, ed. Richard J. Evans (London: Croom Helm, 1978); V. R. Berghahn, *Germany and the Approach of War in 1914* (New York: St. Martin's Press, 1993), 136–143.

39. Derek Leebaert, *The Fifty Year Wound*, 230–231, 243–246.

40. Cf. Robert Caro, *The Years of Lyndon Johnson: Master of the Senate*, vol. 3 (New York: Vintage Books, 2003), 306–334.

41. Cf. Anatol Lieven, "The (not so) Great Game," *National Interest* (Winter 1999/2000). For the later stages of the debate on the Russian threat to India and British responses, see Max Beloff, *Imperial Sunset*, vol. 1, *Britain's Liberal Empire, 1897–1921* (New York: Alfred A. Knopf, 1970), 20–25, 31–39; Aaron Friedberg, *The Weary Titan: Britain and the Experience of Relative Decline, 1895–1905* (Princeton, NJ: Princeton University Press, 1988), 212–280; and David Gillard, *The Struggle for Asia, 1828–1914* (London: Methuen, 1977). For the mid-nineteenth-century origins of the particular British fear and dislike of Russia, see John Howes Gleason, *The Genesis of Russophobia in Great Britain: A Study of the Interaction of Policy and Opinion* (Cambridge, MA: Harvard University Press, 1950).

42. Michael Paris, *Warrior Nation: Images of War in British Popular Culture, 1850–2000* (London: Reaktion Books, 2000), 88–89.

43. Cf. the premise of John Milius's 1984 film of heroic American resistance to a Soviet–Cuban–Nicaraguan occupation, *Red Dawn*.

44. See Stephen W. Mosher and Chuck DeVore, *China Attacks* (West Conshohocken, PA: Infinity Publishing, 2000); Carl Berryman, *2013: World War III*. AuthorHouse, 2004); Ian Slater, *Choke Point: World War III* (New York: Ballantine Books, 2004).

45. Cf. Richard Hofstadter, *The Paranoid Style in American Politics and Other Essays* (1952, repr., Cambridge, MA: Harvard University Press, 1996).

46. Norman Podhoretz, *Present Danger: Do We have the Will to Reverse the Decline of American Power?* (New York: Simon & Schuster, 1980), quoted in Michael Lind, *Up From Conservatism: Why the Right Is Wrong for America* (New York: Simon & Schuster, 1996), 61 (note); cf. also Ehrman, *The Rise of Neoconservatism*. 108–109.

47. Norman Podhoretz, "How to Win World War IV," *Commentary* 113, no. 2 (February 2002).

48. Cf. Craig, *Germany 1866–1945*, 104–113; V. R. Berghahn, *Germany and the Approach of War in 1914* (New York: St. Martin's Press, 1993).

49. For another classic piece of later anti-Soviet paranoia, see Raymond Sleeper, ed., *Mesmerized by the Bear: The Soviet Strategy of Deception* (New York: Dodd, Mead and Co., 1987), with contributions by Jack Kemp and Paul Nitze.

50. For an account of the link between Russian military defeat and the condition of Russian culture and society, see Anatol Lieven, *Chechnya: Tombstone of Russian Power* (New Haven, CT: Yale University Press, 1997).

51. See, e.g., William E. Odom and Robert Dujarric, *Commonwealth or Empire: Russia, Central Asia or the Caucasus* (New York: Hudson Institute, 1996); William E. Odom, "Realism About Russia," *National Interest* (Fall 2001); George Will, "Back in the USSR," *Washington Post*, September 3, 2000; William Safire, "Dangerous Consequences," *New York Times*, November 4, 1999; Bill Gertz, "Defense Official says US still needs nukes; threat remains from Russia, others," *Washington Times*, February 13, 1997; Ariel Cohen et al., "Making the World Safe for America," in *Issues 96: The Candidates' Briefing Book* (Washington, DC: Heritage Foundation, 1996); and Richard Pipes, "Russia's Past, Russia's Future," *Commentary* (June 1996). For a challenge to such views, see Stephen Sestanovich, "Geotherapy: Russia's Neuroses, and Ours," *National Interest* 45 (Fall 1996). For a discussion of these views, see Lieven, *Chechnya: Tombstone of Russian Power*.

52. For the role of institutional vested interests in perpetuating hatred and fear of Russia in the 1990s, see Owen Harries, "The Dangers of Expansive Realism," *National Interest* (Winter 1997/98).

53. Cf. Condoleezza Rice, "Promoting the National Interest," *Foreign Affairs* 79, no. 1 (January/February 2000); press conference by President Bush, February 22, 2001, http://www.fas.org/news/iraq/2001/02/iraq 010222zwb.htm; for a critique of this approach, see Owen Harries, "The Dangers of Expansive Realism."

54. See Ambrose Evans-Pritchard, "Appeasement Is the Proper Policy Towards Confucian China," *Daily Telegraph*, January 22, 2011.

55. Walter Russell Mead, "The Tea Party and American Foreign Policy," *Foreign Affairs* 90, no. 2 (March/April 2011): 36–37.

56. Irwin Stelzer, "Our Broken China Policy," *Weekly Standard* (January 17, 2011).

57. See Michael T. Klare, "Containing China: The US's Real Objective," *Asia Times*, April 20, 2006.

58. The Project 2049 Institute website is at http://project2049.net/.

59. See http://www.house.gov/coxreport; for critiques of the Cox Report, see Walter Pincus, "Hill Report on Chinese Spying Faulted; Five Experts Cite Errors, 'Unwarranted' Conclusions by Cox Panel," *Washington Post*, December 15, 1999. See also the critique by Jack Kemp and Gordon Prather quoted by John McCaslin, "Kemp and Cox," *Washington Times*, July 15, 1999; Tom Plate, "Cox Report was 'an Exercise in Amateur-Hour Paranoia,'" *Los Angeles Times*, July 21, 1999; Editorial, "Lessons of the Cox Report," *Christian Science Monitor*, May 28, 1999. For an overview of relations in the 1990s, see David M. Lampton, *Same Bed, Different Dreams: Managing US-China Relations 1989–2000* (Berkeley: University of California Press, 2001).

60. Quoted in Cal Thomas, "Damage assessments...and duplicity," *Washington Times*, May 28, 1999.

61. Thomas, "Damage assessments,"

62. Juliet Eilperin, "DeLay Assails China, Urges Taiwan Trade Talks," *Washington Post*, June 3, 2003. For the views of conservative Republican colleagues, see, e.g., Representative Dick Armey, "Saying No to China," *Washington Times*, October 30, 1997; and Senator Trent Lott, "Ten Ways to Engage China," *Washington Times*, June 24, 1998.

63. Cf. John Bolton, "Democracy Makes All the Difference," *Weekly Standard* (April 3, 2000); "Beijing's WTO Double-Cross," *Weekly Standard* (August 14, 2000). See also Bush's remarks on China in the South Carolina Republican Primary Debate, February 15, 2000, shown on *Larry King Live*.

64. Nancy Gibbs et al., "Saving Face," *Time* 157, no. 15 (April 16, 2001).

65. Gibbs et al., "Saving Face".

66. Joshua Cooper Ramo, *Time* 157, no. 10 (March 12, 2001); Johanna McGeary, "Dubya talks the talk," *Time* 157, no. 13 (April 2, 2001.

67. Cf. James Lilley and Carl Ford, "China's Military: A Second Opinion," *National Interest* 57 (Fall 1999). This formed part of an exchange with Bates Gill and Michael O'Hanlon, who, in "China's Hollow Military," *National Interest* 56 (Summer 1999), had taken a much more sober view of Chinese power. See also "China Viewed Narrowly," *New York Times*, June 10, 2000; for an extreme anti-Chinese view, see Bill Gertz, *The China Threat: How the People's Republic Targets America* (Washington, DC: Regnery Publishing, 2000). See also the review essay, "Peking Won't Duck," by Tom Donnelly, *Weekly Standard* (December 4, 2000). For the campaign to adopt a strategy of "containment" against China, see Robert G. Kaiser and Steven Mufson, "Blue Team Draws a Hard Line on Beijing; Action on Hill Reflects Informal Group's Clout," *Washington Post*, February 22, 2000; Jay Branegan, "A 'Blue Team' Blocks Beijing," *Time* (April 16, 2000); Johnson, *The Sorrows of Empire*, 82–88.

68. Richard A. Clarke, *Against All Enemies: Inside America's War on Terror* (New York: Free Press, 2004).

69. Kurt M. Campbell (former deputy assistant secretary of defense for East Asian and Pacific affairs), "China Watchers Fighting a Turf War of their Own," *New York Times*, May 20, 2000, quoted in Johnson, *The Sorrows of Empire*, 62.

70. See, e.g., Hillary Clinton's speech to the Council on Foreign Relations on September 8, 2010, http://www.cfr.org/diplomacy/conversation-us-secretary-state-hillary-rodham-clinton/p22896.

71. Xu Yunhong quoted by Claude Arpi, "To Overlook Reality Would Be Stupid," *Indian Defence Review*, March 2, 2011. For the Project 2049's advocacy of an anti-Chinese military alliance including Vietnam, see Dan Blumenthal et al., "Asian Alliances in the 21st Century," http://project2049.net/documents/Asian_Alliances_21st_Century.pdf. See also D. S. Rajan, "China: Media Fears Over India Becoming Part of Western Alliance," South Asia Analysis Group paper 2350, August 29, 2007. For critiques of the idea of an anti-Chinese alliance, see Gwynne Dyer, "US Bending Over Backwards to Secure Indian and Japanese Alliance," *Japan Times*, August 27, 2007; Gregory Clark, "Australia's Anti-China Pact," *Japan Times*, April 12, 2007; Hisane Misaki, "'Alliance of Democracy' Flexes Its Military Muscles," *Asia Times*, March 31, 2007.

72. For neoconservative advocacy of a global alliance of democracies, see Robert Kagan, "The Case for a League of Democracies," *Financial Times*, May 13, 2008, http://www.carnegieendowment.org/2008/05/13/case-for-league-of-democracies/3fp. This is not explicitly directed against China—but would certainly be seen in Beijing as anti-Chinese.

73. Max Boot, "Project for a New Chinese Century: Beijing Plans for National Greatness," *Weekly Standard* (October 10, 2005).

74. See Charles King, "Potemkin Democracy: Four Myths About Post-Soviet Georgia," *National Interest* (July 1, 2001).

75. Cf. Colonel H. R. McMaster, *Dereliction of Duty: Johnson, McNamara, the Joint Chiefs of Staff and the Lies that Led to Vietnam* (New York: Harper Collins, 1997).

76. For Shinseki's views, see Thom Shanker, "Retiring Army Chief Warns Against Arrogance," *New York Times*, June 12, 2003. For the attacks on Shinseki, see Rowan Scarborough, "Wolfowitz Criticizes 'Suspect' Estimate of Occupation Force," *Washington Times*, February 28, 2003; Michael O'Hanlon, "History Will Get the Last Word: Rumsfeld and Shinseki's Tough Relationship," *Washington Times*, June 20, 2003.

77. Cf. Michael T. Klare, "America's Military Revolution: Cold War Government with No War to Fight," *Le Monde Diplomatique* (English edition), July 2001.

78. Cf. David M. Lampton and Kenneth Lieberthal, "Heading off the Next War," *Washington Post*, April 12, 2004.

79. President Bush and Premier Wen Jiabao, remarks to the press, December 9, 2003, http://georgewbush-whitehouse.archives.gov/news/releases/2003/12/20031209–2.html.

80. John Ikenberry, "The End of the Neo-Conservative Moment," *Survival* 46, no. 1 (Spring 2004). See also Martin Walker, "And Now, the End of US Unilateralism," *The Globalist*, March 5, 2004, http://www.theglobalist.com.

81. John Ikenberry, "America's Imperial Ambition," *Foreign Affairs* 81, no. 5 (September/October 2002).

82. Cf. David Frum and Richard Perle, "Beware the Soft-Line Ideologues," *Wall Street Journal*, January 12, 2004; for an early radical nationalist reaction to the change of official wind, see Michael Ledeen, "Grim Anniversary," *National Review Online*, September 11, 2003, http://www.nationalreview.com/search/apachesolr_search/Michael%20Ledeen%20grim%20anniversary.

83. Cf. Leebaert, *The Fifty Year Wound*, 614–616, Johnson, *The Sorrows of Empire*, 57.

84. Ian Williams, "A Faithful Servant," *The Nation* 278, no. 7 (February 23, 2004).

85. NSS, p.15, at http://nssarchive.us/?page_id=32.

86. Johnson, *The Sorrows of Empire*, 34.

87. "X" (George Kennan), "The Sources of Soviet Conduct," *Foreign Affairs* 25 (July 1947).

88. "Mr. Y" (Captain Wayne Porter USN and Colonel Mark Mykleby, USMC), "A National Strategic Narrative," http://www.wilsoncenter.org/MrY.www.wilsoncenter.org.

89. "Mr. Y," "A National Strategic Narrative".

Chapter Six

1. Amos Oz, addressing Israeli Zionist and fundamentalist extremists, in *In the Land of Israel*, trans. Maurie Goldberg-Bartura (New York: Harcourt Brace, 1983), 139.

2. For the texts of the UN General Assembly resolutions and summaries of the debates, see http://www.un.org.

3. Texts of the U.S. Senate and House resolutions of May 6, 2002 www.opencongress.org.

4. "Israeli Prime Minister Gets 29 Standing Ovations in Congress, Sends Message to White House," http://abcnews.go.com/blogs/politics/2011/05/israeli-prime-minister.

5. Cf. the Zogby International Poll of Winter/Spring 2002, cited in Daniel Brumberg, "Arab Public Opinion and US Foreign Policy: A Complex Encounter," testimony to the Committee on Government Reform, Subcommittee on National Security, U.S. House

of Representatives, October 8, 2002; the Pew Research Center for the People and the Press, Global Attitudes: 44-Nation Major Survey (2002); Report of the Advisory Group on Public Diplomacy for the Arab and Muslim World, chaired by Edward P. Djerejian, "Changing Minds, Winning Peace," submitted to the U.S. Congress, October 1, 2003; see also the Saudi polls of 2002 and 2003 cited by Shibley Telhami, "Polling and Politics in Riyadh," *New York Times*, March 3, 2002; and Telhami, "Those Awkward Hearts and Minds," *The Economist*, April 1, 2003.

6. Shibley Telhami, "The 2011 Arab Public Opinion Poll," Saban Center for Middle East Policy, Brookings Institution, November 21, 2011, http://www.brookings.edu/reports/2011/1121_arab_public_opinion_telhami.

7. "Arab Spring Fails to Improve U.S. Image," Gallup, May 17, 2011, http://www.pewglobal.org/2011/05/17/.

8. Quoted in James Blitz, "US-Europe Splits 'Misguided and Dangerous,'" *Financial Times*, March 19, 2003; see also Tony Blair's speech to the U.S. Congress, July 17, 2003, http://articles.cnn.com/2003-07-17/us/blair.transcript_1_joint-session-tragic-prologue-congress-library?_s=PM:US. For a similar U.S. view, see Zbigniew Brzezinski, "Hegemonic Quicksand," *National Interest* (Winter 2003/2004).

9. Issued by the European Council, December 2003, quoted in Ambassador Marc Otte (EU representative for the Middle East peace process), "Towards an EU Strategy for the Middle East," speech in London, March 1, 2004, published by World Security Network, http://www.worldsecuritynetwork.com, March 12, 2004.

10. Timothy Garton Ash, "Anti-Europeanism in America," *New York Review of Books* 50, no. 2 (February 13, 2003).

11. Cf. Dov S. Zakheim, *A Vulcan's Tale: How the Bush Administration Mismanaged the Reconstruction of Afghanistan* (Washington, DC: Brookings Institution, 2011), 39.

12. See "President Bush Discusses Freedom in Iraq and Middle East," speech at the National Endowment for Democracy, November 6, 2003, http://www.ned.org/george-w-bush/remarks-by-president-george-w-bush-at-the-20th-anniversary; and the remarks by Vice President Dick Cheney to the World Economic Forum in Davos, January 24, 2004, http://www.acronym.org.uk/docs/0401/doc18.htm.

13. Cf. Elisabeth Bumiller, "A Partner in Shaping an Assertive Foreign Policy," *New York Times*, January 7, 2004; Robert Kaiser, "Bush and Sharon Nearly Identical on Mideast Policy," *Washington Post*, February 9, 2003.

14. M. J. Rosenberg, "The Full Court Pander," *Israel Policy Forum* 163 (January 9, 2004), http://www.israelpolicyforum.org/commentary/full-court-pander http://www.israelpolicyforum.org.

15. Robert D. Novak, "Politics vs. the Road Map," *Washington Post*, May 26, 2003; for Newt Gingrich's views, see his "Rogue State Department," *Foreign Policy* (July–August 2003); see also Robert Kaiser, "Bush and Sharon Nearly Identical on Mideast Policy," *Washington Post*, February 9, 2003. Thomas Neumann, director of the Jewish Institute for National Security Affairs, quoted in the same article. Ron Suskind, *The Price of Loyalty* (London: Simon & Schuster, 2004), 70–76, 288–290; Philip H. Gordon, "Bush's Middle East Vision," *Survival* 45, no. 1 (Spring 2003); Elisabeth Bumiller, "A Partner in Shaping an Assertive Foreign Policy," *New York Times*, January 7, 2004.

16. Joseph C. Harsch, "Politics and Race," *Christian Science Monitor*, October 27, 1988.

17. Gabriel Weinstein, "The Emergence of Jewish Republicans," November 2, 2010, http://momentmagazine.wordpress.com/2010/11/02/the-emergence-of-jewish-republicans.

18. Roberta Feuerlicht, *The Fate of the Jews: A People Torn Between Israeli Power and Jewish Ethics* (New York: New York Times Book Co., 1983), 166. For worries in the Israeli lobby concerning the domestic U.S. agenda of the Christian fundamentalists and their partly anti-Semitic tradition, see Abraham Foxman, *Never Again? The Threat of the New Anti-Semitism* (San Francisco: HarperCollins, 2003), 133–159; cf. also the study by the Anti-Defamation League, *The Religious Right: The Assault on Tolerance and Pluralism in America* (New York: Anti-Defamation League, 1994).

19. Cf. Joel Benin, "Tel Aviv's Influence on American Institutions," *Le Monde Diplomatique*, July 2003.

20. Richard Perle et al., "A Clean Break: A New Strategy for Securing the Realm," report prepared by the Institute for Advanced Strategic and Political Studies (1996).

21. Elliott Abrams, "Israel and the 'Peace Process,'" in *Present Dangers: Crisis and Opportunity in American Foreign and Defense Policy*, ed. Robert Kagan and William Kristol (San Francisco: Encounter Books, 2000), 219–240.

22. Cf. editorial, "The Olive Branch and the Gun," *Nation* 219, no. 18 (November 30, 1974); see also "UN: Shadow of a Gunman," *Newsweek* (November 25, 1974). For the recognition in the United States after 1991 of the Palestinians' existence as a people, see Kathleen Christison, *Perceptions of Palestine* (Berkeley: University of California Press, 2000), 268ff.

23. *New York Times*/ABC poll of April 1978, cited in William J. Lanouette, "The Many Faces of the Jewish Lobby in America," *National Journal* (May 13, 1978).

24. Cf. the remarks by Irving Kristol on America's ideological duty to support Israel as a democratic state in "The Neoconservative Persuasion," *Weekly Standard* 8, no. 47 (August 25, 2003).

25. Meron Benvenisti, "The Turning Point in Israel," *New York Review of Books* 30, no. 15 (October 13, 1983).

26. Mathew Engel, "Senior Republican calls on Israel to expel West Bank Arabs," *Guardian* (London), May 4, 2002.

27. Tom DeLay, "Be Not Afraid," speech to Israeli Knesset, July 30, 2003, http://www.nationalreview.com/articles/207662/be-not-afraid/tom-delay. See the criticism of DeLay's words by Congressman Chris Bell, reported in Karen Materson, "Houston Lawmakers Plan to Counter House Majority Leader's Speech", *Houston Chronicle*, August 1, 2003, http://business.highbeam.com/5874/article-1G1-119817993/houston-lawmakers-plan-counter-us-house-majority-leader.

28. Cf. Richard Hughes, *Myths America Lives By* (Champaign: University of Illinois Press, 2003), 30–33, 110–123.

29. T. R. Fehrenbach, *Lone Star: A History of Texas and the Texans* (New York: MacMillan, 1968), 712.

30. John Wayne, interview with *Playboy* magazine, May 1971, quoted in Joseph McBride, *Searching for John Ford* (New York: St. Martin's Press, 2001), 296; for the treatment of the Indians over the centuries in American school textbooks, see Frances FitzGerald, *America Revised: What History Textbooks Have Taught Our Children About Their Country, and How and Why Those Textbooks Have Changed in Different Decades* (New York: Vintage Books, 1980), 90–93.

31. Stephen Holmes, *The Anatomy of Antiliberalism* (Cambridge, MA: Harvard University Press, 1996), 66–67.

32. Cf. Christison, *Perceptions of Palestine*, 16–25, 103–104, passim.

33. Senator James Inhofe, Senate Floor Statement, March 4, 2002; see also Chris Mitchell, "The Mountains of Israel," *Christian World News*, January 1, 2003, http://

groups.yahoo.com/group/STANDING_WITH_ISRAEL/message/8259. Strikingly enough, the Jewish American feminist Phyllis Chesler—a figure as utterly different from Senator Inhofe in other ways as can well be imagined—repeats exactly the same bases for Israel's claim to the land of Israel in her *The New Anti-Semitism: The Current Crisis and What We Must Do About It* (San Francisco: Jossey-Bass, 2003), 237.

34. Cf. Pat Robertson, "Why Evangelical Christians Support Israel," speech in Israel, December 17, 2003, http://www.patrobertson.com/Speeches/IsraelLauder.asp.

35. Cf. Asher Arian, *Israeli Public Opinion on National Security 2003* (Tel Aviv: Jaffer Center for Strategic Studies, Tel Aviv University, 2003), http://www.inss.org.il/upload/(FILE)1190276735.pdf; Daniel Pipes, "Does Israel Need a Plan?" *Commentary* (February 2003); for support for the idea of "transfer" on the Right in Israel, see Ehud Sprinzak, *The Ascendance of Israel's Radical Right* (New York: Oxford University Press, 1991), 172–176, 293–298; Ian Lustick, *For the Land and the Lord: Jewish Fundamentalism in Israel* (New York: Council on Foreign Relations, 1988), 178–180.

36. "Survival of the Fittest," Benny Morris interviewed by Ari Shavit, *Ha'aretz*, January 9, 2004. For a liberal Israeli attack on Morris's latest views, see Professor Adi Ophir, "Genocide Hides Behind Expulsion," *Counterpunch*, (January 16, 2004, originally published in *Ha'aretz*).

37. Lustick, *For the Land and the Lord*, vii.

38. Sprinzak, *The Ascendance of Israel's Radical Right*, 13; see also Bernard Avishai, *The Tragedy of Zionism: How Its Revolutionary Past Haunts Israeli Democracy* (New York; Helios Press, 2002), 278–294; Gabriel A. Almond, R. Scott Appleby, and Emmanuel Sivan, *Strong Religion: The Rise of Fundamentalism Around the World* (Chicago: University of Chicago Press, 2003). For the background of these movements in Israeli society and political culture, see the vignettes in Oz, *In the Land of Israel*.

39. *Moral Majority Report*, March 14, 1980, quoted at http://static.justchristians.com/abundantLife/091996/12.html.

40. Sidney Blumenthal, "The Righteous Empire," *New Republic* (October 22, 1984).

41. Hal Lindsey, *The Everlasting Hatred: The Roots of Jihad* (Murrietta, CA: Oracle House, 2002), 59, 127–129; quote from the Book of Job, 39:5–8; Joan Peters, *From Time Immemorial* (New York: Harper and Row, 1984), quoted in Lindsey, *The Everlasting Hatred*, 127, 135–140, 149–158. For the immense audience for fundamentalist and millenarian TV shows, see Grace Halsell, *Prophecy and Politics: Militant Evangelists on the Road to Nuclear War* (Westport, CT: Lawrence Hill, 1986), 11–14.

42. http://www.donfeder.com/articles/0906%20whyKeepTellingUs.htm.

43. Stephen Mansfield, *The Faith of George W. Bush* (Lake Mary, FL: Charisma House, 2003), 126. For the growing relationship between American evangelical fundamentalism and Israeli fundamentalism, see also Gershom Gorenberg, *The End of Days: Fundamentalism and the Struggle for the Temple Mount* (New York: Free Press, 2000); Hassan Haddad and Donald Wagner, eds., *All in the Name of the Bible: Selected Essays on Israel and American Christian Fundamentalism* (Brattleborough, VT: Amana Books, 1986); Paul Boyer, *When Time Shall Be No More: Prophesy Belief in Modern American Culture* (Cambridge, MA: Harvard University Press, 1992), 183–191, 203–208. For the historical origins of American evangelical support for Zionism, see Peter Grose, *Israel in the Mind of America* (New York: Alfred A. Knopf, 1984), 4–15.

44. Colin Shindler, "Likud and the Christian Dispensationalists: A Symbiotic Relationship," *Israel Studies* 5, no. 1 Halsell, *Prophecy and Politics*, 145–160; Gorenberg, *The End of Days*, 238–240.

45. Julia Duin, "Israeli Pits US Politics Against Road Map," *Washington Times*, August 18, 2003.

46. Cf. Pew Research Center for the People and the Press poll, "A Year After the Iraq War," March 16, 2004, http://www.people-press.org/2004/03/16/a-year-after-iraq-war/; Bill Schneider, "Mideast 101: Evolution of US Feelings Towards Israel," CNN, April 17, 2002, http://articles.cnn.com/2002–04–16/world/me101.schneider_1_american-jews-israel-public-support?_s=PM:WORLD.

47. For limitations on debate in the United States, see Paul Findley, *They Dare to Speak Out: People and Institutions Confront Israel's Lobby* (Westport, CT: Lawrence Hill, 1985). For self-censorship in the Jewish community in the United States, see the remarks of General Mattiyahu Peled and Irving Howe, quoted in Feuerlicht, *The Fate of the Jews*, 280, 278–283.

48. See the organization's website at http://www.jstreet.org.

49. Cf. I. F. Stone, "Confessions of a Jewish Dissident," in *Underground to Palestine and Reflections Thirty Years Later* (New York: Pantheon Books, 1978), 229–240.

50. Allyn Fisher-Ilan, "Israeli Ex-Security Chiefs Draft New Peace Plan," Reuters, April 5, 2011, http://www.reuters.com/article/2011/04/05/uk-israel-palestinians-initiative-idUKTRE7344AZ20110405; and Molly Moore, "Ex-Security Chiefs Turn on Sharon," *Washington Post*, November 15, 2003.

51. Cf. the advice to the Israeli government and lobby from the public relations firm Wexner Analysis, "Israeli Communications Priorities 2003," to be found at http://www.adc.org/index.php?id=1789.

52. For a suggestion that Israeli settlement policy has in fact already wrecked the possibility of a two-state solution, and that the only possible and just solution that remains is a unitary binational state, see Tony Judt, "Israel: The Alternative," *New York Review of Books* 50, no. 16 (October 23, 2003); for a rejoinder from a liberal partisan of Israel, see Leon Wieseltier, "What Is Not To Be Done," *New Republic* (October 27, 2003).

53. Cf. "Middle East Partnership Initiative: Arab Press Wary," U.S. Department of State, International Information Program, Foreign Media Reaction, December 20, 2002; see also Augustus Richard Norton, "America's Approach to the Middle East: Legacies, Questions and Possibilities," *Current History* (January 2002), 3–7.

54. Contrast, for example, the discussion of this issue by Quentin Peel, "A Big Idea that Europe Won't Buy," *Financial Times*, February 5, 2004, with that of David Ignatius, "The Allies' Mindless Bickering," *Washington Post*, February 10, 2004.

55. I. L. Kenen, former chairman of the American Israel Public Affairs Committee (AIPAC), links both these assertions in his autobiographical profile of the Israeli lobby and its battles, *Israel's Defense Line: Her Friends and Foes in Washington* (Buffalo, NY: Prometheus Books, 1981), 332 and passim.

56. Zakheim, *A Vulcan's Tale*, 215.

57. Correlli Barnett, *Engage the Enemy More Closely: The Royal Navy in the Second World War* (London: W. W. Norton, 1991), 378–389.

58. Cf. D. C. B. Lieven, *Russia and the Origins of the First World War* (London: MacMillan, 1983), 40–43, 139–151.

59. Stanley Hoffmann, "The High and the Mighty," *American Prospect*, January 13, 2003, f.

60. Quoted in Joyce R. Starr, *Kissing Through Glass: The Invisible Shield Between Americans and Israelis* (Chicago: Contemporary Books, 1990), 225.

61. Conrad Cherry, ed., *God's New Israel: Religious Interpretations of American Destiny* (Chapel Hill: University of North Carolina Press, 1998), epigraph. See especially Samuel Langdon, "The Republic of the Israelites an Example to the American States," in *God's New Israel*, 93–105.

62. For the combination of religious, cultural, and ideological sympathy in the United States for the Zionist movement, see Grose, *Israel in the Mind of America*; for the representative views of Justice Oliver Wendell Holmes, see Edmund Wilson, *Patriotic Gore: Studies in the Literature of the American Civil War* (New York: Farrar, Straus and Giroux, 1977), 784–785.

63. Cf. Justin Vaisse, *Neoconservatism: The Biography of a Movement* (Cambridge, MA: Harvard University Press, 2010), 58–62.

64. Quoted in Halsell, *Prophecy and Politics*, 113–114.

65. Secretary Rumsfeld, Town Hall Meeting, August 6, 2002, http://www.defense.gov/transcripts/transcript.aspx?transcriptid=3573.

66. Cf. David Weisburg with Vered Vinitzky, "Vigilantism as Rational Social Control: The Case of the Gush Emunim Settlers," in *Cross Currents in Israeli Culture and Politics*, ed. Myron J. Aronoff (New Brunswick, NJ: Transaction Books, 1984), 69–88.

67. Amos Elon, *The Israelis: Founders and Sons* (London: Sphere Books, 1972), 232–235; David Hirst, *The Gun and the Olive Branch: The Roots of Violence in the Middle East* (London: Faber and Faber, 1977), 183–184; for a portrait of a similar (unnamed) figure, and his views concerning Israeli policy toward the Palestinians and Arabs, see Amos Oz, "The Tender Among You, and Very Delicate," in *In the Land of Israel*, 85–100. For the comparison with "Indian fighters" see also Uri Avnery, *Israel Without Zionism* (New York: Collier Books, 1971). For the tradition of freelance and vigilante violence on the American frontier, see Joe B. Franz, "The Frontier Tradition: An Invitation to Violence," in *Violence in America: Historical and Comparative Perspectives*, ed. Hugh Davis Graham and Ted Gurr (New York: Bantam Books, 1969), 127–153; H. Jon Rosenbaum and Peter C. Sederberg, "Vigilantism: An Analysis of Establishment Violence," *Comparative Politics* 6, no. 4 (July 1974).

68. Benvenisti, "The Turning Point in Israel."

69. Leon Uris, *Exodus* (New York: Bantam Books, 1959). The conflation of images of the American and Israeli settler in American iconography is rather amusingly illustrated by the cover, showing the Star of David and the ship *Exodus* flanked by two blonde, blue-eyed, square-jawed supposed Jewish fighters in Palestine—the very image of American pioneers from a Hollywood B-movie. See also Christison, *Perceptions of Palestine*, 103–104.

70. Cf. Tony Smith, *Foreign Attachments: The Power of Ethnic Groups in the Making of American Foreign Policy* (Cambridge MA: Harvard University Press, 2000), 16ff; Mitchell Geoffrey Bard, *The Water's Edge and Beyond: Defining the Limits to Domestic Influence on US Middle East Policy* (New Brunswick, NJ: Transaction Publishers, 1991).

71. Cf. Lind, "The Israel Lobby", *Prospect Magazine*, London, April 20 2002, at . http://www.prospectmagazine.co.uk/2002/04/theisraellobby/.

72. Michael Walzer, *Just and Unjust Wars: A Moral Argument with Historical Illustrations* (London: Pelican Books, 1980), 81–85, 216–220, 304, 310n, where the war and expulsions of 1948 and the nature of Israeli military rule over the Occupied Territories are both ignored; and *Exodus and Revolution* (New York: Basic Books, 1985). This highly interesting work, with its sober and moderate rereading of the lessons of the Bible, is

certainly an argument against Israeli extremism. However, it devotes only 3 pages (pp. 141–144) out of 149 to the dispossession and massacre of the Canaanites as described in the Old Testament, and so contorted is the language that after three readings its meaning—if any—for contemporary events and policies is still not clear to me. The words "Palestinian" and "Arab" do not appear.

73. For the philosophy and views of Ahad Ha'am, see Shlomo Avineri, *The Making of Modern Zionism: The Intellectual Origins of the Jewish State* (New York: Basic Books, 1981), 112–124; for Ha'am's views on Jewish treatment of the Arab population of Palestine, see Feuerlicht, *The Fate of the Jews*, 225–226.

74. Nahum Goldmann, *Autobiography: Sixty Years of Jewish Life*, trans. Helen Sebba (New York: Holt, Rhinehart and Winston, 1969), 332–333.

75. For the centrality of the Divine Presence and His worship to the Jewish diaspora communities and traditions, see Rabbi Jonathan Sacks, *A Letter in the Scroll: Understanding Our Jewish Identity and Exploring the Legacy of the World's Oldest Religion* (New York: Simon & Schuster, 2000), 122–180; Irving Howe, *World of Our Fathers: The Journey of the East European Jews to America and the Life They Found and Made* (New York: Harcourt Brace Jovanovich, 1976), 11–14.

76. *Jewish Observer and Middle East Review*, June 10, 1977. Quoted in Feuerlicht, *The Fate of the Jews*, 170; Howe, *World of Our Fathers*, 628; cf. also Goldmann, *Autobiography: Sixty Years of Jewish Life*, 315.

77. Martin Marty, *Pilgrims in Their Own Land: 500 Years of Religion in America* (New York: Penguin, 1985), 462–463; see also Kenneth D. Wald, *Religion and Politics in the United States* (New York: Rowman and Littlefield, 2003), 153.

78. Cf. Carlton J. H. Hayes, *Nationalism: A Religion* (New York: Macmillan, 1960); Hans Kohn, *The Idea of Nationalism* (New York: Macmillan, 1945), 574ff.

79. Cf. Oz, *In the Land of Israel.*

80. Concerning Israel's overall achievements as a state and society—and, like him, leaving aside for the moment Israel's record in the Occupied Territories—I would endorse the glowing assessment by Professor Amnon Rubenstein quoted in Alan Dershowitz, *The Case for Israel* (Hoboken, NJ: John Wiley & Sons, 2003), 225; and indeed expressed, albeit in more wry and ambiguous terms, in Amos Elon's portrait of Israel, *The Israelis: Founders and Sons.*

81. Goldmann, *Autobiography: Sixty Years of Jewish Life*, 299–300.

82. Amos Oz, "From Jerusalem to Cairo: Escaping from the Shadow of the Past," in *Israel, Palestine and Peace: Essays* (New York: Harcourt Brace, 1994), 36–37.

83. Hannah Arendt, "Zionism Reconsidered," *Menorah Journal* 33, no. 2 (Autumn 1945): 213–214.

84. Abba Eban, *Personal Witness: Israel Through My Eyes* (New York: Putnam, 1992), 49–50.

85. Fehrenbach, *Lone Star*, 529.

86. Cf. Feuerlicht, *Fate of the Jews*, 174.

87. Saul Bellow, *To Jerusalem and Back: A Personal Account* (New York: Viking, 1976), 158, 160–163.

88. Dershowitz, *The Case for Israel*, 60; for the amalgamation of the Palestinians and Nazis in Israeli and Israeli lobby rhetoric, see Christison, *Perceptions of Palestine*, 119ff. Concerning the terrible results of such assumptions of collective guilt, see, e.g., Thomas Friedman, *From Beirut to Jerusalem* (New York: Farrar, Straus, and Giroux, 1989), 163, on how the common Israeli elision of the words "Palestinian" and "terrorist" led to indifference to the Sabra and Shatila massacres. For a warning of this risk

in the American "war against terrorism," cf. William Pfaff, "As Captor, the US Risks Dehumanizing Itself," *International Herald Tribune*, January 30, 2002.

89. Quoted in Nahum Goldmann, *The Jewish Paradox* (New York: Grosset and Dunlap, 1978), 99.

90. Cf. Dershowitz, *The Case for Israel*, 78–90.

91. Benny Morris, *The Birth of the Palestinian Refugee Problem, 1947–49* (New York: Cambridge University Press, 1989), and the account of the 1948 conflict in his *Righteous Victims: A History of the Zionist-Arab Conflict, 1881–2001* (New York: Random House, 1999), 191–258. For a discussion of his work and this issue by Israeli and Palestinian scholars, see the essays in Eugene L. Rogan and Avi Shlaim, eds., *The War for Palestine: Rewriting the History of 1948* (Cambridge: Cambridge University Press, 2001). For earlier descriptions of this issue, see the Israeli reports and eyewitness accounts of the expulsions and the terrorization and oppression of the Palestinian population quoted in Hirst, *The Gun and the Olive Branch*, 136–143; Avnery, *Israel Without Zionism*, 223ff; Feuerlicht, *Lone Star*, 242–267; and Edward Said, *The Question of Palestine* (New York: Times Books, 1979), xxxvii, 83–114.

92. "Survival of the Fittest," Benny Morris interviewed by Ari Shavit, *Ha'aretz*, January 9, 2004.

93. Cf. Anatol Lieven, "Divide and Survive," *Prospect* (London) (May 1999).

94. Cf. Anatol Lieven, "Peace Cannot be Fudged," *Financial Times*, September 10, 2003.

95. For a recent denial of the expulsions, coupled with an accusation that talking about this had weakened the national will of Israeli liberal intellectuals and contributed to their futile search for peace in the 1990s, see Efraim Karsh, "Revisiting Israel's 'Original Sin': The Strange Case of Benny Morris," *Commentary* 116, no. 2 (September 2003).

96. *Sunday Times*, June 15, 1969, quoted in Hirst, *The Gun and the Olive Branch*, 264. The important point is not, however, whether there was a fully self-conscious Palestinian nationality in 1948—which is indeed a highly debatable question. Rather, the point is twofold: that in 1948 there was a majority people in Palestine that was well aware that it was different from and threatened by the Jews, and that by 1969 it was already obviously wrong to deny that the Palestinians had developed a clear national identity; in 2004 this would be madness.

97. Quoted in Lanouette, "The Many Faces of the Jewish Lobby in America."

98. For example, Shlomo Avineri's magisterial study of the intellectual bases of Zionism (see above, note 27) contains no reference to "Palestinians." The index entry for Arabs under "Palestine" reads "Palestine: Arab problem in."

99. Said, *Question of Palestine*, 51.

100. Herbert Croly, *The Promise of American Life* (1909; repr., Boston: Northeastern University Press, 1989), 75; for a kind of distillation of the Israeli lobby's presentation of the Israeli–Palestinian conflict—with no mention of the expulsions of 1948 or of any Israeli atrocity—see Phyllis Chesler, "A Brief History of Arab Attacks Against Israel, 1908–1970s," in her *The New Anti-Semitism*, 44–52.

101. Lind, "*The Israel Lobby*."

102. Arnaud de Bochgrave, "Democracy in the Middle East," *Washington Times*, March 5, 2004.

103. Cf. Thomas L. Friedman, "An Intriguing Signal from the Saudi Crown Prince," *New York Times*, February 17, 2002; editorial, "A Peace Impulse Worth Pursuing," *New York Times*, February 21, 2002; editorial, "Support for the Saudi Initiative," *New York Times*, February 28, 2002.

104. Cf. "Israel and the Occupied Territories: Country Report on Human Rights Practices—2003," released by the Bureau of Democracy, Human Rights and Labor, U.S. Department of State, February 25, 2004, http://www.state.gov/j/drl/rls/hrrpt/2003/27929.htm.

105. For the establishment of the settlements and their role in preventing full diplomatic exploitation of the Sadat initiative, see Bernard Avishai, *Tragedy of Zionism: How Its Revolutionary Past Haunts Israeli Democracy* (New York: Helios Press, 2002), 272–296; see also Meron Benvenisti, *Intimate Enemies: Jews and Arabs in a Shared Land* (Berkeley: University of California Press, 1995), 30–37, 52–71; Bernard Wasserstein, *Israel and Palestine: Why they fight and can they stop?* (London: Profile, 2003).

106. Cf. William Safire, "Post-Oslo Mideast," *New York Times*, June 27, 2002; editorial, "Those Arab Peacemakers," *Washington Times*, May 20, 2002; Victor Davis Hanson, "Our Enemies, the Saudis," *Commentary* (July–August 2002); for liberal Jewish American responses in favor of the Saudi offer, see Richard Cohen, "Kristol's Unwelcome Message," *Washington Post*, June 11, 2002; and Henry Siegman, "Will Israel take a Chance?" *New York Times*, February 21, 2002.

107. Daniel Pipes, "Does Israel Need a Plan?," *Commentary* 115, no. 2 (February 2003); Yaacov Lozowick, *Right to Exist: A Moral Defense of Israel's Wars* (New York: Doubleday, 2003); cf. also Daniel Ayalon (Israeli ambassador to the United States), "Israel's Right to Be Israel," *Washington Post*, August 24, 2003.

108. Newt Gingrich, "Barack Obama's Morally Confused Mideast Policies Endanger Israel," June 21, 2011, http://www.jta.org/news/article/2011/06/21.

109. Henry Siegman, "Israel: The Threat from Within," *New York Review of Books* 51, no. 3 (February 26, 2004); cf. also Oz, "Whose Holy Land?," in *Israel, Palestine and Peace*, 91.

110. Elon, *The Israelis: Founders and Sons*, xiii.

111. Cf. Benvenisti, "The Turning Point in Israel."

112. For the background to the failure of the negotiations in 2000–2001, see the debate in the *New York Review of Books* between various participants in the talks: Robert Malley and Hussein Agha: "Camp David: the Tragedy of Errors," August 9, 2001; the exchange of letters with Dennis Ross and Gidi Grinstein in the same issue; Benny Morris's interview with Ehud Barak in the *New York Review of Books* 49, no. 10 (June 13, 2002); Malley and Agha's reply in the same issue, and the further exchange on June 27, 2002. For the role of settlement expansion in the 1990s in undermining Palestinian faith in the peace process, see Christison, *Perceptions of Palestine*, 300ff. See also Deborah Sontag, "Quest for Middle East Peace: How and Why It Failed," *New York Times*, July 26, 2001.

113. Manfred Gerstenfeld, "Anti-Semitism: Integral to European Culture," in *Post Holocaust and Anti-Semitism* 19 (April 1, 2004), published by the Jerusalem Center for Public Affairs; cf. also Nidra Poller, "Betrayed by Europe: An Expatriate's Lament," *Commentary* (March 2004); Marc Strauss, "The New Face of Anti-Semitism," *Foreign Policy* (November/December 2003).

114. Jonathan Tepperman, "The Anti-Anti-Americans," *New York Times Book Review* (December 12, 2004): I would like to express my enduring gratitude to the late Ambassador Bill Maynes and others who wrote to defend me against this repulsive attack. For my own response to Tepperman, see the letters pages of the *New York Times*, January 2, 2005.

115. John J. Mearsheimer and Stephen M. Walt, *The Israel Lobby and US Foreign Policy* (New York: Farrar, Straus and Giroux, 2007). For an attack on the book by a leading representative of the Israel lobby, which attempts to link them to traditional anti-Semitism, see Abraham Foxman, *The Deadliest Lies: The Israel Lobby and the Myth of Jewish Control* (New York: Palgrave Macmillan, 2007). For a critical view of Foxman's leadership of the ADL, see James Traub, "Does Abe Foxman Have An Anti-Anti-Semite Problem," *New York Times Magazine* (January 14, 2007).

116. Jimmy Carter, *Palestine: Peace Not Apartheid* (New York: Simon & Schuster, 2007).

117. Foxman, *Never Again?* 4.

118. Chesler, *The New Anti-Semitism*, 3.

119. Gabriel Schoenfeld, "Israel and the Anti-Semites," *Commentary* 113, no. 6 (June 2002); see also Paul Berman, *Terror and Liberalism* (New York: W. W. Norton, 2003), 186–189; Hillel Halkin, "The Return of Anti-Semitism," *Commentary* 113, no. 2 (February 2002); Robert S. Wistrich, "The Old-New Anti-Semitism," *National Interest* 72 (Summer 2003); Edgar Bronfman and Cobi Benatoff, "Is Darkness Falling on Europe Again?" *Financial Times*, February 19, 2004; Ruth R. Wisse, "Israel on Campus," *Wall Street Journal*, December 13, 2002.

120. Seymour Martin Lipset, *American Exceptionalism: A Double-Edged Sword* (New York: W. W. Norton, 1976), 172.

121. Howe, *World of Our Fathers*, 630–632; see also Roberta Feuerlicht's depressing account of how the Holocaust surfaced as a reason given for Jewish fears of blacks during discussions with blacks in New York in the 1970s, to the stupefaction and fury of moderate black representatives; Feuerlicht, *The Fate of the Jews*, 206–215.

122. Irving Kristol, "The Political Dilemma of American Jews," *Commentary* (July 1984); see also Michael Lind, *Up From Conservatism: Why the Right Is Wrong for America* (New York: Simon & Schuster, 1996), 99–120; David H. Bennett, *The Party of Fear: From Nativist Movements to the New Right in American History* (Chapel Hill: University of North Carolina Press, 1989), 423–425.

123. Nathan Perlmutter, *The Real Anti-Semitism in America*, quoted in Halsell, *Prophecy and Politics*, 154–155. See also Shindler, "Likud and the Christian Dispensationalists"; and David Frum, *Dead Right* (New York: Basic Books, 1994), 159–173.

124. Cf. the booklet issued by the America Israel Public Affairs Committee (AIPAC): Jonathan S. Kessler and Jeff Schwaber, *The AIPAC College Guide: Exposing the Anti-Israel Campaign on Campus*, AIPAC Papers on U.S.–Israel Relations no. 7 (1984).

125. For an excoriating and often justified critique of left-wing attacks on Israel during the cold war, see Conor Cruise O'Brien, *The Siege: The Saga of Israel and Zionism* (New York: Touchstone Books, 1987).

126. Cf. David Corn, "The Banning of Rabbi Lerner," February 10, 2003, http://www.thenation.com/blog/156018/banning-rabbi-lerner; Michael Lerner, "The Antiwar Anti-Semites," *Wall Street Journal*, February 12, 2003, David Friedman, "Democracy and the Peace Movement," *Tikkun*, (May/June 2003); see also the response by Joel Kovel, "Anti-Semitism on the Left and the Special Status of Israel," *Tikkun* 18, no. 3 (May/June 2003).

127. Cf. Joshua Micah Marshall, "The Orwell Temptation: Are intellectuals overthinking the Middle East?" *Washington Monthly* (May 2003).

128. For the use of "straw men" by propagandists for the Israel lobby, see Dershowitz, *The Case for Israel*. This book is structured around a variety of propositions, some of them apparently carefully selected for the ease with which they can be refuted (like "Did

Israel start the Six-Day War?" and "Is Israel the prime human rights violator in the world?"). Of these propositions, 12 are by Edward Said and 8 by Noam Chomsky. One is by Leonid Brezhnev—not, as far as I am aware, one of the leading voices today in the debate over Israel and Palestine. Apart from four by the Israeli peace activist Ilan Pappe, none are by Israelis. The names of Amos Oz, Meron Benvenisti, or any of the other centrist liberal critics of the Israeli occupation of the West Bank and Gaza Strip appear nowhere. Although one proposition is given to Rabbi Michael Lerner, none are given to other leading American liberal critics of unconditional U.S. support for Israel, as represented in the *New York Review of Books*, for example—people who, like Oz in Israel, are strong supporters of Israel's right to exist and defend itself within the borders of 1967. The question of Palestinian rejection of the Barak–Clinton peace proposals is put in stark black-and-white terms ("Was Arafat right in turning down the Barak–Clinton peace proposal?") as is the question given to Chomsky, not to Ambassador Robert Malley or the other U.S. and Israeli moderates who have sought to elucidate this question. The overall effect is, of course, to create an impression of hysterical malignance toward Israel, unqualified by support or sympathy. This is the approach of a ruthless advocate in a court; whether it is appropriate behavior for a professor of law at one of America's leading universities is another matter.

129. Akiva Eldar, "From refuge for Jews to danger for Jews," *Ha'aretz*, November 3, 2003. See also M. J. Rosenberg, "Confusing Criticism with Anti-Semitism," *Israel Policy Forum*, February 6, 2004; Judith Butler, "No, it's not anti-Semitic," *London Review of Books*, August 21, 2003; Henry Siegman, "If Israel's Policies are Unjust, We Should Say So," *Financial Times*, February 10, 2004.

130. Cf. Romano Prodi (president of the EU Commission), "Europe Must Tackle Anti-Semitsim, Xenophobia," *Financial Times*, February 19, 2004.

131. Brian Klug, "The Collective Jew: Israel and the New Antisemitism," *Patterns of Prejudice* 37, no. 2 (June 2003); and "The Myth of the New Anti-Semitism," *The Nation* 278, no. 4 (February 2, 2004).

132. Cf. Chesler, *The New Anti-Semitism*, 33; see also Jerome Chanes, *A Dark Side of History: Anti-Semitism Through the Ages* (New York: Anti-Defamation League, 2000).

133. The notion of an eternal, essentially unchanging anti-Semitism has been called fundamental to much of the philosophy of Zionism, and long predates the latest Israeli–Palestinian conflict and its repercussions; cf. Arendt, "Zionism Reconsidered," 225; Howe, *World of Our Fathers*, 25; Halsell, *Prophecy and Politics*, 131ff.

Conclusion

1. Cf. Clair Brown, *American Standards of Living, 1918–1988* (New York: Blackwell, 2002); Kevin Phillips, *Boiling Point: Democrats, Republicans and the Decline of Middle Class Prosperity* (New York: Harper Collins, 1994); Jeff Madrick, "How New Is the New Economy?" *New York Review of Books* 46, no. 14 (September 23, 1999); Michael Head, "The New, Ruthless Economy," *New York Review of Books* 43, no. 4 (February 29, 1996).

2. Cf. Robert Bellah, *The Broken Covenant: American Civil Religion in a Time of Trial* (New York: Seabury Press, 1975), xv.

3. Stephen M. Walt, "Lessons from the Weimar Republic," *Foreign Policy*, http://walt. foreignpolicy.com/posts/2010/08/23/lessons_from_the_weimar_republic.

References

Abrams, Elliott. 2000. "Israel and the 'peace process.'" In *Present dangers: Crisis and opportunity in American foreign and defense policy*, edited by Robert Kagan and William Kristol. San Francisco: Encounter Books.

Adams, Fay, and Ernest W. Tiegs. 1975. *Our people*, Level 4. Lexington, MA: Ginn.

Adams, John Quincy. 2002. Presidential speech on July 4, 1821, in Walter Russell Mead, *Special providence: American foreign policy and how it changed the world*. New York: Routledge.

Almond, Gabriel A., R. Scott Appleby, and Emmanuel Sivan. 2003. *Strong religion: The rise of fundamentalism around the world*. Chicago: University of Chicago Press.

Alterman, Eric. 2003. *What liberal media? The truth about bias and the news*. New York: Basic Books.

Anderson, Benedict. 1991. *Imagined communities: Reflections on the origin and spread of nationalism*. New York: Verso.

Anderson, Perry. 2002. Force and consent. *New Left Review* 17 (September/October).

Applebome, Peter. 1996. *Dixie rising: How the South is shaping American values*. New York: Times Books.

Arendt, Hannah. 1945. Zionism reconsidered. *Menorah Journal* 33, no. 2.

Armey, Dick, and Matt Kibbe. 2010. *Give us liberty: A Tea Party manifesto*. New York: William Morrow.

Auden, W. H. 1967. "To Keep the Human Spirit Breathing," speech upon acceptance of the 1967 Medal for Literature, Smithsonian Institution, Washington, DC, November 30, 1967 (reproduced in the *Washington Post Book World*, December 24, 1967).

Avineri, Shlomo. 1981. *The Making of Modern Zionism: The intellectual origins of the Jewish state*. New York: Basic Books.

Avishai, Bernard. 2002. *The tragedy of Zionism: How its revolutionary past haunts Israeli democracy*. New York: Helios Press.

Avnery, Uri. 1971. *Israel without Zionism*. New York: Collier Books.

Bacevich, Andrew J., 2004. *American Empire: The Realities and Consequences of US Diplomacy*. Cambridge, MA: Harvard University Press.

Bacevich, Andrew J., 2006. *The New American Militarism: How Americans Are Seduced by War*. New York: Oxford University Press.

Bacevich, Andrew J. *Washington Rules: America's Path to Permanent War*. New York: Metropolitan Books.

Bainbridge, John. 1972. *The super-Americans: A picture of life in the United States, as brought into focus, bigger than life, in the land of the millionaires—Texas*. New York: Holt, Rinehart and Winston.

Balfour, Sebastian. 2002. *Deadly embrace: Morocco and the road to the Spanish Civil War.* Oxford: Oxford University Press.

Bard, Mitchell Geoffrey. 1991. *The water's edge and beyond: Defining the limits to domestic influence on US Middle East policy.* New Brunswick, NJ: Transaction Publishers.

Baritz, Loren. 1985. *Backfire: A history of how American culture led us into Vietnam and made us fight the way we did.* New York: William Morrow.

Barker, Ernest. 1985. "Christianity and nationalism." In *The nation with the soul of a church,* edited by Sidney E. Mead. Macon, GA: Mercer University Press.

Barnett, Correlli. 1991. *Engage the enemy more closely: The Royal Navy in the Second World War.* London: W. W. Norton.

Barry, John M. 1997. *Rising tide: The great Mississippi flood of 1927 and how it changed America.* New York: Simon & Schuster.

Barton, David. 2008. *Original intent: The courts, the Constitution and religion.* Aledo, TX: Wallbuilder Press.

Beck, Glenn. 2011. *The original argument: The Federalists' case for the Constitution adapted for the 21st century.* New York: Threshold Editions.

Becker, Jean-Jacques. 1977. *1914.* Paris: Presses de la Fondation Nationale des Sciences Politiques.

Beeson, Ann, and Jameel Jaffer. 2003. *Unpatriotic acts.* New York: American Civil Liberties Union.

Bell, Daniel. 1963. "The dispossessed—1962." In *The radical right,* edited by Daniel Bell. New York: Transaction Publishers.

Bell, Daniel. 1976. *The cultural contradictions of capitalism.* New York: Basic Books.

Bell, Daniel (ed.). 1963. *The radical right.* New York: Transaction Publishers.

Bellah, Robert N. 1967. Civil religion in America. *Daedalus* 96.

Bellah, Robert. 1975. *The broken covenant: American civil religion in a time of trial.* New York: Seabury Press.

Bellah, Robert, Richard Madsen, William M. Sullivan, Ann Swidler, and Steven M. Tipton. 1985. *Habits of the heart: Middle America observed.* Berkeley: University of California Press.

Beller, Emily, and Michael Hout. 2006. Intergenerational social mobility: The United States in comparative perspective. *Future of Children* 16, no. 2

Bellow, Saul. 1976. *To Jerusalem and back: A personal account.* New York: Viking.

Beloff, Max. 1970. *Imperial sunset.* Vol. I, *Britain's liberal empire, 1897–1921.* New York: Alfred A. Knopf.

Benin, Joel. 2003. Tel Aviv's influence on American institutions. *Le Monde Diplomatique* (July), http://mondediplo.com/2003/07/06beinin.

Bennett, David H. 1989. *The party of fear: From nativist movements to the new right in American history.* Chapel Hill: University of North Carolina Press.

Bennett, William J. 2002. *Why we fight: Moral clarity and the war on terrorism.* New York: Doubleday.

Benson, Lee. 1961. *The concept of Jacksonian democracy: New York as a test case.* Princeton, NJ: Princeton University Press.

Benvenisti, Meron. 1983. "The turning point in Israel." *New York Review of Books* 30, no. 15.

Benvenisti, Meron. 1995. *Intimate enemies: Jews and Arabs in a shared land.* Berkeley: University of California Press.

Berghahn, V. R. 1993. *Germany and the approach of war in 1914.* New York: St. Martin's Press.

Bercovitch, Sacvan. 1975. *The puritan origins of the American self*. New Haven, CT: Yale University Press.

Berman, Paul. 2003. *Terror and liberalism*. New York: W. W. Norton.

Bernstein, David E. 2003. *You can't say that: The growing threat to civil liberties from anti-discrimination laws*. Washington, DC: Cato Institute.

Berryman, Carl. 2004. *2013: World War III*. AuthorHouse.

Bishara, Marwan. 2001. *Palestine/Israel: Peace or apartheid*. New York: Zed Books.

Bishop, Bill. 2009. *The big sort: Why the clustering of like-minded America is tearing us apart*. New York: Mariner Books.

Black, Earl, and Merle Black. 1992. *The vital South: How presidents are elected*. Cambridge, MA: Harvard University Press.

Blackbourn, David. 2003. *History of Germany, 1780–1918: The long nineteenth century*. Oxford: Blackwell.

Blendon, Robert J., J. M. Benson, M. Brodie, D. E. Altman, R. Morin, C. Deane, and N. Kjellson. 2000. "America's changing political and moral values," in *What's God got to do with the American experiment*, ed. E. J. Dionne and John J. Dilulio. Washington, DC: Brookings Institution Press.

Blumenthal, Dan, et al. 2011. "Asian alliances in the 21st century," Project 2049 Institute at http://project2049.net/documents/Asian_Alliances_21st_Century.pdf.

Bork, Robert. 1997. *Slouching towards Gomorrah: Modern liberalism and American decline*. New York: Regan Books.

Bowers, Claude G. 1929. *The tragic era: The revolution after Lincoln*. New York: Blue Ribbon Books.

Boyer, Paul. 1992. *When time shall be no more: Prophesy belief in modern American culture* Cambridge, MA: Harvard University Press.

Brinkley, Alan. 1982. *Voices of protest*. New York: Alfred A. Knopf.

Brock, David. 2002. *Blinded by the Right: The conscience of an ex-conservative*. New York: Three Rivers Press.

Brock, William R. 1974. "Americanism." In *The United States: A companion to American studies*, ed. Dennis Welland. London: Methuen.

Brosseau, Jim, edited by 2002. *A celebration of America: Your helpful guide to America's greatness*.Des Moines: Meredith Publications.

Bruant, Aristide. 1996. "A Biribi." In *Anthologie de la Chanson Francaise: Soldats, Conscrits et Deserteurs*. Paris EPM Musique.

Brubaker, Rogers. 1992. *Citizenship in France and Germany*. Cambridge, MA: Harvard University Press.

Brzezinski, Zbigniew. 2003/2004. Hegemonic quicksand. *National Interest* (Winter)

Bush, George. 1991. "A distinctly American internationalism," speech at the Reagan Presidential Library, Simi Valley, California, November 19.

Bush, George W. 1999. *A charge to keep*. New York: William Morrow.

Bush, George W. 2001. Speech at the Islamic Center of Washington, DC, September 17.

Butler, Judith. 2003. "No, it's not anti-Semitic." *London Review of Books* no. 16, August 21.

Cannon, Lou. 1991. *President Reagan: The role of a lifetime*. New York: Simon & Schuster.

Cantor, David. 1994. *The religious right: The assault on tolerance and pluralism in America*. New York: Anti-Defamation League.

Carlton, David L. 2001. "Rethinking Southern history." *Southern Cultures* 7, no 1.

Carney, Francis. 1971. "A state of catastrophe." *New York Review of Books* 17, no. 5.

Caro, Robert A. 1990. *The Years of Lyndon Johnson.* Vol. 1, *The Path to Power* New York: Vintage Books.

Caro, Robert A. 2003. *The Years of Lyndon Johnson.* Vol. 3, *Master of the Senate.* New York: Vintage Books.

Carpenter, Joel. 1997. *Revive us again: The reawakening of American fundamentalism.* New York: Oxford University Press.

Carter, Jimmy. 2007. *Palestine: Peace not apartheid.* New York: Simon & Schuster.

Cash, W. J. 1991. *The mind of the South.* New York: Vintage Books.

Ceasar, James W. 2000. "The great divide: American interventionism and its opponents." In *Present dangers: Crisis and opportunity in American foreign and defense policy,* edited by Robert Kagan and William Kristol. San Francisco: Encounter Books.

Chanes, Jerome. 2000. *A dark side of history: Anti-Semitism through the ages.* New York: Anti-Defamation League.

Cheney, Lynne, and illust. Robin Preiss Glasser. 2002. *America: A patriotic primer.* New York: Simon & Schuster Children's Publishing.

Cherry, Conrad. 1970. "American sacred ceremonies." In *Social patterns of religion in the United States,* edited by Phillip E. Hammond and Benton Johnson. New York: Random House.

Cherry, Conrad, ed. 1998. *God's new Israel: Religious interpretations of American destiny.* Chapel Hill: University of North Carolina Press.

Chesler, Phyllis. 2003. "A brief history of Arab attacks against Israel, 1908–1970s." In *The new anti-Semitism: The current crisis and what we must do about it,* edited by Phyllis Chesler. San Francisco: Jossey-Bass.

Chesterton, G. K. 1922. *What I saw in America.* New York: Dodd, Mead and Co.

Christison, Kathleen. 2000. *Perceptions of Palestine.* Berkeley: University of California Press.

Clark, Norman H. 1976. *Deliver us from evil: An interpretation of American prohibition.* New York: W. W. Norton.

Clarke, Jonathan. 2001. "The guns of 17th Street." *National Interest* 63 (Spring).

Clarke, Richard A. 2004. *Against all enemies: Inside America's war on terror.* New York: Free Press.

Cliffe, J. T. 1999. *The world of the country house in seventeenth century England.* New Haven, CT: Yale University Press.

Cobb, William J., Jr. 1998. *The American foundation myth in Vietnam: Reigning paradigms and raining bombs.* New York: University Press of America.

Cobban, Alfred. 1990. *A history of modern France, 1871–1962.* London: Penguin.

Coben, Stanley. 1964. "A study in nativism: The Red Scare of 1919–20." *Political Science Quarterly* 79, no. 1

Cohen, Ariel, et al. 1996. "Making the World Safe for America." In *Issues 96: The Candidates' Briefing Book.* Washington, DC: Heritage Foundation.

Cohn, Norman. 1990. *The pursuit of the millennium: Revolutionary millenarians and mystical anarchists of the Middle Ages.* New York, Oxford University Press.

Colley, Linda. 1992. *Britons: Forging the nation, 1707–1837.* London: Yale University Press.

Conger, Kimberley H., and John C. Green. 2002. "Spreading out and digging in: Christian conservatives and state Republican parties." *Campaigns and Elections,* http://www.theocracywatch.org/campaigns_elections_study.htm.

Cook, Rhodes. 1992. "The solid South turns around." *Congressional Quarterly Weekly.*

Cooper, Arthur, trans. and ed. 1973. *Li Po and Tu Fu.* London: Penguin.

Coulter, Ann. 2003. *Treason: Liberal treachery from the cold war to the war against terrorism*. New York: Crown Forum.

Cowan, P. 1979. *The tribes of America: Journalistic discoveries of our people and their cultures*. New York: Doubleday.

Craig, Gordon Alexander. 1978. *Germany 1866–1945*. New York: Oxford University Press.

Croly, Herbert. [1909] 1989. *The promise of American life*. Boston: Northeastern University Press.

Cromartie, Michael, ed. 1993. *No longer exiles: The religious new right and American politics*. Washington, DC: Ethics and Public Policy Center.

Crovitz, L. Gordon, ed. 1989. *The fettered presidency: Legal constraints on the executive branch*. Washington, DC: AEI Press.

Cruise O'Brien, Conor. 1987. *God land: Reflections on religion and nationalism*. Cambridge, MA: Harvard University Press.

Cruise O'Brien, Conor, 1987. *The siege: The saga of Israel and Zionism*. New York: Touchstone Books.

D'Souza, Dinesh. 2002. *What's so great about America*. Washington, DC: Regnery Books.

Davis, Mike. 1998. *Ecology of fear: Los Angeles and the imagination of disaster*. New York: Metropolitan Books.

de Bochgrave, Arnaud. 2004. Democracy in the Middle East. *Washington Times*, March 5.

de Tocqueville, Alexis. [1835] 2000. *Democracy in America*, Vol. I. Translated by Henry Reeve. New York: Bantam Classics.

Dershowitz, Alan. 2009. *The case against Israel's enemies: Exposing Jimmy Carter and others who stand in the way of peace*. New York: John Wiley & Sons.

Diamond, Sara. 1998. *Not by politics alone: The enduring influence of the Christian Right*. New York: Guilford Press.

Doren, Dorothy. 1967. *Nationalism and Catholic Americanism*. New York: Sheed and Ward.

Drury, Shadia B. 1997. *Leo Strauss and the American Right*. New York: St. Martin's Press.

Eban, Abba. 1992. *Personal witness: Israel through my eyes*. New York: Putnam.

Ehle, John. 1988. *Trail of tears: The rise and fall of the Cherokee nation*. New York: Anchor Books.

Ehrman, John. 1996. *The rise of neoconservatism: Intellectuals and foreign affairs, 1945–94*. New Haven, CT: Yale University Press.

Eidsmoe, John. 1995. *Christianity and the Constitution: The faith of our founding fathers*. Ada, MO: Baker Academic Publishers.

Eley, Geoff. 1978. "The Wilhelmine Right: How it changed." In *Society and politics in Wilhelmine Germany*, edited by Richard J. Evans. London: Croom Helm.

Elinson, Howard. 1965. The implications of Pentecostalist religion for intellectualism, politics and race relations. *American Journal of Sociology* 70(4).

Elon, Amos. 1972. *The Israelis: Founders and sons*. London: Sphere Books.

Engel, Matthew. 2002. Senior Republican calls on Israel to expel West Bank Arabs. *The Guardian* (London), May 4.

Epstein, Klaus. 1966. *The genesis of German conservatism*. Princeton, NJ: Princeton University Press.

Erikson, Erik H. 1995. *Childhood and society*. London: Vintage Books.

Farah, Joseph. 2003. *Taking America back: A radical plan to revive freedom, morality and justice*. Nashville, TN: Thomas Nelson.

Farah, Joseph. 2010. *The Tea Party manifesto*. New York: WND Books.

Fastnow, Chris, J. Tobin Grant, and Thomas J. Rudolph. 1999. Holy roll calls: Religious tradition and voting behavior in the US House. *Social Science Quarterly* 80, no. 4.

Fehrenbach, T. R. 1968. *Lone star: A history of Texas and the Texans.* New York: MacMillan.

Fehrenbach, T. R. 1974. *Comanches: The destruction of a people.* New York: Alfred A. Knopf.

Ferguson, Niall. 2003. *Empire: The rise and demise of the British world order and the lessons for global power.* New York: Basic Books.

Feuerlicht, Roberta. 1983. *The fate of the Jews: A people torn between Israeli power and Jewish ethics.* New York: New York Times Book Co.

Fichte, J. G. [1806] 1922. *Addresses to the German nation.* London, Open Court Publishing.

Findley, Paul. 1985. *They dare to speak out: People and institutions confront Israel's lobby.* Westport, CT: Lawrence Hill.

Fischer, David Hackett. 1989. *Albion's seed: Four British folkways in America.* New York: Oxford University Press.

FitzGerald, Frances. 1973. *Fire in the lake: The Vietnamese and the Americans in Vietnam.* New York: Vintage Books.

FitzGerald, Frances. 1980. *America revised: What history textbooks have taught our children about their country, and how and why those textbooks have changed in different decades.* New York: Vintage Books.

Flanagan, Thomas. 2001. "Western star." *New York Review of Books* 48, nos. 19 and 20.

Foner, Eric. 1988. *Reconstruction: America's unfinished revolution, 1863–1877.* New York: Harper and Row.

Foner, Eric. 1998. *The story of American freedom.* New York: W. W. Norton.

Foner, Eric. 2002. *Who owns history? Rethinking the past in a changing world.* New York: Farrar, Straus and Giroux.

Forts, Franklin. 2002. "Living with Confederate symbols." *Southern Cultures* 8, no.1.

Foxman, Abraham. 2003. *Never again? The threat of the new anti-Semitism.* San Francisco: Harper Collins.

Foxman, Abraham H. 2007. *The deadliest lies: The Israel lobby and the myth of Jewish control.* New York: Palgrave Macmillan.

Frank, Thomas. 2004. *What's the matter with Kansas? How conservatives won the heart of America.* New York: Metropolitan Books.

Franz, Joe B. 1969. "The frontier tradition: An invitation to violence." In *Violence in America: Historical and comparative perspectives* Edited by Hugh Davis Graham and Ted Gurr. New York: Bantam Books.

Fredrickson, George M. 1997. "America's caste system: Will it change?" *New York Review of Books*, no. 16.

Fredrickson, George M. 1999. The strange death of segregation. *New York Review of Books* 46, no. 8.

Frey, William H. 2009. "Immigration and the coming 'majority minority'" Washington, DC: Brookings September 18.

Friedberg, Aaron. 1988. *The weary titan: Britain and the experience of relative decline, 1895–1905.* Princeton, NJ: Princeton University Press.

Friedman, Thomas. 1989. *From Beirut to Jerusalem.* New York: Farrar, Straus and Giroux.

Frum, David. 1994. *Dead Right.* New York: Basic Books.

Frum, David, and Richard Perle. 2003. *An end to evil: How to win the war on terror.* New York: Random House.

Fulbright, James William. 2004. *The Arrogance of Power.* New York: Random House.

Gamoran, Adam. 1990. "Civil religion in American schools." *Sociological Analysis* 51, no. 3.

Garton Ash, Timothy. 2003. "Anti-Europeanism in America." *New York Review of Books* 50, no. 2.

Geertz, Clifford. 1993. *The interpretation of cultures*. London: Fontana.

Geller, Pamela, Robert Spencer, and John Bolton. 2010. *The post-American presidency: The Obama administration's war on America*. New York: Threshold Editions.

Gellner, Ernest. 1984. *Encounters with nationalism*. Oxford: Blackwell.

Genovese, Eugene D. 1994. *The southern tradition: The achievement and limitations of an American conservatism*. Cambridge, MA: Harvard University Press.

Genovese, Eugene D. 1998. *A consuming fire: The fall of the Confederacy in the mind of the white Christian South*. Athens, GA: University of Georgia Press.

Gentles, Ian 1992. *The new model army in England, Ireland and Scotland, 1645–1653*. Oxford: Blackwell.

Gerstenfeld, Manfred. 2004. "Anti-Semitism: Integral to European culture." In *Post Holocaust and anti-Semitism*, no. 19, Jerusalem Center for Public Affairs, April 1.

Gerstle, Gary. 2001. *American crucible: Race and nation in the twentieth century*. Princeton, NJ: Princeton University Press.

Gertz, Bill. 2000. *The China threat: How the People's Republic targets America*. Washington, DC: Regnery Publishing.

Gill, Bates, and Michael O'Hanlon. 1999. China's hollow military. *National Interest* 56 (Summer).

Gillard, David. 1977. *The struggle for Asia, 1828–1914*. London: Methuen.

Gingrich, Newt. 1995. *To renew America*. New York: Harper Collins.

Girardet, Raoul. 1983. *Le Nationalisme Francais*. Paris Points.

Glazer, Nathan, and Daniel P. Moynihan. 1979. *Beyond the melting pot: The Negroes, Puerto Ricans, Jews, Italians and Irish of New York City*. Cambridge, MA: MIT Press.

Gleason, John Howes. 1950. *The genesis of Russophobia in Great Britain: A study of the interaction of policy and opinion*. Cambridge, MA: Harvard University Press.

Goldmann, Nahum. 1969. *Autobiography: Sixty years of Jewish life*. Translated by Helen Sebba. New York: Holt, Rinehart and Winston.

Goldmann, Nahum. 1978. *The Jewish Paradox*. New York: Grosset and Dunlap.

Gordon, Philip H. 2003. "Bush's Middle East vision." *Survival* 45, no 1.

Gorenberg, Gershom. 2000. *The end of days: Fundamentalism and the struggle for the Temple Mount*. New York: Free Press.

Graham, Hugh Davis, and Ted Gurr, eds. 1969. *Violence in America: Historical and comparative perspectives*. New York: Bantam Books.

Grant, George. 1996. *The patriot's handbook*. Nashville, TN: Cumberland House.

Greenfield, Liah. 1992. *Nationalism: Five roads to modernity*. Cambridge, MA: Harvard University Press.

Griffin, Larry J. 2001. "The promise of a sociology of the South." *Southern Cultures* (Spring).

Grose, Peter. 1984. *Israel in the mind of America*. New York: Alfred A. Knopf.

Hackney, Sheldon. 2001. "The contradictory South." *Southern Cultures* 7, no. 4 (Winter).

Haddad, Hassan, and Donald Wagner, eds. 1986. *All in the name of the Bible: Selected essays on Israel and American Christian fundamentalism*. Brattleborough, VT: Amana Books.

Halsell, Grace. 1986. *Prophecy and politics: Militant evangelists on the road to nuclear war*. Westport, CT: Lawrence Hill.

Handlin, Oscar. 1979. "American Jewry." In *The Jewish world: Revelation, prophecy and history*, edited by Elie Kedourie. London: Thames and Hudson.

Hannity, Sean. 2002. *Let freedom ring: Winning the war of liberty over liberalism*. New York: Regan Books.

Hannity, Sean. 2004. *Deliver us from evil: Defeating terrorism, despotism and liberalism*. New York: Simon & Schuster.

Hardisty, Jean. 1999. *Mobilizing resentment: Conservative resurgence from the John Birch Society to the Promise Keepers*. Boston: Beacon Press.

Harries, Owen. 1997/1998. The dangers of expansive realism." *National Interest* (Winter).

Harris, Lee. 2004. *Civilization and its enemies: "The next stage of history*. New York: Free Press.

Hart, D. G. 2003. "Mainstream Protestantism, 'conservative' religion, and civil society." In *Religion returns to the public square: Faith and policy in America*, edited by Hugh Heclo and Wilfred M. McClay. Washington, DC: Woodrow Wilson Center Press.

Hartz, Louis. [1955] 1991. *The liberal tradition in America*. New York: Harcourt Brace.

Hastings, Adrian. 1997. *The construction of nationhood: Ethnicity, religion and nationalism*. New York: Cambridge University Press.

Hay, Douglas, et al. 1975. *Albion's fatal tree: Crime and society in 18th century England*. New York: Random House.

Hayes, Carlton J. H. 1960. *Nationalism: A religion*. New York: Macmillan.

Hellmann, John. 1986. *American myth and the legacy of Vietnam*. New York: Columbia University Press.

Herberg, Will. 1956. *Protestant, Catholic, Jew: An essay in American religious sociology*. New York: Doubleday.

Herberg, Will. 1974. "America's civil religion: What it is and whence it comes." In *American civil religion*, edited by Russell E. Richey and Donald G. Jones. New York: Harper and Row.

Herman, Edward S., and Noam Chomsky. 1988. *Manufacturing consent: The political economy of the mass media*. New York: Pantheon Books.

Hertzberg, Hendrik. 2003. Building nations. *New Yorker* (June 9): .

Higham, John. 1974. "Hanging together: Divergent unities in American history." *Journal of American History* 61, no. 1

Himmelstein, Jerome L. 1983. "The new Right." In *The new Christian Right: Mobilization and legitimation*, edited by Robert C. Liebman and Robert Wuthnow. New York: Aldine.

Hine, Robert V., and John Mack Faragher. 2000. *The American West: A new interpretive history*. New Haven, CT: Yale University Press.

Hirst, David. 1977. *The gun and the olive branch: The roots of violence in the Middle East*. London: Faber and Faber.

Hobsbawm, Eric, and Terence Ranger, eds. 1983. *The invention of tradition*. Cambridge: Cambridge University Press.

Hoffmann, Stanley. 1987. "The great pretender." *New York Review of Books* 34, no. 9.

Hofstadter, Richard. [1952] 1996. *The paranoid style in American politics and other essays*. Cambridge, MA: Harvard University Press.

Hofstadter, Richard. 1956. *The age of reform: From Bryan to F.D.R.* New York: Alfred A. Knopf.

Hofstadter, Richard. 1963. *Anti-intellectualism in American life*. New York: Vintage Books.

Hofstadter, Richard. 1963. "The pseudo-conservative revolt—1955." In *The radical Right*, edited by Daniel Bell. New York: Doubleday.

Holmes, Stephen. 1996. *The anatomy of antiliberalism*. Cambridge, MA: Harvard University Press.

Howe, Irving. 1976. *World of our fathers: The journey of the East European Jews to America and the life they found and made*. New York: Harcourt Brace Jovanovich.

Hughes, Richard. 2003. *Myths America lives by*. Champaign: University of Illinois Press.

Hulliung, Mark. 2002. *Citizens and citoyens: Republicans and liberals in America and France*. Cambridge, MA: Harvard University Press.

Humphreys, R. A. 1970. "The rule of law and the American Revolution." In *The role of ideology in the American Revolution*, edited by John R. Howe. New York: Holt, Rinehart and Winston.

Hunt, Michael H. 1987. *Ideology and U.S. foreign policy*. New Haven, CT: Yale University Press.

Huntington, Samuel P. 1968. *Political order in changing societies*. New Haven, CT: Yale University Press.

Huntington, Samuel. 1981. *American politics: The promise of disharmony*. Cambridge, MA: Harvard University Press.

Huntington, Samuel. 1996. *The clash of civilizations and the remaking of world order*. London: Simon & Schuster.

Huntington, Samuel. 2004. "Dead souls: The denationalization of the American elite." *National Interest* 75 (Spring).

Huntington, Samuel. 2004. "The Hispanic challenge." *Foreign Policy* (March/April), http://www.foreignpolicy.com/articles/2004/03/01/the_hispanic_challenge.

Hutchison, William R., and Hartmut Lehmann. 1998. *Many are chosen*. Harrisburg, PA: Trinity Press International.

Ignatiev, Noel. 1995. *How the Irish became white*. New York: Routledge.

Ikenberry, John. 2002. America's imperial ambition. *Foreign Affairs* 81, no. 5.

Ikenberry, John. 2004. The end of the neo-conservative moment. *Survival* 46, no. 1.

Inhofe, James. 2002. Senate floor statement, Washington, DC, March 4.

Ionescu, Ghita, and Ernest Gellner, eds. 1969. *Populism: Its meanings and national characteristics*. London: Weidenfeld and Nicholson.

Isserman, Maurice, and Michael Kazin. 2000. *America divided: The Civil War of the 1960s*. New York: Oxford University Press.

Johnson, Chalmers. 2003. *Blowback: The costs and consequences of American empire*. New York: Holt/Owl Books.

Johnson, Chalmers. 2004. *The sorrows of empire: Militarism, secrecy and the end of the republic*. New York: Metropolitan Books.

Judt, Tony. 2003. "Israel: The alternative." *New York Review of Books* 50, no. 16.

Kagan, Robert, and William Kristol, eds. 2000. *Present dangers: Crisis and opportunity in American foreign and defense policy*. San Francisco: Encounter Books.

Kagan, Robert. 2002. *Of paradise and power: America and Europe in the new world order*. New York: Alfred A. Knopf.

Kaplan, Robert D. 2003. *Warrior politics: Why leadership requires a pagan ethos*. New York: Vintage Books.

Karatnycky, Adrian. 2003. "The 30th Anniversary Freedom House Survey. *Journal of Democracy* 14, no. 1.

Kazin, Michael. 1995. *The populist persuasion: An American history*. New York: Harper Collins.

Kedourie, Elie. 1979. *Nationalism*. London: Hutchinson.

Kehr, Eckart. 1977. *Economic interest, militarism and foreign policy*. Berkeley: University of California Press.

Kelley, Dean M. 1986. *Why conservative churches are growing.* Macon, GA: Mercer University Press.

Kelley, Robert. 1979. *The cultural pattern in American politics: The first century.* New York: Alfred A. Knopf.

Kenen, I. L. 1981. *Israel's defense line: Her friends and foes in Washington.* Buffalo, NY: Prometheus Books.

Kennan, George. 1985. Morality and foreign policy. *Foreign Affairs* 64, no. 2.

Kessler, Jonathan S., and Jeff Schwaber. 1984. "The AIPAC college guide: Exposing the anti-Israel campaign on campus." AIPAC papers on U.S.–Israel relations no. 7. America Israel Public Affairs Committee (AIPAC).

Kevles, Daniel J. 1998. "Darwin in Dayton." *New York Review of Books* 45, no. 18.

King, Charles. 2001. "Potemkin democracy: Four myths about post-Soviet Georgia." *National Interest* 64 (July 1).

Kirk, Stephen. 2011. *Satan as Barack Obama.* Bloomington, IN: AuthorHouse Publishing.

Kirkpatrick, Jeane J. 1982. *Dictatorships and double standards.* Washington, DC: American Enterprise Institute.

Kissinger, Henry. 1994. *Diplomacy.* New York: Simon & Schuster.

Klein, Aaron. 2010. *The Manchurian President: Barack Obama's ties to Communists, Socialists and other anti-American extremists.* New York: WND Books.

Knuckey, Jonathan. 1999. "Religious conservatives, the Republican Party, and evolving party coalitions in the United States." *Party Politics* 5, no. 4.

Kohn, Hans. 1945. *The idea of nationalism.* New York: Macmillan.

Kohn, Hans. 1957. *American nationalism: An interpretative essay.* New York: Macmillan.

Kristol, Irving. [1980] 1983. "'Moral Dilemmas' in Foreign Policy." In *Reflections of a neoconservative: Looking back, looking ahead.* New York: Basic Books.

Kristol, Irving. 1983. "The 'Human Rights' Muddle." In *Reflections of a neoconservative: Looking back, looking ahead.* New York: Basic Books.

Kristol, Irving. 1983. *Reflections of a neoconservative: Looking back, looking ahead.* New York: Basic Books.

Kristol, Irving. 1994. *Neo-conservatism, autobiography of an idea.* New York: Free Press.

Krugman, Paul. 2002. "True blue Americans." *New York Times,* May 7.

Kull, Steven. 2001. "Americans on foreign aid and world hunger: A study of US public attitudes," Program on International Policy Attitudes. February 2.

LaHaye. Tim, and Jerry B. Jenkins. 1995. *Left behind: A novel of the Earth's last days.* Wheaton, IL: Tyndale House Publishers.

Lamont, William, and Sybil Oldfield. 1975. *Politics, religion and literature in the seventeenth century.* London: J. M. Dent and Sons.

Lampton, David M. 2001. *Same bed, different dreams: Managing US-China relations 1989–2000.* Berkeley: University of California Press.

Langdon, Samuel. 1998. "The republic of the Israelites an example to the American states." In *God's new Israel: Religious interpretations of American destiny,* edited by Conrad Cherry. Chapel Hill, NC: University of North Carolina Press.

Le Guin, Ursula K. 1984. *The compass rose.* London: Grafton Books.

Leebaert, Derek. 2002. *The fifty year wound: How America's cold war victory shapes our world.* New York: Little, Brown and Co.

Lemann, Nicholas. 2001. The quiet man (profile of Dick Cheney). *New Yorker* (May 7).

Lepore, Jill. 2011. *The whites of their eyes: The Tea Party's revolution and the battle over American history.* Princeton, NJ: Princeton University Press.

Lerner, Max. 1957. *American civilization: Life and thought in the US today.* New York: Simon & Schuster.

Leslie, Warren. 1998. *Dallas, public and private: Aspects of an American city.* Dallas, TX: Southern Methodist University Press.

Leyburn, James G. 1962. *The Scotch-Irish: A social history.* Chapel Hill: University of North Carolina Press.

Liebman, Robert C. 1983. "Mobilizing the Moral Majority." In *The new Christian Right,* edited by Robert Liebman and Robert Wuthnow. Hawthorne, NY: Aldine Transaction.

Liebman, Robert C., and Robert Wuthnow. 1983. *The new Christian Right.* Hawthorne, NY: Aldine Transaction.

Lieven, Anatol. 1983. *The Baltic revolution: Estonia, Latvia, Lithuania and the path to independence.* New Haven, CT: Yale University Press.

Lieven, Anatol. 1997. *Chechnya: Tombstone of Russian power.* New Haven, CT: Yale University Press.

Lieven, D. C. B. 1983. *Russia and the origins of the First World War.* London: MacMillan.

Lilley, James, and Carl Ford. 1999. "China's military: A second opinion." *National Interest* 57(Fall).

Lind, Michael. 1995. *The next American nation: The new nationalism and the fourth American revolution.* New York: Simon & Schuster.

Lind, Michael. 1996. *Up from conservatism: Why the Right is wrong for America.* New York: Simon & Schuster.

Lind, Michael. 2003. *Made in Texas: George Bush and the southern takeover of American politics.* New York: Basic Books.

Lindsey, Hal. 2002. *The everlasting hatred: The roots of jihad.* Murrietta, CA: Oracle House.

Lindsey, Hal. 2002. *The late great planet Earth.* Murrietta, CA: Oracle House.

Lindsay, Vachel. 1963. *Selected poems,* edited by Mark Harris. New York: Macmillan.

Lipset, Seymour Martin. 1976. *American exceptionalism: A double-edged sword.* New York: W. W. Norton.

Lipset, Seymour Martin, and Earl Raab. 1970. *The politics of unreason: Right wing extremism in America, 1790–1970* New York: Harper and Row.

Lizza, Ryan. 2011. "Leap of faith: The making of a Republican front-runner." *New Yorker* (August 15).

Lonnrot, Elias. 1989. *The Kalevala: An epic poem after oral tradition,* translated by Keith Bosley. New York: Oxford University Press.

Lozowick, Yaacov. 2003. *Right to exist: A moral defense of Israel's wars.* New York: Doubleday.

Lustick, Ian. 1988. *For the land and the Lord: Jewish fundamentalism in Israel.* New York: Council on Foreign Relations.

MacCurtain, Margaret. 1972. *Tudor and Stuart Ireland.* Dublin: Gill and Macmillan.

Magraw, Roger. 1983. *France 1815–1914: The bourgeois century.* London: Fontana.

Maher, Bill. 2003. *When you ride alone you ride with Bin Laden: What the government should be telling us to help fight the war on terrorism.* Beverly Hills, CA: Phoenix Books.

Malley, Robert, and Hussein Agha. 2001. "Camp David: The tragedy of errors." *New York Review of Books* (August).

Mann, James. 2004. *Rise of the Vulcans: The history of Bush's war cabinet.* New York: Viking.

Mansfield, Stephen. 2003. *The faith of George W. Bush.* Lake Mary, FL: Charisma House.

Marsden, George. 1993. "The religious Right: A historical overview." In *No longer exiles: The religious new Right and American politics,* edited by Michael Cromartie. Washington, DC: Ethics and Public Policy Center.

Marty, Martin. 1985. *Pilgrims in their own land: 500 years of religion in America*. New York: Penguin.

Marx, Karl, and Friedrich Engels. 1967. *The Communist manifesto*, translated by Samuel Morse. London: Penguin Books.

Mayer, Jane. 2010. "Covert operations: The billionaire brothers who are waging a war against Obama." *New Yorker* August 30).

McBride, Joseph. 2001. *Searching for John Ford*. New York: St. Martin's Press.

McClosky, Herbert. 1964. "Consensus and ideology in American politics." *American Political Science Review* 58, no. 2.

McDougall, Walter A. 1997. *Promised land, crusader state: American encounters with the world since 1776*. New York: Houghton Mifflin.

McGirr, Lisa. 2002. *Suburban warriors: The origins of the new American Right*. Princeton, NJ: Princeton University Press.

McMaster, Colonel H. R. 1997. *Dereliction of duty: Johnson, McNamara, the Joint Chiefs of Staff and the lies that led to Vietnam*. New York: Harper Collins.

McMurtry, Larry. 1966. *The last picture show*. New York: Simon & Schuster.

McMurtry, Larry. 1987. *Texasville*. New York: Simon & Schuster.

McMurtry, Larry. 1999. *Duane's depressed*. New York: Simon & Schuster.

McMurtry, Larry. 2000. *Roads: Driving America's great highways*. New York: Simon & Schuster.

McMurtry, Larry. 2001. *In a shallow grave: Essays on Texas*. New York: Touchstone Books.

McMurtry, Larry. 2001. "Separate and unequal." *New York Review of Books* 48, no. 4.

McNeill, William H. 1986. "The care and repair of public myth." In McNeill, *Mythistory and other essays*. Chicago: University of Chicago Press.

McWhiney, Grady. 1988. *Cracker culture: Celtic ways in the Old South*. Tuscaloosa: University of Alabama Press.

Mead, Sidney E. 1985. *The nation with the soul of a church*. Macon, GA: Mercer University Press.

Mead, Walter Russell. 1999/2000. "The Jacksonian tradition." *National Interest* 58 (Winter).

Mead, Walter Russell. 2002. *Special providence: American foreign policy and how it shaped the world*. New York: Routledge.

Mead, Walter Russell. 2011. "The Tea Party and American foreign policy: What populism means for globalism." *Foreign Affairs* 90, no. 2.

Mearsheimer, John J., and Stephen M. Walt. *The Israel lobby and US foreign policy*. New York: Farrar, Straus and Giroux.

Melville, Herman. 1967. *White-Jacket*. New York: Holt, Rinehart and Winston.

Merk, Frederick. 1978. *History of the westward movement*. New York: Alfred A. Knopf.

Merton, Robert K. 1957. *Social theory and social structure*. Glencoe, IL: Free Press.

Michelet, Jules. 1973. *The people*, translated by John P. McKay. Champaign: University of Illinois Press.

Miller, Zell. 2003. *A national party no more: The conscience of a conservative Democrat*. Atlanta: Stroud and Hall.

Minogue, Kenneth. 1997. *Nationalism*. New York: Basic Books.

Mommsen, Wolfgang J. 1995. *Imperial Germany 1867–1918: Politics, culture and society in an authoritarian state*, translated by Richard Deveson. New York: Arnold.

Monaghan, Robert R. 1970. "Three faces of the true believer: Motivations for attending a fundamentalist church." In *American mosaic: Social patterns of religion in the United States*, edited by Phillip E. Hammond and Benton Johnson. New York: Random House.

Moore, R. Laurence. 1986. *Religious outsiders and the making of Americans*. New York: Oxford University Press.

Moorhead, James H. 1998. "The American Israel: Protestant tribalism and universal mission." In *Many are chosen*, edited by William R. Hutchison and Hartmut Lehmann. Valley Forge, PA: Trinity Press International.

Morgan, Edmund S. 2001. The price of honor. *New York Review of Books* 48, no. 9.

Morison, Samuel Eliot. 1994. *The Oxford history of the American people*. New York: Penguin Books.

Morison, Samuel Eliot, Henry Steele Commager, and William E. Leuchtenburg. 1969. *The growth of the American republic*. Vols. 1 and 2. New York: Oxford University Press.

Morone, James A. 2003. *Hellfire nation: The politics of sin in American history*. New Haven, CT: Yale University Press.

Morris, Benny. 1989. *The birth of the Palestinian refugee problem, 1947–49*. New York: Cambridge University Press.

Morris, Benny. 1999. *Righteous victims: A history of the Zionist-Arab conflict, 1881–2001*. New York: Random House.

Mosher, Stephen W., and Chuck DeVore. 2000. *China attacks*. West Conshohocken, PA: Infinity Publishing.

Mosse, George L. 1988. *Nationalism and sexuality: Middle class morality and sexual norms in modern Europe*. Madison: University of Wisconsin Press.

"Mr Y" [Captain Wayne Porter, USN, and Colonel Mark Mykleby, USMC]. 2011. "A National Strategic Narrative," Woodrow Wilson International Center, Washington, DC, http://www.wilsoncenter.org/sites/default/files/A%20National%20Strategic%20Narrative.pdf.

Muravchik, Joshua. 1991. *Exporting democracy: Fulfilling America's destiny*. Washington, DC: American Enterprise Institute.

Myrdal, Gunnar. 1996. *An American dilemma: The negro problem and modern democracy*. Piscataway, NJ: Transaction Publishers.

Naipaul, V. S. 1989. *A turn in the South*. London: Viking.

Nash, Gary B., Charlotte Crabtree, and Ross E. Dunn. 1997. *History on trial: Culture wars and the teaching of the past*. New York: Alfred A. Knopf.

Nelson, Lars-Erik. 2000. "Military-industrial man." *New York Review of Books* 47, no. 20.

Niebuhr, Reinhold. 1952. *The irony of American history*. New York: Charles Scribner's Sons.

Niebuhr, Reinhold. 1985. "A note on pluralism." In *The nation with the soul of a church*, edited by Sidney Mead. Macon, GA: Mercer University Press.

Niebuhr, Reinhold. 1986. "The children of light and the children of darkness." In *The essential Reinhold Niebuhr: Selected essays and addresses*, edited by Robert McAfee Brown. New Haven, CT: Yale University Press.

Niebuhr, Reinhold. [1943] 1998. Anglo Saxon destiny and responsibility In Conrad Cherry, ed., *God's new Israel: Religious interpretations of American destiny*. Chapel Hill: University of North Carolina Press.

Niebuhr, Richard. 1957. *The social sources of denominationalism*. Cleveland, OH: Meridian Books.

Nye, Russel. 1966. *This almost chosen people: Essays in the history of American ideas*. East Lansing: Michigan State University Press.

Odom, William E., and Robert Dujarric. 1996. *Commonwealth or empire: Russia, Central Asia or the Caucasus*. New York: Hudson Institute.

O'Hara, John M., and Michelle Malkin. 2011. *A new American tea party: The counterrevolution against bailouts, handouts, reckless spending and more taxes*. New York: John Wiley & Sons.

Oz, Amos. 1983. *In the land of Israel*. Translated by Maurie Goldberg-Bartura. New York: Harcourt, Brace and Co..

Oz, Amos. 1994. "From Jerusalem to Cairo: Escaping from the shadow of the past." In *Israel, Palestine and peace: Essays*, edited by Amos Oz. New York: Harcourt, Brace and Co.

Padover, Saul, ed. 1943. *The complete Jefferson*. New York: Irvington Publishers.

Palin, Sarah. 2009. *Going rogue: An American life*. New York: Harper Collins.

Palin, Sarah. 2010. *America by heart: Reflections on family, faith and flag*. New York: Harper Collins.

Paris, Michael. 2000. *Warrior nation: Images of war in British popular culture, 1850–2000*. London: Reaktion Books.

Patterson, Lt. Colonel (ret.) Robert "Buzz." 2003. *Dereliction of duty: The eyewitness account of how Bill Clinton compromised America's national security*. Washington, DC: Regnery Publishing.

Patterson, Orlando. 1997. *The ordeal of integration: Progress and resentment in America's "racial" crisis*. New York: Basic Civitas.

Pei, Minxin. 2003. The paradoxes of American nationalism. *Foreign Policy* (May–June).

Perdue, Theda. 2000. "Cherokee women and the Trail of Tears." In *American encounters: Natives and newcomers from European contact to Indian removal, 1500–1850*, edited by Peter C. Mancall and James H. Merrell. New York: Routledge.

Perlmutter, Nathan. 1984. *The real anti-Semitism in America*. Westminster, MD: Arbor House.

Perlstein, Rick. 2001. *Before the storm: Barry Goldwater and the unmaking of the American consensus*. New York: Hill & Wang.

Persinos, John F. 1994. Has the Christian Right taken over the Republican Party? *Campaigns and Elections* 15, no. 9.

Peters, Joan. 1984. *From time immemorial*. New York: Harper and Row.

Pfaff, William. 2000. *Barbarian sentiments: America in the new century*. New York: Farrar, Strauss and Giroux.

Phillips, Kevin. 1969. *The emerging Republican majority*. New York: Arlington House.

Phillips, Kevin. 1994. *Boiling point: Republicans, Democrats and the decline of middle class prosperity*. New York: Harper Perennial.

Phillips, Kevin. 1999. *The cousins' wars: Religion, politics and the triumph of Anglo-America*. New York: Basic Books.

Phillips, Kevin. 2004. *American dynasty: Aristocracy, fortune and the politics of deceit in the house of Bush*. New York: Viking.

Phillips-Fein, Kim. 2009. *Invisible hands: The making of the conservative movement from the New Deal to Reagan*. New York: W. W. Norton.

Plato. 1976. *The republic*, translated by by Desmond Lee. London: Penguin.

Podhoretz, Norman. 2002. "How to win World War IV." *Commentary* 113, no. 2.

Podhoretz, Norman. 1980. *Present danger: Do we have the will to reverse the decline of American power?* New York: Simon & Schuster.

Porch, Douglas. 1983. *The conquest of Morocco*. New York: Alfred A. Knopf.

Potter, David Morris. 1976. *The impending crisis, 1848–1861*. New York: Perennial.

Prestowitz, Clyde. 2003. *Rogue nation: American unilateralism and the failure of good intentions*. New York: Basic Books.

Pumpurs, Andrejs. 1988. *Lacplesis, a Latvian national epic*. Riga: Writers Union.

Ravitch, Diane. 2003. *The language police: How pressure groups restrict what students learn*. New York: Alfred A. Knopf.

Reed, John Shelton. 1972. *The enduring South*. Lexington, MA: Lexington Books.

Reed, John Shelton. 1982. *One South: An ethnic approach to regional culture.* Baton Rouge: Louisiana State University Press.

Reed, John Sheldon. 2002. "The banner that won't stay furled." *Southern Cultures* 8, no 1.

Reed, Ralph. 1994. "The future of the religious right," in *Christian political activism at the crossroads,* edited by William R. Stevenson Jr. Lanham, MD: University Press of America.

Reed, Ralph. 1998. "Separation of church and state: 'Christian nation' and other heresies." In *God's new Israel: Religious interpretations of American destiny.* Chapel Hill: University of North Carolina Press.

Reichley, A. James. 2003. "Faith in politics." In *Religion returns to the public square: Faith and policy in America,* edited by Hugh Heclo and Wilfred M. McClay. Baltimore: Johns Hopkins University Press.

Remini, Robert V. 2001. *Andrew Jackson and his Indian wars.* New York: Penguin.

Remini, Robert V. 2001. *The life of Andrew Jackson.* New York: Harper Collins.

Renan, Ernest. 1996. *What is a nation?* (1882), translated by Martin Thom. In *Becoming national: A reader,* edited by Geoff Eley and Ronald Grigor Suny. New York: Oxford University Press.

Rice, Condoleezza. 2000. "Promoting the national interest." *Foreign Affairs* 79, no 1.

Richardson, Joel. 2010. *The Islamic antichrist: The shocking truth about the real nature of the beast.* Los Angeles: WND Books.

Robertson, Pat. 1996. *The end of the age.* Dallas, TX: Word Publishing.

Rogan, Eugene L., and Avi Shlaim, eds. 2001. *The war for Palestine: Rewriting the history of 1948.* Cambridge: Cambridge University Press.

Rogger, Hans J., and Eugen Weber. 1965. *European right: A historical profile.* Berkeley: University of California Press.

Rorty, Richard. 1998. *Achieving our country: Leftist thought in twentieth century America.* Cambridge, MA: Harvard University Press.

Rose, Richard. 1985. National pride in cross-cultural perspective. *International Social Science Journal* 37, no. 1.

Rosenbaum, H. Jon, and Peter C. Sederberg. 1974. "Vigilantism: An analysis of establishment violence." *Comparative Politics* 6(4).

Rossiter, Clinton. 1962. *Conservatism in America.* New York: Random House.

Rousseau, Jean-Jacques. 1978. *The social contract,* translated by Maurice Cranston. London: Penguin.

Rozell, Mark J., and Clyde Wilcox. 1996. "Second coming: Strategies of the new Christian Right." *Political Science Quarterly* 111, no. 2.

Sacks, Rabbi Jonathan. 2000. *A letter in the scroll: Understanding our Jewish identity and exploring the legacy of the world's oldest religion.* New York: Simon & Schuster.

Said, Edward. 1979. *The question of Palestine.* New York: Times Books.

Schoenbaum, David. 1980. *Hitler's social revolution: Class and status in Nazi Germany, 1933–1939.* New York: W. W. Norton.

Schoenfeld, Gabriel. 2002. "Israel and the anti-Semites." *Commentary* 113, no. 6.

Sestanovich, Stephen. 1996. "Geotherapy: Russia's neuroses, and ours." *National Interest* 45 (Fall).

Sharpe, J. A. 2004. *Crime in early modern England, 1550–1750.* New York: Longman.

Shils, Edward. 1958. "Ideology and civility: On the politics of the intellectual." *Sewanee Review* 66, no. 3.

Shindler, Colin. 2000. "Likud and the Christian dispensationalists." *Israel Studies* 5, no. 1.

Shipler, David K. 1998. *A country of strangers: Blacks and whites in America.* New York: Alfred A. Knopf.

Siegman, Henry. 2004. "Israel: The threat from within." *New York Review of Books* 51, no. 3.

Simkins, Francis Butler, and Charles Pierce Roland. 1972. *History of the South.* New York: Alfred A. Knopf.

Simms, J. G. 1986. *War and politics in Ireland, 1649–1730.* London: Hambledon Press.

Slater, Ian. 2004. *Choke point: World War III.* New York: Ballantine Books.

Slotkin, Richard. 1973. *Regeneration through violence: The mythology of the American frontier, 1600–1800.* Norman: University of Oklahoma Press.

Slotkin, Richard. 1985. *The fatal environment: The myth of the frontier in the age of industrialization.* Norman: University of Oklahoma Press.

Slotkin, Richard. 1998. *Gunfighter nation: The myth of the frontier in twentieth century America.* Norman: University of Oklahoma Press.

Smidt, Corwin. 1983. "Born again politics." in *Religion and politics In the South: Mass and elite perspectives,* edited by Tod A. Baker, Robert B. Steed, and Laurence W. Moreland. New York: Praeger.

Smidt, Corwin. 1988. Evangelicals within contemporary American politics: Differentiating between fundamentalist and non-fundamentalist evangelicals. *Western Political Quarterly* 41, no. 3.

Smidt, Corwin E., ed. 1989. *Contemporary evangelical political involvement: An analysis and assessment.* Lanham, MD: University Press of America.

Smith, Anthony D. 2001. *Nationalism.* Oxford: Blackwell.

Smith, Oran P. 1997. *The rise of Baptist Republicanism.* New York: New York University Press.

Smith, Tony. 1994. *America's mission: The United States and the worldwide struggle for democracy in the twentieth century.* Princeton, NJ: Princeton University Press.

Smith, Tony. 2000. *Foreign attachments: The power of ethnic groups in the making of American foreign policy.* Cambridge, MA: Harvard University Press.

Sprinzak, Ehud. 1991. *The ascendance of Israel's radical Right.* New York: Oxford University Press.

St. Jean de Crevecoeur, Hector. 1926. *Letters from an American farmer.* New York: Dutton.

Stampp, Kenneth M. 1965. *The era of reconstruction, 1865–1877.* New York: Alfred A. Knopf.

Starkey, Armstrong. 1998. *European and Native American warfare 1675–1815.* Norman: University of Oklahoma Press.

Starr, Joyce R. 1990. *Kissing through glass: The invisible shield between Americans and Israelis.* Chicago: Contemporary Books.

Stern, Fritz. 1974. *The politics of cultural despair.* Berkeley: University of California Press.

Stockman, David. 1986. *The triumph of politics: Why the Reagan revolution failed.* New York: Harper Collins.

Stockton, Ronald R. 1989. "The evangelical phenomenon: A Falwell:Graham typology." In *Contemporary political involvement: An analysis and assessment,* edited by Corwin E. Smidt. Lanham, MD: University Press of America.

Stone, I. F. 1978. "Confessions of a Jewish dissident." In *Underground to Palestine and reflections thirty years later,* edited by I. F. Stone. New York: Pantheon Books.

Stone, Lawrence. 1965. *The crisis of the aristocracy, 1558–1641.* Oxford: Oxford University Press.

Strauss, Marc. 2003. The new face of anti-Semitism. *Foreign Policy* (November/December).

Suskind, Ron. 2004. *The price of loyalty.* London: Simon & Schuster.

Taggart, Paul. 2000. *Populism.* Philadelphia: Open University Press.

Talmon, J. L. 1960. *The origins of totalitarian democracy.* New York: Praeger.

Talmon, J. L., ed. 2002. *Totalitarian democracy and after.* New York: Frank Cass and Co.

Tate, Allen, et al. 1930. *I'll take my stand: The South and the agrarian tradition.* New York: Harper

Taylor, William R. 1963. *Cavalier and Yankee: The Old South and American national character.* New York: Anchor Books.

Telhami, Shibley. 2002. *The stakes: America and the Middle East.* Boulder, CO: Westview Press.

Turner, Helen Lee, and James L. Guth. 1989. "The politics of Armageddon: Dispensationalism among Southern Baptist ministers." In *Religion and political behavior in the United States,* edited by Ted G. Jelen. New York: Praeger.

Tweed, Thomas A. 2002. Our Lady of Guadeloupe visits the Confederate Memorial. *Southern Cultures* 8, no. 2, (Summer).

Uris, Leon. 1959. *Exodus.* New York: Bantam Books.

Vaisse, Justin. 2010. *Neoconservatism: The biography of a movement.* Cambridge, MA: Harvard University Press.

Woodward, C. Vann. 1968. *The burden of Southern history.* Baton Rouge: Louisiana State University Press.

Woodward, C. Vann. 2003. *The strange career of Jim Crow.* New York: Oxford University Press.

Wald, Kenneth D. 2003. *Religion and politics in the United States.* New York: Rowman and Littlefield.

Wald, Kenneth, Dennis E. Owen, and Samuel S. Hill, Jr. 1988. "Churches as political communities." *American Political Science Review* 82, no. 2: 531–548.

Walker, Mack. 1998. *German home towns: Community, state and general estate, 1648–1817.* Ithaca, NY: Cornell University Press.

Walt, Stephen M. 1999. "Rigor or rigor mortis? Rational choice and security studies." *International Security* 23, no. 4.

Walzer, Michael. 1980. *Just and unjust wars: A moral argument with historical illustrations.* London: Pelican Books.

Walzer, Michael. 1985. *Exodus and revolution.* New York: Basic Books.

Warner, W. Lloyd. 1974. "An American sacred ceremony." In *American civil religion,* edited by Russell E. Richey and Donald G. Jones. New York: Harper and Row.

Washington, James Melvin, ed. 1986. *A testament of hope: The essential writings of Martin Luther King, Jr.* New York: Harper and Row.

Wasserman, Ira M. 1989. "Prohibition and ethnocultural conflict: The Missouri Prohibition referendum of 1918." *Social Science Quarterly* 70, no. 4.

Wasserstein, Bernard. 2003. *Israel and Palestine: Why they fight and can they stop?* London: Profile.

Weber, Eugen. 1976. *Peasants into Frenchmen: The modernisation of rural France, 1870–1914.* Stanford, CA: Stanford University Press.

Weber, Timothy P. 1979. *Living in the shadow of the second coming: American premillennialism, 1875–1925.* New York: Oxford University Press.

Wehler, Hans-Ulrich. 1997. *The German Empire 1871–1918.* Leamington Spa: Berg Publishers.

Weisburg, David, with Vered Vinitzky. 1984. "Vigilantism as rational social control: The case of the Gush Emunim settlers." In *Cross currents in Israeli culture and politics,* edited by Myron J. Aronoff. New Brunswick, NJ: Transaction Books.

Weiss, John. 1977. *Conservatism in Europe, 1770–1945: Tradition, reaction and counter-revolution.* London: Thames and Hudson.

Whitman, Walt. 2009. *Democratic vistas*. Charleston, SC: BiblioBazaar.

Williams, Peter W. 2002. *America's religions from their origins to the 21st century*. Champaign: University of Illinois Press.

Williamson, Joel. 1993. *William Faulkner and Southern history*. New York: Oxford University Press.

Wills, Garry. 1987. *Reagan's America: Innocents at home*. New York: Doubleday.

Wills, Garry. 1992. "The born again Republicans." *New York Review of Books* 39, no 15.

Wilson, Edmund. 1977. *Patriotic gore: Studies in the literature of the American Civil War*. New York: Farrar, Straus and Giroux.

Wilson, William A. 1990. *Folklore and nationalism in modern Finland*. Bloomington: Indiana University Press.

Wood, Gordon S. 1970. "Republicanism as a revolutionary ideology." In *Role of ideology in the American Revolution*, edited by John R. Howe. Toronto: Holt, Rinehart and Winston.

Woods, Randall Bennett. 1994. "Dixie's dove: J. William Fulbright, the Vietnam War and the American South." *Journal of Southern History* 60, no. 3.

Woodward, Bob. 2002. *Bush at war*. New York: Simon & Schuster.

Wright Mills, C. 1959. *The power elite*. New York: Oxford University Press.

Wyatt-Brown, Bertram. 1986. *Honor and violence in the Old South*. New York: Oxford University Press.

"X" [George Kennan]. 1947. "The sources of Soviet conduct." *Foreign Affairs*.

Zeldin, Theodore. 1980. *France 1848–1945: Intellect and pride*. New York: Oxford University Press.

Zernicke, Kate. 2010. *Boiling mad: Inside Tea Party America*. New York: Henry Holt.

Zunes, Stephen. 2003. *Tinderbox: US Middle East policy and the roots of terrorism*. Monroe, ME: Common Courage Press.

Index